The Oscillatory Nature of Language

Drawing on cutting-edge ideas from the biological and cognitive sciences, this book presents both an innovative neuro-computational model of language comprehension and a state-of-the-art review of current topics in neurolinguistics. It explores a range of newly emerging topics in the biological study of language, building them into a framework which views language as grounded in endogenous neural oscillatory behaviour. This allows the author to formulate a number of hypotheses concerning the relationship between neurobiology and linguistic computation. Murphy also provides an extensive overview of recent theoretical and experimental work on the neurobiological basis of language, from which the reader will emerge up to date on major themes and debates. This lively overview of contemporary issues in theoretical linguistics, combined with a clear theory of how language is processed, is essential reading for scholars and students across a range of disciplines.

ELLIOT MURPHY is a research associate at the Vivian L. Smith Department of Neurosurgery, McGovern Medical School, University of Texas Health Science Center, at the Texas Institute for Restorative Neurotechnologies. He has published widely on the neurobiology of syntax, language evolution, and current topics in semantics, pragmatics and philosophy.

T0382277

The Oscillatory Nature
of Language

Elliot Murphy

McGovern Medical School, University of Texas Health Science Center

Shaftesbury Road, Cambridge CB2 8EA, United Kingdom

One Liberty Plaza, 20th Floor, New York, NY 10006, USA

477 Williamstown Road, Port Melbourne, VIC 3207, Australia

314–321, 3rd Floor, Plot 3, Splendor Forum, Jasola District Centre, New Delhi – 110025, India

103 Penang Road, #05–06/07, Visioncrest Commercial, Singapore 238467

Cambridge University Press is part of Cambridge University Press & Assessment, a department of the University of Cambridge.

We share the University's mission to contribute to society through the pursuit of education, learning and research at the highest international levels of excellence.

www.cambridge.org
Information on this title: www.cambridge.org/9781108818889

DOI: 10.1017/9781108864466

First published 2021
First paperback edition 2023

A catalogue record for this publication is available from the British Library

Library of Congress Cataloging-in-Publication data
Names: Murphy, Elliot, author.
Title: The oscillatory nature of language / Elliot Murphy, University College London.
Description: Cambridge, UK ; New York : Cambridge University Press, 2020. | Includes bibliographical references and index.
Identifiers: LCCN 2020026174 (print) | LCCN 2020026175 (ebook) | ISBN 9781108836319 (hardback) | ISBN 9781108864466 (ebook)
Subjects: LCSH: Biolinguistics. | Neurolinguistics. | Psycholinguistics. | Neuropsychology. | Cognitive neuroscience.
Classification: LCC QP360 (print) | LCC QP360 (ebook) | DDC 612.8–dc23
LC record available at https://lccn.loc.gov/2020026174
LC ebook record available at https://lccn.loc.gov/2020026175

ISBN   978-1-108-83631-9   Hardback
ISBN   978-1-108-81888-9   Paperback

'Yes, a key can lie forever in the place where the locksmith left it, and never be used to open the lock the master forged it for.'

– Ludwig Wittgenstein, *Culture and Value* (1977, 54)

'I fear those big words, Stephen said, which make us so unhappy.'

– James Joyce, *Ulysses* (1998, 31)

Contents

Preface

This book is the culmination of a five-year effort to develop a series of linking hypotheses between components of the language faculty – principally, its computational basis – and components of neurobiology, namely oscillatory behaviour. First conceived in November 2014, I began researching ways to approach a monographic treatment of this topic. In order to achieve this, it would first be necessary to discover a feasible means to decompose 'narrow syntax' considerably further than it has typically been in the literature. For instance, the generative grammar literature mostly takes Merge to be an elementary operation rather than a complex of, at least, *search*, *combine*, *categorise* and *maintain*. Next, one would need to identify neural mechanisms (and not purely regions) putatively capable of carrying out these operations. This gradually developed into an effort to go beyond what soon became the field's go-to neural mechanism for phrasal comprehension, oscillatory 'entrainment' – what is regarded in this book as only the first step in a complex network-level process of endogenous cross-frequency couplings (based on ideas proposed in Murphy 2015b, 2016a).

Soon after, my aim became to distinguish between theoretical formulations in the neurolinguistics literature that don't really carry much explanatory weight (and are used to re-describe the output of statistical analyses performed on neuroimaging datasets, rather than account for them) and forms of theoretical formulations that really don't carry much explanatory weight. A general trend has emerged whereby – to take a common example – amplitude increases in a particular, canonical frequency band are coded as underlying complex cognitive processes, and yet there are no neurobiologically realistic computational roles being ascribed to such frequencies. Or, when we reach a moment when even the decidedly specific process of δ-β phase–amplitude coupling is being associated with both motor control inhibition during the processing of task-relevant abstractions and the effects of paternal (but not maternal) caregiving behaviours on the brains of preschool children, it seems clear that a momentary departure from data collection is required. Successful model formulation is not achieved by constructing new labels for well-established abstractions, as when Hagoort (2019, 55) proposes a re-naming of *operations* to 'elementary linguistic operations (ELOs)' and a re-naming of *representations* to 'elementary linguistics units (ELUs)', a move which brings with it no new insights into the nature of operations and representations.

Although certain studies have begun to show that particular linguistic operations are indexed by specific neural behaviour in certain cortical regions, what is currently lacking in the field is a comprehensive explanatory account for why we find the neural signatures that we do. For instance, why do γ oscillations appear to index successful semantic composition? Pointing to the fact that γ typically indicates local cortical processing is not sufficient, since the gap in abstraction level between semantic processing and high-frequency action potential firing is not something that will be bridged automatically or seamlessly.

As I began developing preliminary versions of an empirically and theoretically defensible oscillatory model of phrase structure building throughout 2014–2019, similar spectres emerged: an unjustified cortico-centric emphasis in standard neurolinguistic models, sidelining the crucial role of subcortical structures in language; an inability for standard models to account for neuroplasticity; a neurobiologically unrealistic insistence that a specific subregion of Broca's area is the 'seat of syntax'; and a hidebound focus on localisation of function (as when, in his Foreword to Friederici's recent monograph, Chomsky claims that 'it is the ventral part of B44 [sic] in which basic syntactic computations – in the simplest case Merge – are localized'; Friederici 2017, x), as opposed to the construction of a more dynamic neural code for language, potentially realisable across multiple neural systems.

Early on in this process, a more fundamental goal had been achieved: isolating the components of language suitable for potential neurobiological grounding. Having reviewed existing ethological research into non-human cognitive capacities, I isolated primarily the *labelling* component in natural language as being of sufficient granularity (being a form of categorisation and object maintenance) to map onto postulated computational properties of certain oscillatory processes. Other components, such as representational storage in a derivational workspace and intrinsic representational complexity, were proposed as candidates for neural mapping. In brief, the goal has been to accommodate language-specific components postulated by theoretical syntax within a particular framework of neural computation.

By 2020, it became increasingly clear across a number of fields in the neurobiology of cognition that cellular and oscillatory mechanisms, once believed to be highly domain-specific, are in fact recruited in the service of computationally analogous processes operating over distinct representational domains. This book has attempted to apply this insight to language, pushing this approach as strongly for the 'broad' faculty of language (e.g. the sensorimotor system, representational storage) as it does for the 'narrow' faculty (phrase structure building via labelling).

It is my sincere hope that by turning away from rhetorical re-formulations and towards theoretical neurobiology, and synthesising the wealth of currently available empirical findings concerning the oscillatory nature of language, this book can encourage others to pursue the paramount task of model formulation, and thereby ground the computational nature of language within intrinsic neural processes.

Introduction

There are numerous neurobiological models of language, ranging from those concerned with speech perception, white matter structure and the function of dorsal and ventral streams. Departing somewhat from typical neurolinguistic terrain, this book is aimed to serve as a comprehensive, state-of-the-art compendium on the oscillatory basis of language, with the central focus being on phrase structure building. Along with providing an extensive overview of the theoretical and experimental work done in recent decades into the electrophysiological basis of language, it will also formulate a number of novel hypotheses concerning the potential relationship between neurobiology and linguistic computation, and will propose a specific neurocomputational model of language comprehension argued to be empirically justifiable and neurobiologically feasible. Much of the book is formulated as a literature review, and theoretical discussions and evaluations of this literature are ideally aimed at graduate students and experts in the field of psycholinguistics, neurolinguistics and evolutionary linguistics. Advanced undergraduate students could follow the core arguments and narrative while stepping over some of the more technical details concerning, for instance, phase-coupling and migrating oscillations. For the experts, this book provides a synthesis of current knowledge in a new format, centred on the perspective of theoretical linguistics, and executed alongside the presentation of novel theoretical proposals and research directions. In particular, the latter half of the book will suggest a theory of the mapping between oscillatory activity in different frequency bands (e.g. delta, theta, alpha, beta and gamma) and syntactic and semantic primitives. The book will assume audience familiarity with some general notions from linguistics, but will foreground much of this discussion (further explanation of key terms is presented in the Glossary).

While a core motivation will be to review the literature, this will not be a purely dispassionate process. The range of empirical overviews presented in each chapter will also be used to embed oscillatory discussions of language within an evolutionary framework in order to construct a series of hypotheses concerning how language is implemented in the brain. Early parts of the book will briefly explore the computational and evolutionary nature of language in order to properly set up the later discussion of the oscillatory nature of language, given that this latter investigation will in turn impact our understanding of linguistic computation and language evolution – at least, that is the hope.

From a biological perspective, language is a peculiar, complex form of behaviour with a number of unique properties, where we can take *behaviour* to mean the following, assuming an apt definition from Levitis et al. (2009): 'Behavior is the internally coordinated responses (actions or inactions) of whole living organisms (individuals or groups) to internal and/or external stimuli, excluding responses more easily understood as developmental changes.' The question for neurolinguists then centres on what exactly the 'internally coordinated responses' are in the brain which produce language. This book will suggest that these responses come in the form of *neural oscillations*.

While perhaps novel to linguists and cognitive scientists, the potential existence of a relationship between language and neural oscillations was discussed as early as 1978 in O'Keefe and Nadal's monumental work *The Hippocampus as a Cognitive Map* (O'Keefe & Nadal 1978). Here, the authors discuss Chomsky and Jackendoff's work on syntax and the semantic representation of space, attempting to draw links between how the hippocampus appears to represent vectors and how the language system appears to represent space. O'Keefe and Nadal attempted to show how their theory of cognitive maps could account for certain properties of linguistic 'deep structure' and semantic long-term memory. In effect, this book is an attempt to expand on O'Keefe and Nadal's seminal suggestions, broadening both the neurophysiological and computational landscape that these authors set down and discussing a wide number of cortical and subcortical structures and how they might implement elementary linguistic operations.

Neural oscillations (also commonly called *brain rhythms*) 'have come of age', as Buzsáki and Freeman (2015, v) put it. They reflect synchronised fluctuations in neuronal excitability and are grouped by frequency, with the most commonly (and classically, based on clinical research) rhythms being delta (δ: ~0.5–4Hz), theta (θ: ~4-8Hz), alpha (α: ~8–12Hz), beta (β: ~12–30Hz) and gamma (γ: ~30–150Hz). These are generated by various cortical and subcortical structures, and form a hierarchical structure since slow rhythms phase-modulate the power of faster rhythms. Oscillations can fluctuate in amplitude, and do so in a gradual (phasic) or rapid (tonic) manner, with this behaviour potentially reflecting coordinated computations. It has been known since at least Wilson and Bower (1991, 498) that 'the phase and frequency of cortical oscillations may reflect the coordination of general computational processes within and between cortical areas'. Fast γ oscillations can be found at different levels of complexity, ranging from single neurons to neural clusters to electroencephalography (EEG) recordings (Biasiucci et al. 2019), suggesting that γ activity has a broad functional range. Moreover, slow rhythms below 10Hz have been found to dominate the cortex in both wakefulness and sleep, suggesting that they have a clear role in global coordination and information integration, not least because these slow rhythms were additionally found to be coupled to the amplitude of faster rhythms across all cortical layers (Halgren et al. 2017).

Relatedly, the slow-oscillating cortical layers mediate global processing due to feedback connections and diffuse thalamocortical matrix afferents (Rubio-Garrido et al. 2009). Berger (1929) first introduced α and β to, respectively, denote any amplitude below and above 12Hz (his interest in brain physics was ultimately grounded in his urge to verify his beliefs in telepathy, a quite distinct motivation from the one behind this book), and his demarcations have since been adopted and refined. This classificatory system is in many ways too simplistic: a frequency band may be produced by multiple, distant mechanisms, and a given region can also produce multiple rhythms (Ainsworth et al. 2011). Brain rhythms are today studied not simply via EEG, but also in vitro and in vivo electrophysiology, optogenetics and magnetoencephalography (MEG). Signals measured via M/EEG reflect the mean activity of medium-sized (thousands) or large-sized (millions) clusters of neurons, and their activity is characterised by coordinated postsynaptic fluctuations in the membrane potentials of pyramidal neurons which are physically grouped in parallel cross-cortically. In general, slower rhythms are thought to synchronise distant brain regions, while faster γ rhythms are thought to activate local neuronal assemblies (Buzsáki & Draguhn 2004; Yan & Li 2013).

Neural oscillations are increasingly being implicated in a number of basic and higher cognitive faculties. Oscillations enable the construction of coherently organised neuronal assemblies through establishing transitory temporal correlations. These ideas will be explored in considerable detail here. After exploring the elementary operations of the language faculty in Chapter 1, Chapters 2–3 will comprehensively explore empirical work into the oscillatory basis of language and propose an oscillatory model of linguistic computation. It will be argued that the universality of language is to be found within the extraordinarily preserved nature of mammalian brain rhythms employed in the computation of linguistic structures. The extent to which brain rhythms are the suitable neuronal processes which can capture the computational properties of the human language faculty will be considered against a backdrop of existing cartographic research (where 'cartographic' refers to the neuroimaging sense, and not the syntactic sense, e.g. Cinque 1999) into the localisation of linguistic interpretation, leading to clear, causally addressable empirical predictions. More specifically, I will propose a model according to which a broad range of migrating δ couplings with the amplitude of θ, β and γ rhythms constitute the basis of phrase structure building.

Given this outline, why focus exclusively on oscillations? Their relevance for cognitive neuroscience has been well established, and they are increasingly being implicated in a wide range of functions. For instance, oscillations seem to play a causal role in perception. When detecting visual targets, adults are not aware of visual stimuli that is presented during the *trough* of an α wave (i.e. the least excitable phase, when the fewest number of neurons are firing) in the parietal cortex. They are most likely to detect targets at the *peak* of the ongoing wave. Visual data arriving during the trough do not reach conscious awareness.

With respect to language, oscillations have been implicated in speech perception (Giraud & Poeppel 2012; Kayser et al. 2014) non-verbal emotional communication (Symons et al. 2016) and, as we will see, a range of other linguistic processes. According to Giraud and Poeppel's temporal linking hypothesis, oscillation-based decoding segments information into 'units of the appropriate temporal granularity' (2012, 511). Oscillations may consequently explain how the brain decodes continuous speech. The γ, θ and δ rhythms, respectively, correspond closely to (sub)phonemic, syllabic and phrasal processing, as Giraud and Poeppel note, restricting their experimental enquiry to the γ and θ bands. In addition, the neural dynamics implementing basic elements of sentence comprehension may be obscured by the processing of external sensory events like speech, and so different experimental designs have since been deployed to control for this, as the following pages will discuss.

Oscillations have also been linked to the timing of cortical information processing (Klimesch et al. 2007). Synchronous oscillatory activity has been suggested as a viable, neurobiologically feasible mechanism of top-down and bottom-up information propagation across cortical levels (Bressler & Richter 2015). As Vaas notes, '[i]ntrinsic oscillatory electrical activities, resonance and coherence are at the root of cognition' (2001, 86), with the condensing and dissolving of oscillatory bursts possibly explaining the 'cinematic' nature of subjective experience (Freeman 2015) and providing some mechanistic basis for experiencing what Fernando Pessoa called 'the everythingness of everything'. It is therefore not surprising that Henry Bergson's (1911, 332) writings also invoked the notion of a 'cinematograph' in relation to the role of the oscillations in cognition:

We take snapshots, as it were, of the passing reality ... Perception, intellection, language so proceed in general ... we hardly do anything else than set going a kind of cinematograph inside us.

We conventionally view our eyes, writes McGilchrist (2010, 162):

[L]ike the lens of a camera of a moving swivel, perhaps a bit like a film-maker's camera – just as our model of thinking and remembering is that of the computer, with its inert memory banks. The image suggests that we choose where we point our attention; in that respect we see ourselves as supremely active, and self-determining.

Yet the brain samples the environment periodically, in its own good time, and so even sustained visual attention is never really sustained (Fiebelkorn et al. 2018, Helfrich et al. 2018). This suggests, amongst other things, that cognition is far more complex than sustained neuronal spiking, and that something much more dynamic is at play: chiefly, its oscillatory activity, which grounds and perpetuates the brain's dynamism. Expanding on Giraud and Poeppel's (2012, 511) goal of establishing a 'principled relation between the time scales present in speech and the time constants underlying neuronal cortical oscillations', one of the central challenges will be to draw up relations between oscillatory time constants and the time scales of linguistic computation.

Cognitive neuroscience research into oscillations was given a substantial boost over a quarter of a century ago by Gray and Singer (1989), who discovered that when multiple features of a visual scene were interpreted by an individual as belonging to the same object, the neuronal temporal impulses were synchronised in the regions assumed to subserve each featural component. I think the potential for these mechanisms to shed light on, and perhaps even constitute part of, the human faculty of language is considerable; indeed, Gray and Singer were surprised by oscillatory coupling at neuronal groups 7mm apart, but by now it has been established that coupling can occur at much greater distances, and so the potential explanatory scope of oscillatory activity has dramatically increased over recent years.

Along with reviewing traditional topics in linguistics, this book will also be concerned with emerging themes in *neurolinguistics*. From a researcher's perspective, neurolinguistics studies how language is implemented in the brain, and uses the modern imaging tools of neuroscience to investigate the neural basis of particular linguistic processes. Yet from a conceptual standpoint, there are currently no direct connections between the structures posited by neuroscientific theories (dendrites, ionic channels, nodes of Ranvier) and those posited by linguists (lexical features, syllables, nouns). Indeed, a coherent research programme has not been agreed upon by the field. When it comes to the visual or olfactory systems, researchers largely agree on what the basic components of analysis are – not so for the widely diverse and often controversial approaches to the various subcomponents of language.

The *human-specific* feature of language will also be a recurrent theme in the book. Although Darwin successfully managed to bridge many of the classical gulfs separating humans and other animals, many of his contemporaries, such as the linguist Müller (1866), complained that 'language is the Rubicon, which divides man from beast, and no animal will ever cross it'. While Müller may be correct to point to the ultimate species-specificity of language, it will be shown throughout this book that non-humans have many of the core articulatory and cognitive faculties required for language, and that it may simply be the way these discrete faculties are arranged that gives rise to the heralded Rubicon.

But what precisely are the computational primitives of language that we would like to investigate at the oscillatory level? This question is purely a task for linguists, since only they can provide details about the structure of the language system – and, furthermore, only they are in the business of appropriately decomposing notions like 'grammar' and 'communication'. The assumption of many contemporary linguists is that part of the complexity of the world's languages is encoded in the human computational system. In one of the most prominent branches of linguistics, the Minimalist Program (the current model of generative grammar; Chomsky 1995), the operation, to which language's human-unique aspects may reduce, is termed 'Merge'. This constructs a new syntactic object out of the two already formed. Assimilating standard accounts (Chomsky 2013, 2019a) with more recent definitions which assume elements are merged to a workspace (Chomsky et al. 2019), we can define the operation as follows:

MERGE
Select two lexical items α and β and form the set $\{\alpha,\beta\}$ in a workspace.

This involves searching for discrete elements in the lexicon and then merging them to a workspace. Merge is a computational operation in the traditional sense that it is being described at a higher level of abstraction than algorithmic procedures and the implementational level of neurons and dendrites (Marr 1982). Early minimalism (1990s) held that when Merge targets two syntactic objects, α and β, forming a new object, Γ, the label of Γ is either α or β. That is, when two lexical items (LIs) are merged, one of them 'wins' (so to speak) and is projected as the *head* or *label*: $\mathbf{M}(\alpha,\beta) = \{\alpha\{\alpha,\beta\}\}$ or $\{\beta\{\alpha,\beta\}\}$. With *red car*, the label is *car* since this word determines the category of the phrase (a noun phrase, not an adjectival phrase). Narita (2011, 191) summarises this 'old intuition' by writing that 'it is simply an ordinary fact about language that "noun phrases" are interpreted in a "nouny" way'. Or, as Narita and Fukui (2016, 20) summarise, 'major properties of a verbal phrase *read a book* are determined by its head verb *read*, yielding its event-predicatehood and θ-roles, among others'. Consider the structures [C [TP...]], [T [*v*P...]] and [V [*n*P]]. These 'head-complement' structures involve a prominent head (Complementiser, Tense and Verb) determining the semantic characterisation of the configuration: C determines the clausal force (e.g. declarative, interrogative), T feeds tense and modal properties, while V determines lexical and aspectual properties of the event and assigns a θ-role to its complement. The label therefore indicates the structure's meaning to what generative linguists term the conceptual-intentional (CI) system (an axiom assumed in Chomsky 2013, Epstein et al. 2014 and much other work). To put it plainly, 'labelling' is the operation that chooses what lexical features select the phrasal category, yielding an unbounded array of hierarchically organised structures and the capacity for discrete infinity. As Fitch (2010a, 105) notes, 'many of the hotly debated differences among syntacticians are not particularly relevant to questions in the biology and evolution of language'; such as the debates between lexical functional grammar, generative grammar or head-driven phrase structure grammar. As such, we will focus on the elementary computational architecture, much of which is shared across frameworks (all of which, for instance, rely on structure-dependent rules).

Due to the existence of labelling, a sentence cannot be analysed simply as a linear combination of words. It rather possesses some form of hierarchical structure. In a sentence like *The man left*, the words *The* and *man* are associated in a way in which *man* and *left* are not. The first two words are grouped together as a single labelled phrase, since they can be substituted for a 'pro-form' like *He*. This substitution operation cannot apply to *man left*. In addition, an adverb like *quietly* can be inserted between *man* and *left* but *the man* cannot be broken up in this way (Lasnik 2017).

Since human beings are the only species who seem capable of this phrase structure building capacity, the structural information and interpretations which emerge from phrase structure configurations amount to a uniquely human type of thought. Certain patterns of long-distance dependencies, conceptual categorisations or recursively embedded hierarchical structures are a peculiar subset of human cognition. This makes investigations of the neural basis of phrase structure building pertinent to a range of fields, since it demands attention to how the human brain organises itself to uniquely contribute these modes of thought.

Computational models of syntactic, semantic and phonological knowledge are likely not going to be reduced fully to neural tissue, but George Box's famous saying that 'all models are wrong, but some are useful' should remind us that the ultimately 'incorrect' nature of neurocomputational models can at least provide a useful function in directing future research. The study of language should take advantage of whatever sciences could enhance its own hypotheses and methodologies. In the Enlightenment period, developments in philosophy of mind contributed to an understanding of some fundamental linguistic concepts like *self*. In the 1950s, developments in meta-mathematics contributed to an understanding of language's grammatical architecture. Today, with the proliferation of the brain sciences, it is likely that other features of language can now be explored, such as the way different linguistic representations are combined together and maintained in memory.

Yet this proliferation can come with certain risks, often not acknowledged by researchers. Jonas and Kording (2017) used standard neuroscientific research methods to try and understand the MOS 6502 microchip (the processor in, amongst other things, the Commodore 64), which contains 3,510 transistors as it is able to run only the most primitive, vintage video games. Their results should generate a fair degree of humility: they discovered only that the chip has a clock and is able to read and write to memory. Nothing else was uncovered about it via the standard methods of neuroscience ('lesioning' transistors, analysing individual transistors and local field potentials, performing Granger causality analysis, and so forth). Jonas and Kolding discovered general-purpose operations which transistors could perform, but they found no 'Donkey Kong transistor' or 'Space Invaders transistor', i.e. transistors essential and exclusive to a given game. And while the chip is purely deterministic, neurons can exhibit random behaviour. The lessons are clear, with Jonas and Kolding's work serving as a further motivation for abandoning the classical 'cartographic' models of language comprehension, which propose one-to-one mappings between brain regions and (often fairly complex) cognitive operations, fixating on the traditional 'language areas', Broca's and Wernicke's areas. We are often told that certain linguistic operations 'take place' at a given region, or are 'interpreted' along a particular pathway, yet the story of what exactly the brain is doing to derive these localised interpretations is left unanswered. Instead of the standard image of neuroscience being data-limited, it appears that the field is rather theory-limited. The physical sciences place a great deal of emphasis on the importance of theoretical physics, and not just, for instance, experimental particle physics. There is no reason why neuroscientists should not afford the same respect to theoretical neurobiology, yet the drive for experimental innovation is currently by far the dominant force in the field. Neurolinguistic research has often used violation paradigms, using stimuli which violate certain phonological, syntactic or semantic rules, using these forms of atypical language processing to yield insights into its neurobiological structure. In particular, there is an increasing interest in combining techniques such as repetitive transcranial magnetic stimulation (rTMS) and EEG to assess how distinct brain areas are coupled together via oscillatory activity. Though illuminating, there is surprisingly little theoretical understanding of how normal language comprehension proceeds (as Moro 2015 persuasively argues).

Jonas and Kording's work hints at another major limitation of contemporary computational neuroscience: We do not even have a solid conception of what it would mean to *understand* the brain. The most sophisticated proposals amount to, for instance, Marr's (1982) and Marr and Poggio's (1976) three-level approach of the computational, algorithmic and implementational levels (see also Neeleman 2013), and Lazbnick's proposal that understanding arises at the moment when it becomes possible to fix a certain implementation in a system. The multidisciplinary perspective adopted here (encompassing higher-order psychological models of the language system and lower-order models of neurophysiological architecture) is in line with Hochstein's (2018, 1105) conclusion: namely that '[g]iven that no model can satisfy all the goals typically associated with explanation, no one model in isolation can provide a good scientific explanation. Instead we must appeal to collections of models'. Going further, this book will attempt to satisfy the five (rough and not exhaustive) criteria Hochstein (2018, 1106) associates with an explanatory scientific theory, although even with this generous offering only four will be the major focus, and three the minor focus:

1. Successfully conveying understanding about the target phenomenon, or making it intelligible, to an audience or enquirer.
2. Determining when a given phenomenon is expected to occur, and under what conditions.
3. Identifying general principles or patterns that all instances of the explanandum phenomenon adhere to and/or constraints that the phenomenon must conform to.
4. Identifying the particular physical mechanisms that generate and sustain the target phenomenon.
5. Providing information sufficient to control, manipulate and reproduce the target phenomenon.

This book, pessimistically enough, will therefore approach the problem of implementing language in the brain with a number of crucial caveats. The models and hypotheses put forward may not ultimately produce a degree of understanding Marr or Lazbnick would appreciate, but enquiry needs to have its limits, and being able to recognise these limits (whatever they may be) does not as a result invalidate a given theoretical enterprise. For instance, a major problem discussed in philosophy and the language sciences concerns how the human mind is able to 'detach' itself from perceptual experience and generate predictions and hypotheses about possible states of the world. This level of independence of conceptual structures from sensorimotor representations (a topic which closely relates to free will) is a topic this book will not even attempt to explore through any mechanistic, lower-level approach. Instead, we will focus only on the most primitive, elementary features of linguistic computation, leaving aside the realm of perceptual experience.

    In a recent review article, Pylkkänen (2019, 64) poses a stark question for contemporary neurolinguistics:

Is there a neurally implemented computation that builds syntactic structure and does not compute any meaning – a mechanism that, upon encountering "angry bird," composes the representation of the adjective category with the representation of the noun category to yield a representation of a noun phrase, with no information about the meanings of the elements that were combined?

A positive answer will be given to this fundamental question. Most notably, it will be proposed that the MERGE function is grounded in particular interactions (specifically, cross-frequency interactions) between θ and γ rhythms, which in turn interact with δ rhythms. Although we will not present the specific details until Chapter 2, to briefly summarise the model, the data structures involved in linguistic computation (syntactic and semantic features, ranging from Masculine to Third Person to Animate to Case features) are indexed by discrete γ cycles which are 'embedded' within the slower θ and δ cycles, such that oscillations are used to cluster these features together, as when MERGE clusters certain features together within a local set during a syntactic derivation. Aspects of the δ phase and its coupling with cross-cortical γ and parahippocampal and temporal θ are proposed to be responsible for indexing syntactic categorial information, abstracted away from semantics. In addition, within the context of our human-specific brain shape (i.e. a globular shape relative to other primates), these oscillations can be shown to 'travel' across portions of cortex and subcortex, and it is argued that this grants certain computational properties to the language system's more fundamental oscillatory basis. One of the implications of this model is that the processing constraints imposed on the language faculty arise 'for free' from the raw frequency bands that MERGE is implemented through. In addition, the derivational workspaces will be decomposed into distinct oscillatory subroutines, such that interactions between δ and θ will code for one workspace (namely, a maintenance workspace), and interactions between θ and γ will code for another (namely, a 'live' construction workspace which feeds to the maintenance space). All of these proposals, in particular the latter concerning workspace architecture, will be motivated by and grounded within contemporary theoretical linguistics, which is – and, as will be argued, should always be – the core guide for neurolinguists.

One question which naturally arises for linguists, psycholinguists and neurolinguists is 'What is your evidence?' This book will effectively present two forms of empirical evidence in favour of the model ultimately developed:

(1) Indirect empirical support from non-linguistic neuroimaging work which taps into cognitive processes hypothesised to be recruited by the language faculty. This is a form of 'bottom-up' model construction.

(2) Direct empirical support from neuroimaging studies designed to explicitly explore how the brain executes the fundamental computational operations of the language faculty, either through carefully controlled experimentation or through naturalistic language stimuli calling upon normal comprehension processes. This is a form of 'top-down' model construction.

In addition, a further motivating factor will come from pre-existing models of neural computation, typically from the fields of computational neuroscience and theoretical neurobiology. That is to say, a range of theoretical models have already been used to motivate computations similar or analogous to aspects of phrase structure building. Although the evidence presented for the model constructed will inevitably come from a wide range of sources, the main forms of evidence will include studies suggesting that delta-theta (δ-θ) interactions are a computationally feasible means to generating, indexing and maintaining sets of hierarchically organised linguistic features ('phrases'), and also research pointing to the existence of human-specific richness in possible cross-frequency couplings in these slow frequency bands.

As mentioned, throughout this book we will be concerned with the topic of brain dynamics. Complex, systems-level interactions have been observed across the brain at a number of levels, from microscopic cells (Schroeter et al. 2015) to macroscopic regions (Zalesky et al. 2014). Evidence for the brain's dynamism comes in many forms, such as the findings that focal changes in neural activity via transcranial magnetic stimulation effect not only the targeted region, but also between-system interactions (Cocchi et al. 2015). In the following chapters, I will outline a number of hypotheses about the systems-level neural basis of language. These neurolinguistic hypotheses are necessarily constrained by biology. For instance, the principles that explain how changes in local neural activity alter communication with distant regions remain a mystery, and knowledge of these principles is essential to understanding how information is sent across the brain (see Gollo et al. 2017 for comprehensive discussion). Given the widespread nature of dynamic systems, it is somewhat surprising that language scientists have only recently explored the relevance of them for language processing in the brain. Despite these and other glaring gaps in our knowledge of the brain, I will suggest that enough is currently known to outline a large-scale neurocomputational architecture accounting for elementary linguistic processes, even if an understanding of how these systems-level computations arise from the cellular level is currently lacking.

As Petersen and Sporns (2015, 207) emphasise, most accounts of cognition have 'focused on computational accounts . . . while making little contact with the study of anatomical structures and physiological processes'. Since '[t]he fact that a theory is computationally explicit does not automatically render it biologically plausible' (Bornkessel-Schlesewsky et al. 2014, 365), Chapter 1 will decompose the computational operations of language down to a small set of (potentially generic) sub-operations, attempting to achieve an appropriate level of granularity from which computational-processing connections can be constructed. As such, we will hope to answer Genon et al.'s (2019, 362) question positively: 'Can currently available cognitive ontologies be mapped onto the brain? That is, will we find that specific cognitive concepts can be mapped onto specific biological units?'

In order to be in a position to draw up a comprehensive neurolinguistic model of language, this book will be concerned primarily with defending the following three postulated principles:

Principle I
The functions of language can be decomposed into elementary sub-operations which can adequately describe the computational properties of natural language grammars.

Principle II
The functions of the brain are manifested via oscillatory activity and information transmission across the brain can be measured as a function of phase coherence.

Principle III
The computational operations of language can be explained through the oscillatory activity of the brain and how our species-specific oscillatory profile evolved.

These principles are motivated by what Poeppel (2017, 164) terms 'the desire to identify the smallest, "primitive" or "atomic" representations and computations' of mental life. If Alcalá-López et al. (2018) are right to conclude that functional neuroimaging suggests that 'no brain region or network is exclusively devoted to social processes', then it is reasonable to assume that, after decomposing language into its elementary processes, we would expect to find a similar state of affairs for other cognitive domains, and we would encounter no such thing as a 'language area' to be targeted by subsequent evolutionary and neuroanatomical hypotheses. Nevertheless, as Uriagereka (2012, 8) has already pointed out, expecting a one-to-one mapping between higher-order computational or psycholinguistic theories and neurobiology is similar to expecting a one-to-one mapping between cosmic background radiation and the Big Bang – certainly possible, but highly unlikely.

Exploring these principles will help neurolinguistics shift from a state of description to a more desirable state of explanation, possibly shedding light on a major, unanswered question: How do neurons code for syntactic structures? The search for the neural code in animal neurophysiology has seen a marked transition from the analysis of individual spike timings to larger patterns of synchronisation (Siegel et al. 2015), and the study of language should readily embrace these systems-level developments in the field. Ultimately, this book will argue that if we do not have a story about the neural code for linguistic computation, then we do not have a story at all; we will only have cartographic directions for the approximate location of particular representations.

This book will also aim to extend the scope of enquiry into language evolution by demonstrating the clear relevance of a number of fields in the cognitive and life sciences which have previously not entered into most discussions of the topic. As Karakaş and Barry (2017) argue in a recent review paper, oscillations can serve as robust biomarkers of a number of cognitive faculties, and yet, as they put it, 'the field of psychology is still making limited use of neuro-oscillatory dynamics for a bio-behavioral understanding of cognitive-affective processes'. As of May 2020, a PubMed search for publications concerning *neural oscillations* published by scholars associated with departments of *language* yielded only sixty articles, and seventeen for departments of *linguistics*. Friederici's (2017) monograph, *Language in Our Brain*, devotes five pages to the topic of neural oscillations. Yet Karakaş and Barry's (2017) point remains, as illustrated by the fact that cross-frequency coupling is decreased in Alzheimer's disease patients relative to healthy controls and that this coupling is more strongly correlated to the scores of cognitive tests than what the strength of functional connectivity is (Sotero et al. 2019), suggesting that oscillatory coupling can provide greater explanatory insight into the neural basis of cognition than functional connectivity measures (e.g. broadband interactions as opposed to cross-frequency coupling).

The following chapters will be a language-centred attempt to correct for this generally limited engagement, discussing a number of fruitful theoretical and experimental directions for oscillatory research. Once we pass beyond the divisive gates of cross-disciplinary terminology, we will find that a number of important similarities between cognitive systems can be found. For instance, the *Select*, *Merge* and *Spell-Out* operations of generative syntax (Chomsky 1995; Narita 2009, 2014a; Fukui 2017) are in many ways computationally identical to the *Load*, *Maintain* and *Read-Out* operations discussed in the working memory literature (Machens et al. 2005; Dipoppa et al. 2016), and so it may be possible to draw legitimate inferences about the implementational basis of one system given emerging findings concerning another. More fundamentally, I will assume with Sengupta et al. (2013) that 'any transformation of information can be regarded as computation, while the transfer of information from a source to a receiver is communication'. Since oscillations seem capable of indexing information transfer, we will explore the possible alignment between abstractly formulated linguistic processes and endogenous brain activity.

The general goals of this book are essentially *exploratory* (a comprehensive review of the current state of the art) and *explanatory* (discussing the potential particular aspects of brain dynamics have for explaining basic features of linguistic cognition). It will be argued that only by adopting a pluralistic, multidisciplinary perspective on the language system will biologically plausible and evolutionarily realistic models be developed. This interdisciplinary perspective will complement a central philosophical assumption running through the oscillatory investigation of language presented here: namely, the suggestion in Bates et al. (1979, 3) that 'language is a new machine built out of old parts'.

Otto Koehler (1951) was one of the first to realise that only a highly inter-disciplinary investigation into the biology of language would provide serious insights, and this perspective has been carried forward by most contemporary researchers. In their recent, comprehensive review of the current state of systems neuroscience, Bassett and Sporns (2017, 353) write the following:

Neuroscience is entering a period marked by a rapid expansion in the size, scope and complexity of neural data acquired from large portions of nervous systems and spanning multiple levels of organization. Much of these 'big data' represent networks comprising the relations or interconnections that link the many elements of large-scale neurobiological systems. Examples include ... synaptic connections and anatomical projections among brain areas, dynamic patterns of neural signaling and communication associated with spontaneous and task-evoked brain activity ... Notably, these data often cross multiple levels of organization (neurons, circuits, systems, whole brain) or involve different domains of biology and data types (for example, anatomical and functional connectivity ... [and] activity in distributed brain regions in relation to behavioral phenotypes).

Pursuing this interdisciplinary goal, the chapter divisions in this book will take the following format. Chapter 1 presents a brief introduction to the biological study of language (*biolinguistics*) and will lay out the conceptual and philosophical terrain to be covered in subsequent chapters. In particular, it will sketch out the main set of evolutionary frameworks typically adopted by researchers, arguing that any attempt to explore the oscillatory basis of language needs to be properly embedded within an understanding of how certain oscillatory features emerged. With respect to the philosophical topics of interest, some fundamental issues in cognitive neuroscience are explored in order to properly ground what the implications an oscillatory model of language might be for these domains. Major topics in animal cognition and animal communication are explored in order to narrow down possible language-specific components. The core computational architecture of the language faculty is compared alongside existing accounts of non-human primates, songbirds and a number of other species. What is termed the 'Labelling Hypothesis' is put forward, which proposes that the ability to generate hierarchical phrase structures is the defining feature of the human computational system. This allows us to settle on a small list of computational primitives to later be explored from an oscillatory perspective – a necessary step for any explanatory neurolinguistic model.

Chapter 2 will explore functional neuroimaging and brain dynamics and introducing core concepts from each domain, both theoretical and experimental. The chapter will provide the first major monograph treatment of the oscillatory basis of language, as well as providing a thorough review of debates in structural neuroanatomy. Classical frameworks, centred on Broca's and Wernicke's areas, will be contrasted with more recent accounts embracing elements of brain dynamics and hypotheses concerning the non-specialised nature of particular hub regions in language processing. Extensive experimental evidence will be put forward to support various novel claims about the oscillatory implementation of linguistic computation; specifically, it will be claimed that basic linguistic combinatorics involves (amongst other things) θ-γ interactions, cyclic 'chunking' involves α-inhibition and β increases, and phrase structure building involves the embedding of multiple oscillations inside δ rhythms. The notion of a *neural code* will be argued to be highly relevant to language. When Stanley (2013, 260) notes of the imperative to 'identify a clear biophysical mechanism to propagate . . . codes across microcircuits and across regions', we will point to oscillations as being representative of these underlying mechanisms. It will additionally be argued that it was the embedding of this specific neural code inside a uniquely globular braincase that gave rise to hierarchical phrase structure. It is hoped that this satisfies a more general point raised by authors such as Chen et al. (2019, 2), who note that syntactic labelling 'is proposed mainly within the framework of linguistics', and that '[t]he neural substrate of dynamically using . . . [labelling] to process syntactic structures still needs to be explored'.

Chapter 3 elaborates on the hypotheses presented in the previous chapter by refining the proposed neural code for language, with particular focus on hierarchical phrase structure (as opposed to bare set-formation and semantic combinatorics). A number of original hypotheses will be introduced concerning the functional role of oscillations in language, supported by extensive literature from across the cognitive and biological sciences. A more intensive review of the computational properties of discrete oscillation bands is presented, and a number of attempts are made to reconcile the present neural code with more traditional cartographic neurolinguistic models. The chapter will expand on the notion that certain interactions between oscillations generated via 'cross-frequency coupling' and oscillatory 'migrations' are responsible for linguistic computation. It will be suggested that linguistic phrase structure building is implemented not simply via sustained neuronal activity, but rather via discretised, rhythmic pulses of coordinated neuronal firing. Other implications for future research are discussed, such as the possibility that the present set of oscillatory hypotheses can serve as a model for the neural formatting of human thought. An extensive number of language-relevant neuroanatomical and oscillatory differences between humans and our closest relatives will be presented, along with an evolutionary timeline of their likely development. The chapter ends with a discussion of the neuroethological implications of the book, returning to some concerns raised in the first two chapters.

Chapter 4 concludes and presents a number of future research directions.

1 Theory and Praxis

Perhaps the most striking feature of language is how distinct and isolated it is in the biological world. While thematic agent–patient relations (Reinhart 2002), properties of general reasoning, and the capacity to count small numbers and execute elementary arithmetical operations have all been documented in monkeys (Hauser et al. 1996), pigeons (Rugani et al. 2011) and a number of other animals, the ability to construct hierarchically organised sets of representations and combine them with further sets of similar structural complexity remains the exclusive property of humans. Humans seem particularly competent at constructing and interpreting hierarchies. Just as we can combine two sentences into a larger one, we can also combine representations of social hierarchies into larger units, combining multiple hierarchically organised political organisations (e.g. national governments) into larger structures (e.g. the European Union), which themselves can be decomposed and altered (e.g. Brexit). These forms of hierarchies seem to be subserved by distinct neural systems, with the hippocampus and medial prefrontal cortex being implicated in processing visual, spatial and social hierarchies, and regions in the left inferior frontal gyrus being implicated by many researchers in linguistic hierarchies. While environmental stimuli play an important role in determining how language develops in a child, the language sciences have also shown that there must be a certain degree of 'innateness' to language design. The general research programme geared towards exploring these and other topics (including the implementation and development of language in the brain and language pathologies) has been referred to as *biolinguistics*. This term was putatively coined in 1974 at an interdisciplinary meeting at Dedham, Massachusetts, by its organiser, Massimo Piattelli-Palmarini (1974), around the time that researchers began exploring the neural basis of language using emerging methods, focusing on cerebral asymmetries (Jenkins 2000, LeMay & Geschwind 1975).

Although language evolution typically occupies centre stage, biolinguists concern themselves with a wide number of different research questions, employing frameworks general to evolutionary theory, typically (and reasonably) not claiming that language requires some special, new form of evolutionary theory and can be accommodated by existing models (e.g.

adaptationism, anti-adaptationism, saltationism, exaptation or spandrel models). For instance, language acquisition is assumed to undergo a 'growth' period from an innate, initial state (termed *Universal Grammar*, UG), which proceeds through to an intermediate stage as the child fixes the parameters of their grammatical principles, and finally reaches a level of mature grammatical competence. UG is used to refer to the biological basis of whatever capacity is deemed essential and unique to language, examining the nature of 'I-language' (the internal, individual and intensional structure of language – a purely cognitive perspective) rather than 'E-language' (any other conception of language distinct from I-language, typically 'external', extra-mental conceptions of language like 'English' or 'a collection of utterances', something which could not possibly exist in the physical world). While many claim to hold views on the evolution of language, it is often the case that they are rather exploring *language change*. For instance, Deutscher's (2005) outstanding monograph bears the title *The Unfolding of Language: The Evolution of Mankind's Greatest Invention*, but as is clear from the intentional language, the text explores how (E-)languages themselves have changed over the centuries (e.g. French, English), consulting no biological frameworks.

The extent to which properties of language are innate is often overlooked in the literature. Considering the development of the lexicon, words involving polysemy (*book, newspaper, city, lunch*) involve associating semantically distinct senses for which there is no immediate evidence in the environment (e.g. a lunch can be an abstract event or a physical item of food), and simply associating a sound with a 'thing' in the world will not suffice to generate this knowledge in children (Murphy 2017a). Yet a commitment to a certain number of innate factors does not entail commitment to some form of gene-centrism, since the environment also plays an important role. *Language* and *cognition* are therefore thought to be parts of the natural world on a par with *chemical, optical* and *electrical* aspects, being just as amenable to naturalistic enquiry (Ueda 2016). Seeking the biological basis of language is in this sense comparable to exploring the visual system. As Epstein et al. (2017a, 51) make perfectly clear, 'vision scientists are not directly engaged in trying to account for *what* people might decide to look at'; rather, they are interested in explaining how we use our eyes to see in the first place. While the classical nature–nurture debate resulted in much division but little substantial progress, contemporary discussions of nativism and empiricism typically focus on emerging paradigms that employ this dichotomy in the service of certain continua, or particular spectra of developmentally achievable states modulated by environmental pressures and physical constraints, such that we no longer have to choose between either nature or nurture.

Whichever research topic is pursued, there are by necessity three independent factors which interact to generate the final state of any biological property related to language (Chomsky 2005): (1) genetic endowment, (2) environment ('stimuli', 'data') and (3) principles not specific to language (general physical law). As a subordinate concern, this book will occasionally discuss some of these 'third factors' (general physical law) in language design, such as the efficient wiring of the brain (e.g. dynamical system constraints) and electro-physiological dependencies between brain waves. For instance, Fermat's principle of least time seems to apply to how light travels and also to how insects such as fire ants navigate space (via the shortest path) (Oettler et al. 2013). These principles of efficiency are based on natural law, not natural selection, and it will be of interest to see if similar principles influence the design of language and how much of the language system's biology we can derive 'for free', directly from physics. This motivation is closely aligned with the more general goal of science, which the physicist Jean Baptiste Perrin defined as the attempt to reduce complex visibles to simple invisibles; namely, explaining large-scale phenomena in terms of general laws and principles. Another possible example of a third factor is the Input Generalization by Holmberg and Roberts (2014), the learning strategy which generalises from detection of one instance of a category to all future instances, for example, after seeing a black bat, assume all bats are black until contrary evidence presents itself. Further evidence for principles of efficient computation operating at the individual level comes from Terzi et al. (2019), who show that five- to eight-year-old children with autism spectrum disorder avoid the use of pronominal subjects, which can be taken as evidence that they use a strategy to avoid infelicitous reference.

Like these general laws, language becomes open for evolutionary study once we acknowledge that it is not 'embedded' somehow in a speech community but is rather part of a speaker's mental life, and therefore part of their physical existence. This *internalist* focus on the mental faculty of language (Berwick 2017) is in stark contrast to the *externalist* focus on the output of language, such as speech and communication. Fisher (2016) and Fisher and Vernes (2015), along with many others, have explored in admirable detail the genetics of *speech*, but it is unclear whether this relates to language evolution if language is understood in the computational/representational terms we will outline here. Distinguishing speech from language (and from communication) is an essential first step in exploring the biological basis of higher cognition. Not doing so results in confusion, as when Bichakjian (2017, 119) claims that '[t]he fossil evidence from the development of central and peripheral speech organs provides . . . no support for the alleged existence of a fateful event that would have dubbed a speechless ancestor into a speech-vested mutant', and uses this to make invalid claims about the evolution of language. 'Minimalism' and 'internalism' (which stress the importance of structural complexity over external shaping effects) is also the standard position in physics: the solar system has no 'function', but it does have an internal structure, dictated by natural law. Even in 1968 it was recognised by Sklar (1968) that linguistics 'is really theoretical biology' – a perspective maintained throughout this book.

1.1   Language Architecture

The nineteenth-century philosopher Wilhelm von Humboldt stressed how language is not a product (*Ergon*) but an activity (*Energeia*), or what linguists today would call a process of syntactic combinatorics and not the work of externalising them into products/words (Underhill 2009, 58). Humboldt claimed that language makes infinite use of finite means, such that it can construct an unbounded number of expressions from a limited number of elements. After successfully popularising Humboldt's formulation amongst the linguistics community, Chomsky later proposed that a language user's knowledge amounts to a finite set of representations and a finite set of combinatorial operations (informally, grammatical rules). This system was embedded within a broader architecture, according to which 'a grammar contains a syntactic component, a semantic component, and a phonological component. The latter two are purely interpretive' (Chomsky 1965, 141). Since we are viewing language as a generative procedure relating sounds (or signs) and meanings via syntax, we will be primarily concerned with what Trotzke (2015, 124) – following many others (e.g. Arbib 2006; Benítez-Burraco et al. 2014; Kenneally 2007) – refers to as the 'computational approach to language evolution'. Adopting these ideas throughout the modern history of linguistics involved what Freidin (2012, 893) calls 'a shift in focus from the external forms of a language to the grammatical system that generates it, a system that is assumed to exist in the mind of the speaker'. While the ultimate range of hierarchically organised syntactic structures is achieved most likely through processes of cultural evolution (a main focus of what we might call the 'communicative approach to language evolution'), the actual capacity to produce these structures in the first place is a separate topic, and the one taken up in this book.

There is also a (regrettably coarse) distinction in the field between those who believe language is mostly representational and innate, and those who believe it is mostly communicative and learned. As will soon become clear, I will side with the former position (see Fujita 2016, 2018 for arguments against the common claim that language was originally, and remains, primarily an instrument of communication, with Fujita arguing that language is, and likely remains, primarily an instrument of thought). As Chomsky has reversed Aristotle's dictum, language is not *sound with meaning*, but rather *meaning with sound* (i.e. externalisation is a secondary concern). With respect to innateness, this will bear on the topic of oscillations insofar as it will be suggested that certain language-specific oscillatory behaviour is genetically determined, as opposed to being learned in development via statistical analysis. With respect to the representational, cognitive structure of the language system, this will bear on the topic of oscillations insofar as the particular oscillatory model for language defended here will be constructed to some extent out of non-linguistic oscillatory behaviour putatively responsible for aspects of higher cognition like memory, attention and combinatorial processing.

Many linguists assume that each human is endowed with a *language faculty* (constructed from UG), a component of their mind/brain which permits the generation of an unbounded number of hierarchically structured expressions. Each expression is a pairing of phonological and semantic objects, which determines an association of a sound (or sign) with a 'meaning' (the activation of a given set of linguistic representations and semantic associations, e.g. First Person, Masculine). These expressions are composed of individual lexical items stored somewhere in the mind/brain. The procedures involved in current language processing are extremely difficult to tease apart. The emergence of phrase structure has no clear explanation and certainly requires more elaboration than Bybee's (2011, 536) proposal: 'Once two words can be strung together, the process of grammar creation can begin.' It is possible that every single subcomponent of language is shared with other species and that humans have simply integrated a disparate range of cognitive capacities in novel ways. This book will address this crucial topic and provide evidence that there are in fact unique properties of the human brain responsible for the human-specific subcomponents of language, although these neurobiological components are indeed likely recycled and restructured in some fashion from pre-existing components shared with a range of other species. Indeed, it is now understood that even neural tissues did not create their abilities from scratch, but rather optimised capabilities already present in ancestors: 'Unicellular creatures and non-neural metazoan tissues were already solving problems, maintaining physiological and anatomical homeostasis, and constantly trying to improve their lot in life – long before nervous systems evolved' (Pezzulo & Levin 2017; see also Burkhardt & Sprecher 2017). The molecular basis of development is highly conserved (Carroll 2006), and so there are strong reasons to assume that comparisons between species will reveal convergently evolved traits, such as vocal learning.

1.2   The 'Mechanical Power' of Language

As mentioned, we will be concerned with the following core question: *How is language implemented in the brain?* This book will have a strong computational, ethological and neuroanatomical content, necessary to explore these broader, general principles structuring language processing, and also language evolution. The dominant focus will gradually shift towards neuroscience and electrophysiology: a decision motivated by a number of factors to be discussed, one of which being, as Aboitiz (2017, 2) puts it, the fact that all accounts concerning language, 'including genetic, cultural or linguistic accounts, will eventually have to be subordinated to an explanation of how our brains construct language'.

Long before such advances could even be imagined, David Hume (1902, 108) wrote the following concerning human knowledge:

But though animals learn many parts of their knowledge from observation, there are also many parts of it which they derive from the original hand of nature; which much exceed the share of capacity they possess on ordinary occasions; and in which they improve, little or nothing, by the longest practice of experience. These we denominate Instincts, and are so apt to admire as something very extraordinary, and inexplicable by all the disquisitions of human understanding. But our wonder will, perhaps, cease or diminish, when we consider, that the experimental reasoning itself, which we possess in common with beasts, and on which the whole conduct of life depends, is nothing but a species of instinct or mechanical power, that acts in us unknown to ourselves; and in its chief operations, is not directed by any such relations or comparisons of ideas, as are the proper objects of our intellectual faculties.

What is the 'species of instinct or mechanical power' underlying language? We can think of the *species of instinct* as the genetic basis of language, while the *mechanical power* can be referred to as the real-time implementation of language in the brain. Exploring these domains demands a careful decomposition of language into a number of subcomponents, as well a careful focus on the individual language user as the output of a long evolutionary history rather than simply focusing on their linguistic output. For instance, in the vision sciences an exploration of eye morphology and maturation, rather than simply individual differences and environmental factors, has resulted in remarkable advances.

This leads us to a central topic of contemporary linguistic research, one which brings with it a number of evolutionary implications: language variation. Linguists have recently discovered that it is highly likely that all of language variation can be reduced to morphophonological changes: different languages, 'dialects' and so forth differ only insofar as they have distinct morphophonological implementations. This idea, that all variation is post-syntactic, has been formalised by Boeckx (2011):

Strong Uniformity Thesis
Principles of narrow syntax are not subject to parametrisation: nor are they affected by lexical parameters.

Recent work in ethology gives credence of the idea that variation in externalisation – dynamically ranging between generalisation and specificity – is not human-specific, being found also in birdsong (Farias-Virgens & White 2017; Tian & Brainard 2017). Generalisation in this context is the ability to identify or articulate a motor gesture in multiple sequential contexts, while specificity refers to the ability to do so in a certain sequential context. We will return to the implications of these findings below.

1.3   Language Evolution: Conflicting Models

As soon as we recognise that language is a biological capacity which must be accounted for in biological terms, we are forced to frame our investigation within a particular evolutionary model. Beginning with a major late twentieth-century framework, the neo-Darwinian synthesis (closely related to function-alist and adaptationist models of evolution, which use a biological system's putative function to direct enquiry into its origins) has great power with regard to explaining survival, but it provides few insights when investigating the form and structure of organic systems. Indeed, functionalism and the neo-Darwinian synthesis, by focusing on function rather than form, face certain difficulties even with supposedly simple structures like bones, which simultaneously provide bodily support but also store marrow and calcium for producing red blood cells, and so could be regarded as part of the circulatory system. As Zeder (2017) summarises:

> In the [modern neo-Darwinian synthesis] natural selection is recognized as the pre-eminent and ultimate causal force in evolution that sorts variation arising through random mutation, and passes on adaptive variations at a higher rate than less adaptive ones, resulting in an evolutionary process that proceeds at a gradual pace made up of small microevolutionary changes in the composition of individual genes and alleles within genes.

Moving beyond these strictures, Fuentes (2016) pushes for an 'Extended Evolutionary Synthesis', which takes into account the full range of biological, cultural and psychological factors underpinning the evolution of the human condition. Certain strands of evolutionary biology have moved beyond the 'micro mutational' gradualist perspective best symbolised by the 'hill-climbing' metaphor (derided by William James as 'Pop-Darwinism' in his critique of Herbert Spencer). Separate research programmes generate separate research methods, and in evolutionary psychology (aligned to a large extent with functionalism) assuming a priori that a given trait is an adaptation is an experimental heuristic, an assumption not always made in other strands of evolutionary theory. Adaptationism assumes that language has evolved to fulfil a particular function given some form of pressure/requirement. But what are often viewed as adaptive problems are also not necessarily so, but rather the 'regularities   of   the   physical,   chemical,   developmental,   ecological, demographic, social, and informational environments encountered by ancestral populations during the course of a species' or population's evolution' (Tooby & Cosmides 1992, 62). Adaptationism at times seems to hearken back to August Weismann's (1893) argument for the *Allmacht*, or omnipotence, of natural selection over other evolutionary forces.

In addition, phylogenetic evidence suggests that language does not necessarily evolve from simple to complex stages. Di Sciullo et al. (2013) present a range of evidence from the phylogeny of several Indo-European languages that while prepositional phrases can indeed become complex by hosting postpositions, adpositions or circumpositions, this variety of complexity is in fact minimised as a given language changes over time. Under a non-adaptationist view, language likely constitutes a spandrel, namely a feature not directly selected for but a by-product of evolution (Piattelli-Palmarini 1989).

As a result of the conclusions drawn from this brief foray into evolutionary biology, we will not stick purely to adaptationist and functionalist explanations. These models may be useful in exploring certain aspects of language evolution (for instance, imitation and speech perception), but we will also see that relying on lower-level accounts derived from general laws of form can provide novel insights into the evolution of mental faculties. As we will see, both neo-Darwinian and formalist accounts are useful in constructing theories of language evolution. Viewing the mind not just as a *modular* system (in which various modules collaborate to solve various tasks) but also as a product of adaptive pressures can shed light on certain aspects of language that the formalist account can provide little insight into, and vice versa. We will see how far the view that language is an array of distinct computational machinery can take us, and to what extent positing the innateness of language-specific computations within certain neural processes can improve on neighbouring accounts. The competition between functionalism and 'formalism' (to use nineteenth-century terminology, focusing on physical form and structural complexity independent of environment) will be ever present, as it is in much of biology: Discussing the physical genesis of multicellular forms, Newman et al. (2006, 290) conclude that, 'rather than being the result of evolutionary adaptation, much morphological plasticity reflects the influence of external physico-chemical parameters on any material system and is therefore an inherent, inevitable property of organisms'. While functionalism is concerned with structural use, formalism stresses the importance of physical principles determining organic structural complexity. Whereas many have characterised the central debate in nineteenth-century biology as being between evolutionists and creationists, a more accurate classification (as Darwin himself noted) would distinguish teleologists (who regarded adaptation as the single most important aspect in evolution) with morphologists (who held that commonalities of structure were the defining biological characteristic) – a dichotomy stressed by E. S. Russell's *Form and Function* (1916). These internalist concerns are also found in the perceptive words of the seventeenth-century German physician Daniel Sennert (1650, 765):

> Always in vain does anyone resort to external causes for the concreation of things; rather does it concern the internal disposition of the matter ... On account of their forms ... things have dispositions to act ... They receive their perfection from their form, not from an external cause. Hence also salt has a natural concreation ... not from heat or cold, but from its form, which is the architecture of its domicile.

L. T. Hobhouse remarked in his classic study *Mind in Evolution* that the chaotic motion both of long grass and of 'the white blood-corpuscle' are 'only very complicated results of the same set of physical laws in accordance with which the grass bows before the wind' (1901, 11–12).

Lewontin's 'Triple Helix' (of environment, genes and the organism), Gould's (2002) 'historical', 'functional' and 'formal' causal influences on the creation of natural objects, and Chomsky's 'three factors' in language design of data, genetic endowment and natural law lead to a familiar approach in biology: examine organism-internal constraints, with any analysis of environmental events taking place only within these constraints. We should not ignore the possibility (even likelihood) that there exist 'fourth factor' effects currently unknown and which may altogether lie beyond the grasp of physical enquiry.

In brief, the evolutionary linguist seeks to investigate the properties of a natural system, largely ignoring questions of ontology or disciplinary labels like *linguistics*, *psychology* or *biology*, which are purely honorific. As Peter Kropotkin (2010[1908]) put it:

> And to the question once asked by the Russian physiologist, Setchenov: 'By whom and how should psychology be studied?' science has already given the answer: 'By physiologists, and by the physiological method.' And, indeed, the recent labors of the physiologists have already succeeded in shedding incomparably more light than all the intricate discussions of the metaphysicists, upon the *mechanism of thought*; the awakening of impressions, their retention and transmission.

In modern linguistic theory, assumptions of computational efficiency regarding the computational system of language embrace the possibility that an 'inherently global principle of computational optimisation further forces syntactic derivation to adopt some sort of computational cycles, such as *phases*, constituting a kind of heuristic "computational trick" that syntax uses for restricting computational domains locally and thus reducing the computational load' (Narita & Fujita 2010, 385; see also van Gelderen 2018 and Cecchetto & Donati 2015 for the implications of cyclicity for contemporary linguistic theory). This leads to a number of questions, addressed in subsequent pages: How has the brain evolved the capacity to chunk information across modalities? How do other species do this? Is there anything unique about linguistic 'chunks', or does the novelty reside in the procedure of constructing and relating these chunks?

The popular focus on natural selection is of course justified to some extent, since positive selection is well known to have acted on the human genome (Sabeti et al. 2006), and brain areas putatively advantageous or crucial for language processing (such as the frontal lobe and Broca's and Wernicke's areas) are under substantial genetic control and are highly heritable (Thompson et al. 2001). But focusing on natural selection should not lead to the exclusion of other evolutionary forces. Many contemporary philosophers and intellectuals like Daniel Dennett and Steven Pinker propose a stark choice between God and natural selection (e.g. Dennett 2018, 277), which somewhat misses the point for the purposes of constructing accurate evolutionary theories. As Hinzen (2006, 96) points out, the functionalist doctrine articulated by Pinker ('[H]ow well something works plays a causal role in how it came to be' (1999, 162)) 'flies in the face of the Darwinian doctrine that neither adaptation nor natural selection are sources of genetic change. Mutations are the sources of novelty, their causes are internal, and they are crucially undirected, hence not intrinsically functional'. These Spencerian distortions have been revived by Dennett, who regards Spencer as 'an important clarifier of some of Darwin's best ideas' (1995, 393), despite the fact that Darwin himself favoured a Kropotkin-style view of human nature in which concepts like mutual aid play a central role, and believed wholeheartedly in 'the intimate connection between the brain, as it is now developed in us, and the faculty of speech' (Darwin 1871, 58). Every individual in a given population possesses genes, many of which will be shared with others. Yet for evolution to take place, some genes must differ between individuals, with distinct chemical variants of genes (alleles) providing this variation. Parents pass their genes to offspring, and the procedure of recombination merges parts of each parent's chromosome, yielding genetic variation; mutations also produce variation. Evolutionary linguists over the past decade or so have begun to stress the need for addressing the evolution of language from a highly interdisciplinary perspective, avoiding just-so stories of the kind found in evolutionary psychology – what William Blake would have called '*the* Science, of Imaginary Solutions' (Bloom 1997, 42).

More recently, Dennett (2018) has put forward perhaps his most clear and well-developed theory of language evolution in his monograph *From Bacteria to Bach and Back: The Evolution of Minds*. The two chapters largely dedicated to this topic (2018, 176–204, 248–281) do not provide a detailed model of language evolution. Dennett's theory effectively reduces to the idea that language evolution involved discovering different 'ways of speaking' (forms of learned behaviour) modified from the time of proto-languages to modern languages, involving refinements of our vocal apparatus and various cognitive capacities involved in speaking to conspecifics, which Dennett in turn explains solely through natural selection. For Dennett, weighing up the role of natural selection against other evolutionary forces constitutes proof that linguists (in particular those who he derides as formulating their ideas 'in typical MIT style'; 2018, 188) have 'staunchly resisted evolutionary thinking' (2018, 187). He adds that 'Chomskyans ... want to dismiss all evolutionary approaches to language as mere "just-so stories" unfit for scientific assessment' (2018, 248); where 'evolutionary approaches' refers only to adaptationist, neo-Darwinian frameworks.

Other texts concerning language implementation and evolution currently explore a range of topics such as physiology, genetics, and functional neuroi-maging. One landmark text, Fitch's *The Evolution of Language* (2010a), explored ethology, palaeontology, musical protolanguage and the evolution of the human vocal tract – but no subsequent text has moved far beyond these domains. For instance, Fitch (2017, 597) himself argues that Berwick and Chomsky's (2016) monograph 'offers a biased and faulty guide to the large and rapidly growing literature on language evolution'. Further, many texts including Berwick and Chomsky's have made assumptions about the conceptual capacities of non-humans based purely on communication data (call sequences, gestures, etc.), and not data from studies of animal cognition. Indeed, one of the core innovations of generative grammar was the observation that the complexity of human cognition is not limited to the serial output of linguistic externalisation. It is odd, then, that many generativists follow Bolhuis et al. (2014) and Hauser et al. (2002, 2014) and draw their conclusions about non-human primate cognition based on discoveries concerning their communication systems, not affording bonobos and chimpanzees the same privileges they afford humans (we will return to this point in Chapter 3). This constitutes an unusual double standard, considering how generativists claim that externalisation is only secondary to mind-internal syntax.

Pinker and Bloom (1990, 717), in their paper which has largely and rightly been credited with reviving the study of language evolution, critique certain anti-adaptationist stances of the time by pointing out that they could not explain 'how any specific aspect of grammar might be explained, even in principle, as a specific consequence of some developmental process or genetic mechanism or constraint on possible brain structure'. This was arguably a legitimate criticism in 1990. But, three decades later, we are now seeing signs that certain components of anti-adaptationist critique are bearing fruit.

1.4   Past, Present and Emerging Terrain

One of the major divisions in the scientific world is between the natural and cognitive sciences. The aspiration of many in both domains is to breach the gap between them, to the extent that the 'mental' world is explained to the same degree of empirical precision achieved by those who study the 'external' world. Advancing the cognitive sciences will require grounding them within the natural sciences, bridging the divide between a number of descriptive levels, ranging from neural implementation to algorithmic execution to general behaviour. As Pinker (2015, 85) notes, any theory attempting to bridge the implementational level of biology and the computational level of linguistic theory via some form of neurocomputational algorithm 'faces a formidable set of criteria: it must satisfy the constraints of neurophysiology and neuroanatomy, yet supply the right kind of computational power to serve as the basis for cognition'. It is increasingly being recognised that cognitive processes are emergent properties of the brain's eighty-six billion neurons. Advances in computational neuroscience have provided some answers concerning how particular neural networks give rise to firing patterns and what computational properties can be ascribed to them (i.e. what function these networks appear to have). The evolution of cognitive science into a natural science – that is, one that makes causal/explanatory connections with lower-level physics (see Chomsky 2001a, 2001b for related discussion) – is something that Başar (2006) sees as pivotal to the contemporary scene:

Due to its breadth and impact, Newtonian dynamics has become the metaphor of all natural sciences. The relevance of the prestimulus EEG as a causal factor in attention, perception, learning and remembering has important parallels with Newton's ... first law of motion where the state of a moving body is a causal factor for the further evolution of its movement. The application of this law to electrophysiology is the following: The state of the brain as reflected in the prestimulus EEG is the causal factor for the later brain responses.

Language is undoubtedly one of the most complex and well-examined cognitive faculties. It has been argued by some to be the origin of complex thought and imagination. Tattersall (2017) writes:

This symbolic capacity of ours resonates in every realm of our experience, and in combination with the complex ancestral foundation of intuitive intelligence and association-making on which it is superimposed ... it is the fount not only of our imagination and creativity, but of all those other cognitive peculiarities that set us apart from even our closest living relatives in nature.

As Tattersall's words suggest, the study of the neural basis of language (neurolinguistics) concerns the biological basis of internalised syntactic, semantic and phonological structures, and not more complex, cultural phenomena. It should be noted, though, that it is possible (as will be discussed later) that language is not in fact the necessary centre of complex thought, even if it does enhance it (another candidate includes the Multiple Demand system; Duncan 2013). Rather, it is likely that language is at the centre of a particular format of complex thought: namely, hierarchically organised and cyclically structured representations (e.g. phrases). One major tradition in contemporary linguistics, arguably founded by Chomsky (1957), proposes that humans are genetically endowed with a mental computational system that can generate an infinite number of hierarchical expressions, contributing to human-specific mental powers. This system interfaces with conceptual systems (for meaningful interpretation) and articulatory systems (for expression).

A range of novel findings support the claim that part of this knowledge concerning syntactic structures is biologically innate. For instance, Goldin-Meadow and Yang (2016) studied a deaf child who had received no linguistic input and who had consequently acquired no spoken language. Instead, they used gestures ('homesigns') to communicate, and the authors discovered that these gestures were in fact combinatorial in nature, implementing recursive procedures such that the child could create an unbounded number of expressions. Instead of applying rote memorisation operations to the signs they received, the child was able to use their homesigns creatively – the hallmark of human syntactic combinatorics. In contrast, non-human primates exposed to linguistic input can only memorize certain symbols and do not generate a productive computational system. The authors comment:

> The urge to communicate using a productive combinatorial system is so weak in chimpanzees that they do not even see productivity in the combinatorial communication systems to which they are exposed. In contrast, this urge is so strong in human children that they will create a system with combinatorial productivity even if not exposed to one.

Experiments with English-speaking children also indicate that 'children are genetically predisposed to rule out structure-independent options' when forming *yes/no* questions involving auxiliary inversion (Sugisaki 2016, 126). Language differs from animal systems of communication in that it is not stimulus-driven, nor does it have a specialised function like alarm calls or seduction songs. Hauser and Watumull (2017) have recently argued that the more fundamental generative capacity is equivalent to a universal Turing machine (in principle, given unlimited memory) which interfaces with a number of different conceptual systems: morality, mathematics, music and language. Each of these systems has a unique representational base (numbers for mathematics, notes for music, action patterns for morality, lexical features for language) and imposes distinct interface demands. Linguists study 'event structure', moral theorists study 'moral structure'; both generated using the same recursive computational procedure. This framework of assuming the existence of this core computational system (what Hauser and Watumull call the *Universal Generative Faculty*, UGF) produces a mental architecture through which distinct representational domains access a universal Turing machine which provides a number of generative procedures, which differ based on which representational domain interfaces with UGF: recursion for language and music, iteration for motor routines, and the successor function for mathematics. As the authors put it (Hauser & Watumull 2017):

Computability is common to all generative systems, and *definition by induction* is ubiquitous in the generation of hierarchical structure. Thus it is possible for a system to be computable but not generative of hierarchy (e.g., Lashley's motor routines), as well as computable and generative of hierarchy but not unbounded (e.g., birdsong or human phonology).

What this suggests is that the generative procedures of UGF are available to different representational domains in humans, though not in other species. Since cognitive faculties are generated by the brain, it follows that there must be something unique about the human brain that gives rise to this 'sharing' of UGF with representational domains which are predominantly spread out across a range of cortical and subcortical structures. For instance, morality seems to access concepts which are only derived from *content* words like nouns and verbs, with most moral judgements involving certain actors doing things to others. *Functional* elements, like determiners, auxiliaries and copulas, seem language-specific, and indeed the combination of content and functional elements seems to be the core representational feature of human language syntax (Miyagawa et al. 2013). Indeed, while function words are very often derived from content words, content words are virtually never descended from function words, suggesting a clear evolutionary trajectory for the complexity and organisation of language (Hurford 2014).

In line with the notion of UGF, Collins (2015a, 740) discusses a similar hypothesis and rightly notes that 'nonhuman animals might possess something akin to Merge, or some device falling under the Chomsky hierarchy, which fails to be integrated with other systems so as to be unused for general cognition or communication, or is restricted in some fashion'. Milne et al. (2018, 44) have also compared structured sequence learning across sensory modalities in humans and, in line with the proposed existence of UGF, conclude that 'humans do not possess a single, domain-general system that operates identically over all auditory and visual sequences. Rather the system appears to be more complex and operates under modality and stimulus-specific constraints.' For independent reasons, Gallego and Orús (2017, 18) come to a similar conclusion, writing that 'the human abilities of language, mathematics, and probably others, may actually be different manifestations of a fundamental single ability of the human brain, namely, *the ability to organize and process information according to different physical scales*'. The notion of physical scale will be returned to throughout this book, in particular with respect to discussions of brain oscillations.

Of clear relevance for us is an important finding discussed by Petersson and Hagoort (2012, 1977), pointing the way to particular dynamic perspectives on neural activity to account for linguistic computation (see also Siegelmann 1999):

[A]ny Turing computable process can be embedded in dynamical systems instantiated by recurrent neural networks that are closer in nature to real neurobiological systems. The fact that classical Turing architectures can be formalized as time-discrete dynamical systems provides a bridge between the concepts of classical and nonclassical architectures.

An assumption of the 'cognitive revolution' of the 1950s and 1960s was that many forms of human behaviour rely on mind-internal representations and processes which are performed highly efficiently by the brain. As Lobina (2017, 4) puts it, 'Chomsky's whole *oeuvre* can be seen as an attempt to follow the rather sensible view that it is a prerequisite of cognitive science to understand the nature of the organism ... before analysing the behaviour it produces.' Relatedly, the standard approach in evolutionary psychology is to search for genetically determined cognitive solutions to environmental challenges. As a result, emphasis is often placed on special-purpose, domain-specific neural modules. Yet, the evolutionary and neuroscientific evidence increasingly points towards a more nuanced account, revealing a set of limited, generic procedures which can be reused in dynamic ways. Indeed, the pervasive nature of neural 'reuse' should lead us to reject the neural version of the modularity thesis, or the idea that the brain is composed of segregated, functionally dedicated modules. As Anderson (2016, 2) explains:

Not every cognitive achievement – not even achievements as central to the life of a species as natural language is to ours – need be supported by a specific targeted adaptation. In fact, the principle of parsimony would appear to dictate that, *ceteris paribus*, we should prefer accounts that show how 'higher-order' cognitive processes (such as language and mathematics) marshal existing neural resources and behavioral strategies in unique ways over accounts that posit unique adaptations.

Mechanisms such as neural reuse are also likely responsible for the recently discovered shared substrates between language and spatial navigation systems. Vukovic and Shtyrov (2017) used electroencephalography (EEG) to monitor activity in subjects performing spatial navigation and sentence-picture matching tasks. They identified a common network consisting of 'frontal, motor and premotor, temporo-occipital and extrastriate regions associated with the computation and maintenance of allocentric and egocentric perspectives at an inter-individual level, which mediate integration of perceptual features into sentence-derived semantic representations' (Vukovic & Shtyrov 2017, 130). Upon the emergence of the human-specific feature of phrase structure building, it appears to have exploited existing networks to perform certain computationally similar tasks. Neural reuse also likely explains the existence of the visual word-form area in left occipito-temporal sulcus, since writing systems are only 7,000 years old. This area seems consistent across the world's language users, and therefore orthography is likely constrained by visual working memory – which indeed seems the case, given Dehaene and Cohen's (2007) finding that individual characters in alphabetic systems across the globe consist on average of three strokes, with the intersection contours of these strokes adhering to the same frequency distribution (e.g. Y, N, K, Z).

While the revolution in linguistics emerging in the 1950s and 1960s firmly placed the field within the broader, emerging domain of cognitive science, this brought with it a certain cost, substantially alienating the study of language from neuroscience. Proponents of generative grammar have always stressed their core belief that *language is an organ of the mind* and hence *linguistics is biology at a higher level of abstraction*, but concrete linking hypotheses with biology have been lacking. If more theories of linguistic behaviour made predictions and generated hypotheses about brain circuits, then a richer field of neurolinguistics would surely emerge. The development of a mechanistic theory of elementary linguistic computation requires more than data from correlational functional neuroimaging studies concerning where in the brain particular operations appear to be implemented; it requires an understanding of how the brain in fact functions. As Ramón y Cajal said, 'To observe without thinking is as dangerous as to think without observing.'

Many linguists have recently claimed that they are beginning to engage much more with the biology literature at various levels. But this almost always amounts to literature reviewing, rather than genuine engagement. The importance of a broad, multidisciplinary approach to the neural basis of language cannot be underestimated. Welch (2017, 263) succinctly and powerfully summarises some of the core problems of evolutionary biology, which we can generalise to the study of language and the brain:

[T]he variety of living things and the complexity of evolution make it easy to generate data that seem revolutionary (e.g. exceptions to well-established generalizations, or neglected factors in evolution), and lead to disappointment with existing explanatory frameworks (with their high levels of abstraction, and limited predictive power). ... [T]his research needs distinct tools, often including imaginary agency, and a partial description of the evolutionary process. This invites mistaken charges of narrowness and oversimplification (which come, not least, from researchers in other subfields), and these chime with anxieties about human agency and overall purpose.

The issue of evolutionary complexity, and what it can tell us about appropriate ways to theorise about the biological basis of language, should be front and centre of the biolinguistics enterprise (Samuels 2011, 2015). Yoshimi (2012, 373) notes that 'physical systems aggregate into increasingly complex structures, existing at different levels of organization'. Perhaps reacting to a similar intuition, Plato believed intelligibility was to be found only in the world of geometry and mathematics, with the complex world of sensation being unapproachable. An effective study of astronomy, in his view, requires that 'we shall proceed, as we do in geometry, by means of problems, and leave the starry heavens alone' (1945, 248–249; see also O'Meara 1981). In more recent times, Plato's belief in the importance of higher-order abstractions to properly characterise complex behaviour echoes in Krakauer et al.'s (2017) analysis of the current state of neuroscience. These authors propose that behavioural experiments are vital to the field, providing a level of computational understanding lower-level approaches cannot. Neuroscientific experiments can give us interesting data, which can indicate what level we need to be investigating: the same level, a higher level or a lower level. We might find out that we need to go lower, into the 'connectome' (the set of neural connections in a given nervous system; Sporns et al. 2005) from brain dynamics, for instance.

1.5   Simplicity and Neural Organisation

A guiding theme throughout this book will be that neural functional localisation (typically via functional magnetic resonance imaging (fMRI) and electroencephalography (EEG)) is an inadequate paradigm in developing neurolinguistics theories. Different parts of our brain may well selectively respond to different aspects of our sensorium, but as Jackendoff (2007, 13) has already noted, 'even if we know *where* a structure is localized in the brain – the sort of information that neural imaging can provide – we do not know *how* the brain initiates the structure'. A neurolinguistic theory is 'incomplete if it does not offer genuine solutions to the problems of combinatoriality, structural hierarchy, and binding among structures' (2007, 15). Summarising a large number of neuroimaging studies, Grimaldi (2012, 318) provides some general conclusions about the linguistic importance of certain regions: '[T]he temporal lobe controls memorizing operations (learning new and retrieved stored linguistic primitives), the parietal lobe controls analysing sublexical linguistic units and converts sensory subunits to motor subunits, and the frontal lobe integrates linguistic units in motor sequencing with the lateral prefrontal cortex, and Broca's area in particular is specialized to process complex linguistic hierarchies efficiently.' How these regions actually implement the analysing and integrating of linguistic units remains less well understood.

The urge to map linguistic modules (e.g. binding, movement operations) to specific areas of the brain is a common one, but the project has been, from a neurocomputational perspective, a failure. As discussed later, the brain has no dedicated networks for complex cognitive and linguistic modules like theta-role assignment (Reinhart 2002), and its computational and representational primitives seem far more fine-grained. Complicating matters, a number of core linguistic components can arguably be eliminated in favour of a core set of elementary operations impacting external memory, interpretive and articulatory systems (see, for instance, Hinzen 2016 for an attempt to eliminate binding, in the traditional sense in which *a* binds *b* iff *a* and *b* are coindexed and *a* c-commands *b*).

Along with Lenneberg's 1967 *Biological Foundations of Language* (see also Lenneberg 1964), Chomsky's 1965 *Aspects of the Theory of Syntax* hinted at a minimalist-style approach to language, noting the importance of 'principles of neural organization that may be even more deeply grounded in physical law' (1965, 6). Unfortunately, those looking for robust connections between linguistics and such principles have been repeatedly disappointed. For instance, in a recent special issue on the biology and evolution of language, Friederici (2016) points solely to neuroanatomical studies of functional correlations between linguistic manipulations and BOLD responses on fMRI scans. These correlational studies are doubtless informative, but are couched in a necessarily delimited, restrictive theoretical framework. Likewise, Friederici's monograph *Language in Our Brain* comes to the conclusion that species-specific brain differences may be at the root of language evolution (Friederici 2017). Yet the picture she presents is undeveloped from a neurocomputational perspective, focusing on cartographic hypotheses such as the claim that a white matter dorsal tract connecting syntax-relevant regions may be the missing link affording human language. Instead of placing rather heavy explanatory burdens on individual regions, this book will rather argue that species-specific structures such as this dorsal tract are only a small part of the missing link.

In addition, Chomsky's comment in *Aspects* about organisational principles is a very general one, effectively a kind of programmatic statement. Indeed, in 2017 similar comments were made (Bassett & Sporns 2017, 356): '[T]he brain is inherently a spatially embedded network, and physical constraints resulting from that embedding underlie functionally important network characteristics, such as efficient network communication and information processing.' These comments are accurate, but moving beyond generalisations requires particular hypotheses about individual levels of complexity.

The limitations of the cartography-without-rhythmicity approach (i.e. brain imaging without any electrophysiological or neurocomputational direction) cannot be underestimated. Recent work (Blank et al. 2016a) has shown that left hippocampus is involved in hierarchical linguistic interpretation (individuals with hippocampal amnesia also display particular language deficits; Duff & Brown-Schmidt 2012). Yet even if it transpired that a substantially greater number of cortical and subcortical structures were deeply involved in recursive phrase structure building, this would only tell us something about anatomical functional distribution. The problem of how these regions neurally implement these computations remains. Unless theoretical advances are made on this front, the emerging field of oscillatory research into language could soon slip into the same mistakes made by the previous generation of functional neuroimaging studies, fixating only on correlations between brain states and cognitive tasks rather than drawing any neurocomputational conclusions from such data.

As such, I will consequently approach the problem of implementing language in the brain with a number of crucial caveats. Neurolinguistics has been awash with new data over recent years but it has also seen a lack of conceptual or theoretical innovation to account for this data. Many researchers continue to apply the intuitive cartographic mindset to newly emerging levels of analysis, with Bastiaansen and Hagoort (2015) coming to the neurobiologically implausible conclusion that γ rhythms are responsible for something as complex as 'semantic unification' because they detected γ increases during semantically well-formed structures. Notice that this theory is in fact purely a redescription of the data, and an explanation for *why* we see γ increases is a separate issue, which Bastiaansen and Hagoort (2015), to their credit, do attempt to provide, if only briefly. Brown (2014) summarizes the current situation well in a brief report:

> If we really care about the question of how the brain works, we must not delude ourselves into thinking that simply collecting more empirical results will automatically tell us how the brain works any more than measuring the heat coming from computer parts will tell us how the computer works. Instead, our experiments should address the questions of what mechanisms might account for an effect, and how to test and falsify specific mechanistic hypotheses.

Filling the gap between new data and neurobiological and evolutionary theory, I will argue, is a particular neurocomputational multiplexing algorithm supported by an understanding of how the brain dynamically operates in real time. This will be presented in Chapters 2 and 3. Helfrich and Knight (2016) review how non-linear dynamics such as cross-frequency coupling, phase resetting and exogenous entrainment can contribute to the transmission of information through multiple information streams to be reconstructed downstream (the essence of multiplexing), all of which will be implicated in phrase structure building in the discussion to follow. More broadly, Helfrich and Knight (2016, 916) summarise that 'the functional architecture of cognition is profoundly rhythmic', and the implications of this for theories of higher cognition are just beginning to come to fruition. Currently, the most sophisticated attempts to theorise about the oscillatory basis of language amount to claims related to how certain slow rhythms such as δ 'reflect chunking processes' (Bonhage et al. 2017). *Reflect* is a metaphor and does not specify anything concrete; *chunking* is ill-defined in much of the literature (what is the size of a chunk?); and *processes* leaves open the neural mechanisms of parcellation. Phrases like 'reflect chunking processes' should be treated with scepticism when not backed up with modelling (they are at best examples of reverse inference), and it is unfortunate that rhetorical constructions such as these often constitute attempted explanations for experimental data.

What are the other underlying motivations for approaching the study of language in this manner? General concerns over simplicity factor here. The search for elegance and simplicity in science has its roots in classical thought. Olympiodorus claimed that 'nature does nothing superfluous or any unnecessary work'. Formulating his first rule of reasoning in 'natural philosophy' (early modern science), Newton wrote that 'nature is pleased with simplicity, and affects not the pomp or superfluous causes' (1687, ii. 160ff). A recognition of the limits of naturalistic science can also be found during Copernicus's exposition against the geocentric theories of Ptolemy (1952, I.8, 519):

Why therefore should we hesitate any longer to grant it the movement which accords naturally with its form, rather than put the whole world in a commotion – the world whose limits we do not and cannot know? And why not admit that the appearance of daily revolution belongs to the heavens but the reality belongs to the Earth?

The pluralism discussed by Giere (2006, 34) adds further impetus for linguists to embrace the field of neural dynamics and investigate the computational properties of brain rhythms:

If one is studying diffusion or Brownian motion, one adopts a molecular perspective in which water is regarded as a collection of particles. . . . However, if one's concern is the behavior of water flowing through pipes, the best-fitting models are generated within a perspective that models water as a continuous fluid. Thus, one's theoretical perspective on the nature of water depends on the kind of problem one faces. Employing a plurality of perspectives has a solid *pragmatic* justification. There are different problems to be solved, and neither perspective by itself provides adequate resources for solving all the problems.

Simplicity of theory may be a desirable outcome (as in Friederici's hypotheses about white matter dorsal tracts), but in all likelihood an explanation for the human capacity for sentence comprehension will have to be distributed across a number of brain regions, time scales and levels of neural interconnection (as Friederici has also noted in a number of places). Following Lakatos (1970, 69), we should maintain that 'the history of science has been and should be a history of competing research programmes ... the sooner the competition starts, the better for progress'. What does this mean in practice? To take an example of competing programmes, Aboitiz (2017) claims that language evolved due to the expansion of the phonological loop. This can likely explain the *object maintenance* aspect of phrase structure generation (i.e. the need to hold a set of lexical items in memory during sentence comprehension), but not the *property attribution* aspect (i.e. the existence of hierarchically organised sets). Yet Aboitiz's observations can also assume a different rationale. What syntacticians term Internal Merge (reorganising objects within an already-existing set) places greater demands on working memory than External Merge (placing two objects into a workspace), with the former involving a mildly context-sensitive grammar and a linear-bounded automaton, but the latter requiring only pushdown memory. Hence, Aboitiz's account of an expanded phonological loop in humans could go some way to explaining the emergence of certain components of Internal Merge – a highly desirable move. Research into this question is only just being initiated, yet even this account is insufficient for reaching the full range of syntactic complexity universally displayed by human languages.

Departing from this somewhat, Chomsky (2019b) argues that External Merge involves 'massive search' given that it involves searching the lexicon, whereas he argues that Internal Merge is a less computationally intensive operation since its units of manipulation are already present in the workspace. However, this sidelines the role of workspace *maintenance*, which given the internal complexity of most lexical items would be considerable in cases of Internal Merge, whereas External Merge involves maintaining fewer items for a shorter period. In addition, and as already mentioned, the distinct formal grammar profiles of these operations lead me to depart from Chomsky's (2019b) claim about Internal Merge simplicity. In brief, Chomsky's (2019b) account only addresses *Search*-related computational cost, and not other forms of computation distinguishing External and Internal Merge.

An expanded phonological loop can also potentially account for the rapid, cyclic implementation of certain elementary phonological computations, which must be constantly active during language processing. For instance, consider the need to compute identity. Reiss (2003) notes that a number of phonological processes require an operation which detects whether two segments (e.g. two consonants surrounding a vowel) are identical or not, since there are procedures which apply only if two segments are identical and there are other procedures which apply only if they are different. This requires a function with two arguments, IDENTICAL(x, y), with the variables being one of the segments. In reality, this operation must apply simultaneously at multiple phonological levels, since the aforementioned procedures apply at both the segment and subsegment level. An expanded phonological loop could likely deal with this burden.

In this connection, Sedivy (2019) provides interesting, albeit indirect, insights into whether the phrase structure mechanism or the expanded phonological loop emerged first. Sedivy concludes that complex syntactic constructions emerged only recently, and that throughout most of human history very simple (yet still hierarchically organised) structures were employed in oral production. I think this suggests that any sensitivity found in the brain to complex syntax (e.g. in Broca's area) is most likely the result of cultural evolution involving language change and selection for greater phonological loop memory load. Picking up on earlier concerns, natural selection can here explain the recent emergence of this particular human-specific feature of language. But it cannot explain the seemingly rapid, initial emergence of phrase structure, which is required to generate and interpret any phrase at all, simple or complex; the title of a recent paper by Idsardi (2018) summarises it best: 'Why is phonology different? No recursion.' This also exposes why many debates about natural selection and third factors are highly contentious – researchers are not decomposing language down to a sufficient level of granularity. Other important considerations when exploring language change, and when investigating why language's syntactic structures have only recently become more elaborate, include the relatively increased range of contexts for language use since the cultural shifts brought about by the Upper Paleolithic Revolution (i.e. a broader range of social scenarios), the faster rate of technological innovation (more inventions lead to new names for objects and processes) and an increase in non-iconic language.

But before turning to broader issues, it is necessary to introduce more thoroughly the architecture of the language faculty.

1.6   A System of Discrete Infinity

Having set the scene with respect to the general cognitive architecture, I will now suggest that asymmetric hierarchy is created by labelling such that the process of establishing a phrasal identity automatically produces a hierarchical relation between phrasal elements, and furthermore that this process is species-specific. To briefly illustrate the latter point, even though it has been well established that birds can chunk song units, these do not appear to contain the properties out of which the chunks are composed. The *warble-rattle* chunks of chaffinches (Riebel & Slater 2003) do not host the properties of either of the individual song units. There are no 'warble phrases' or 'rattle phrases', just sequences of warbles or rattles. In contrast, EEG studies have shown that children utilise prosodic boundaries for phrase structure building at around three years of age (Männel & Friederici 2011), while adult-like phrase formation develops at around six years of age (Wiedmann & Winkler 2015). Nothing remotely similar occurs with non-humans. Labelling is thus a true example of *autapomorphy*, a derived trait existing only in our lineage.

Tomalin (2007, 1784) observes in his account of the development of the theory of recursive functions that 'even if a label-free system is proposed, the essential constructional process remains the same'; that is, set-formation and labelling are essential for the construction of 'a potentially infinite set of hierarchical structures'. The concerns of linguists also bear directly on

Tinbergen's (1963) seminal ethological research programme, which aimed to explore development (ontogenesis), how a behaviour develops in an organism, and evolutionary history (phylogenesis), how it developed in the species. By following his 'aims and methods', what ethology has revealed about the cognition of non-human animals has been highly instructive (see Boeckx & Grohmann 2007). Relatedly, many other researchers have called for an inter-disciplinary approach to language evolution, but with some caveats. For instance, Christiansen and Chater (2017) call for a broad, 'integrated science of language', calling on all scientists to contribute, with the notable exception of one camp: generative linguists. Christiansen and Chater provide no moti-vated reasons for rejecting generativism (indeed, their paper includes not a single citation from generativism, while their monograph, Christiansen & Chater 2016, uses the phrase 'language itself' to refer to an externalised conception of language as a shared sociocultural construct, rather than an internal generative system).

As Hochstein (2016) notes of neuroscientific history, 'the assumption that there is a single ideally correct way of classifying or categorizing mental phenomena, and that neuroscience and psychology should adhere to this correct scheme, runs counter to productive scientific practices in these domains'. Distinct categorisational schemes require distinct goals and meth-odologies (hypothesis testing, design, pattern identification and prediction are just some of their uses), and so there is simply no way of showing a priori that linguistic concepts should be abandoned, to be replaced in full by implementa-tional processes. Similarly, many generative linguists have misinterpreted Marr (1982) through prioritising computational and algorithmic investigations over implementational research (e.g. Abels 2013) and believing that the three levels should be explored independently, despite the absence of anything in Marr which suggests this; indeed Marr's programme was geared towards bridging these levels of analysis, not segregating them.

1.6.1   Concatenation

Having rejected certain frameworks for interpreting the notion of 'language itself', we will now briefly present the core computational architecture of language assumed in this book.

The operation Merge, presented earlier, can be decomposed into a number of suboperations, including Concatenation and Label (Hornstein 2009). Hornstein and Pietroski (2009, 113) elaborate that COMBINE(A,B) consists of LABEL [CONCATENATE(A,B)]. Concatenation takes two objects and forms from them an unordered set, $\{\alpha\ \beta\}$. This is a case of what Epstein et al. (2014, 471) call Simplest Merge, noting that 'composite operations are in general unwelcome as we search for the primitive, minimal, undecomposable operations of NS [narrow syntax]'. Labelling then imposes order after searching for a head, say β. The 'copy' of β, <β>, is also typically assumed to be left after β has been concatenated in a new position: $\{_\beta \alpha\, \beta\} \rightarrow \{_\beta \beta\, \{_\beta \alpha <\beta>\}\}$. This can represent certain forms of question formation, where a copy of the *wh*-phrase is left in its initially concatenated position, for reasons of interpretability during semantic interpretation: 'What did you see <what>?'

1.6.2   Agree

Consider the sentences in (1):

(1)   a. There seems likely to be a man in the house.
         b. There seem likely to be men in the house.

In such *there*-expletive constructions, the main verb exhibits long-distance number agreement with an associate noun phrase. This featural covariation cannot be delivered by pure set-formation, and so an independent operation, Agree, has often been appealed to, in which a Probe with an unvalued feature searches its domain for an eligible Goal with a valued feature to match (e.g. Number). The value of the Goal is copied onto the Probe, establishing syntactic covariance. Another perspective deems Agree reducible to what is termed *minimal search*, through which it is framed as a top-down process which simply relates matching features to generate a degree of symmetry between syntactic objects, such as in cases where X and Y share a matching feature that is equally prominent in both X and Y (Chomsky 2015b; Narita et al. 2017). The main thesis presented in this book will not be dependent on the adoption of either of these specific claims, and so this matter will be left for the syntacticians. Indeed, it will soon become clear that linguistic features are difficult to currently embed neurobiologically; hence, my focus will largely be on computations (but see Chapter 3.6.4).

1.6.3   Natural Numbers

If Chomsky (2012) and Hinzen (2009) are right that Merge yielded the natural numbers via the successor function (a claim often adopted in generative circles), then it must be free of 'triggers' and should be executed freely. The natural numbers do not appear to require labelling, as Tomalin (2007, 1795) notes: '[T]he objects generated by the repeated application of Merge are not associated with labels ... and therefore the computational processes of arithmetic do not seem to require the same information concerning hierarchical structure that is required by the computational procedures that generate syntactic objects.' It is also possible that the acquisition of number concepts employs linguistic mechanisms; the successor function is 'a generative procedure that recursively assigns semantic meanings to number concepts' (Yang 2018, 2), yielding a productive numeral system. Despite exhibiting some competence for a number sense, 'non-human species never develop an infinite number system precisely due to the absence of a linguistic system' (Yang 2018, 16). Nevertheless, Hiraiwa (2017) notes that grammatical number and numerals do not in fact exhibit the successor function, but he acknowledges that the computation of natural numbers possibly does.

In terms of their neuroanatomy, mathematical knowledge and language appear to involve distinct cortical networks (Amalric & Dehaene 2019). Despite this, it may be that the computational similarities between aspects of syntax and aspects of mathematics can be explained by shared oscillatory codes operating over distinct networks (i.e. same computation, distinct representations); we will briefly return to this issue later.

1.6.4   Adjuncts

If Concatenate/set-formation is not human-specific (Scott-Phillips 2015, 43, discusses how 'there is no particular reason to think that combining existing signals is in any way cognitively challenging'), the sentential structures formed by it may effectively be residues of ape cognition. Since Concatenate is a simpler computational operation than Merge, we would expect its semantics to be simpler. This prediction seems to hold true, as Pietroski (2002, 2005, 2008, 2018) discusses in the context of Neo-Davidsonian event semantics. If Concatenate generates no hierarchy, simian cognition may be capable of processing modificational structures like '(the) [brown [heavy [stick]]]'. Non-hierarchical adjuncts may have arisen from pre-existing combinatorial capacities, while argument structure requires a labelling mechanism. Language provides certain formats for structuring concepts, which suggests that when these concepts do not enter into linguistic computations – in their rudimentary, 'bare' form – they are likely shared with other animals which either do not have complex syntax or do not establish an interface between syntax and their various conceptual systems. Humans are likely unique in being able to construct concepts like THE OBJECT SECOND TO THE LEFT OF THE BROWN CHAIR, but are not unique in having the discrete concepts which make up this structure.

Building on these and related insights, Blümel (2017) presents a rich array of evidence from comparative syntax demonstrating that unlabelled structures created via adjunction can participate in ongoing derivations. This suggests that adjoined unlabelled structures remain unlabelled when the rest of the generated material is transferred to the conceptual and articulatory interfaces from the syntactic system. Adjoined structures are therefore 'exempt from requiring a label' (Blümel 2017, 284). Thus, the mental representations derived from ancient simian cognition appear to have been left substantially intact, not being required to undergo the recent transformation into a form of labelled existence of the kind exhibited by most other linguistic structures. This also potentially speaks in favour of a rapid, saltationist and non-adaptationist model of language evolution, since clearly the influence of the core human-specific feature of language (labelling) has only spread so far across the computational landscape of the human mind.

Finally, labelling alone is sufficient to account for morphological Spell-Out: Taking the ambiguous sentence 'Visiting relatives can be dangerous', 'visiting' can be labelled a verbal noun in 'Visiting relatives is a nuisance' or a verbal participle in 'Visiting relatives are a nuisance', depending on the meaning. In this sense the different projections required for compositional semantics can directly explain the different patterns in agreement ('is'/'are') in morphology (Huybregts 2017; see also Oseki & Marantz 2017). This leads us to the computational properties of labelling.

1.6.5   Labelling

Some linguists (notably Hornstein 2009, Adger 2013) have suggested that the headedness/endocentricity generated by labelling (through which one element determines the identity of the larger phrase) is a language-specific feature. Chomsky (2013, 2014, 2015a, 2015b) likewise proposes that head detection can be reduced purely to minimal search, while labelling must take place at the point of transfer to the interfaces from syntax (Chomsky 2015a), obeying least effort principles. Narita (2012, 156) terms this minimal head detection. The notion of prominence here refers to those aspects of a lexical item which allow the labelling algorithm (Chomsky 2013) to identify it as an atom to be headed (Narita 2011, 190).

Minimal Head Detection
For any syntactic object Σ, the head of Σ is the most prominent LI within Σ.

We will return to other components of labelling later, but we can conclude that a supposedly simple operation like Merge in fact requires considerable breakdown into (at least) the following components: *generate* a feature, *select* the feature, *enter* the feature into a workspace, *generate*, *select* and *enter* another feature into the workspace, *concatenate* the two through attributing the constructed set some form of identity, and *transfer* the information cluster to a particular cognitive system for *labelling*.

Recent proposals have suggested that even <φ, φ> and <Q, Q> structures can be labelled (e.g. Chomsky 2015a), in which an object exhibits agreeing φ-features or Q-features, as when one member is from the Q-feature of a *wh*-word and the other is from the Q-feature of the interrogative complementizer. The labelling algorithm is assumed to search not only for categorial features of heads but also any agreeing features shared by two heads. Yet, as Shim (2018) demonstrates, postulating the latter type of search process by the labelling algorithm (i.e. locating agreeing features) adds computational burden by forcing the language system to 'perform two different types of search, namely, a "comparison search" in addition to the widely agreed-upon Minimal Search'. Shim presents an alternative analysis under which only minimal search is required, such that the empirical facts about acceptability can be derived through only invoking categorial head detection. A more conceptual difficulty for the 'dual search' model of labelling, Shim notes, is that $<\varphi, \varphi>$ structures likely do not contribute to semantic interpretation at the conceptual interface, being non-categorial. How exactly are $<\varphi, \varphi>$ structures interpreted?

A possible rebuttal to Shim (2018) is that $<\varphi, \varphi>$ and $<Q, Q>$ structures may still be able to be labelled as such, and that the language system simply recruits a more ancient search computation (namely, *comparison search*, which is found across a number of cognitive domains and pre-exists the evolution of labelling) to establish a phrasal identity. An interesting question then arises concerning how these two search procedures interface. Still, Shim's (2018) rebuttal of dual-labelling appears empirically convincing, allowing us to likely keep to the minimal search conception proposed in standard labelling theory.

1.7   Animal Syntax

What are the computational capacities of non-human animals, and do they in any way approximate those of humans? Any neurobiological programme aiming to explore human-specific features of language will need to at least have some coherent response to this question. The following sections will present a selection of interesting examples to more forcefully ground the language system within broader ethological research.

1.7.1   Formal Languages

To begin with, consider that birdsong notes of Zebra finches often combine into multi-element syllables, which combine into motifs, which string together into song bouts (Cynx 1990). They are sung in response to potential mates or rivals, and the order of notes becomes increasingly jumbled as the singer becomes more agitated. Grey parrots demonstrate processing capacities in some ways comparable to those of five- to six-year-old children, being able to learn simple vocal patterns and referential elements – but only through social interaction (Pepperberg 2007). Birdsong seems to be a holistic communication system, rather than a compositional one like human language (Okanoya 2012, 2013). Song bouts exhibit hierarchical structure, but there is no labelling, no mapping of complexes into lexical equivalence classes. Okanoya (2013, 515) proposes a reasonable evolutionary scenario according to which natural selection would have favoured a simpler syntax for wild birdsong since 'songs are needed to identify species in the wild, requiring that songs avoid phonological and syntactic complexity'. It would follow that mutations leading to greater song complexity would not have become fixed.

We can interpret any findings about animal communicative complexity from the perspective of the traditional hierarchy of formal languages (see Jäger & Rogers 2012):

Chomsky Hierarchy (Chomsky 1956b, 1957, 1963)
Type 0: Unrestricted systems (Turing machine)
Type 1: Context-sensitive systems (linear-bounded automaton; sets of sets of symbol sequences)
Type 2: Context-free systems (pushdown automaton; sets of symbol sequences)
Type 3: Regular systems (finite-state automaton; symbol sequences)

Formal language theory can be a useful tool in exploring the computational resources of and patterns from different cognitive domains. For instance, Type 2 context-free phrase structure grammars were proven insufficient for human language in the 1980s (Shieber 1985). Human language is thought to lie beyond Type 2 as mildly context-sensitive (MCS) but below Type 1 languages (Joshi 1985), which cannot be parsed in polynomial time. MCS languages are distinguished from Type 3 languages by their narrow number of overlapping dependencies and their ability to nest clauses inside clauses of indiscriminate depth. Phrase structure grammars assume a counting mechanism, implemented by pushdown stack memory, and so can generate A^nB^n structures of the kind A^iB^i $i \leq 4$, a finite subset of this language in which n is no greater than 4. Finite-state grammars cannot achieve this (Chomsky 1956a), although they can generate $(AB)^n$ languages. A^nB^n languages are thus not necessarily Type 3, but can make use of Type 2 computations. Type 1 and 2 grammars require a working memory space, dealing with dependencies between constituents. Song sequences are usually non-random but are also non-deterministic, with the probability of a song type depending on one or more preceding types (Catchpole & Slater 2008, 208–209). If dependents are further back than the immediately preceding type, then a higher-order Markov chain is required (Dobson & Lemon 1979), not a context-free grammar.

What are the uses of this framework? To give a clear example, European starlings (*Sturnus vulgaris*) can supposedly distinguish A^nB^n auditory sequences from those with an $(AB)^n$ structure, at least according to an influential study by Gentner et al. (2006) (returned to later), and nightingales can sing motifs with notes embedded within looped chunks (Todt & Hultsch 1998). An

$(AB)^n$ structure is a case of a regular/finite-state grammar and is in the Strictly Local class, SLk, being constructed from a finite alphabet with a beginning ($\ltimes$) and end ($\rtimes$). $(AB)^n$ is an SL2 stringset definable by a set of two factors (Rogers & Hauser 2010, 9–10): D(AB)n = {$\ltimes$A,AB,BA,B$\rtimes$}. Set-formation and the atomisation of call units are displayed, then, but a labelling operation is absent. Call unit α can be concatenated with unit β, forming the linear sequence <α, β>, but this structure is never given an independent structural identity. Abe and Watanabe (2011, 1070) claim that finches can distinguish syllable strings constructed by context-free grammars, supposedly being sensitive to centre-embedded structures.

It is important to stress that embedding and recursion are not equivalent (Fitch 2010b; Watumull, Hauser & Berwick 2014; Watumull, Hauser, Roberts et al. 2014), even if memory constraints permit and motivate recursion and chunking. Chomsky (1959, 148) defined self-embedding as in the following (where I is the identity element, zero, and $\Rightarrow$ refers to a rewrite operation):

A language L is *self-embedding* if it contains an A such that for some φ, ψ ($\varphi \neq I \neq \psi$), $A \Rightarrow \varphi A \psi$

Mastering $A^n B^n$ structures involves comparing two sequences of elements, which is potentially achievable by competent short-term memory and not necessarily Type 2 (Ojima & Okanoya 2014, 166–170, present critical commentary). MCS languages also go beyond this by generating $A^n B^m C^n D^m$ stringsets with cross-serial dependencies; no human language is known to require further power. Consequently, any ethological model which attempts to show the context-freeness of non-human syntax needs to demonstrate that the As and Bs are paired together. Merely showing that the number of distinct elements is equal, as in the Gentner et al. (2006) model, does not entail a dependency. In this vein, Fitch and Friederici (2012, 1943) document that counting and comparing across phrases, the computation required to recognise $A^n B^n$, is 'difficult or impossible for most tested non-human species'. They also suggest that the concept of bilateral/mirror symmetry requires a context-free grammar capable of recognising $A^n B^n$ structures and, as a result, able to engage in mirror symmetry detection (2012, 1943–1944). $A^n B^n$ languages, though context-free, can still be recognised by some finite-state automata augmented with a simple counter (Jäger & Rogers 2012, 1962, Zimmerer et al. 2014), bringing into question what computational capacities ethologists are in fact investigating. As Zuidema (2013) observes, Gentner et al. (2006) presented stimuli to teach starlings to distinguish $A^n B^n$ from $(AB)^n$, but no stimulus was presented which would allow them to exclude $A^n B^m$, leading to ambiguities over whether the starlings could actually learn Type 2 languages.

Repeating these errors, Suzuki et al. (2016) also claim that the Japanese tit (*Parus minor*) possesses a compositional syntax since in their experiments the birds responded to novel sequences of calls in particular call orderings. Yet, as Fukui (2017) notes in his critique, 'their experiments show at best that bird syntax is only narrowly based on linear order, whereas it is well attested that human language is dependent on hierarchy instead of (or in addition to) linearity'.

A further problem with many experiments (e.g. Abe & Watanabe 2011; Ten Cate & Okanoya 2012) is their lack of specificity about the object of investigation, not clearly distinguishing between the ability to implement, learn and exhibit a preference for a Type 2 language. The mild context sensitivity of non-humans has not been well tested, with ethologists typically favouring the search for identification of nesting. Work by Kershenbaum et al. (2014) suggests only that non-Markovian dynamics like the 'renewal process' (a strong tendency to repeat elements) may characterise the vocalisations of seven taxa including Bengalese finches, rock hyraxes and killer whales, rather than Markovian processes or, indeed, context-free grammars. Further research is needed to determine whether birds can recognise Type 2 languages and which family of Type 2 or 3 languages matches their auditory cognition; for instance, can finches recognise a more complex finite-state pattern such as $A^1(BA^1)^1$, where 1 indicates paired elements?

For now, it at least seems clear that, lacking a lexicon or identifiable semantics (Catchpole & Slater 2008), birdsong is best characterised as 'phonological syntax' (Marler 1998), resembling most strongly human sound structure. Birdsong might turn out to be linked to some form of complex semantic system, and it would be worthwhile investigating this, but no evidence currently exists to support this notion. Although human phonological structure is characterisable via finite-state machines (Johnson 1972; Rogers et al. 2010), there the similarities appear to end with birdsong syntax. Gentner and Hulse (1998), for instance, proved that a first-order Markov model serves to describe the majority of starling motif sequences, with every motif being predictable by its immediate predecessor. Producing sequential vocal elements is certainly a strong behavioural parallel that birdsong shares with human speech, but there appear to be no other legitimate parallels involving combinatorial syntactic complexity. The inherited acoustic signals of songbirds appear to be mediated by the dorsomedial subregion of nucleus intercollicularis and the central mesencephalic grey (Dubbeldam & Den Boer-Visser 2002). Low-threshold microstimulation of the nucleus intercollicularis elicits simple call-like vocalisations in adult male zebra finches and canaries (Vicario & Simpson 1995).

Concerning the evolutionary basis of these capacities, Wilson et al. (2013) studied two species which differ in their evolutionary distance from humans; marmosets and macaques, with the latter enjoying a closer distance. Both species learnt an artificial grammar with non-deterministic word transitions.

While marmosets displayed a sensitivity to simple violations, macaques were sensitive to more complex violations, suggesting that closer relatives to humans demonstrate a more sophisticated artificial grammar processing capacity. Chapter 3 will return to these issues and discuss them within the electro-physiological context provided in Chapter 2.

1.7.2   Hierarchy

A brief clarification should be presented here about the nature and scope of *hierarchy*. As mentioned, the songs of Bengalese finches are markedly predictable in that each sequence is constructed purely from concatenating a new subsequence to the end of another (see Dawkins 1976 for a discussion of the efficiency of hierarchical organisations of common subroutines). This constitutes a form of trivial tail recursion (Fitch 2010a). Bengalese finches are also capable of segmentation and chunking, basic processes thought to be involved in human language acquisition (Takahasi et al. 2010, 481). As with phonological syntax, labelling is not necessary for hierarchy. There is no endocentric labelling in syllables which have a nested [σ[onset] [ρ [nucleus] [coda]]] structure; further, there is no repeated nesting (syllables within syllables).

It has been claimed that wild mountain gorillas appear to prepare nettles for eating in a hierarchical procedure (Hurford 2011), free of endocentricity:

Nettle preparation (adapted from **Byrne & Russon 1998**)
Find patch → Collect leaf-blades; Enough? ↺ → [Strip stem; Enough? ↺ → Tear-off petioles] → Clean → Fold blades. [Eat nettles]

Byrne and Russon conclude that 'great apes suffer from a stricter capacity limit than humans in the hierarchical depth of planning' (1998, 667). Indeed, as Fitch and Friederici (2012, 1936) comment, 'as our understanding of neural computation in vertebrates progresses, it seems likely that different hierarchies will arise'. Pulvermüller (2014) even suggests that locality conditions in syntax may impose constraints on the 'syntax of actions' and motor planning (see Moro 2014 for objections, and Boeckx & Fujita 2014 for a review).

Be that as it may, what appears to be hierarchical may simply be automated, with the brains of wild mountain gorillas possibly having created a looped routine characterisable in Markovian terms (see Penn et al. 2008, 117, for criticisms of attributing hierarchical forms of cognition to non-humans). Furthermore, while motor routines may implement concatenative functions, it is inaccurate to describe this as true recursion, which defines its output value in terms of the values of all of its previous applications, grounded in the initial application. This self-referential quality of recursion is clearly found in language, but there is nothing homologous in motor routines. As Bolhuis et al.

(2018) review, there is currently no serious evidence of syntax-determined meaning in non-humans.

1.7.3   Compositionality

Language and primate vocal calls share many features, being forms of coordinated activity relying to a large extent on similar neural mechanisms, and also involving an extensive array of pragmatic inferential processes (Seyfarth & Cheney 2017). Returning to issues of combinatorics, free-ranging male Campbell's monkeys have been shown to respond to disturbances with around twenty loud calls and six call types: *krak, krak-oo, hok, hok-oo, wak-oo* and *boom* (Ouattara et al. 2009). The majority of sequences include a series of *krak-oo* calls which are occasionally concatenated with other types, while the tempo is modulated by the sense of emergency (i.e. *krak* is uttered in emergencies, *krak-oo* in non-emergencies). The contact calls of female Campbell's monkeys can be externalized as single units (ST1, SH2 etc.), combined (e.g. Concatenate (ST1,SH2) = {CT}) or distinguished by a suffix (e.g. Concatenate(SH2,frequency-modulated-arch) = {CH6}). These sequences are used to communicate narrow contextual information, the content of which can be strongly modified by slight changes (Lemasson et al. 2013, see also Zuberbühler 2019 for a brief review).

The computational capacities required for such concatenation do not seem to extend beyond Type 3 systems, and it appears that the monkeys are restricted to a single application of concatenation. Schlenker et al. (2014) have developed a formal semantic analysis of the calls of free-ranging Campbell's monkeys, proposing that *krak* and *hok* are 'roots' which independently convey information (and can have attributed to them a propositional semantics, 'type t') and which can be optionally affixed with *-oo*, whilst calls which begin with *boom boom* indicate a non-predatory context. *Krak* appears to have different 'lexical entries' (conceptual content) for two different groups of monkeys in Tai forest (Ivory Coast) and on Tiwai island (Sierra Leone), and so seems to be 'underspecified' in the way that many human language constructions require pragmatic *strengthening* and *saturation*, providing further impetus to look in places beyond pragmatics for human-specific features of language. These call combinations can be generated by a finite state grammar (Schlenker et al. 2014, 454), with a 'leopard call', for instance, having the following structure ('*' = multiple occurrences, 'K' = *krak-oo*, 'k' = *krak*):

Leopard call: k K*, k k*

The 'cognome' (i.e. the set of computational operations able to be implemented by a particular system; Poeppel 2012) of white-handed gibbons also permits the concatenation of a finite set of units to yield duet and predator songs (Clarke et al. 2006), utilising combinatorial rules to advertise pair bonds and repel conspecific intruders.

One final study sheds new light on these issues. Jiang et al. (2018), for the first time, trained two rhesus macaques to generate structured sequences through hitting a touchscreen at certain locations arrayed around a circle. After intensive training, the macaques learned to produce mirror sequences of an ABC|CBA pattern, and generalized this to sequences of varying lengths. These grammars have been shown to require supraregular computational abilities, going beyond regular or finite-state grammars. This suggests that, in the domain of visuospatial reasoning, macaques can execute working memory processes akin to human language. However, Jiang et al. also tested five- to six-year-olds, who learned these grammars after only around five demonstrations, vastly outperforming the macaques (who needed tens of thousands of trials). It is possible, then, that the neural processes and computations employed reflex-ively by human children are of a completely different type from those deployed by macaque brains, who likely deployed various cognitive resources from distinct domains to implement the mirror grammars. Only future neuroimaging and behavioural work can address this topic.

We can conclude from this section that the evidence in favour of non-human MCS grammars is either non-existent or based on speculation and misrepre-sentation, while the evidence for Type 2 grammars is limited, although this may be due more to the methodological flaws of a young field (Fitch & Hauser 2004 being the first major study) than the computational properties of its objects of enquiry. Some non-human conceptual systems may be compositional, but only human language simultaneously exhibits compositionality and productivity. These issues will be discussed in a neurobiological context in Section 3.7.

1.8   Mapping Syntax and Sentence Processing

One final issue needs to be addressed before we can progress to the next chapter, and this concerns the relationship between models of sentence proces-sing (psycholinguistics) and models of linguistic knowledge (syntax). The approach to language processing that will be outlined in the next chapter is consistent with the 'one-system' contention of Lewis and Phillips (2015) that grammatical theories and language processing models describe the same cog-nitive system, as evidenced by the fact that grammar-parser misalignments only seem to occur as a consequence of limitations in domain-general systems such as memory access and control mechanisms, and as also evidenced by the convergence between online and offline responses to grammatical anomalies (Sprouse & Almeida 2013). This supports the hypothesis that 'online and offline representations are the product of a single structure-building system (the grammar) that is embedded in a general cognitive architecture, and misalignments between online ("fast") and offline ("slow") responses reflect the ways in which linguistic computations can fail to reflect the ideal performance of that system' (Lewis & Phillips 2015, 39; see also Lightfoot 2020). It will be claimed in the next chapter that the interactions between different neural oscillations at different time scales allows the brain to flexibly achieve the rapid parsing of linguistic structures, with an average reader comprehending 250–300 words per minute (Rayner et al. 2012).

While real-time processing data is typically consistent with theoretical considerations, it is also the case that the considerably vast range of psycholinguistic results are only occasionally related to generative models of linguistic knowledge. For instance, one author points out that we often find 'theoretical linguistics often proceeding without drawing on experimental results, and psycho-/neurolinguistics limitedly relying on linguistic theory' (Mancini 2018, 1). This is partly due to many researchers assuming that the Marrian levels of analysis (computation, algorithm, implementation) are to be investigated in isolation, as mentioned earlier. Yet, if we assume the one-system contention of Lewis and Phillips (2015), we immediately get a transparent mapping between syntax and sentence processing; namely, the computational level denotes the offline properties of the system (it can search, merge, copy, label, etc.) and the algorithmic level denotes it real-time execution. Any system of language processing needs a precise specification of the formal properties of, say, merging and labelling, and any model of language processing would need to state how real-time steps are executed.

We do, however, sometimes find misalignments between online and offline responses to grammaticality, i.e. a sentence might be ungrammatical, in terms of its agreement relations, but is nevertheless processed with no obvious difficulty. Yet, as Mancini (2018) proposes, it is possible that online and offline responses represent 'distinct snapshots of a process that unfolds in time and that goes through different computational stages'. If this is the case, then there is no need to invoke a 'two-systems' model of the parser and grammar.

The reason why this topic is relevant to our concerns is that, as discussed below, recent research has shown that patterns of neural oscillations are sensitive to hierarchical syntactic structure. The implications of this for models of sentence processing, and psycholinguistics more broadly, are quite substantial. For instance, these findings suggest that the real-time structure-building mechanism (the parser) can incrementally group linguistic units in a Merge-like way. This supports the one-system contention of Lewis and Phillips (2015) and suggests that the computational/derivational component of language can be implemented in a left-to-right fashion (as Phillips 2003 contended).

However, language processing involves not just bottom-up generative procedures, but also top-down processes of prediction. It will be argued below that this top-down predictive component is also implemented via neural oscillations, alongside the structure-building component. How might this be implemented at the algorithmic level? Martorell (2018) makes a plausible suggestion about this issue, noting that since sentences are potentially infinite it is likely that the most parsimonious strategy would be for the language system to avoid predictions relating to optional syntactic elements (like adjuncts) and only generate predictions related to core structural elements such as verbs and their arguments. As such, the processing of adjuncts would involve bottom-up processing with no prior activation (see Martorell 2018 for empirical evidence, such as the finding that arguments lead to faster reading times than adjuncts; Tutunjian & Boland 2008).

Another topic relevant to the alignment of linguistic theory with processing models is Minimalist Grammars (MGs) (Stabler 1997). These provide an explicit formulation of the computational machinery of generative grammar (Merge, Move, Agree, etc.), and there has been work using MGs as the basis for psycholinguistic modelling (i.e. as a way of explaining patterns in behavioural data during sentence processing experiments). To take an interesting and recent example, consider Hunter et al. (2019). These authors note how psycholinguistic research increasingly suggests that human parsing of moved syntactic elements is 'active', or even 'hyper-active', such that leftward-moved objects are related to a verbal position rapidly (rather than the parser delaying such interpretive procedures until necessary), possibly before the transitivity information associated with the verb is available to the comprehender. In an attempt to align this feature of the parser with the minimalist/generative computational architecture of the language system (and, hence, to ultimately provide support for the one-system contention), Hunter et al. embed within the search space of MGs branching points that can be identified as the locus of the decision to perform active gap-finding. Effectively, this imposes on the parser certain syntax-specific points of interpretive action, in line with what psycholinguistic work is revealing about how humans seem to implement movement operations.

To illustrate, a typical *filler-gap* dependency involves a pronounced element (*filler*) and a subsequent position in the sentence which is 'silent' and not pronounced in any way (*gap*). In 'What did John buy yesterday?', the silent space between 'buy' and 'yesterday' is the *gap*, since this is the object of 'what', with 'buy' taking a direct object – yet the parser has to determine this independently, with no help from the speaker. Recent research, including some of my own, has shown that comprehenders posit gaps as a 'first-resort' strategy, rather than leaving open the possibility that an alternative interpretation for the upcoming words could arise.

In brief, these forms of potential alignments between linguistic theory and processing models invite further efforts from the domains of neurobiology and electrophysiology to achieve specific unifications, in particular given that

psycholinguistic models have in turn been grounded in specific electrophysiological and neuroanatomical components.

1.9   Homo Projectans

This chapter has concluded that the labelling capacity is human-specific. The
remaining chapters will explore the implications of assuming what I will term
the *Labelling Hypothesis*:

Labelling Hypothesis
Labelling constitutes the evolutionary novelty which distinguishes the human cognome
from non-human cognomes.

As such, exploring the neurobiological basis of elementary representational
combination (Merge) will not be enough to derive the properties of language,
since a separate computational procedure is required, not just a freeing of
concepts from their selectional restrictions (as in Boeckx 2014a). This permits
us to explain certain lexical content in terms of labelling choices; a 'red ball' is
an object (NP/DP), not a property (AP), and 'John ran' is an event (*v*P), not
a special kind of thing (NP/DP). Labelling is required if only because there is
nothing in the set-theoretic definition of Merge which leads to symmetry-
breaking. This is a primary motivation behind Hornstein and Pietroski's
(2009, 133) claim that, semantically, 'concatenation is an instruction to conjoin
monadic concepts, while labelling provides a vehicle for invoking thematic
concepts, as indicated by the relevant labels'. Dyadic concepts like INTERNAL
(E,X) can be introduced by labels, with lexical items delivering the required
information to fill in the thematic content. Nevertheless, labelling is still
predominantly seen as a side effect of Merge. A monograph by Citko (2011)
bears the title *Symmetry in Syntax: Merge, Move, and Labels* – the pluralisation
in 'labels' reflects this tendency to relegate the labelling operation itself and
focus on its products.

   Labels, Epstein et al. (2014, 472) comment, are 'arguably a natural requirement necessary for CI [conceptual-intentional] interpretation'. Shim (2013)
formalises this observation in his Single Label Condition on Interpretation:

Single-Label Condition on Interpretation
An expression must have a single label to be interpreted at the interfaces.

What Hinzen and Sheehan (2013, 101) call the 'substantive content' in language is found not simply in recursion, but rather in the way labelling provides
the means to introduce to atomic conceptual roots functional structures which
serve as the hosts of conceptual notions like predicate and argument. As Ursini
(2011, 215) phrases it, 'language represents a "neutral" logical space, a model

of knowledge representation in which different concepts can be freely combined' – a process of cyclic combination permitted by labelling.

With these background assumptions in place concerning *what* language is, we can now progress further afield to construct an understanding of *how* these computational capacities are implemented.

2 Brain Dynamics of Language

> It is for certain the principal organ of our soul and the instrument with which it executes formidable things: the soul believes that it has penetrated everything outside of itself, such that there is no limit to its knowledge; however, when the soul enters its own house, it would not know how to describe it, and it does not know itself anymore. One only has to dissect the big mass of matter that makes up the brain to have reason to lament this ignorance. On the surface, you see an admirable diversity, but when you have entered it, you cannot see a thing.   Nicolaus Steno, *Discours sur l'Anatomie du Cerveau*, 1669

How the human brain differs from the brains of other species is a major topic of research, though our knowledge is still currently very limited. Topics under consideration range from protein emergence, extensive sequence editing, retrotransposon activity and multiple non-coding RNA functions (Bitar & Barry 2018), but none of these have so far yielded any direct consequences for language evolution. As such, this chapter will be concerned largely with higher-order constructs like general neuroanatomy and oscillatory brain dynamics.

There is, as Somel et al. (2013, 119) put it, 'accumulating evidence that human brain development was fundamentally reshaped through several genetic events within the short time space between the human-Neanderthal split and the emergence of modern humans'. While I will largely be concerned with the neuroanatomical and electrophysiological properties of the human brain, there are many other legitimate avenues through which one could explore human uniqueness in relation to the evolution and neural implementation of language. For instance, it has been suggested that protein-coding changes in cell cycle-related genes are highly relevant candidates for human-specific traits (Pääbo 2014). Genes with fixed non-synonymous changes in humans are often expressed in the ventricular zone of the developing neocortex, compared with fixed synonymous changes (Kuhlwilm & Boeckx 2019), and genes involved in axon-guidance, myelination and synaptic vesicle endocytosis (implicated in sustaining high rates of synaptic transmission) appear to number highly in gene sets proposed to be responsible for human-specific neural features.

Given that the hierarchy of brain oscillations appears to have remained extraordinarily preserved during mammalian evolution (Buzsáki et al. 2013), the construction of a new substitute for the Chomsky Hierarchy (see Section 1.7.1), which makes brain activity and computational operations like set-formation and labelling commensurable, is an urgent challenge. As Fitch (2010a, 108) comments on the history of formal language theory, many linguists lost interest in the Chomsky Hierarchy 'when it became apparent that the remaining open questions addressable within this formal framework had little relevance to the details of natural language and its implementation in human brains'. This chapter will explore how brain oscillations can enhance understanding of information chunking (ideas perhaps most forcefully proposed, in the context of language, by Giraud & Poeppel 2012), and could therefore act as a bridge between neurobiology, ethology and the algorithmic and computational levels of syntax. It is the aim of this chapter to present how exactly this research has been, and can continue to be, fruitful.

2.1   Theoretical Overview

2.1.1   Anatomy

In their recent review of the neurolinguistics literature, Friederici et al. (2017, 719) conclude that the task for future research centres on 'finding the explanatory link between the neuroanatomical data, the electrophysiological data, and the formal properties of human syntax'. We will here present a number of relevant debates surrounding language processing in the brain before proposing a range of such explanatory links. The core question explored in order to achieve such links will be: What are the neural underpinnings of language? Or, to return to Hume's terminology, what is the *mechanical power* of language?

In an attempt to address this, a wide range of studies have recently shown that the task of syntactic processing is not relegated to Broca's area alone, but implicates a specific left frontotemporal network involving Broca's area (in the left inferior frontal gyrus), parts of Wernicke's area (in the posterior superior temporal cortex) and the pathways connecting these regions. Indeed, a closer inspection of the neuroimaging results that implicate Broca's area in syntactic processing actually reveal that the activation profile of the posterior temporal lobe is almost always coupled with Broca's area (Matchin et al. 2017). This had led some to emphasise the importance of posterior temporal and also parietal regions (Pillay et al. 2017). Cytoarchitectonically, Broca's area is split into a posterior portion (pars opercularis, BA 44) involved in syntax, and an anterior portion (pars triangularis, BA 45) involved in lexical-semantic processing (Price 2010). White matter fibre bundles connect Broca's and Wernicke's areas, with a dorsal pathway connecting BA 44 to the temporal cortex and a ventral pathway connecting BA 45 (Friederici 2011). A very striking effect has been found in the literature: The greater the degree of syntactic complexity, the greater is the activation in BA 44 (Makuuchi et al. 2009). The involvement of the dorsal pathway connecting BA 44 to the posterior superior temporal cortex seems clear from diffusion-weighted brain imaging, which has revealed an increase in myelin and behavioural performance during the processing of syntactically complex sentences (Skeide et al. 2016); though whether or not it is crucial for the elementary computations which construct basic phrases is another issue, to be addressed later.

As is widely understood, the left hemisphere processes phonology, morphology, lexical information and syntax. Damage to it causes speech devoid of meaning and comprehension problems. The right hemisphere processes intonation, non-literal aspects of language (jokes, etc.) and emotion, with damage to it causing inference problems and impaired emotional interpretation (although both hemispheres have been implicated in a combination of these functions, there is nevertheless clear dominance). Wernicke's area receives input for auditory and visual cortexes, and is the locus of semantic processing. Broca's area deals with speech planning and production, controlling both inflectional and functional morphemes and is connected to Wernicke's area by the arcuate fasciculus. This is a bundle of nerve fibres that was first described in the early eighteenth century by Johan Cristian Reil and which run around the superior border of the Sylvian fissure, encompassing the superior temporal and inferior parietal and frontal areas. Damage to this tract typically leads to conduction/associative aphasia, resulting in intact auditory comprehension and largely intact speech production but degraded speech repetition. The arcuate fasciculus has more extensive nerve fibres in the left relative to the right hemisphere, even in newborns (Perani et al. 2011). Along with this, Catani et al. (2013) discovered another tract relevant to language processing, the frontal aslant, which is a vertical fibre bundle connecting the supplementary and pre-supplementary motor areas in the superior frontal gyrus with the inferior frontal gyrus. This tract is affected in a subset of patients with primary progressive aphasia, a chronic loss of speech fluency.

The mechanisms behind semantic interpretation are lateralised throughout the brain from ages two to three, with Chiarello (2003, 236) commenting: 'Although the right hemisphere seems to retain information about the perceptual characteristics of words, we do know that words presented to either hemisphere are comprehended (although not necessarily in the same way). Hence word meaning access is bilateral.' Nevertheless, there are recently discovered limits to this purely cartographic focus on lateralisation, with Bradshaw et al. (2017, 1) reviewing the fMRI literature on language lateralisation and concluding that 'the current high level of methodological variability in language paradigms prevents conclusions as to how different language functions may lateralise independently'.

2.1.2   Granularity

As one can perhaps already notice, focusing on anatomy as a means of grounding linguistic competence can be a confusing and potentially unenlightening experience. One of the arguments of this chapter will be that recent developments in brain dynamics and neurochemistry can provide the type of framework needed to meet Poeppel and Embick's (2005) challenge of 'granularity' mismatch, or the problem of reconciling the primitives of neuroscience with the primitives of linguistics, in ways superior to that of simple one-to-one mappings between anatomy and computation (see also Poeppel 2011; Fitch 2009).

In 1996, Poeppel noted of cell assemblies (neurons firing transiently with each other, regardless of whether they are synaptically connected) and oscillations that 'it is unclear whether these are the right biological categories to account for cognition' (1996, 643), but by now the oscillation literature has sufficiently expanded to incorporate numerous cognitive processes. Indeed, it is becoming somewhat vogue to attempt to replace fundamental linguistic concepts in favour of grounding them in biology – a highly desirable move, if properly executed. Consider Martins's (2017) attempt to eliminate the notion of 'markedness' from linguistic theory in favour of lower-level biological factors:

The concept of markedness in particular, though probably very advantageous in [a] utilitarian sense to many linguists, doesn't seem to do much for the understanding of the phonological component when we start wondering about its place in biology and evolution, even if we don't pursue those curiosities much further.

Linguistics can direct the brain sciences insofar as its insights into the universality of operations like Merge inform the goals of neurobiology, while the brain sciences can direct linguistics insofar as they place constraints on what possible operations neuronal assemblies and their oscillatory behaviour can perform (see Badin et al. 2017 for an exploration of the notion of a neuronal assembly, which they see the defining feature of as being 'one of dynamism'). While linguists should focus on making their claims about language biologically feasible, neuroscientists should conversely ensure that they do not sideline the notion of computation, as stressed by Gallistel and King (2009).

In order to explore this issue, I will adopt a multidisciplinary approach which endorses an interweaving of the sciences concerned with the following topics: the computations performed by the human nervous system (the cognome, discussed earlier; Poeppel 2012), brain dynamics (the 'dynome'; Kopell et al. 2014), neural wiring (the 'connectome'; Seung 2012; or the 'neurome'; Bota et al. 2015) and genomics. Every time we move from one level of description to another, a specific linking hypothesis is needed to explain and motivate the transition. The connectome (i.e. anatomy) constrains the *kinds* of operations performed by the nervous system, but it cannot reveal *what* operations in particular are performed. What is needed, as Seung himself has explained, is not just a comprehensive model of neural wiring, but also neural computation, which is what a theory of the cognome can contribute (see Reimann et al. 2015 for a proposed algorithm to predict the connectome of neural microcircuits). As Swanson and Lichtman (2016, 212) put it:

The problem stems from the intrinsic lack of intelligibility of connectomics data. The inherent complexity of data that simultaneously show thousands of streams of informa-tion flowing into and out of each of many nodes (individual neurons, neuron types, or regions) is likely beyond any individual human's comprehension. Making sense of such data may therefore be beyond the limits of the explanatory power of the human mind. The long-debated challenge of bridging the divide between mind and brain is unfortu-nately not likely to be overcome by a detailed accounting of each and every synaptic connection in the brain.

Furthermore, research into complexity and data compression indicates that any object is no more complex than the total information of the source programme and data that defines its construction (Chaitin 1977), and so the actual complex-ity of the brain is likely far less than what the results of connectomics might suggest. Achieving a theory of brain function will instead require developing algorithmic neurobiological models at a level of abstraction appropriate to the computations under investigation. Disassembling the brain into its elementary components by no means leads to a necessary enhancement of higher-level theories concerning its functioning. As Tsien (2016) puts it, 'this relentless push – or downward spiral – into ever finer details has created its own attrac-tion – or black holes – from which too many of us may find too hard to resist intellectually and professionally'. Connectomics has no computationally rig-orous answers, for all its impressively wide phenotypic coverage – witness the birth of the 'ferretome', the connectome of the ferret (Sukhinin et al. 2016) – but it nevertheless crucially reduces the hypothesis space. As Swanson and Lichtman (2016, 198) put it, connectomics 'constrains the range of function-ality and hypotheses of underlying mechanisms' and in addition 'provides the neuroinformatics skeleton for organizing related molecular, genetic, physiolo-gical, behavioral, and cognitive data'. But still, the central questions remain: *What* computations are executed (addressed in Chapter 2) and *how* exactly are they executed?

This chapter will suggest that the most currently appropriate level of abstrac-tion is to be found in what I have elsewhere called the 'oscillome' (Murphy 2016c). While the dynome is the level of brain dynamics, encompassing electrophysiology and neural oscillations, the oscillome addresses a subset of these oscillations which can be ascribed computational roles relevant to cogni-tion (not every feature of brain dynamics will be related to language, attention, memory and so forth). The dynome explores 'not only *what* is connected, but *how* and in what directions regions of the brain are connected' (Kopell et al. 2014, 1319). The cartographic literature (e.g. fMRI and DTI studies) discusses neural 'activation', 'firing' and 'pathways', keeping at a connectomic level of spatiotemporal brain nodes and edges (Bressler & Menon 2010). Indeed Eklund et al. (2016) found an extraordinary 70 per cent of false-positives when analysing imaging data with standard fMRI softwares, pointing out that the results of around 40,000 previous studies are therefore potentially suspect. More broadly – and perhaps more bizarrely – many standard fMRI analyses assume that every repeated appearance of a given stimuli in an experimental environment will, somehow, lead to the same brain response every time, not taking into consideration familiarity/expectancy effects. Since 'a function of network oscillations is to control the flow of information through anatomical pathways' (Akam & Kullmann 2014, 111), connectivity issues will be key to understanding how the brain implements language. But the oscillome adds to such a 'functional connectome' an understanding of the regions involved in producing and processing brain signals. For example, Kamigaki and Dan (2017) exposed the role of vasoactive intestinal peptide (VIP$^+$) neurons in the dorsomedial prefrontal cortex in working memory modulation, but the way the firing of these cells synchronise with other brain regions requires an understanding of brain dynamics – the connectome alone will not suffice.

Although I will focus on brain rhythms with respect to the oscillome, it should be noted that the dynome extends beyond neural oscillations and includes other temporal structures (Larson-Prior et al. 2013). Moreover, fMRI has recently been shown to be able to directly map fast neural oscillations throughout the brain (Lewis, Setsompop et al. 2016), extending its potential use in oscillatory investigations. fMRI results are increasingly being interpreted alongside neural oscillations, with part of the BOLD signal being seen by Scheeringa and Fries (2019) as feedback signalling via α and β influences travelling from infragranular cortical layers to layer 4, such that future fMRI studies could in fact be used to test predictions derived from studies using the major time-sensitive neurophysiological methods, M/EEG.

As mentioned, we will explore how the universality of language lies within the extraordinarily preserved nature of mammalian brain rhythms (the oscillations of mice and rats have the same pharmacological profiles as humans) likely arising from the deployment of long-diameter axons of long-range neurons (Buzsáki et al. 2013; see also Calabrese & Woolley 2015). Such cortical and subcortical structures are 'among the most sophisticated scalable architectures in nature' (Buzsáki et al. 2013, 751), with scalability referring to the ability to perform the same operations with increasing efficiency despite escalating organisational complexity. Sensory inputs help the brain adjust its 'internal connectivity and computations to the spatial and temporal metrics of the external world' (Buzsáki 2006, 11), with oscillations being a primary method of detecting these metrics. Brain rhythms, yielded in part by such structures, would therefore be expected to be capable of complex forms of information transmission and integration.

2.1.3   Cartographic Directions

So far, we have outlined the various ways that distinct levels of analysis can interact, and the limitations in particular of purely anatomical/connectomic descriptions. We will now focus greater attention on these cartographic (localisation-based) themes in order to help direct our enquiry into brain dynamics.

In Chapter 1, it was claimed that the ability to label linguistic structures with a categorial identity (e.g. determiner, verb and adjective), having merged them into an unordered set and transferred them in a cyclic fashion to the conceptual interface, is the defining property of the human computational system. This perspective will be maintained here. It will be argued that modifications in oscillatory couplings and the cell assemblies targeted by such oscillatory operations are a viable candidate for what brought about what could be regarded as a phase transition from single-instance set-formation (of the kind seen in monkey calls) to unbounded set-formation. For instance, the phase/non-phase rhythm (where syntactic 'phases' are chunks of merged representations cyclically transferred to the interfaces for labelling and externalisation) – [C/T [v/V[D/N]]] – emphasised by Richards (2011), Uriagereka (2012) and Boeckx (2013), may translate well into the rhythmic processes of neural oscillations.

Beginning with general methods, since the origins of modern cognitive neuroscience, linguistic processes have been claimed to elicit numerous event-related potentials (ERPs) by psycholinguists using M/EEG As time-frequency analysis and its Fourier transforms developed into a mainstay of 'ERPology' (Luck 2014) in the 1990s and 2000s, it became possible to test the involvement of distinct brain regions and the concomitant electrical activity associated with various linguistic processes, given the standard assumption that language is a cognitive system. The ERP community has spent a great deal of time decomposing the major components, such as the P600 and N400. It is taken for granted that the level of analysis provided by these components does not suffice at the electrophysiological level to describe generic linguistic sub-operations. The urge to seek a finer level of granularity, then, is clearly manifested in the ERP community through M/EEG investigations (Lau et al. 2008), but this objective is often not found in cartographic neuroimaging research. At the same time, a standard assumption in the ERP literature is that activity not phase-locked to a particular event should be deemed as noise, but this leads to a severely impoverished view of the neural activity underlying cognitive processes, shutting out a lot of potentially interesting data. Examining induced oscillatory activity via

M/EEG does not lead to this limitation. To take a recent case, Schneider and Maguire (2019) used EEG to investigate how eight- to nine- and twelve- to thirteen-year-olds process semantics and syntax in naturally paced, auditory sentences compared to adults. Participants listened to semantically and syntactically correct/incorrect sentences. When processing a semantic error, developmental differences were observed in the θ band, but not in the N400 component, suggesting that ERPs 'may be too gross a measure to identify more subtle aspects of semantic development that occur in the school years'. Moreover, M/EEG investigations do not suffer from some of the major pitfalls of neuropsychological patient investigations, since lesions used to investigate the basis of language are typically extensive and affect white matter tracts, and are also highly idiosyncratic in their involvement of different forms of rapid recovery and neural reorganisation. Recent work has even shown the benefits of using MEG jointly with transcranial alternating current stimulation (tACS), a non-invasive form of brain stimulation which modulates spike timing and which can add a greater level of detail with respect to exposing the precise areas involved in generating oscillatory signatures (Witkowski et al. 2016).

Relatedly, there are a number of methodological motivations for investigating brain rhythms as opposed to other possible markers of neural activity. For instance, there seem to be certain computations which are not open to fMRI investigation. Dubois et al. (2015) showed that while facial identities could be decoded from posterior regions of ventral occipital cortex using fMRI and direct neuronal recordings, this was not the case in anterior regions, where information could be decoded only via neuronal signals. It is likely that the computational basis of more complex cognitive capacities like language will also remain undetectable via similar neuroimaging techniques.

Reviewing recent technological and analytical advances, Baillet (2017) proposes the following:

MEG is the modality with the best combination of direct and noninvasive access to the electrophysiological activity of the entire brain, with sub-millisecond temporal resolution and ability to resolve activity between cerebral regions with often surprising spatial and spectral differentiation and minimum bias. Indeed, unlike EEG, the accuracy of MEG source mapping is immune to the signal distortions caused by the complex layering of head tissues, with highly heterogeneous conductivity profiles that cannot be measured with precision in vivo.

The experimental results from the oscillation literature also appear to be much more robust than much of the cartographic neuroimaging literature, which is currently facing something of a replication crisis, with experimental findings often not being repeated in follow-up studies by separate authors (for instance, see the findings discussed in Roux & Uhlhaas 2014). Intensifying the problem, Matchin et al. (2017, 120) discuss their fMRI results from an investigation into non-word lists, two-word phrases and sentential structures and note that a number of crucial contrasts were unable to reach significance, commenting:

> One possibility is that the BOLD response is simply not the right method for identifying the brain basis for syntactic operations. This may be because the BOLD signal is not sensitive to the neural activity that builds basic syntactic representations or because the cortical area is not the right level [of] neuroanatomical granularity for syntactic mechanisms.

There are also naturally many limitations to MEG investigations, such as the fact that a minimum of 10,000–50,000 cells are required to produce an MEG-detectable signal (Murakami & Okada 2006) – it is possible that particular low-level computations relevant to language are carried out below this threshold.

Be that as it may, the importance of oscillatory investigations, tracking the real-time processing properties of language, should be clear. Moving to an area that neuroscientific research has been able to enrich, at the most general anatomical level, the increased processing speeds of intelligent brains appears to be related to greater grey matter densities (Neubauer & Fink 2009), particularly in the frontal and parietal lobes (Jung & Haier 2007). In recent decades, neuroanatomical enquiry into the structures responsible for syntactic processing has led to a number of revelations concerning the biology of language which range beyond these general levels of description. Petersson et al. (2012) reveal the inadequacy of the classical Broca-Wernicke-Lichtheim language model of the brain (under which Broca's and Wernicke's areas are responsible for production and comprehension, respectively) by noting how the language network extends to substantial parts of superior and middle temporal cortex, inferior parietal cortex, along with subcortical areas such as the basal ganglia (Balari & Lorenzo 2013), the hippocampus and the thalamus (Theofanopoulou & Boeckx 2016; Kepinska et al. 2018). The network is also implicated in more general cognitive systems like the default mode network and the multiple demand system. As Iaria and Burles (2016, 722) discuss in the context of the neural correlates of Developmental Topological Disorientation (DTD), 'attempting to ascribe cognitive functions to specific brain regions is especially unsuitable for dealing with such behaviorally and cognitively complex concepts as a "cognitive map", a representation that is typically believed to be supported by the hippocampus and place cell assemblies'. In the context of language, such correlational methods remain insufficient.

Pushing these cartographic methods further, BA 44 and the posterior superior temporal cortex appear to be involved in a pathway which supports core syntactic computations (Friederici et al. 2006; see also Santi & Grodzinsky 2010; Tettamanti & Weniger 2006), with the combinatorial network being identified by Poeppel (2014) as aMTG and aITS. Lieberman's (2006) Basal Ganglia Grammar model proposes the existence of a pattern generator whose excitation/inhibition mechanism is located in the basal ganglia. This interfaces with working memory space located in Broca's area (Santi et al. 2015). Lieberman estimates that the dorsolateral prefrontal circuit is involved in sentence comprehension, projecting from the prefrontal cortex towards the lateral dorso-medial region of the globus pallidus, and the thalamus, which projects back to the prefrontal cortex. β coherence has also been reported between the prefrontal cortex and thalamus during working memory maintenance (Parnaudeau et al. 2013), while optogenetic suppression of the medio-dorsal thalamus suppresses cortical delay activity (Schmitt et al. 2017), findings which suggest a crucial role for thalamocortical connections in cognition. Balari and Lorenzo (2013, 100–102) have suggested that this may be the circuit used as language's computational system operating within a structure of working memory networks (Balari et al. 2012). The importance of this circuit, and its neurocomputational relevance, will be a topic developed later. For now, we will continue to present a more general overview of topics relevant to the brain dynamics of language, such as the place that the oscillome can occupy within philosophy of biology.

2.1.4   Evo-Devo Directions

As the theory of evolution expands beyond the Modern Synthesis and into areas such as evolutionary-developmental (evo-devo) biology (Carroll 2006; Bolker 2008) there is in turn more space for linguists to find their place within biology. Evo-devo research has exposed how local genetic changes can influence the expression of other genes, leading to dramatic phenotypic consequences after the impact of developmental influences. Developing some concerns raised above, in the evo-devo programme, following the lead of traditional formalists such as Vicq-D'Azyr, Goethe and Owen (Amundson 1998, 2006), natural selection is 'a constantly operating background condition, but the specificity of its phenotypic outcome is provided by the developmental systems' (Pigliucci & Müller 2010, 13). Evo-devo departs from neo-Darwinian adaptationism (NDA), or 'phylogenetic empiricism' (Chomsky 1968), in that it takes the saltationist view that species are the result of punctuated genetic changes. The functionalism of NDA should also be rejected, since functions do not typically pre-exist organic form (Müller 2008), which is determined by morphogenetic parameters such as the viscoelastic properties of cellular matrices and the kinetic activity of cellular diffusion (what Alberch termed 'morphological evolution'), and which at best have what Balari and Lorenzo call a 'functional potential' (2013, 37). Contrary to ideas in Dawkins (2006, 202) and Lieberman (2015), laws governing the conservation of developmental pathways should be 'acknowledged with a creative character similar – if not superior – to that of natural selection' (Balari & Lorenzo 2013, 115; although, interestingly, Dawkins 2015, 382–384, embraces the idea that recursive language emerged from a small number of genetic mutations rather than through a gradual process of natural selection). Form often precedes function, then, and natural selection acts as a 'filtering condition on pre-existent variants'; thus, 'arrival of the fittest, instead of survival of the fittest, is the core issue in any evolutionary study' (Narita & Fujita 2010, 364; see also Bertossa 2011). Philosophers of biology typically distinguish functions based purely on natural selection. For instance, Dennett (1987) proposes that functions are in the mind of the beholder, but that natural selection is somehow one of those beholders, and acts for him with no restrictions on its scope upon the diversity found in populations yielded by genetic point mutations.

What are the implications of this? Perhaps most importantly, evo-devo encourages us to focus on the specific neural or oscillatory *form* that higher cognition may take, sidelining secondary speculations about their adaptive benefits and why they may have been selected for. For instance, under evo-devo, one would assume that the form of a neural system can very often dictate its function, such that the properties of certain cognitive systems may arise from the formal structure of the connectome or dynome.

Closely connected to evo-devo, the goals of 'Theoretical Morphology' (classical biological formalism), outlined by George McGhee (1998, 2), are likely the closest to those of the form of biolinguistics I will be proposing here:

The goal is to explore the possible range of morphologic variability that nature could produce by constructing n-dimensional geometric hyperspaces (termed 'theoretical morphospaces'), which can be produced by systematically varying the parameter values of a geometric model of form. [. . .] Once constructed, the range of existent variability in form may be examined in this hypothetical morphospace, both to quantify the range of existent form and to reveal nonexistent organic form. That is, to reveal morphologies that theoretically could exist [. . .] but that never have been produced in the process of organic evolution on the planet Earth. The ultimate goal of this area of research is to understand why existent form actually exists and why nonexistent form does not.

The notion of 'why existent form actually exists and why nonexistent form does not', I will argue, is tied directly to form and limitations of oscillatory interactions. But to briefly speculate somewhat beyond this, how can the above frameworks be applied to areas of linguistics ranging outside our narrow concern of syntactic computation? Consider the sensorimotor interface. Recent research in avian genomics suggests that the evolution of externalisation may not be as difficult as typically considered by generative grammarians. Pfenning et al. (2014, 1333) demonstrated that the profiles of transcription genes in vocal learners can be aligned, with fifty genes being shared between humans and birds which are 'enriched in motor control and neural connectivity functions'. Both humans and birds appear to have converged on identical solutions to vocal learning, a remarkable finding considering the 310-million-year gap separating birds from humans. Nevertheless, there is currently insufficient evidence for one-to-one homologies between avian and mammalian brains (Jarvis et al. 2005). Field L2 in the avian forebrain receives auditory connections from the thalamus, and projects onto Field L1 and L3. These two areas, respectively, project to the caudomedial mesopallium and caudomesial nidopallium. Some have argued that this general complex (Field L) may be homologous to the mammalian primary auditory cortex, which also receives thalamic input and is composed of three core regions (Bolhuis & Gahr 2006).

How best to move beyond these abstract, programmatic ideas? A focus on more specific neurobiological differences is useful here. Rakic and Kornack (2001) observe that the phase of asymmetric cell division yielding neuronal cells differs in timing between humans and monkeys to the extent that human neuronal populations are thought to be between eight to sixteen times larger than those of monkeys. Human-specific neuronal traits include the protein ApoE4, providing stronger synaptic connections (Bufill & Carbonell 2004). Parker and McKinney (1999) detail how the myelinisation of the neocortex occurs in humans until the age of twelve, but lasts for only 3.5 years in rhesus monkeys. Moreover, the timing of myelination appears to be strong predictor of computational abilities in higher cognitive faculties like language and theory of mind (Mars et al. 2018). Can the nature of higher cognitive faculties be due to these formal, structural differences?

2.2   Oscillations as Functional Units

How much physiological detail is required to capture the operations of the language faculty? At the most general mesoscopic physiological level of local neuronal groups, synchronised firing patterns result in coordinated input into other cortical areas, which gives rise to the large-amplitude oscillations of the local field potential. Oscillations may arise due to alternating excitation-inhibition of neurons, pacemaker cells or subthreshold membrane oscillation. Pacemaker neurons typically operate in a characteristic frequency range and are located in pattern generator circuits controlling rhythmic motions such as locomotion, peristaltic movements and swimming (Grillner 2006). Inhibitory interneurons play an important role in producing neural ensemble synchrony by generating a narrow window for effective excitation and rhythmically modulating the firing rate of excitatory neurons. Interneurons place constraints on the oscillations responsible, as argued here, for computation. Subthreshold membrane potential resonance may also contribute to oscillatory activity by facilitating synchronous activity of neighbouring neurons. As Cannon et al. (2014, 705) note, 'The physiology underlying brain rhythms plays an essential role in how these rhythms facilitate some cognitive operations.' I should stress that 'function' here is a purely honorific term, since ultimately oscillations themselves do not, of course, have any functions – indeed, they don't 'have' anything, they simply exhibit certain properties. But speaking of oscillations as 'having functions' seems at least appropriate for the purposes of model-formation; oscillations themselves seem to index certain lower-level neuro-chemical computations, and so speaking of them as 'having computational properties' is, again, an indirect way of talking about more fundamental (but yet-to-be-determined) computations. For instance, Canolty and Knight (2010) speak of the functions of cross-frequency coupling, and this seems to be a wholly justified use of the term.

Recent debates about the origins of ERP component generation have led some (Tass 2000; Makeig et al. 2002) to propose that components do not arise purely from latency-fixed polarity responses which are additive to continuing EEG responses, but rather arise through a superposition of oscillations which reset their phases in reaction to sensory input (see Lu et al. 2017 for a review, and Sauseng et al. 2007 for the methodological limitations of particular phase resetting claims). ERP components may effectively be taking credit for the hard neurocomputational work carried out by underlying oscillations. Phase resetting involves the realignment of ongoing oscillatory phases in relation to a given reference point, either endogenous or exogenous (Voloh & Womelsdorf 2016). For our purposes, it is worth noting that this phase reset model was the first to propose a strong dependency between components and oscillations, introducing to brain dynamics a functional and not purely electro-physiological role. This immediately granted researchers the ability to transfer understanding of components (which are in turn linked to cognitive faculties) to brain rhythms whilst correspondingly inferring the nature of components from an emerging understanding of oscillations. While cognitive electrophysiologists have embraced this integrally reciprocal perspective (Klimesch et al. 2004), linguists often remain hostile (understandably, given the lack of general discussion in the field about implementation) to the claim that the nature of mental computations – like components – can be explored explicitly through biophysics.

Nevertheless, the oscillome, with its operations of information segregation and spike timing organisation, can in some sense be seen as a Marr-style algorithmic level (Marr 1982), implemented by the cellular structures of the connectome. These Marrian concerns become more vivid when we consider with Martins and Boeckx (2014) that syllables, which are unique to humans, evolved from primate lip-smacking. In terms of brain rhythms (amplitude fluctuations), they are both identical, yet one is human-specific and another is not. The implications for the exploration of the present Labelling Hypothesis are clear: only comparative investigations of domain-general neurophysiological mechanisms, and the context in which they operate (and their oscillatory couplings), will lead to enhanced understanding of human-specific computations. Indeed, as Hasson et al. (2018) eloquently note, many language-specific interpretations of experimental neurophysiological and electrophysiological data might be better seen as implementations of clusters of highly generic processes, like monotonic integration of information, establishment of coherence, prediction and representational binding.

In this connection, there are two central approaches to the cognome-oscillome one could adopt: reconstruct the cognome from the bottom-up, or import linguistic constructs into a model of the oscillome. I will be primarily concerned with the latter methodology, though the material reviewed and the model outlined open up the possibilities of using neurophysiology to guide linguistic investigations. Indeed, as Anderson (2016, 6) makes clear, proceeding in a thoroughly top-down fashion would be futile:

Different neural patterns indexing different perceptual states, action choices, preferences, reward estimations, other predictions, and so forth, do not combine syntactically in the manner of compositional linguistic structures. Neither are the functional parts of the brain always best understood as components with stable, intrinsic input-output mappings and well-defined interfaces supporting the exchange of content-carrying symbols.

Likewise, as Bolhuis and Wynne (2009, 833) put it: 'As long as researchers focus on identifying human-like behaviour in other animals, the job of classifying the cognition of different species will be forever tied up in thickets of arbitrary nomenclature that will not advance our understanding of the mechanisms of cognition.' The study of language evolution constitutes a careful balancing act between top-down cognitive preconceptions and bottom-up biological constructs.

2.2.1   Neural Syntax

At the most general level of analysis, neural oscillations emerge from the tension between the two most central principles of the brain: segregation of function and dynamic integration (De Pasquale et al. 2012). Human brains are highly complex dynamical systems with principles of cellular and electrochemical organisation which range across a hierarchy of scales. The brain cannot function purely through anatomical connections – the *locus classicus* of standard neuroimaging studies – but additionally requires dynamic functional connectivity, putatively achieved through oscillatory synchronisation. Frequency bands alone are not sufficient for computation; rather, it is their interactions which are significant. Intuitive prejudices against studying complex systems in these dynamical terms abound: for instance, chemical dynamics are typically thought about in terms of reaction kinetics, being stipulated as preformed stable variables, ignoring the molecular composition/ decomposition process. While external cues can influence internal dynamics, it is exclusively brain-intrinsic processes that implement functions such as memory and spatial navigation. An understanding of the biological basis of higher cognition therefore requires an exploration of such brain-intrinsic processes, with oscillatory dynamics being a major feature in this respect.

A core feature of the brain's functional complexity is created by rhythms generated in different cortical and subcortical tissue. Oscillations denote distinct states of brain activity, while oscillatory activity reflects a dynamic interplay between the dissimilar cell types of discrete circuits (Buzsáki 2006). Brain rhythms, with their inter-wave hierarchies, provide 'a syntactical structure for the spike traffic within and across circuits at multiple time scales' (Buzsáki & Freeman 2015, viii). 'Phase synchronisation' will additionally be a central notion in the present discussion, referring to a consistent phase coupling between two neuronal signals oscillating at a given frequency. γ band synchronisation (GBS) in particular has been intensively studied due to its apparent role in phase coding and perceptual integration (Fries 2009), and is thought to be a major process subserving a fundamental operation of cortical computation implicated in various cognitive functions. Which functions are involved will depend ultimately on the neural circuits GBS operates over.

The need for computational understanding at any level of neurophysiological enquiry was expressed well in the following passage from Longuet-Higgins (1972, 256):

In so far as the neurophysiologist is concerned to understand how the brain works, he must equip himself with a non-physiological account of the tasks which the brain and its peripheral organs are able to perform; only then can he form mature hypotheses as to how these tasks are carried out by the available 'hardware' – to borrow a phrase from computing science.

With this in mind, we will now (re-)outline the core computational properties of language and discuss potential ways they could be implemented at the level of oscillations.

2.2.1.1 Basic Combinatorics: The θ-γ Code   In order to construct or interpret any linguistic structure the human brain needs to, at a minimum, combine two distinct pieces of lexical information into a larger unit. Although it is not typically seen as falling within the fields of neurolinguistics, psycholinguistics or evolutionary linguistics, I will argue here that language scientists should embrace the substantial research in cognitive neuroscience which explores the neural correlates of combinatorial processes. As Deco, van Hartevelt et al. (2017, 197) summarise this research: 'The integration of information is likely to take place in a functionally coherent, yet distributed network of brain regions, where computations are highly segregated.' Such computations require a certain degree of global and temporal coherence, and so turning to neural oscillations seems justified. Single-word comprehension is associated with the left temporal pole and adjacent anterior temporal cortex (Mesulam et al. 2015), but how does the brain deal with combinations of words? A recent summary of the field concludes that the anterior superior temporal gyrus and the frontal operculum support bi-item combinatorics regardless of structure (a claim in line with the finding that the frontal operculum is a phylogenetically older part of the brain compared to Broca's area and is involved in simple sequence detection; Sanides 1962), while the ventral portion of the inferior frontal gyrus 'supports initial phrase structure building' (Friederici 2017, 59).

Recent studies have also shown that the anterior temporal lobe is implicated in basic semantic combinatorics, while the angular gyrus appears to be implicated in semantic representations that are more complex and anomalous (Molinaro et al. 2015), with combinatorial semantics more generally increasing the coupling strength between these two regions. More specifically, the left angular gyrus was recently found to be more activated in complex sentential syntax relative to simple phrases and words (Sheng et al. 2019).

Given these findings, it is perhaps unsurprising to learn that the evolution of the temporal lobe appears to have played a significant role in enhancing the combinatorial flexibility of human cognition. Bryant and Preuss (2018) adopt a comparative perspective and show that among primates 'humans possess a temporal lobe that has significantly expanded'. Since linguistic combinatorics and semantic memory are largely based in the temporal lobe, the evolution of this structure seems pertinent to neurolinguistics. The author discovered 'modifications to external morphology (gyri and sulci), preferential expansion of association areas, and elaboration of white matter fasciculi, distinguishing the human temporal lobe from those of Old World monkeys'. The neuroanatomical details surrounding the precise nature of the expansion are only beginning to be explored, and it will be of great interest to see if a more specific molecular and oscillatory profile can be extracted from future research.

Enhancing these preliminary ideas, the central proposal of the model I will develop here is that the interaction of oscillations yields linguistic computation. Lower frequencies such as the α range are known to synchronise distant cortical regions; procedures which may represent the substrates of linguistic cross-modular transactions (Kinzler & Spelke 2007). The set-forming operation Merge constructs a new syntactic object out of two already formed (Chomsky 1995). In Murphy (2015b) I suggested that since lower frequencies are known to synchronise distant cortical regions, this may represent the oscillatory implementation of Merge. I assumed that thalamic and occipital α embeds cross-cortical γ to generate, or 'lexicalise', individual representations (see Raichle et al. 2001) before these γ-individuated units were themselves embedded within hippocampal and parahippocampal θ (see Wilson et al. 2008 for evidence that parahippocampal gyrus is involved in auditory language comprehension).

The data structures involved in basic combinatorics are linguistic features, as in contemporary minimalist syntactic theory (Chomsky 1995; Adger & Svenonius 2011) or optimality theory for the phonological system (Heinz et al. 2009); that is, atomic, elementary components manipulated by the generative computational system, such as Tense features, Person, Number, Gender features, semantic features, and other features assumed to be generic in syntactic theory. I have assumed that these are each to be represented by γ-individuated items.

In this connection, we should consider the possibility that many of these data structures are shared with the representational systems of other species. For example, Golston (2018) reviews evidence that all the major φ-features (Person, Number, Gender) are shared with primates, and some with vertebrates, and that there are no φ-features unique to humans. While it is difficult to believe that neuter gender features are cognisable by vertebrates, as Golston (2018, 84) claims, there is indeed sound evidence that the other φ-features are known in some sense to other species, thus allowing us to appropriately narrow our focus on other capacities in search for human-unique language features. Other, 'indirect' grammatical features such as case, declension, conjugation and finiteness seem unique to natural language, however (Mithun 2015).

The decoupling of γ from α would be achieved through the activity of the thalamic reticular nucleus. These forms of cross-frequency interactions are typically implemented through slower rhythms (extended across the cortex) modulating faster ones (localised in smaller regions) (Lakatos et al. 2005; Canolty & Knight 2010). Of great relevance to the pursuit of such a model, Schmitt et al. (2017) demonstrated that mediodorsal thalamic input can modulate prefrontal cortical connectivity, 'enabling rule-specific neural sequences to emerge and thereby maintain rule representations'. The authors explain that these findings expose 'a previously unknown principle in neuroscience; thalamic control of functional cortical connectivity', indicating that the role of the thalamus in cognition is much wider than has typically been assumed. What exactly this wider role constitutes will be discussed in greater detail later in the chapter. The cellular and synaptic mechanisms that regulate thalamic oscillations also appear to have a role in controlling local and global brain rhythms (Fogerson & Huguenard 2016; Acsády 2017).

There is increasing evidence for the relevance of θ interactions in language – indeed, leaving aside interactions and focusing purely on θ power, a recent MEG study of verbal working memory (Proskovec et al. 2019) found that during encoding of letter strings to be committed to short-term memory for a variant of the Sternberg task, stronger frontal θ increases (substantially left-lateralised) were found for the more memory-intensive condition (six letters vs. four letters), indicating the rhythm's apparent role in constructing online representations of stimuli (see also Onton et al. 2005 for related results). While Proskovec et al. (2019) only found frontal θ increases during encoding, and not maintenance, other studies have only found θ increases during maintenance of items structured by some form of temporal order (e.g. n-back tasks; Scharinger et al. 2017); hence, for natural language, we would expect to find similar results.

The assemblies implicated by the γ range may have been influenced by the extended neocortical myelinisation discussed earlier, with direct effects on the network of information stored across such regions. This is consistent with recent claims that α is responsible for the binding of visuo-spatial features (Roux & Uhlhaas 2014) and is deployed in the service of determining successful lexical decisions (Strauss et al. 2015), and so this rhythm might also be implicated in storing lexical representations in short-term memory while θ carries out the work of combining representations. Moreover, in contrast to the θ-γ code for working memory, Roux and Uhlhaas (2014) suggest that an α-γ code involving phase–amplitude coupling (where the amplitude of the higher band is coupled with the phase of the lower band) exists for maintaining various sensory features. (As with visuo-spatial features, there is growing evidence that certain kinds of features posited by linguists are also neurobiologically plausible: Mesgarani et al. (2014) discovered that groups of neurons are sensitive to the phonetic features of speech, although this level of neurobiological granularity has not currently been found for distinctive syntactic or semantic features.) Following Deco, Cabral et al.'s (2017) functional exploration of what they refer to as 'binding regions' (regions responsible for significant amounts of temporal binding) and regions typically referred to as belonging to the 'rich club' (regions exhibiting dense anatomical interconnectivity), other potentially important regions for featural concatenation (i.e. regions which are in both camps) include the left mid-occipital cortex, putamen and precuneus, and the right superior frontal gyrus, hippocampus and putamen. Suppression of the α rhythm over parieto-occipital EEG sites also appears to be crucial for generic working memory operations like *Search* (van Driel et al. 2017), likely forming part of the core Merge operation.

Corcoran et al. (2018a) review recent advances in accurately modelling individual α frequencies using a Savitzky-Golay filter, which is open source and easily available on popular programming languages like MATLAB and Python. Despite these important advances, Yael et al. (2018) discuss how filter-based phase shifts (common to virtually all analysis techniques in neuroimaging) can distort neuronal timing information, such that claims made about cross-frequency coupling (CFC) (amongst many other things) post-filtering can often be misleading. The authors discuss a number of ways neuroscientists can restore original timing information through circumventing these filter-induced phase shifts.

Bringing further modifications to our understanding of the oscillatory basis of language, Segaert et al. (2018) observed EEG responses to syntactic binding operations, finding α increases over a left-lateralised cluster of fronto-temporal electrodes during successful binding (and not during word list processing). The authors note that we may therefore need to add 'an additional mechanism' to α, although they did find α increases across different sites to those found in van Driel et al. (2017), suggesting that only slight modifications may need to be made. Leszczynski et al. (2017) also discovered that in epilepsy patients broadband γ in the ventral and dorsal visual streams occurred across broader α phase ranges when task-relevant information was maintained in a simple visual match-to-sample task, likely reflecting longer excitable duty cycles. It is possible that this mechanism is generic and domain-general and might explain the findings in Segaert et al. (2018) such that syntactic maintenance results in longer duty cycles implicated in $\{α(γ)\}$ coupling (where the amplitude of the rhythm inside parentheses is coupled to the phase of the rhythm inside brackets), with increased α power being one result of that.

Finally, since it has been suggested that elementary mathematical procedures could be derived from language (by restricting Merge to single-instance applications, producing the natural numbers; a proposal which effectively goes back much further than modern linguistics; see Section 1.6.3), a brief examination of mathematical knowledge is required. Amalric and Dehaene's (2018) systematic review indicates that brain activity during mathematical reflection spares perisylvian language-relevant areas and instead implicates bilateral intra-parietal and ventral temporal regions involved in the 'number sense' core knowledge system. Nevertheless, these regions overlap substantially with the presently discussed concatenation-relevant regions, suggesting some potential for rooting the number sense in regions involved in early-stage linguistic computations (i.e. pre-phrase formation) and lending support to the existence of the broader Universal Generative Faculty (Hauser & Watumull 2017) discussed earlier. The evolutionary implications of these studies are far from clear, although the fact that mathematics seems to be embedded in a more ancient cortical network at least points to a general timeline, with reflective mathematical knowledge likely emerging relatively late in human development, as Russell (1919, 3) speculated: 'It must have required many ages to discover that a brace of pheasants and a couple of days were both instances of the number 2: the degree of abstraction involved is far from easy.'

2.2.1.2 Cyclicity: α-Inhibition and β-Maintenance   Recent work has suggested that individual differences in chunking abilities in working memory act as a strong predictor of individual differences in language processing (McCauley et al. 2017), and so exploring the oscillatory basis of memory and its potential relation to language seems well motivated.

Linguists take concatenation to occur in cyclic chunks (Chomsky 2008; Chomsky et al. 2019). I will discuss the ways in which this process may be realised, taking as a starting point the aforementioned parahippocampal coupling between θ and cross-cortical γ. Note that discussions of cyclicity require no commitments to particular theoretical architectures (e.g. minimalist syntax, according to which syntactic structures are passed over and interpreted by a semantic system) and we will assume only that constructed semantic objects need to be interpreted in some fashion by external conceptual and memory systems, a process we can refer to as cyclicity for convenience (but see Hinzen 2016 for arguments in favour of 'interface-free' architectures, according to which grammatical structures have a more direct impact on semantic interpretation than is typically assumed). More broadly, it will be suggested here that the existence of cyclic computation in language is a direct consequence of properties of neural systems, with the brain making optimal use of electrophysiological constraints (e.g. the eigenfrequencies of cortical networks), in this sense grounding phrase structure building in 'third factors'.

In order for $\{θ(γ)\}$ embedding to take place, γ likely needs to be decoupled from the α band through the activity of the thalamic reticular nucleus. Both types of Spell-Out/Transfer operations discussed in the linguistics literature – one to the sensorimotor systems, another to the conceptual interface – will be subsumed under this approach, which at a minimum involves this desynchronisation of α-generated structures and subsequent θ-synchronisation. Though the thalamic reticular nucleus is here identified as a core component of desynchronisation, other regions may also be involved. Due to its involvement in $\{θ(γ)\}$ embedding in auditory processing (Nosarti et al. 2004), the posterior corpus callosum is also likely to be heavily involved in cyclicity. Recent experimental work which supports this model includes Elmer and Kühnis's (2016) EEG study comparing simultaneous interpreters (SIs; individuals who are trained in translating a source language into a target language virtually simultaneously) with multilingual controls during an auditory semantic decision task. For the SIs, they found increased left-hemispheric θ phase synchronisation compared to controls during early processing states, suggesting the involvement of this rhythm in preactivating speech representation during translation from one language into another. Given the role of hippocampal θ in working memory processes, it is also likely that this region, along with subcortical θ- and α-oscillating regions like the thalamus, contributes to the rapid lexical access abilities of simultaneous interpreters. θ is also capable of coupling cell assemblies across regions and information 'chunking' (Colgin 2013, Jensen & Colgin 2007), and frontal and temporal θ appears essential to good performance on the Sternberg memorisation task (Raghavachari et al. 2001). Maintaining mentally constructed visual objects in memory (i.e. combining a small number of basic shapes into a larger unit), in contrast to 'whole' objects, also leads to greater fronto-parietal θ synchronisation, and so this rhythm seems well-suited to the maintenance of complex objects generated – likely by fast γ – in fronto-parietal circuits (Ewerdwalbesloh et al. 2016).

After the initial decoupling of γ from α, it seems plausible to suggest that subsequent α increases have an additional role in working memory *Clear* operations (as defined in Dipoppa et al. 2016) through selective inhibition, emptying the existing cognitive set of content and thereby generating a form of cyclicity, something the language system might recruit. Indeed, Dipoppa et al.'s suggestion that *Load* operations are implemented via γ/β, *Maintain* via θ and *Clear* via α, resonates to a certain degree with the present suggestions for the language faculty. α increases have been linked to the selective inhibition of brain areas not currently task-relevant (Jensen & Mazaheri 2010), and indeed a broader reach for this rhythm resulting from human-specific braincase globularity may have enhanced selective attention to a point permitting pre-existing cognitive resources to be implemented more efficiently (Murphy 2018a, 2018b). This model is an improvement on existing theories of working memory operations (e.g. Lisman & Idiart 1995) which do not address *Clear* operations. Dipoppa and Gutkin's (2013) oscillatory model of working memory also invokes γ/β oscillations to access and load memories, θ oscillations to maintain memories, and finally α oscillations in rapid memory clearance. In summary, the claim that α is responsible for at least the final stages of cyclicity operations seems well supported.

More broadly, slower rhythms like θ and δ appear to increase in power during the selection of lexical information (Brunetti et al. 2013), suggesting that increasing global phase synchronisation (something only slower rhythms can achieve) may recruit global cortical regions in the service of semantic analysis. This aligns with Sanchez-Vives et al.'s (2017, 993) assessment of slow oscillations, which to them are 'a collective phenomenon with a dynamical origin not only rooted in the features of single neurons but also determined by the synaptic reverberation of the spiking activity at the mesoscopic (cell assemblies/cortical columns) and macroscopic (cortical areas/whole brain) levels'.

Finally, θ is involved in engaging functionally distinct subregions of the medial prefrontal cortex, integrating information from the output of different cognitive operations (Mas-Herrero & Marco-Pallarés 2016), a function potentially optimised for generating cycles of lexical feature-sets and dealing with Christiansen and Chater's (2016) *Now-or-Never bottleneck*, or the problem of rapidly encoding linguistic material given its natural propensity to vanish from working memory. Given the current lack of evidence for the conceptual-intentional interface in the human brain and how it might operate, oscillatory investigations into the syntax-semantics interface will be crucial in the years ahead if the field of evolutionary neurolinguistics is to make substantial strides.

2.2.1.3 Phrase Structure Building: δ-Nesting   As the previous chapter reviewed, along with concatenation and cyclicity there is also labelling. Labelling is monotonic in that once a set has been labelled (e.g. as a VP), its identity is sustained when embedded inside another set. Since labelling must take place at the point of transfer to the interfaces (to prevent a structure being a VP at the conceptual systems but a different phrase at the sensorimotor systems), labelling must be seen as a core operation of language (Piattelli-Palmarini & Vitiello 2015), and not emerging epiphenomenally at the interfaces.

Although additional details to the oscillatory model for phrase structure building will be outlined later, with the present section being preliminary given the scope of the model ultimately defended in this book, for now I will defend the position that labelling is implemented via the slowing down of γ to β followed by $\{\delta(\beta)\}$ coupling involving a cortico-basal ganglia-thalamo-cortical loop through which cortical input is received at the striatum (a major basal ganglia structure, in turn projecting to the smaller pallidum) and then chan-nelled back to the cortex via the thalamus (see Cannon et al. 2014 for the rhythmogenesis of β in the basal ganglia, and also Cole & Voytek 2017 for the non-sinusoidal properties of motor cortical β). This would disinhibit the tha-lamic medio-dorsal nucleus via the β band. This frequency coupling arises from a relationship between oscillations which form a hierarchy such that the speed of the slower rhythm controls the power of the faster rhythm, as noted earlier. The involvement of the cortico-basal ganglia-thalamo-cortical loop would be due to its being a major source of the brain's core timing system, with a core feature of labelling being rhythmicity (compare Bartolo et al. 2014 with Chomsky 2008, who both stress the importance of cyclicity). Recent work also indicates that the temporal precision of self-generated timed actions (i.e. generating a time interval in the absence of sensory input) is controlled by α-β phase–amplitude coupling (Grabot et al. 2019), further involving this core oscillatory multiplexing mechanism in time-related cognition. Grabot et al. (2019) more generally conclude that α and β 'cooperate for content mainte-nance'. The proposed role of basal ganglia β is in line with Okanoya and Merker's (2007, 421) claim that string segmentation is broadly implemented by 'bottom-up statistical learning by basal ganglia and top-down rule extraction by the prefrontal cortex'.

When γ-itemised representations are coupled to parahippocampal θ, I will assume that some of them ultimately slow to β to be maintained in short-term memory as the existing cognitive set (see Engel & Fries 2010 for evidence that β is responsible for such maintenance operations, and also Armeni et al. 2019 for evidence that unexpected words lead to β decreases, disrupting the maintenance of the set). Evidence that this process is neurophysiologically plausible comes from Gollo et al. (2017), who showed that after cortical regions are coupled together, their oscillatory frequency changes as a result of network interactions, such that 'slower hub regions speed up, and faster peripheral regions slow down their activity'. Moreover, the hippocampus is highly effective at 'generating ordinal cell assembly sequences relevant to the particular situation', be that a spatial, temporal, auditory or memory-related function (Buzsáki & Llinás 2017, 484). The domain-generality of its computational power indicates a likely crucial role in linguistic feature-set combinatorics.

Findings reported in Gehrig et al. (2019) also support the particular role of β in phrasal identity proposed here. These authors investigated speech memory representations using direct cortical recordings in the left perisylvian cortex during delayed sentence reproduction in patients undergoing awake tumor surgery. Based on the memory performance of patients, they found that the phase of fronto-temporal β oscillations represents sentence identity in working memory. The very notion of sentential identity presupposes a labelled structure (CP, TP, VP…), seemingly represented by fronto-temporal β.

In addition, there is evidence that θ and β show remarkable levels of co-maturation during childhood (Rodríguez-Martínez et al. 2015). Since the only other rhythms which display this level of co-maturation are high β and γ, these results may well reflect the development of the oscillatory language system proposed here. An assessment of the CFC of these rhythms with respect to language processing during development would be needed to substantiate these ideas (as Buzsáki 2006, 351 notes, 'relatively little research has been devoted to the problem of cross-frequency coupling').

The role of the thalamo-cortical network as a slow rhythm generator, and hence a single dynamic and functional unit of brain oscillations, has been recently supported by Crunelli et al.'s (2015) review of the EEG literature, and extensive, reciprocal anatomical connections exist between the thalamus and cortex (Jones 2007). Accumulating evidence suggests that β holds objects, whereas γ generates them (Martin & Ravel 2014). Dean et al. (2012) relatedly show how β is an excellent candidate for comparing old and new information from distinct modalities due to its wider temporal windows, likely drawing on different conceptual representations and hence different 'core knowledge systems' and brain regions (Spelke 2010). Related both to Balari and Lorenzo's (2013) claim that the basal ganglia is the centre of their 'Central Computational Complex' and Jouen et al.'s (2013) findings that this structure is implicated in acquiring the serial response order of a sequence, it is likely that this region holds one of the γ-supported items before slowing it down to the β frequency as a consequence of the conduction delays resulting from the surrounding neural regions. Thus, the β band accomplishes the role of labels, a claim supported by findings that β activity maintains existing cognitive states (Engel & Fries 2010).

More broadly, the basal ganglia and the striatum are implicated in sequencing and chunking, with striatal structures operating at the β range (Leventhal et al. 2012). The core position occupied by the basal ganglia in this labelling model also fits well with imaging studies which have revealed the region's involvement in 'syntactic complexity', specifically the processing of type-identity intervention of matching labels, being activated in a recent fMRI study when a noun phrase similar to the dependency head in a long-distance dependency intervenes in the dependency (Santi et al. 2015).

Moving to a different brain structure, there are emerging evolutionary frameworks which point to human-specific properties of the striatum, and it is therefore possible that these properties contribute to phrase structure building. Sousa et al. (2017) performed transcriptome sequencing of sixteen regions of adult human, chimpanzee and macaque brains, revealing regional and cell type-specific expression differences in genes representing distinct functional categories. Notable in their findings were rare subpallial-derived interneurons (TH^+ interneurons) expressing dopamine biosynthesis genes highly enriched in the human striatum relative to non-human primates (chimpanzees in the present study) and completely absent in the non-human African ape cortex (macaque monkeys). Given their well-known contribution to oscillatory function, the evolution of these particular kinds of striatal interneurons should be studied further in order to establish their impact on brain function and their possible relation to language. Furthermore, TH^+ interneurons are depleted in patients with Parkinson's disease, suggesting a role in higher cognition (Fukuda et al. 1999). Sousa et al. (2017, 1032) further note that TH^+ interneurons of macaques 'may have lost their ability to deviate to the cortex from the rostral migratory stream. Indeed, some human TH^+ interneurons migrating via the rostral migratory stream to the olfactory bulb divert to the prefrontal cortex.' In the context of language evolution, the globularisation of the human brain could explain the success of these migratory streams, permitting more efficient, or at least newly structured, pathways.

Turning again to another structure, the cortico-basal ganglia-thalamo-cortical loop is especially appealing with respect to its potential role in labelling given the finding that different 'stations' on the loop can be responsible for information integration from distinct cortical sources: convergence appears to occur at the pallidum (Yelnik et al. 1984), subthalamic nucleus (Haynes & Haber 2013) and thalamus (Theyel et al. 2010). These stations also display a degree of functional specificity, and it is likely that different features of linguistic representations (phonological, semantic, and so forth) are integrated into the phrase structure building process in a procedural manner. The anterior thalamus, for instance, is already being considered a major site of memory formation (Sweeney-Reed et al. 2015), going against standard cortico-centric and hippocampal-centric models. Wojtecki et al. (2017) also demonstrated a significant α-θ power increase and enhanced α-θ coherence between the subthalamic nucleus and the frontal EEG sites during a verbal generation task. The fact that lesions to Broca's area do not always result in syntactic impairments or modulations in sentential processing competence (Mohr et al. 1978) also suggests that other, possibly non-cortical circuits are (or at least can be) implicated in phrase structure building. Reviewing related literature, Klostermann et al. (2013) conclude that 'malfunction of the BG [basal ganglia] leads to deficits in applying combinatorial rules to linguistic messages, compatible with proposed superordinate BG functions, such as the sequencing or time-critical selection of input signals in general'.

Overall, the computational roles ascribed here are supported by a range of experimental findings, such as the general claims in Ketz et al. (2015) that θ is related to recollective/episodic memory processes (confirmed by recent experimental work showing θ phase synchronisation binding associative memories; Clouter et al. 2017), β is related to familiarity and executive control, and α is related to the gating of sensory information into higher-order systems.

A necessary feature of language is that its structure-building processes (elementary syntax) need to have direct access to the categories of the items being combined and stored together as a larger unit. It is highly likely, then, that the posterior inferior frontal gyrus (being involved in processing hierarchically organised linguistic structures; that is, labelled structures) and the temporal lobe (being implicated in categorisation processes in phonology, semantics and conceptual storage; Overath et al. 2015; Clarke & Tyler 2015), in particular the posterior middle temporal gyrus, dynamically interact during the construction and maintenance of linguistic representations, generating the human-specific trait of labelling. The posterior middle temporal gyrus likely decodes sequences of auditory phonological representations in the posterior superior temporal gyrus into hierarchical structures, and links them to a conceptual/ entity knowledge hub in the anterior temporal lobe and an event knowledge hub in the angular gyrus (see Matchin & Hickok 2019 for support and a detailed architectural proposal along these lines). Interesting support for this idea comes from Hanna et al.'s (2014) study of the syntactic mismatch negativity (sMMN) ERP component involved in the processing of simple two-word phrases. Previously localised only in temporal regions (Bakker et al. 2013), Hanna et al. (2014) for the first time revealed an inferior frontal gyrus source for the sMMN at around 150–190ms. In primates, conceptual categorisation appears to involve the coordination of temporal and frontal cortex (Freedman et al. 2003), and it is possible that the human language system recruited this more ancient categorisation capacity in the service of categorising the source of multiple streams of linguistic information into a labelled structure. Since it is involved in interactions between syntax and semantics, the posterior superior temporal cortex (Bornkessel et al. 2005) is almost certainly involved in what we could call the wider 'labelling network'.

Following the lead of much of contemporary linguistic theory, if we distinguish between the syntactic category and the representational content of a lexical item, we can assign distinct functions to the dorsal and ventral streams connecting temporal and frontal regions. The processes involved in interpreting hierarchically organised sequences implicate the dorsal stream (in particular the arcuate fasciculus), whereas the combinatorics of human semantics implicate the ventral stream. Importantly, unlike the dorsal stream the combinatorics exhibited by the ventral stream is limited to basic associative cognition and strictly linear sequences (Bemis & Pylkkänen 2013). Thanks to recent principal component analyses of lesion-symptom mappings (Fridriksson et al. 2016), we can now anatomically define these dual streams with some confidence: The ventral stream, involved in form-to-meaning mapping, involves lateral temporal lobe structures extending to the inferior parietal lobe in addition to the inferior frontal lobe via the uncinated fasciculus. The dorsal stream, a form-to-articulation pathway, extends from anterior speech areas, such as the pars opercularis, to posterior regions in the supramarginal gyrus, and reaches into the edge of area Spt of the planum temporale.

Cues about conceptual combinatorial processes and related forms of associative learning trigger anterior temporal and anterior frontal cortices (Scharinger et al. 2015), whereas cues about syntactic structure engage areas connected via the dorsal stream (Goucha & Friederici 2015). In non-human primates, the dorsal stream is used in an exclusively modality-specific fashion, being hardwired for vocal processing, with the dorsal prefrontal cortex also being implicated in gestural processing (Aboitiz 2012). In humans, dorsal processing of syntactic structures is modality-independent, being used in spoken and sign language (MacSweeney et al. 2005). From an oscillatory perspective, the coordination of different streams of dorsal and ventral combinatoric outputs could have boosted both the conceptual and syntactic capacities of anatomically modern humans.

Human-specific dorsal extensions into Geschwind's territory (Boeckx 2017) also likely permitted this structure-building mechanism to interface with other modules in the parietal and temporal lobes, a claim compatible with the 'functional constraints hypothesis' of the evolution and development of phenotypic traits, which claims that 'correlated change reflects the action of selection on distributed functional systems connecting the different sub-components, predicting more complex patterns of mosaic change at the level of the functional systems and more complex genetic and developmental mechanisms' (Montgomery et al. 2016). Major brain regions consequently evolve together due to the fact that functional systems extend across them. Even though dorsal connections may be implicated in constructing hierarchical phrase structures, other recent work compatible with the present approach suggests that the basal ganglia and thalamus act as network hubs forming a core circuit supporting large-scale integration (Acsády 2017; Bell & Shine 2016); indeed, large-scale information integration is 'a key computational priority' of the subcortex, for Bell and Shine. This model lends further weight to the idea that dorsal stream circuits can extend into subcortical regions to participate in maintenance/memory processes executed by slow θ, α and β rhythms.

In many ways, this should force researchers such as Friederici et al. (2017) to substantially revise their maps of the 'structural connectivity between language regions' (Friederici et al. 2017, 715, Fig. 1), since the 'language regions' can no longer be regarded as being restricted to BA 44, BA 45 and the posterior temporal cortex. Indeed, Friederici et al. (2017) provide little in the way of a neurolinguistic theory, noting only that BA 44 'subserves' syntactic processing; how it does so is not addressed. Noting how the neural network of BA 44 and its temporal connections does not fully develop and myelinate until late childhood (between seven and ten years of age), Friederici et al. (2017) suggest that early language acquisition (naturally involving the interpretation and production of complex phrases and sentences) is implemented via anterior BA 44, which supports single-instance Merge applications and the processing of canonical sentences. This is certainly a possibility. Another, simpler possibility is to assume that the BA 44-posterior temporal cortex dorsal pathway is not in fact crucial for recursive labelling operations, and that parts of the broader language network proposed here mature earlier and take on this responsibility (including posterior temporal cortex, but also subcortical structures like the basal ganglia, thalamus and parahippocampal regions).

A recent study by Davey et al. (2016) provides an additional node for this map. The posterior middle temporal gyrus was found to act as a hub integrating the default mode network with goal-oriented cognition located in a fronto-parietal multiple-demand circuit. This process has been claimed to impose a level of constraint and order onto the 'self-generated' representations of the default mode network (Sato et al. 2016), and may consequently play a role in particular elements of semantic representations built from these fronto-parietal networks. A recent line of research also points to human-specific parietal connections between Broca's and Wernicke's areas which add to white matter pathways shared with other primates (Hecht et al. 2013; Mendoza & Merchant

2014), and it is likely that this boosted the human capacity for constructing complex clusters of representations.

Another anatomical issue worth addressing concerns the origins of multi-modal communication, since human language is known to be externalised with equal complexity across a number of distinct modalities (speech, sign, touch), each with core common neural correlates in left inferior frontal regions. It remains unknown how sounds and signs were paired to achieve multimodal forms of externalisation, and how they were paired to phrasal construction processes in the brain. Interesting comparative directions have recently emerged, which may permit novel research directions: Activation of the homo-logous Broca's area in chimpanzees in both attention calls and gestures may suggest a multimodal origin of language (Taglialatela et al. 2011). Multimodal communication also appears to exist in birds, which communicate simulta-neously through pairing sounds with synchronised beak, feet and wing move-ment (Pika & Bugnyar 2011; Hoepfner & Goller 2013; Soma & Mori 2015).

Recent analyses of data from severe global aphasia also indicate that lan-guage is not necessary for complex thought (Fedorenko & Varley 2016). What this suggests is that the oscillatory mechanisms of syntactic computation can readily operate independently of any lexical representations. The theoretical implications of this kind of scenario have already been touched on (i.e. it lends weight to Hauser and Watumull's concept of a Universal Generative Faculty), but the experimental implications are also quite clear. No longer should lin-guists interested in the neural basis of syntactic computation focus solely on language. This may seem as if linguists are in fact no longer studying language, but in fact this kind of move is highly desirable; indeed, *geometry* originally referred to the study of land mass, before it became more theoretically sophis-ticated and began to abstract away from its original object of study and into more general mathematical principles. Likewise, if linguists can find numerous ways to move beyond the study of language in the sense of grammar and communication, this would also reflect a similar theoretical advance.

Finally, the rhythmic division of complexity following from the aforemen-tioned proposals is supported by Honkanen et al. (2015), who demonstrated that simple objects represented in visual working memory employ the γ band, while more complex objects are represented by the β band. The role attrib-uted here to γ assemblies additionally finds some support in Bastiaansen and Hagoort's (2015) EEG study of semantic unification, which detected larger γ-band power for semantically coherent than semantically incongruent sen-tences. Larger β-band power was also found for syntactically correct sen-tences relative to ungrammatical sentences, lending support to the hypothesised labelling power assigned to β in the present model. But this γ-semantics and β-syntax framework is impoverished not only with respect to the experimental data, but also with respect to neurobiological and algorithmic plausibility (as we will see, β increases are also consistent with incrementally accurate prediction processes). Directly associating large-scale, complex computations like 'sentence processing' and 'semantic interpretation' with particular rhythms (and not their interactions and modulations) may actually constitute a form of *regression* from the standard, much derided cartographic conclusions in the neuroimaging literature, since at least fMRI studies can provide some form of detailed source localisation, unlike the low levels of spatial resolution found in the EEG literature. Egidi and Caramazza (2014) even show that the processing of consistent vs. inconsistent discourse content is executed across very different networks depending on the mood of the comprehender, implying the existence of alternative routes for the core language network, and reinforcing the importance of seeking a neural code rather than a neural network.

2.2.2   Theory vs. Data Redescription in the Study of Language

Having outlined a series of working hypotheses, what of the algorithmic models connecting these levels of analysis? Drawing a related linking hypothesis between psycholinguistics and neurobiology, Martin (2016) suggests that cue integration, a mechanism from vision and multisensory perception which incorporates probabilistic estimates of a cue's reliability, may serve to aid the interpretation of linguistic structures from the phonemic to phrasal levels. The core suggestion of this model is that the basic parsing operations found in psycholinguistic models (e.g. cue-based retrieval and expectation-based parsing frameworks) can be implemented by a single neurobiological principle of cue-integration. Martin makes use of the Discovery of Relations by Analogy (DORA) algorithmic model of relational concept development (Doumas et al. 2008), which uses associative learning to generate hierarchical relational concepts out of linear inputs and is a symbolic-connectionist model of relational reasoning. As Martin (2016) discusses, DORA can learn multiple argument predicates using time or onset of activity in sub-nodes, or the synchrony/asynchrony of sub-node firing, where sub-nodes represent an individual argument. Indeed, Martin's decomposition of the cue integration mechanism into two generic neural processes (normalisation and summation) leads to similar levels of neurocomputational granularity as that achieved by the aforementioned decomposition of labelling. The DORA model can elegantly capture not only the binding of roles to their fillers, but the inherently dynamic and flexible nature of this binding relationship, such that in natural language we often find the rapid creation of bindings (i.e. the labelling of a phrase as a DP or a VP) followed swiftly by their destruction and rebinding (i.e. a change in phrasal status of a given construction during, for instance, ambiguity resolution).

More recently, Martin and Doumas (2017) tested this DORA model against the oscillatory results documented in Ding et al. (2016) (namely, the finding of 2 Hz 'entrainment' to phrases, and 1Hz entrainment to sentences), showing a close alignment between the structure-building processes of DORA and the particular δ entrainment features in Ding et al. What is particularly interesting about entrainment is that it involves an alignment between endogenous brain oscillations and the rhythm of stimulus, which seems to reflect the brain's goal of aligning optimal moments of excitatory activity (processing) with input deemed relevant to some particular perceptual or cognitive domain. Note that the phase-locking involved in entrainment may be lagged and does not imply phase synchrony/identity, but simply that the phases co-vary. The findings in Martin and Doumas (2017) suggest that DORA is a feasible neural network model – if the entrainment hypothesis can be maintained (see also Lakatos et al. 2008 for the role of oscillations in attention). Recent work suggests that it can, at least for certain aspects of language processing (namely, speech processing): The modulation of oscillations which can lead to entrainment can be achieved via three rhythmic stimulation methods: sensory stimulation, non-invasive electric/ magnetic stimulation, and invasive electrical stimulation (Hanslmayr et al. 2019). Riecke et al. (2018) used 'speech-envelope-shaped transcranial current stimulation' (envTCS) to conduct two experiments involving a cocktail party–like scenario and a listening situation devoid of any speech–amplitude envelope input. The results suggest effects on listeners' speech recognition performance, implying the existence of a causal role for speech-brain entrainment in speech processing. Application of envTCS seemed to reset the phase of δ, disrupting entrainment. In addition, Bauer et al. (2018) used EEG to investigate the temporal evolution of entrainment during short and long periods of stimulation in the auditory cortex, showing that stimulus-brain phase aligns dynamically over a period of several seconds. Di Liberto et al. (2018) also lend a more precise temporal dimension to the mechanisms of entrainment, using MEG to show that δ-driven cortical entrainment to the speech envelope emerged in left inferior frontal gyrus at ~50 ms and at Heschl's gyrus at ~100ms, being sustained until ~250ms.

Even saccades appear to be phase-locked to α oscillations in the occipital and medial temporal lobe during successful memory encoding in humans, 'suggesting a mechanistic role for alpha oscillations in coordinating the encoding of visual information' (Staudigl et al. 2017). It will be of interest to examine oscillatory dynamics in non-human primates during saccadic movements associated with similar memory processes, determining whether saccades might serve to parcellate visual working memory units.

Yet despite all this, syntactic information does not have a counterpart in the external speech stream, and so it follows that exogenous entrainment and perceptual tracking will not be sufficient for the construction of phrasal and sentential meaning. It is possible, as I have discussed elsewhere, that linguistic entrainment is not entrainment proper but rather what Meyer et al. (2019) call entrainment 'in disguise'. The lack of invariant amplitude cues below the rate of syllables suggests that rhythmicity results from perceptual inference of higher-level structural meaning, i.e. endogenous information. In other words, it is likely that only minimal levels of exogenous entrainment are needed (probably only in auditory cortex) to activate the higher-order endogenous rhythms proposed in the model developed in this chapter, which 'take over' immediately from the speech stream. Indeed, upon the activation of this endogenous code for a particular structure, this process may stabilise perception of the sensory signal. As Ohki and Takei (2018) independently conclude, 'oscillations play a significant role in extracting and maintaining higher-level information and applying it to the processing of novel information'. Meyer et al. (2019) elaborate a similar general framework, but do not provide any concrete examples or a model of endogenous linguistic computation to match against the literature on exogenous entrainment; they only point towards the existence of endogenous activity responsible for guiding language comprehension; and, even here, their talk of 'synchrony' should more accurately be interpreted as 'partial synchrony', following core principles of non-linear dynamics (e.g. see Guevara Erra et al. 2017). As such, partial synchrony permits phase shifts between synchronised signals, referring to how correlated the activity of these underlying networks is. Falling short of the granularity standards typically expected in neurolinguistics, Meyer et al. (2019) provide no clear oscillatory model or neuroanatomical framework, and they suggest only that intrinsic (partial) synchronicity in frontal-posterior networks is associated with abstract linguistic processes. Indeed, the dual entrainment-synchrony model in Meyer et al. (2019) was already proposed in Murphy (2016a, 2016c), although Meyer et al. (2019) explore some interesting, context-specific implementations (e.g. noisy bottom-up signals can be compensated by top-down inferences, like in the context of a nightclub), and this dual model has also been developed by others (e.g. the excellent work of Nicola Molinaro; see Molinaro & Lizarazu 2018). A question which remains open is how partially synchronous endogenous mechanisms influence or direct entrainment; another area where CFC may be invoked, returning to earlier hypotheses about the importance of coupling in Arnal et al. (2014) and Murphy (2015b).

According to the model developed in this book (and in earlier publications; Murphy 2015b, 2016a), what might appear to be entrainment on the outside might simply reflect a phase resetting based on the internally synchronised behaviour of endogenous oscillations. Indeed, future work could explore to what extent there is a dynamic interplay between exogenous entrainment (or resonance) and endogenous synchronicity, with both mechanisms being used flexibly based on the nature of current input. Despite these limitations in applying entrainment to complex syntactic and semantic processes, entrainment is highly likely to be involved at least in tracking speech rhythm (Peelle et al. 2013), and can work in tandem with internal partial synchronicity, and possibly other endogenous mechanisms.

Oscillatory circuits also have a propensity to be entrainable by periodically modulated inputs: 'Pulse sequences whose frequency is close to the preferred frequency of the oscillator or its harmonics, entrain the oscillator and shift its frequency until it oscillates in synchrony with the inducing pulses' (Singer 2017). What the precise neurocomputational properties of the oscillations documented by researchers such as Ding et al. are still remains unexplored in the literature, however. Relatedly, Teng et al. (2018) show that θ rhythms are capable of more than entrainment, being involved in active auditory chunking.

Moving to more theoretical concerns, Martin and Doumas (2017) propose DORA as a response to the current gap between cortical and cognitive computation: '[The DORA-based] hypothesis would shed light on whether the observed cortical signal reflected "mere" tracking of hierarchical linguistic representations or whether it, in fact, reflects the online generation of hierarchical linguistic structure.' But these two options – mere tracking versus the reflection of structure generation – still leave the neurocomputational properties of oscillations at a distance. More worryingly, Frank and Yang (2017, 2018) point to a notable flaw of Ding et al.'s (2016) study. They observe that in the Ding et al. stimuli the occurrence frequency of phrases is identical to the occurrence frequency of nouns (one per two words), and the occurrence frequency of transitive verbs is identical to the occurrence frequency of sentences (one per four words). Instead of finding cortical entrainment to syntactic structure, Ding et al. may have simply found entrainment to lexical information, with distinct rhythms triggering representations of distinct lexical categories stored in different brain regions. Using a model for lexical information and comparing it to Ding et al.'s data for their English stimuli, Frank and Yang's (2017, 2018) results were virtually identical to Ding et al.'s. This lexical explanation is simpler than the entrainment account; however, it is also not incompatible with the syntax-based account. Ding et al.'s finding of increased δ for real words compared to pseudo-words was also not replicated in Mai et al. (2016), and so further work is needed to clarify these issues. Indeed, Brookshire et al. (2017) found entrainment to visual oscillations for American Sign Language speakers at around 1-5Hz over occipital and parietal EEG sites, peaking at ~1Hz, approximately the same range found in Ding et al., suggesting that the phrase structure building process resulted in the same underlying dynamics independent of modality. Unfortunately, current work in the field continues to reproduce the standard syntax-driven interpretation of Ding et al. (2016) despite its fundamental issues; Adger's (2019a, 59–60) monograph claims that Ding et al.'s experiments 'quite conclusively' showed that '[c]ertain brain rhythms synced with the abstract structure of sentences'.

That being said, as luck would have it (for Adger and others) Jin et al. (2019) revealed in late 2019 that the 1 Hz-sentence and 2Hz-phrase sensitivity (at least, in English, with different timings for Chinese) initially claimed to exist in Ding et al. (2016) can in fact be replicated in a new stimuli set (in MEG) modelled in spirit on Ding et al.'s stimuli but crucially including a control for semantic/ lexical information. The authors also controlled for the semantic relatedness of adjacent words, ensuring that any neural response they found could not be due to this factor (e.g. a decrease at Word 2 after the semantically related Word 1 appeared). They found that 1–2Hz activity tracks multiword chunks that are constructed based on chunking rules rather than lexical properties or semantic relatedness.

At this point it is worth noting an important qualification, presented most forcefully in an excellent critique of recent oscillation research by Frank and Christiansen (2018). These authors note that, contra Ding et al. (2016) and Jin et al. (2019), it may not be the case that language comprehenders necessarily construct a hierarchy of linguistic structures in any given instance of inter- pretation. Frank and Christiansen (2018, 1214) suggest that 'abstraction from the input can remain limited to what is required for comprehension . . . (e.g. frequent multiword strings can be analysed as a whole, so no internal structure is assigned, even if the string also retains its sequential character)'. Context is also important: It is likely that the language system will impose a more super- ficial analysis on an informal conversation than on a reading of a carefully- crafted legal document. In fact, this perspective is wholly in line with standard generative and minimalist assumptions about computational efficiency (note that Ding et al. 2016 support the generative project and insist that comprehen- ders 'must' construct hierarchies to the phrase level in any scenario); that is to say, minimalist principles of economy are clearly adhered to by a language system which invokes what Frank and Christiansen (2018) term 'minimal abstraction', only resorting to complex hierarchical phrase structure building when statistics and memory are insufficient: 'If a sequential explanation suf- fices this should be preferred because of the lower level of abstraction involved' (Frank & Christiansen 2018, 1215). This is a sensible guideline, though it is also the case that a recent comparison between sequential and hierarchical models of language processing revealed that measures of hier- archical structure building can better explain unique variance in neural activa- tion (Nelson et al. 2017, although see later in the chapter). As such, the cognitive reality of hierarchical structure-building processes for language seems well supported at the moment, even if we concur with Frank and Christiansen (2018) that not every aspect of language processing will require the use of the full neural code for hierarchical language comprehension presented in this book.

It is possible that the oscillatory interactions proposed in this chapter (and expanded on in Chapter 3) are responsible for the low δ entrainment found by Brookshire et al. (2017), Ding et al. (2016) and Jin et al. (2019). Whether or not this claim can be substantiated, it at least appears to be the case that the data reported in Ding et al. (2016), although not discussed by Brookshire et al. (2017), cannot be accounted for based on special properties of auditory cortex or speech perception. Rather, it is likely that a more generic neural code is exploited by the language system to interpret certain informational peaks (~1/ 2Hz) corresponding to the construction of grammatical sentences/phrases. Nevertheless, further experimental work is needed to resolve this particular issue. Indeed, Ding et al. (2017) apply the stimuli set from Ding et al. (2016) to EEG, and in doing so reveal the usefulness of the more prevalent technology (compared to MEG); however, they present no new theoretical insights alongside their replicated entrainment findings. Since no study has currently reported intelligible speech processing without some form of neural entrainment, Kösem and van Wassenhove (2017, 538) justifiably argue that 'low-frequency entrainment may be the hallmark of a necessary (but not sufficient, and not language-related) mechanism used for speech comprehension'.

In Chapter 3, we will propose a number of more specific δ interactions (namely, δ-θ CFC) as being responsible for phrase structure building, and we will also discuss the limitations of the current entrainment debates in the literature. Rather than focusing purely on the properties of δ entrainment, it will be suggested that a broad range of migrating δ couplings are the basis of phrase structure building. For further motivation in this direction, Boucher et al. (2019) examined how δ (for them, <3Hz) entrains to three types of stimuli: tones, nonsense syllables and utterances. They found δ oscillations at frontotemporal sites entrained to temporal groups in meaningful utterances, but also meaningless syllables, suggesting that δ – in isolation – may support but does not directly bear on content processing, and that entrainment is rather used for more generic sensory chunking. Indeed, it has long been known that ERPs associated with the grouping of words into implicit phrases appear with a regularity not requiring periodic exogenous prosodic cues (Steinhauer et al. 1999; Roll et al. 2012).

Indeed, it is probably due to the role of δ entrainment in this generic sensory chunking that over the past decade various authors have implicated it in the processing of virtually every conceivable linguistic unit: 'intonation', 'prosody', 'sentences', 'phrases', 'accent phrases', 'prosodic processing', 'metrical stress', 'long syllables' and, of course, 'words'. As discussed later in the chapter, it is much more likely that certain rhythmic interactions are responsible for processing more specific units of language.

Alongside these current limitations, the EEG dynamics of anaphor resolution (involving the relationship between pronouns and other discourse elements) have only recently been explored. Meyer et al. (2015) explored the retrieval of an antecedent either across a single or a double clause boundary, and found θ increases after a double clause relative to a single clause boundary, likely calling upon additional working memory and lexical access demands. Nieuwland and Martin (2017) showed increased γ power for referentially coherent expressions compared to referentially problematic expressions across a number of modalities. They argue that the observed γ increases reflect successful referential binding and resolution, which links incoming informa- tion to antecedents through an interaction between the brain's recognition memory networks and frontal-temporal language network. During successful anaphor resolution, the authors found increased γ power first across posterior parietal cortex at around 400–600ms post-anaphor, then across fronto-temporal cortex at around 500–1000ms. The authors suggest that these progressions reflect connections between the brain's parietal recognition systems and its fronto-temporal language regions, as if the anaphor is recognised and then subsequently computed into the discourse. Not finding any N400 modulations, the authors concluded that their results were most likely not due to prediction generation, but rather reflected the implementation of anaphor retrieval and discourse insertion. More compellingly, the authors did not find any significant θ increases during referentially coherent expressions compared to referentially incoherent ones, suggesting that this rhythm is strictly involved in featural combinatorics and not in the antecedent reactivation process, as the model proposed above predicts.

This seems to be a cartographically well-motivated account, what the authors call a 'nascent corticohippocampal theory of reference.' What this account is lacking is an algorithmic model of what operations these γ rhythms are executing. Under the model developed in this chapter, Nieuwland and Martin's results can be accounted for if we assume that the legitimate anaphor resolutions involve a successful integration of new lexical features into the discourse, represented by the γ-itemisation pro- cess, and that illegitimate/mismatched φ-feature associations (as in 'John said she was happy', where the pronoun is intended to refer to 'John') naturally involved fewer such features being integrated by the $\{\theta(\gamma)\}$ code. What is needed is a follow-up experiment (broadening the range of stimuli to involve a greater variety of featural mismatches) analysing phase codes and CFCs. Nieuwland and Martin's 'nascent corticohippocampal theory of reference' is a redescription of a dataset and one-to-one mappings between regions of interest and previous functional neuroimaging findings. 'Gamma-band increases' reported in the Results section transform into 'successful referential binding' in the Discussion section, but a motivated connection is absent. The neurocomputational steps required to get from γ increases to Binding Theory are not laid out. Gamma-band increases should of course be documented when found, but as Stankovski et al. (2017) point out, '[a]lthough neural interactions are usually characterized only by their coupling strength and directionality, there is often a need to go beyond this by establishing the functional mechanisms of the interaction' – with the authors giving the prime example of 'the coupling functions of neural oscillations', the core mechanism proposed in this book to be responsible for hierarchical phrase structure.

In another recent MEG study of the oscillatory nature of reference, Brodbeck et al. (2016) add a much-needed time course to successful reference resolution, but like Nieuwland and Martin (2017) they proceed no further than data redescription, with little in the way of a broader neurocognitive architecture or model being proposed. By presenting a global model and exploring the causal-explanatory power of the $\{\theta(\gamma)\}$ code, it is hoped that the discussion in this chapter goes beyond Nieuwland and Martin (2017) in that it cannot be reduced purely to a correlational finding about γ increases during particular linguistic manipulations; rather, it attributes to brain rhythms certain neuro-computational properties (or, to repeat again, brain rhythms index more fundamental neurochemical computations, indirectly) which help explain why we find such oscillatory responses. The general cognitive processes used to resolve linguistic dependencies may also be used to resolve music and action sequences (van de Cavey & Hartsuiker 2016), and future experimental work could address whether the oscillatory coupling mechanisms are also similar.

Like Nieuwland and Martin's work, a recent study by Nelson et al. (2017) presents novel experimental data in the absence of a compelling theoretical account. Nelson et al. attempt to investigate the electrophysiological basis of Merge and found γ decreases in posterior superior temporal sulcus sites at phrasal boundaries (a site Goucha et al. 2017 implicate more specifically, and likely more accurately, in labelling) but do not discuss the intrinsic computational properties of the γ activity they discovered. They use their data to support pre-existing higher-level conceptions of Merge (hence, Chomsky et al. 2019 cite Nelson et al. 2017 approvingly). Despite claiming to have found the neural basis of Merge, Nelson et al. (2017) rather demonstrated that well-known sentence-final 'wrap-up' effects (which are themselves potentially a consolidation process or a form of cyclicity) also occur after phrases (see Stowe et al. 2018). This is unsurprising given recent work in syntax (Chomsky 2015a) showing that clausal structures have many parallels with smaller phrasal structures (arguably a form of symmetry). The idea that Merge (i.e. both its combinatorial and phrasal attribution features) simply boils down to γ decreases is far from tenable. Indeed, high γ power was in fact the only band Nelson et al. reported, not carrying out an analysis of any other rhythms, and the main effect they found was localised to a single electrode in a single patient. Another limitation is that Merge is assumed by Nelson et al. to occur only at phrase boundaries (which, in their experimental materials, are often quite distant from each other), while according to contemporary theoretical syntax both Merge *and* labelling occur much more frequently (i.e. Merge is said to occur after every lexical item). Unfortunately, Nelson et al.'s study has readily been embraced, and cited approvingly and uncritically, across the language sciences, despite its analytical and theoretical flaws.

In another recent study of Merge, Segaert et al. (2018) used EEG to compare the oscillatory responses of processing successful binding (pronoun + pseudoverb, e.g. 'she dotches') versus unsuccessful binding (two pseudoverbs, e.g. 'pob dotches'). Increased α power over a left-lateralised cluster of frontal-temporal electrodes was found at the second word in the successful binding condition, which the authors suggest is 'related to syntactic binding taking place'. While this novel finding points to a role for α not just in inhibition (as in the model pursued earlier) but also in some other, distinct process, the authors do not explore this possibility, nor do they explore *how* α increases might be related to binding.

Relatedly, Wang et al. (2018) used MEG to observe the dynamics of predic- tion processes in language comprehension, comparing predictable sentence endings with unpredictable sentence endings. With sentences providing enough information for listeners to easily predict upcoming words, Wang et al. found coupling between posterior α and frontal γ oscillations (a form of coupling proposed here to be involved in early stages of lexical combination). They conclude their study by claiming that 'language processing might be supported by the coupling between the alpha and gamma activities' – a very real possibility, although a proposal about *how* is absent.

Moving to another area of language processing, while our understanding of how the brain processes adjective-noun combinations is still in its infancy, an MEG study by Fyshe et al. (2016) revealed that the neural representations of adjectival semantics entrain to α. They conclude that 'during semantic compo- sition, oscillatory activity is used to coordinate brain areas, to retain and to recall information as it is needed'. This notion is not developed further.

A greater level of engagement with syntactic, semantic and phonological computations will also be required of future oscillatory experiments, with Mai et al. (2016) claiming imprecisely that γ increases are representative of 'lexical memory retrieval' and 'processing grammatical word categories'. Unless the computational sub-operations of lexical retrieval and featural combination are acknowledged and explored, the task of reducing complex, multifaceted cog- nitive processes to neurobiological primitives will be hindered.

Developing the theoretical discussion somewhat further, Whitford et al. (2017) have shown that the production of an inner phoneme (during inner speech) is associated with an efference copy of the phoneme; namely, it is associated with an internal duplicate of the movement-producing neural signals required for the given phoneme. This suggests that inner speech is associated with efference copies with detailed motor properties, lending weight to an old suggestion of Jackendoff's that inner speech should be properly construed as *internalised externalisation*, or the inner reproduction of externalised sound. As Whitford et al. (2017) phrase it, 'inner speech may ultimately be '*a kind of action*', and a special case of overt speech'. If inner phonemes are electrophysiologically closely related to heard phonemes, then inner phrases and sentences may well have the same kind of existence, adding further impetus for moving beyond entrainment.

Keitel and Gross et al. (2018) provide some additional insight into the core issue addressed in this section. They analysed speech tracking in source-localised MEG data by focusing on timescales extracted from statistical regularities in the speech stimuli. They found that the following structures were tracked at particular bands: phrases (0.6–1.3Hz), words (1.8–3Hz), syllables (2.8–4.8Hz) and phonemes (8–12.4Hz). Correctly comprehended trials resulted in stronger tracking for phrases in the left premotor cortex and for words in the left middle temporal cortex. In addition, the slow δ rhythm which tracked phrases was coupled with β power in motor areas, which likely implements top-down speech predictions. Though this particular study did not find that δ coupled with any other bands, other studies by the same lab group (discussed later) did (see also Steinmetzger & Rosen 2017 for δ increases during intelligible speech but not unintelligible speech).

The cartographic details of Keitel et al. (2018) (and much other work) map on to the findings of Iwabuchi et al. (2019), who used fMRI to show that the neural substrate for syntactic processing is functionally located in a distinct region from the substrate for verbal working memory. Japanese sentences with an Object-Subject-Verb (OSV) structure were contrasted with canonical SOV sentences, with the latter exhibiting less hierarchy in syntactic structure due to no movement occurring. They found that the posterior part of Broca's area and the left posterior middle temporal gyrus exhibited specific activation for hierarchical structure building, with these left temporal regions overlapping with Keitel et al.'s (2018) results. Modulations in verbal working memory load (through adding modifiers to the subject or object noun phrases) resulted in activation in the op9, a structure in the frontal operculum adjacent to Broca's area, suggesting a clear segregation of phrase structure processing from verbal working memory. These findings also speak to the possibility of a 'dual workspace' for language, i.e. some form of construction workspace interfacing with a maintenance/storage workspace, since verbal working memory does not share a common resource with phrase structure memory (an issue we will return to in Chapter 3). Relating this more directly to current models of syntax, op9 is likely involved in processing linear distance in syntax, while the left posterior middle temporal gyrus is likely involved in processing structural (hierarchical) distance. Recent support for the general architecture of a linguistic dual workspace comes from Berger et al. (2019), who found sustained activity in inferior frontal gyrus, middle temporal gyrus and hippocampus when electrocorticography (ECoG) subjects maintained a low and high tone in memory, possibly suggesting that the more complex forms of phrasal memory piggyback off a lower-level memory architecture. That is to say, part of the initial construction workspace may be anchored in parahippocampal and temporal regions, while the maintenance workspace may be anchored across parahippocampal and inferior frontal regions. Indeed, Vanier et al. (2019) discovered that, relative to apes and monkeys, the human hippocampal formation shows an increase in size in the CA3, subiculum and rhinal cortex regions, and also an increase in the neocortex; expansions which might underlie our unique episodic memory capacity, as the authors speculate, but also our unique ability to string together large clusters of neocortical linguistic features into coherent lexical items and phrases (following the role of θ-γ interactions postulated here).

Finally, Molinaro and Lizarazu (2018) contrasted cortical entrainment to natural speech compared to qualitatively different control conditions (amplitude-modulated white noise and spectrally rotated speech), finding that while θ entrainment largely reflected perceptual processing (and likely other computations relevant for feature-set combinatorics, following the model in this chapter), only δ entrainment involved higher-order language-related processes (although their continuous speech stimuli did not reveal which particular features of speech entrain to δ, and as mentioned earlier, these findings can be explained via a more generic sensory chunking role for δ entrainment). Indeed, they note that '[t]he information extracted from this "entrainment step" would then be available to higher-order cognitive processes that are not necessarily phase-synchronized with the external input' – precisely the type of perspective developed here, and which justifies further work oriented around exploring theoretical commensurability between neurobiology and linguistics rather than purely pursuing novel experimental directions.

Overall, oscillation-based linking hypotheses might also provide a substantive response to Revonsuo's (2001, 51) comment that in contemporary neuroscience 'the main efforts are concentrated on the description and systemisation of data and the utilisation of the data for clinical purposes. No radically new theoretical purposes, comparable to the neuron doctrine, have emerged from this enterprise as yet.' As Snyder (2015) reviews, oscillations are increasingly being shown to play a causal, and not correlational, role in the perceptual segregation of sound patterns (though it should be stressed that numerous other oscillatory mechanisms likely do not play a causal-functional role in cognition). As such, the number of avenues that one might take to go beyond data redescription – of the kind reviewed in this section – is increasing.

2.3   Applications and Consequences

2.3.1   *Autism and Schizophrenia: The 'Price' We Paid for Language*

If these language-oscillation hypotheses are along the right track, this would give a justification to the related hypothesis that language deficits can be oscillatory in nature. For instance, Murphy and Benítez-Burraco (2016, 2017) and Benítez-Burraco and Murphy (2016) suggest that language deficits in schizophrenia and autism spectrum disorders can be explained by assuming that their abnormal CFC profiles impair (among other things) the domain-general ability to extract particular items from memory. Disruptions of neurotypical oscillatory activity may reflect what Mohammad-Rezazadeh et al. (2016) call the 'tendency of the brain to become "stuck" (versus flexibly adaptive) in a redundant pattern of functional connectivity', which may 'relate to motor and cognitive systems in autism spectrum disorder (ASD) which are also "stuck" in a series of repetitive behaviors or restricted interests'. Interestingly, Kessler et al. (2016) conducted an extensive literature review and hypothesised that 'especially low delta-theta frequency long-range phase coupling should be affected in ASD in conjunction with reduced local PAC and possibly inter-trial phase coherence during high-level social cognition that requires complex signal integration over time'. Recent evidence also suggests that tACS can modulate cross-frequency interactions (Herrmann et al. 2016) and can increase long-range (posterior-anterior) α Granger causal connectivity beyond a twenty-four-hour period in humans, an occurrence which brought with it sustained reductions in anxious arousal (Clancy et al. 2017). The clinical applications are extremely promising, with Clancy et al. (2017) being the first to document long-term oscillatory effects. A highly important application of interventionist strategies to brain stimulation can be found in network stimulations to treat mental diseases (see Salimpour & Anderson 2019; Wilkinson & Murphy 2016), with CFC in particular being a potential therapeutic target in disease states. Overall, these ideas are commensurable with recent moves in neuroscience to view psychiatric illnesses as oscillatory connectomopathies (Vinogradov & Herman 2016; Cao et al. 2016), and are also compatible with the more general (and plausible) claim that autism and schizophrenia were the 'price' that humans paid for acquiring language (Sikela & Searles Quick 2018), since the arrival of such a complex system brings with it the risk of malfunction, with many of the core traits of these disorders arguably being linguistic in nature.

2.3.2   *Prediction and Binding*

We concluded in the previous chapter that, from a psycholinguistic perspective, there are very good reasons to maintain that the label-driven mechanism of language processing should include a predictive component that generates expectations for core structural elements (and not optional elements like adjuncts). But how is this system implemented? We can now apply our understanding of the functional role of neural oscillations to an overview of two major processes relevant for language: prediction and binding. These respectively map on to the top-down and bottom-up processes of expectation generation and structural combinatorics. The former seems to be implemented via β increases, the latter via δ and θ. Beukema and Verstynen (2018) claim that these two processes constitute interacting algorithms supporting the consolidation of sequential motor skills. As with language, the learning and execution of habitual motor sequences demands the interpretation and implementation of serially ordered actions. It also demands what the authors term 'fast prediction of transition probabilities between events and slower binding of serial actions into unified sets' – computations closely aligned to linguistic processes. They classify 'predicting serial order' as involving *fast, associative* and *extrinsic* features, while 'set building' (binding) demands *reinforcement, efficiency* and *intrinsic* computations (Beukema & Verstynen 2018, 99, fig. 1). The fast detection of serial ordering appears to rely on the medial temporal lobe, in particular the hippocampus. A sub-population of hippocampal cells are tuned for the temporal associations between event sequences (MacDonald et al. 2011).

In line with this subcortical focus, Henderson et al. (2016) present evidence, through a joint eye-tracking and fMRI study of syntactic surprisal, that the network responsible for syntactic prediction is widely distributed, spanning bilateral inferior frontal gyrus and insula, and fusiform and right lingual gyri, reaching far beyond the classical regions. Shain et al. (2020) also found with fMRI language-specific predictive coding in naturalistic sentence comprehension, such that sentence processing mechanisms in left inferior frontal regions generate predictions about upcoming words using processes sensitive to hierarchical structure and specialised for language. Blending these cartographic and oscillatory perspectives, this leads to the clear prediction that β increases across this broad perisylvian network may interact, via coupling, in specific ways with the oscillatory system implementing sentence comprehension (reviewed in Chapter 3).

More recently, Beukema and Verstynen (2018, 100, fig. 2) have noted of the binding-prediction learning process that, 'once the transition probabilities between serially ordered items [...] becomes deterministic, it is computationally efficient to group sensorimotor decisions into unified sets, for example, a "chunk", where the entire set is represented as a single, generative sensorimotor decision'. Likewise, motivations of computational efficiency (invoked most forcefully by generative linguistics) likely structured the evolution of phrase structures, which also appear to be hierarchically organised (i.e. labelled) through a process of efficient computation ('least effort') termed *minimal search* (see Chapter 1). Indeed, this may reflect a more general 'third factor' in evolution: Employing an optimal control theory framework, Ramkumar et al. (2016) discuss how binding represents an optimal solution to controlling complex sequences of movements through minimising global computational cost during learning. They show that as animals become more proficient at a sequential skill, efficiency increases as the number of chunks decreases, reflecting an increased number of bound elements in each chunk. Moreover, in line with what has already been reviewed, Jin et al. (2014) reviewed the range of action sequence-linked cell types in the striatum and concluded that during learning the striatum facilitates concatenation.

Why are these findings of computational efficiency relevant for us? Since I have proposed that these chunking mechanisms are implemented via neural oscillations, and furthermore that these processes seem to be optimised in various ways, it is noteworthy that encoding information in the timing of action potential spikes incurs a lower metabolic cost than encoding information in other possible ways, facilitates rapid processing, and can also be used to disambiguate simultaneously-presented stimuli (VanRullen et al. 2005). Consequently, there seems to be something of a causal chain from information-encoding optimisation at the spike-timing level, to the oscillatory level, and finally to the computational (in this case, binding) level.

Sengupta et al. (2013) make a more fundamental point:

The repertoire and speed of biological computations are limited by thermodynamic or metabolic constraints: an example can be found in neurons, where fluctuations in biophysical states limit the information they can encode – with almost 20–60% of the total energy allocated for the brain used for signalling purposes, either via action potentials or by synaptic transmission.

How the imperative for neurons to 'optimise computational and metabolic efficiency' (Sengupta et al. 2013) influences higher-order oscillatory processes – and thereby linguistic processes – is a promising topic for future enquiry. For now, it seems clear from Ramkumar et al. (2016) that breaking compound movements into chunks (or in the language domain, collections of words into phrases) reduces overall computational complexity. Furthermore, Ramkumar et al. invoke learnability as a core motivation for chunking, being a cost-efficient learning strategy and limiting the cost of computation; a possible explanation for the format/size of phrase structures.

There are some directions in the literature, however, which make novel theoretical headway with respect to these core processes. Christiansen and Chater's (2016, 99–114) *chunk-and-pass* model of language processing effectively mirrors a prediction-binding system, albeit one which explains, for the authors, the origins of language-specific processing chunks. Interestingly, their *chunk-and-pass* model reinterprets some classical linguistic constraints as simple constraints on processing, a highly desirable and feasible approach. Instead of invoking some abstract grammatical rule, when considering the contrast in (2), we can explain this 'if we view the structure of language as emerging from countless individual processing episodes' (2016, 245); every word originates and develops in different grammatical structures, with these (irregular) origins later impacting the acceptability of constructions such as (2) ('*' = unacceptable):

(2)   a. Mary gave a book to the library.
        b. Mary gave the library a book.
        c. Mary donated a book to the library.
        d. *Mary donated the library a book.

Much of the learned linguistic structure discussed by syntacticians, semanticists and phonologists can likely be explained through the real-time demands of processing during language acquisition and use, as Christiansen and Chater (2016) argue – even if this leaves the origin and neural implementation of linguistic computations and representations at a distance (see also Ott 2017).

Some recent advances documented in Daffertshofer et al. (2018) can sharpen this picture even further. These researchers used MEG to investigate whether the scaling properties of the resting brain (signified by scale-free temporal correlations) differ between amplitude and phase fluctuations, which may reflect different aspects of cortical functioning. They discovered power law scaling for the collective amplitude and for phase synchronisation, both capturing whole-brain activity. They summarise that 'temporal changes of the amplitude comprise *slow, persistent memory processes*, whereas phase synchronisation exhibits less temporally structured and more complex correlations, indicating a *fast and flexible coding*' (emphasis added). This pattern accords with the oscillatory model of language defended in this chapter, and also supports previous findings about phase–amplitude coupling, with, for instance, the rapid, online processing of phrase structure identity being implemented by phase-coupled δ and θ rhythms, whereas gradual amplitude increases over the course of discourse interpretation (as in the case of documented β and γ increases during syntactically and semantically well-formed sentences) also seem to be well characterised in this manner.

Along with its putative role in syntactic prediction, we should also consider the evidence that β plays a crucial role in sensory prediction through being modulated by unpredicted pitch stimuli 200–300ms post-onset (Chang et al. 2016), and it is conceivable that a domain-general updating procedure is carried out by ensembles oscillating in this range, with both sensation and language requiring perceptual and structural property updates (see Palmer et al. 2016 for further evidence that β power reflects sensorimotor uncertainty estimates). Abel et al. (2016) detected robust and focal β increases at the left and right anterior temporal lobe during the retrieval of names for people and tools, and Chang et al.'s (2016) EEG experiment of unexpected pitch processing suggested that induced β power in auditory cortex is sensitive to unpredicted changes in pitch even when the pitch is presented at a predicted time. These studies seem to indicate that β is implicated in predicting both what and when sensory experiences will occur, and that it is also involved in the accurate selection and maintenance of lexical representations. Brennan and Pylkkänen (2017) provide additional evidence from MEG that the dynamics of the anterior temporal lobe play a role in semantic composition during sentence comprehension, and that this region implements an incremental 'left-corner' parsing strategy (through which constituents are postulated after the left-most member of a constituent has been encountered).

2.3.3   Empirical Consequences

This section will explore further applications and consequences of assuming an oscillatory basis for language. For instance, what can we say of the interplay between neuroimaging and oscillatory frameworks? Among many other forms of imaging and behavioural data, it seems clear from the earlier discussion that neuroimaging studies should be used as a guide for time-frequency analyses. The experimental implications of this are quite direct. With respect to linguistic computation, the left anterior temporal lobe has been implicated in basic conceptual combinatorics (concatenation) and phrasal construction (labelling) (Bemis & Pylkkänen 2013; Westerlund & Pylkkänen 2014; Clarke & Tyler 2015; Molinaro et al. 2015), while the posterior middle temporal gyrus seems to be involved in lexical access (lexicalisation) and ambiguity resolution (Turken & Dronkers 2011). Nevertheless, evidence from neuropsychological studies on patients with anterior temporal lobe degeneration, damage or resection reveals that while these patients have severe conceptual-semantic impairments, basic sentence comprehension and production remains intact (Wilson et al. 2014), suggesting only a possible partial role in combinatorial processing but not a necessary role in phrase structure generation. The left anterior temporal lobe plays a major role in the processing and combining of concepts, being implicated in the interpretation of lexicosemantic information (Binney et al. 2010) and in the interpretation of linguistic structures seemingly of all sizes, from phrases to well-formed meaningful sentences (Zhang & Pylkkänen 2015). Given the present oscillatory perspective, the much-discussed fronto-temporal language network would consequently be purely an *output* system of the above-mentioned operations, not a 'core syntax region', to quote Friederici (2012, 265). Friederici (2012) holds that distinct regions of the left inferior frontal gyrus are responsible for different types of syntax, arguing, for instance, that the dorsal stream is only implicated in embedded structures or structures deviating from normal ordering. Yet, as the above-mentioned model makes clear, the basic combinatorics are universal across syntactic structures, whether simple or complex.

Despite having noted the limitations of cartographic studies, an area of ongoing neurolinguistic research is the spatial scales of brain rhythms. Emerging technologies to experimentally test and refine the present oscillatory model include high-density electrode recordings and optogenetic tools (Chow et al. 2010). Bemis and Pylkkänen (2013) showed that between 200 and 300ms after the presentation of a word which can be combined with a previous item, the left anterior temporal lobe is activated, implicating this region in semantic composition. This would consequently be a good estimate of when oscillation studies might detect labelling effects to arise, given the role of labels in semantic composition (Hornstein & Pietroski 2009). At the most general level of lexical comprehension, M/EEG studies would also predictably find coherent oscillatory activation of large neuronal assemblies when processing words relative to processing pseudowords, as Pulvermüller et al. (1994) found.

A level of cortical entrainment would also be predicted for non-syllabic, phrasal and sentential structures during the auditory presentation of simple stimuli; structures which are not part of any speech stream but are rather internally constructed by the comprehender. Entrainment of auditory cortex to speech has recently been used to gauge how well the brain encodes the properties of speech. Such auditory entrainment has been linked to speech comprehension (Peelle & Davis 2012) and is more generally considered a central component of how the brain encodes, segments and parses speech features like prosody and syllables. On the psychoacoustic side, θ has been claimed to reflect syllabic structures due to the natural syllabic rate of speech closely matching the θ range (Giraud & Poeppel 2012; Ding & Simon 2014), while slower δ rhythms have been associated with processing supra-segmental prosodic features such as acoustic stress (Goswami & Leong 2013; Kayser et al. 2015).

Empirical predictions can also be generated for non-human oscillatory behaviour. As noted, the oscillatory phenomenon of entrainment is increasingly being used to enrich more traditional, cartographic models of the functional organisation of speech perception. This has typically been associated with the dorsolateral temporal lobes. In primates, these areas are implicated in both hierarchical and parallel processing (Rauschecker 1998). Primary auditory cortex (the 'core') is surrounded by belt and parabelt fields, and is organised into rostral and causal projections. These projections have been described as processing 'streams', much akin to the ventral and dorsal visual streams. Indeed, in non-human primates rostral auditory areas are sensitive to conspecific vocalisations (what has been termed the 'what' stream) while causal areas are sensitive to the spatial location of the sounds (the 'where' pathway) (Tian et al. 2001). Posterior-medial auditory areas respond to speech production even in the absence of sound (in the event of 'mouthing' sounds), and these areas have been associated with working memory processes for rehearsing speech and non-speech sounds (Hickok et al. 2003). Regions along the superior temporal sulcus in mammals appear to exhibit stronger representational bias for conspecific vocalisations in rhesus macaques (Tian et al. 2001), marmosets (Sadagopan et al. 2015) and humans (Fecteau et al. 2004), with the temporal pole also being implicated in this bias in marmosets, rhesus macaques, chimpanzees and humans (see Andics & Miklósi 2018 and references therein).

2.3.4   Feeble Currents

Kopell et al. (2014, 1319) stress that connectome–dynome linking hypotheses need to be supplemented with 'the biological details that relate this connectivity more directly to function'. In this section, I will attempt to briefly depart from analyses which remain at the levels of the dynome and cognome (e.g. Sporns 2013). Recent results indicate that the physiological processes underlying oscillations contribute to the gating of signal flows within and among regions (Cannon et al. 2014), and it is at this lower-level connectomic level that more robust linking hypotheses with the rest of the biological sciences (for instance, genetics) can begin to be established. As Mišić and Sporns (2016, 5) put it:

> An emerging theme in network neuroscience emphasizes representations and models that not only embody the topological organization of the brain, but also capture the complex multi-scale relationships that link brain topology to its origins in genetics and development, and to the rich cognitive-behavioral repertoire it supports.

Kopell et al. (2014, 1324) further note that 'an immersion in the physiology supporting temporal dynamics suggests mechanisms that would not be obvious if one were thinking abstractly about computation and rhythms', a statement which carries urgent lessons for theoretical linguistics and neuroimaging research.

This section will use the oscillome alongside neurochemistry as tools to construct a neurobiologically feasible cognome, pursuing the methodological naturalism often discussed by linguists and philosophers (Chomsky 2000, 2018a, 2018b; McGilvray 2013; Collins 2015b). As I hope to have shown, oscillatory studies of language have the potential to progress neurolinguistics beyond the situation described by Szathmáry in 1996: 'Linguistics is at the stage at which genetics found itself immediately after Mendel. There are rules (of sentence production), but we do not yet know what mechanisms neural networks are responsible for each rule' (1996, 764). So far, I have presented some suggestions for how to embed the cognome within the dynome (yielding the oscillome), but it is also vital to ground the dynome within the connectome and microlevel analyses, in turn addressing Szathmáry's concern.

It has been shown that neuronal populations can synchronously discharge due to an internal or external event, and additionally as a result of dynamic interactions between reciprocally coupled networks, which serve to 'tag the responses of neurones that need to be related to one another', as König (1994, 31) put it in his seminal assessment of oscillations. This synchronous activity further tends to be oscillatory in nature (Liu et al. 2010). Oscillations have also been linked to neurochemistry (Muthukumaraswamy et al. 2009). While oscillatory electrical activity in cell assemblies has been observed since the 1920s beginning with Berger's (1929) groundbreaking work, inspired by the Liverpool surgeon Richard Caton's (1875) studies of the 'feeble currents' generated by rabbit and monkey brains, its role in cognitive capacities has been intensively explored only since the turn of the century (Jensen et al. 2002; Ossandón et al. 2011), largely down to theoretical, technological and optogenetic advances. Updating Caton's imagery, McCormick et al. (2015, 133) summarise that brain rhythms are generated through 'the interaction of stereotyped patterns of connectivity together with intrinsic membrane and synaptic properties'.

At the most common level of investigation, time-locked frequency analysis can decompose an EEG signal and identify changes in oscillations. But the widespread use of non-invasive and high-temporal resolution MEG, and recent advances in its source localisation power (Wipf et al. 2010), have led to enhanced understanding of the spatiotemporal dynamics of oscillations and how they operate within neural networks. Recent work has begun to deliver an increasingly precise account of how, for instance, different classes of GABAergic interneurons in the hippocampus coordinate activity giving rise to network oscillations (Allen & Monyer 2015). $GABA_B$ receptors also perform time integration of cell assemblies (classically defined as a set of neurons exhibiting stronger within-group connectivity than with other connected neurons; Hebb 1949) from the subsecond to second scale (Deisz & Prince 1989), a vital function in computing conceptual and linguistic information representations.

More recently, Hardingham et al. (2018) review how differences in transcriptional responses to synaptic activity between humans and mice likely contributed to lineage-related cognitive capacities, and mapping how genes can be transcriptionally induced by synaptic activity will be a major challenge for this line of work:

The discovery of operational changes in activity-regulated transcription in evolution caused by lineage-related divergence in promoter architectures provides the mechanistic basis for a new conceptual framework that may help us to understand the evolution of cognitive abilities. According to this hypothesis, species-specific activity-regulated transcriptomes may both specify the construction of neuronal networks during development and determine their capacity for structural and functional plasticity in the adult.

Further advances can be made through mapping brain rhythms to the numerous interneuron classes, which are defined based on cell body location, expression of marker proteins, axonal arborisation and other properties (Klausberger et al. 2005; Somogyi & Klausberger 2005; Whittington & Traub 2003). Korotkova et al. (2010) attempted to reach such a goal by showing how the removal of NMDA receptors in parvalbumin-expressing (PV) interneurons reduced the power of θ oscillations in the CA1 hippocampal region, while also reducing the γ-power modulation by θ oscillations. PV interneurons and somatostatin-expressing (SOM) interneurons preferentially synapse, respectively, onto the cell bodies and proximal dendrites of pyramidal cells and the distal dendrites of pyramidal cells (Royer et al. 2012). The silencing of PV interneurons, but not SOM interneurons, altered the θ phase precession in the brains of mice running on a treadmill belt in the experiments conducted by Royer and colleagues, suggesting that PV interneurons are highly fit to control the firing phase of principal neurons during θ oscillations.

It should be noted, however, that PV and SOM expression is common to numerous hippocampal interneuron classes, and so further optogenetic work is needed in order to establish the role of individual interneuron classes in oscillation generation. Fruitful prospects can be found in recent advances in juxtacellular recordings, permitting the monitoring of a single interneuron in vivo. To take a relevant case, Lapray et al. (2012) discovered that PV basket cells – providing inhibition to the pyramidal cell body and proximal dendrite – fire preferentially at the descending θ phase (findings reproduced by Varga et al. 2012), while ivy cells – providing inhibitory currents onto pyramidal cell dendrites – fire preferentially during ascension and at the trough. These studies reveal that during a single θ cycle the inhibitory power onto distinct pyramidal cell sectors varies systematically (see also Brandon et al. 2014).

Results from modelling studies by Neymotin, Lee et al. (2011) and Neymotin, Lazarewicz et al. (2011) suggested that a computational model including pyramidal cells, fast-spiking basket cells and oriens-lacunosum moleculare interneurons can reproduce θ-γ modulation. Nevertheless, the neurophysiological basis of oscillatory interactions remains under investigation.

Viewing cell assemblies as the fundamental unit of computation rather than single neurons can arguably be justified in that assemblies can tolerate noise by not being redirected in their trajectory, unlike single or small clusters of neurons (which would also be impacted by spike transmission failures), intensifying the justification for placing such assemblies at the centre of the oscillome. Given the information chunking and feature merging roles attributed to γ cycles, Buzsáki suggests metaphorically that episodes of γ oscillations, which contain strings of cell assemblies, 'may be regarded as a neural word' (2010, 365), that is, a discrete unit of information. If induced γ is also responsible for constructing coherent conceptual objects by synchronising neural discharges binding together distant brain regions, as proposed by Tallon-Baudry and Bertrand (1999), then oscillations may also be responsible for certain forms of polysemy demanding the simultaneous association of multiple representations.

A slightly tangential topic, but one which is still vital for any neurobiological theory of cognition, concerns the precise computational properties of cell assemblies implicated in neural oscillations. Xie et al. (2016) discuss an elegant, simple mathematical rule of organising cell assembly architectures into specific-to-general primitives of the kind easily exploitable by the brain. The 'Theory of Connectivity' they outline postulates that within individual computational blocks ('functional connectivity motifs', FCMs) the maximum number of principal projection-cell cliques with distinct inputs follows a power-of-two-based permutation logic of $N = 2^i\text{-}1$, where N denotes the number of distinct neural cliques that can cover all possible permutations and combinations of specific-to-general input patterns, with i denoting the number of distinct information inputs. As a result, 'each FCM consists of principal projection neuron cliques receiving specific inputs, as well as other principal projection neuron cliques receiving progressively more convergent inputs that systematically cover every possible pattern using the power-of-two-based permutation logic' (2016, 2). Generalised neural cliques can discover patterns relating to semantic and categorical knowledge, and so this neural logic should be detectable across cortical and subcortical circuits and should also be developmentally preconfigured – concrete predictions confirmed by Xie et al.'s experimental work.

What should be of particular interest for linguists is how the Theory of Connectivity can explain the emergence of generalised concepts like *meal* through the combinatorial logic provided by the $N = 2^i\text{-}1$ equation which merges individual experiences and memories like *blueberry, pancake* and *milk*. The specific-to-general cell assembly architecture provided by this logic permits pattern-extraction, pattern-discrimination and pattern-categorisation. Under Xie et al.'s model, when a group of similar neurons form a clique to interpret basic computations like recognising food and friends, groups of such cliques cluster into FCMs which permits them to deal flexibly with each putatively basic representational unit. An exception to this general logical rule was found by Xie et al. in the dopamine neurons of reward circuits, which seem to be structured along a more basic logic and did not use the specific-to-general coding logic – possibly explaining why these cells typically contribute to binary judgements like 'good' versus 'bad'.

It seems, then, that the brain does not simply employ a basic one-to-one direct mapping solution to information processing, where information (i) is mapped to coding units (n) such that $i = n$. Nor does it seem as if information is stored in a totally random wiring fashion. Rather, it appears that a substantial portion of the brain's information processing power is implemented via a highly conserved principle of logic. Interestingly, the principal projection neuron cliques which constitute FCMs are ultimately combined to form larger categorical structures which permit abstraction over a set of basic representations, forming *meal* from a cluster of cells representing *blueberries*, *pancakes* and *milk*.

As this section has shown, our understanding of the neurobiological basis of oscillations is fairly limited (hence the lack of attention I have paid to it). Nevertheless, is there any indication that certain computational properties of language can be implemented at the cellular level? To my knowledge, there is little published work in this domain; indeed, the arguments in this book rest on the assumption that oscillations should be centred in models of linguistic computation. Papadimitriou and Vempala (2019) provide novel proposals in this direction, however. The specific details of their work go beyond the scope of this book, but it is worth briefly noting their line of reasoning: These authors note that neuronal assemblies are formed when clusters of cells project (from one layer to another, for instance), and this process creates a new assembly. They then propose that when two distinct assemblies project and 'meet' at the projection site, this might form the basis of Merge for natural language, since two (neuronal) objects have made some form of contact. This is a potentially interesting idea, but it is also difficult to imagine how theoretical advances could be made with a model that assumes such a simple, generic operation as assembly projection to derive a very domain-specific process. In addition, it assumes that merged elements must be stored within projection distance, and therefore the brain cannot merge representations from distant cortical sites.

2.3.5   Cross-Frequency Coupling

As mentioned, CFC is a core oscillatory component of brain function, and likely linguistic computation, as suggested in the model presented earlier in this chapter and recent empirical work. It has been suggested that this generic operation coordinates spatiotemporal neural dynamics (Canolty & Knight 2010; Lisman & Jensen 2013), resolving a long-standing problem over how neural activity is synchronised. With larger neuronal populations oscillating at lower frequencies and smaller populations doing so at higher frequencies, CFC would enable their synchronisation. Phase–amplitude coupling thus estimates the statistical dependence between the phase and an amplitude of local field potentials. In particular, it has been shown that via phase–amplitude CFC the phase of the lower frequency modulates the amplitude of the higher-frequency component, a process claimed to be involved in information transfer for faculties such as memory (Tort et al. 2009; Malekmohammadi et al. 2015; though see Aru et al. 2015 for current limitations of phase–amplitude modelling). Bergmann and Born (2017) review very compelling evidence that phase–amplitude coupling constitutes a general mechanism for memory processing/consolidation and synaptic plasticity. In short, with phase–amplitude CFC the phase of the slower rhythm modulates the computations implemented at the speed of the faster rhythm. Phase–amplitude coupling has been experimentally detected in at least ten combinations of bands in humans and non-humans: δ-θ, δ-α, δ-β, δ-γ, θ-α, θ-β, θ-γ, α-β, α-γ and β-γ.

Jensen et al. (2016) also present examples of genuine CFC, in contrast to more spurious cases involving non-sinusoidal or non-zero-mean waveforms. Although, as Cole and Voytek (2017) note, non-sinusoidal waves may have computational properties distinct from sinusoidal waves, and may therefore be relevant to cognition. Eliav et al. (2018) review how even though bat hippocampal neurons do not exhibit rodent-like θ oscillations, and instead exhibit arrhythmic synchronisation and phase precession in their place cells, they found non-oscillatory phase coding (conserved across bats and rodents) which seemingly encode the animal's spatial position. This emphasises the importance of focusing on specific forms of phase coding, as opposed to assuming a priori that cognitive computations are executed rhythmically.

Refining our understanding of this contentious issue, Siebenhühner et al. (2020) used a unique dataset of stereo-EEG (SEEG) and source-reconstructed MEG to chart resting-state CFC networks in humans. A novel graph-theoretic model was used to distinguish inter-areal coupling from potentially false positive coupling, and they found that the human resting state exhibits genuine phase–amplitude coupling and $n{:}m$-cross-frequency phase synchrony (a form of phase synchronisation characterised by a stable phase-difference between oscillations having an integer $n{:}m$ frequency ratio). They also found that coupling was stronger in superficial cortical layers relative to deep layers, and that resting-state phase-amplitude coupling for α-β and α-γ coordinated areas along the anterior-posterior brain systems.

{θ-β(γ)} CFC increases significantly during linguistic tasks such as active/passive listening to phonemes and words, word production and visual reading (Canolty et al. 2006). While the lower-level mechanisms responsible for {θ-β(γ)} CFC remain unknown, sensible and realistic suggestions have nevertheless been made. For example, since the phase of θ rhythms matches the time course of membrane potential fluctuations, and since the power of β and γ rhythms reflects local neural excitability, it may well be that {θ-β(γ)} CFC represents the regulation of neural excitability at time points modulated by the θ phase (Schroeder & Lakatos 2008). This suggests that tracking changes in oscillatory dynamics can serve as a proxy for lower-level connectivity changes. CFC consequently appears to be intrinsically linked to synaptic potentiation of the kind implicated in higher cognitive functions. It seems, then, that studies of oscillatory dynamics can complement and enhance existing functional neuroimaging work, with growing evidence suggesting that distinct neural processes yield spectrally isolated β and γ rhythms and spectrally broader θ (along with α and δ) rhythms.

In brief, while much is known about the biophysical substrates of individual frequency components, the cellular mechanisms behind frequency *interactions* like CFC remains opaque. Slower oscillations (θ through to β) appear ubiquitous in infragranular layers of the neocortex (5 and 6), whereas faster γ rhythms have been detected in granular layer 4 and supragranular layers 2/3 and 1 (Ninomiya et al. 2015). Using laminar electrodes to measure activity in monkey primate visual cortex, Spaak, Bonnefond et al. (2012) found that α phase in infragranular layers modulates γ amplitude in supergranular layers (see also Friston 2008); similar to how thalamic nuclei oscillating at the α band synchronise distant cortical regions oscillating at higher frequencies. As Aru et al. (2015) note, the most elegant theory to account for these findings is that periodic membrane potential fluctuations generate low-frequency oscillations which subsequently gate the incidence of higher-frequency activity in a phase-specific fashion. From a functional perspective, the nested γ cycles invoked in the present oscillatory model could act as multiplexing mechanisms (Buzsáki 2006, 356) for sustaining working memory representations by sending multiple representations as a single complex message to be recovered and 'unpacked' downstream, such that information encoded by the faster rhythm would be integrated over the time scales of the slower rhythm, precisely as is seen in syntactic labelling and cyclicity (see also Hyafil et al. 2015 for empirical support that $\{\theta(\gamma)\}$ coupling is involved in speech de-multiplexing, and Baddeley et al. 2014 for a review of working memory mechanisms).

2.3.6   Free Energy and the Hidden States of the World

A more fundamental consequence of assuming an oscillatory perspective of language is that linguistic computation must operate within certain fundamental constraints on neural dynamics, such as the free-energy principle (following seminal insights from Friston 2010) through which the homeostatic brain minimises the dispersion (entropy) of interoceptive and exteroceptive states. If entropy is the average of 'surprise' over time, then the brain will choose appropriate sensations to minimise surprise, and in so doing 'the brain is implicitly maximizing the evidence for its own existence' (Bastos et al. 2012,

702), a notion not too far removed from Vaas's assessment that the brain is 'a self-referential, closed system, a functional reality emulator that constructs the world, rather than reconstruct it' (Vaas 2001, 88). This form of 'predictive coding' conforms to the free-energy principle and the image of the brain as a *constructive organ*, assembling and inferring linguistic representations. Studies of chaotic itinerancy (Tsuda 2013, 2015), many-body physics and thermodynamics (Vitiello 2015) may also prove indispensable in describing the high-dimensional state space of cortical activity implicated in computation (see the essays collected in Ohira & Uzawa 2015 for discussion). Yet as Kirmayer (2017) notes, principles such as free energy may provide great generality, and '[f]ree energy minimization may be a necessary condition for life, but it is not sufficient to characterize its goals, which vary widely and, at least at the level of individual organisms or populations, clearly can run counter to this principle for long stretches of time'. Be that as it may, many biological and cognitive principles of efficiency may well be special cases of a variational principle of free energy. As Friston has argued, this should allow researchers from distinct disciplines to re-evaluate their hypotheses and empirical evidence in terms of lower-level free energy. This will result in a number of alternative and competing process/implementation theories for linguistic computation in the brain which can all adhere to free energy but can also be compared against emerging empirical evidence from, for instance, systems neuroscience and neurolinguistic experimentation.

Although most research concerning free energy has focused largely on sensory perception, in a recent expansion of the active inference model Friston et al. (2017) apply it to the reading of a narrative, tentatively aligning their concerns with those of neurolinguists in ways which seem quite promising and illuminating. Considering hierarchical models with deep temporal structure, active inference is applied to state transitions, or sequences over time, permitting the authors to apply free energy to *sequential scene construction* of the kind found in reading a narrative. The core idea is that 'equipping an agent or simulated subject with deep temporal models allows them to accumulate evidence over different temporal scales to find the best explanation for their sensations' (Friston et al. 2017, 388). The authors associate perisaccadic updating with neurobiological activity such as delay period activity and perisaccadic local field potentials, accounting for how epistemically rich information is judiciously sampled by the eyes. In brief, their generative model (not to be confused with generative grammar; Friston et al. employ 'generative' to mean a probabilistic mapping from causes to an observed consequence) proposes that sequences of hierarchically nested *hidden states* (e.g. the location and category of an object, or some other unknown variable) are generated by the brain using probability transitions specified by a particular *policy* (action or plan), such that hidden states can influence expected free energy and thus influence policies determining transitions among subordinate states. As with phrase structure generation, which uses multiple memory buffers to maintain phrasal identities while also constructing new ones (to be embedded), a given hidden state entails a sequence of embedded hidden states, similar to how a TP entails a VP, and a VP an NP. Friston et al.'s model generates outcomes over nested timescales, as when phrases, words and syllables are parsed simultaneously via oscillatory entrainment to distinct frequencies. More generally, within this context active inference denotes the optimisation of expectations regarding hidden states and policies with respect to variational free energy. This yields a 'deep dynamic narrative' to the trajectories of hidden states (Friston et al. 2017, 390; see their fig. 5). In short, under this model agents infer the hidden states under each policy that they entertain before evaluating the evidence for each policy based on observed outcomes and beliefs. Posterior beliefs about policies are used to inform a Bayesian model average of the next outcome, realised via action.

Assimilating this model with the hierarchical anatomy of cortico-basal ganglia-thalamic loops described in Jahanshahi et al. (2015), Friston et al. (2017, 392) claim that passing messages of belief propagation (concerning the nature of hidden states) results in a situation in which 'competing low level (motor executive) policies are evaluated in the putamen; intermediate (associative) policies in the caudate and high level (limbic) policies in the ventral striatum. These representations then send (inhibitory or GABAergic) projections to the globus pallidus interna (GPi) that encodes the expected (selected) policy.' These expectations are subsequently communicated to superficial cortical layers via thalamotorical projections, most probably matrix thalamocortical circuits that 'appear to be specialized for robust transmission over relatively extended periods, consistent with the sort of persistent activation observed during working memory and potentially applicable to state-dependent regulation of excitability' (Cruikshank et al. 2012, 17813). It was discussed earlier how the labelling mechanism employs cortico-basal ganlia-thalamic loops via particular oscillations, and it is likely that Friston et al.'s (2017) detailed model of belief propagation is recruited by the language system to generate policies concerning the identity of current syntactic structures.

Sequential scene construction accounts for the semantic processing and prediction involved in sentence comprehension (we have already seen that the language network seems to carry out predictive processing, supporting the idea that prediction is a 'canonical computation' implemented in domain-specific circuits; Keller & Mrsic-Flogel 2018) – but the wilful generation of recursive hierarchies resulting from labelling (e.g. in sentence production) are kept at a distance. This is hardly a limitation of Friston et al.'s model as it stands (indeed, the authors make it clear that 'we are not concerned with computational linguistics *per se* but the more general problem of *epistemic foraging*', examining 'how subjects use accumulated beliefs about the hidden states of the world to prescribe active sampling of new information to resolve their uncertainty quickly and efficiently'; Friston et al. 2017, 388), but it does point proponents of free-energy in new directions. In particular, applying the related concept of Markov blankets to phrase structure (which, like all phenomena Markov blankets are applied to, exhibits *boundaries* between what counts as a certain phrase and what counts as lying outside its domain) may prove most fruitful. Friston et al. (2017, 399) conclude by plausibly speculating that in order to capture 'the dynamic character of language comprehension and production' (including compositional recursive rules) neurobiologists should attempt to develop 'deeper generative models that may entail some structure learning'.

More related to our concerns, I suggest that the existence of syntactic structures in natural language constitutes a unique form of epistemic foraging, minimising surprise and variational free energy. Epistemic foraging aims to reduce uncertainty about the environment, and this is precisely what lexical categories and syntactic phrases do. A reduction does not, of course, result in an elimination of uncertainty, and so natural language can still exhibit ambiguities, both syntactic and lexical. Discussing rodent models, Corcoran et al. (2018b) summarise that, via the active inference framework, '[o]nce ambiguity or uncertainty has been sufficiently resolved, the rodent may then switch to policies that exploit the resources availed by the environment' – a process familiar to the exploitation of syntactic phrasal identities in natural language (for interpretation and subsequent action).

2.3.7   Communication-through-Coherence

An emerging consensus regarding the validity of the communication-through-coherence (CTC) hypothesis lends further impetus to the claim that oscillations bring about linguistic computation (Bastos et al. 2015). CTC claims that rhythmic synchronisation, especially in the β and γ bands, modulates the efficacy of anatomical connections, and that oscillations are necessary for long-distance assembly formation (König et al. 1995; Fries et al. 2008). CTC can be complemented with recent developments in the understanding of the functional role brain rhythms play, with assembly formation being the core operation at the connectome level required to establish the kinds of cross-modular representational structures seen in natural language (Lopes-dos-Santos et al. 2011). γ band activity, for instance, has been associated with numerous cognitive functions such as memory and selective attention. With γ bands arising from an interplay of inhibition (produced by GABAergic neurons) and excitation (produced by glutamergic neurons) mediated by NMDA and AMPA receptors, Bosman et al. (2014) propose that these bands have their origin in basic functional motifs conferring an advantage for low-level system processing and multiple cognitive functions (see also Bartos et al. 2007; Buzsáki & Wang 2012). While slow rhythms are typically needed for long-distance oscillatory synchronisation across the brain, γ rhythms have also been found to synchronise between distant cortical regions of the same hemisphere during attention (Gregoriou et al. 2009).

The broad functionality of γ makes it an ideal candidate, along with the thalamus (discussed later), for being the conductor of language's cross-modularity. The role of γ synchronisation in visual feature integration (Bosman et al. 2009), for instance, makes it a prime candidate to be the mechanism carrying out the forms of conceptual assimilation seen in natural language semantics. If linguistic computations are in fact responsible for this cross-modularity, then language can perhaps be more closely aligned to dominant descriptions of consciousness and working memory (Dehaene et al. 2014), even if we are forced to remain 'virtually mute' (Chomsky 1998, 440) about the nature of experiential content (Strawson 2008, 2010). Indeed, Crick and Koch (1995) already noted the likelihood of cortical oscillations having a prominent role in conscious experience. Likewise, volition is also an inherently network-level phenomenon, and so oscillations are a prime candidate for its implementation (as opposed to single-cell models) – with creative language production famously being the classical example of volitional control.

In addition, γ synchronisation has been shown to support certain low-level functions in the hippocampus which may be vital to particular cognitive functions attributed to this region, such as memory encoding and retrieval (Bosman et al. 2014). As mentioned, the hippocampus is the site of $\{\theta(\gamma)\}$ coupling in that multiple γ waves are typically embedded within a single θ cycle (Bragin et al. 1995). The hippocampus seems particularly suited to facilitate these cross-modular interactions, since it has been argued to play a role in integrating 'what' and 'where' information in the perirhinal cortex through the lateral entorhinal cortex and the postrhinal cortex through the medial entorhinal cortex (Fernández-Ruiz & Oliva 2016; see also O'Neill et al. 2017 for the role of the entorhinal cortex in spatial and episodic memory, which seems to be able to act independently of the hippocampus). Along with the standard phase-locking operation through which higher waves occur at stable phases in cycles of lower waves (Lachaux et al. 1999; Belluscio et al. 2012), this allows spike coordination and may consequently be partly responsible for low-level oscilla-tory operations like phase coding.

As Lisman and Jensen (2013) review, dual γ and θ oscillations form a code for representing multiple items in an ordered way (see also Lisman & Buzsáki 2008). Since each θ cycle contains four to eight nested γ cycles, different forms of spatial information (such as a series of events from short-term memory, constituting an 'episode') can be represented and sequentially coordinated within a given cycle, with discrete items being encoded and replayed at certain phase angles. The neuronal subsets that constitute the assemblies activated by each γ cycle also form circuits that tend to coactivate. As such, memory items are thought to be expressed by a transient, rapid γ wave. This seems to fit the recent revision of working memory from the classic five to nine items to four items (Cowan 2001), and also recent revisions to visual working memory capacity as being fixed at three to four items (Jost et al. 2011). There is increasing evidence that this θ-γ memory model is applicable to the human brain (Sauseng et al. 2019), as when Axmacher et al. (2010) discovered that an increase in the number of visual items (faces) to be retained by subjects resulted in a slowing down of the θ waves that there coupled with nested γ, suggesting that more memory items require a larger θ wave to be nested in.

I have claimed elsewhere – and will maintain here – that this process may constrain the number of lexical features able to be transferred in a given derivational cycle, and may constitute a mechanism for combining linguistic features. It is likely that brains capable of rapidly adapting (and slowing down) the phases of slow rhythms (e.g. θ, but also δ, as already discussed) will become more competent language users, being able to fine-tune the representational binding and maintenance necessary for language comprehension.

Other work suggests that CFC between frontal θ and posterior γ is enhanced during visual stimuli encoding (Friese et al. 2013). Through the coding scheme discussed by Lisman and Jensen, the cell assembly that fires during a given γ cycle forms a topographic pattern representing a particular item from memory. Interaction between rhythms supports neural communication and plasticity, ensemble formation, and the formation of long-term memories (Buzsáki & Draguhn 2004). Phase-coupling preferences also correlate with behaviour and neural function, remaining stable over numerous days, suggesting that oscillations aid in the selective control of distant functional cell assemblies (Canolty et al. 2010). Along with the development of a neural code for linguistic computation, investigations of memory decay will also likely be crucial to understanding the limitations of syntactic phrase structure building, with the factors influencing information maintenance placing direct constraints on any algorithm used to construct phrases. In the most recent research in this tradition, Pinotsis et al. (2018) modulated the number of items a group of monkeys had to hold in memory (one to three objects in the same visual hemifield), and these modulations changed the connectivity in the prefrontal cortex-frontal eye fields-lateral intraparietal area network. Feedback (top-down) coupling broke down when the number of objects exceeded cognitive capacity.

The number of γ cycles able to be embedded within a θ cycle may be a major constraint, then, of working memory limits (Kamiński et al. 2011). Other research compatible with this hypothesis includes the finding that increases in memory load result in decreases in the power of the slower rhythm during phase–amplitude coupling (Axmacher et al. 2010). Roux and Uhlhaas (2014) make the related claim that oscillatory activity ensures the maintenance of working memory information. This explanation exhibits the kind of granularity linguists should seek to capture syntactic operations like labelling, which involves storing conceptual roots in memory.

In brief, and returning to issues outlined earlier, if intrinsic coupling across cortical oscillations is responsible for the hierarchical combination of computations at the syllabic and phonemic levels, 'restoring the natural arrangement of phonemes within syllables' (Hyafil et al. 2015), then this leads to the possibility that hierarchical syntactic computations result from similar mechanisms.

These operations are all conserved from early in mammalian evolution, with the above-mentioned interplay between excitation and inhibition being found in crustaceans (Nusbaum & Beenhakker 2002) and major phyla dating back 350 million years (Katz & Harris-Warrick 1999). Bosman et al. (2014) draw on such considerations in claiming that the evolutionary acquisition of this excitation–inhibition interplay led to the selection of these γ waves as a principal element of computation. If the γ synchronisation mechanism was a 'direct, inevitable consequence of early circuitry organization' (Bosman et al. 2014, 1994), then it may be that it is an exaptation (being co-opted, as when gills are transformed into jawbones or ear ossicles) in that it was later afforded a functional role in systems of memory and learning (for seminal proposals concerning exaptation, see Gould & Vrba 1982). Further, top-down neocortical processes implicated in particular higher cognitive faculties like working memory (Buschman & Miller 2007) and free-choice reach (Pesaran et al. 2008) also appear to be carried out by interareal synchrony in the β rhythm (Bressler & Richter 2015), increasing the electrophysiological validity of the functional roles attributed to this wave above.

Summarising briefly, it appears that the developed interneurons and dendritic spinal strength proposed by Geschwind and Rakic (2013) fortified long-distance assembly connections and, in turn, the mechanisms of CFC and other neuronal processes necessary for the rhythmic interactions claimed earlier to be the source of computations like labelling and cyclic transfer. The targeting of the perisomatic region of pyramidal neurons by inhibitory interneurons in particular leads to the formation of γ rhythms and their concomitant properties of conceptual combination.

*2.3.8   Operations and their Constraints: Merge, Anti-identity, and * {t,t}*

There is one final topic relating directly to the applications and consequences of assuming an oscillatory model of language: how to model the *constraints* on language.

In the same way that γ oscillations 'arise simultaneously and inevitably with inhibitory-excitatory interplay, and are neither an epiphenomenon nor a separate cause of the functionality beyond the underlying circuits' (Bosman et al. 2014, 1995), this book has so far suggested that linguistic computations are to be seen as identical to the operations of the oscillome. While I hope to have shown that distinct oscillatory phases segregate discrete units of information (visual, olfactory, semantic, etc.), there remains the possibility that they also serve computations spanning multiple oscillatory cycles. Oscillatory phases may be the means through which different lexical features (e.g. φ-features, Tense) are processed or time-locked with other features, leading to agreement relations, the resolution of filler-gap dependencies, feature inheritance and other familiar syntactic operations.

What about the process of 'feature valuation', through which certain features on lexical items are retrieved from the lexicon unvalued and undergo valuation via the presence of the same (valued) feature on a different lexical item? Consider one possibility: Cell assemblies implicated via cycle skipping in the features of two merged elements may undergo phase-locking, leading to oscillatory synchronisation of two discrete units of information. When this occurs, feature valuation takes place and the derivation can converge. If this process is barred in virtue of rhythmic coupling restrictions and the limits of assembly synchronisation, then feature valuation, and hence concatenation, does not take place. If the distribution of unvalued features, $[uF]$, also contributes to the demarcation of phases (Narita 2014a), then the dynamics of feature valuation would likely align closely with the account of cyclicity given earlier, since valuation, Agree and other copy-forming operations such as Internal Merge apply as a fundamental part of Transfer. Notice that this model at once implies specific neurobiological limitations, in that the hypothetical coupling responsible for feature valuation should occur after the cross-cortical $\{\alpha(\gamma)\}$ embedding proposed to be the substrate of set-formation.

As a secondary concern, I will assume, as is commonly done, that feature valuation (along with feature inheritance and Agree) are both cases of a more generalised Search operation, which forms relations between identical feature complexes (Kato et al. 2014; Ohta et al. 2013). Kato et al. (2014) even go as far as claiming that Search is in turn just an instance of Merge, and that the human language faculty may reduce to pure Merge (implemented via minimal search). The ideas sketched earlier and Kato et al. consequently yield different predictions about oscillatory behaviour.

Moving to constraints, Richards' (2010) Distinctness Condition, prohibiting the presence of multiple lexical units of the same label within a single phase complement, may be the consequence of how many distinct rhythms it is possible to couple in specific actions. These *XX-like structures (e.g. structures containing multiple phase-internal nouns such as '*John Mary ate apples') may be ungrammatical because of the oscillatory patterns local language regions can sustain (Boeckx 2013). This forms the core of a more general observation in the linguistics literature; that elements of the same type are typically not syntactically adjacent (with the obvious exception of listed adjectives, which are adjacent in terms of linear order but are part of the same syntactic constituent) but separated by tokens of distinct types. The Obligatory Contour Principle (Odden 1986), Double Determiner Filter (*[D1...D2] where no lexical head intervenes between D1 and D2; Davis 2010, 23), Similarity Avoidance (Frisch et al. 2004) and other related principles share this overlapping feature. Indeed, constraints on identity are found not just in natural language, but artificial language too (Nevins 2010), and van Riemsdijk (2008, 242) goes so far as to argue that 'Identity Avoidance is a general principle of biological organization'. For instance, Lefebvre et al. (2012) document that protocadherins underlie dentritic self-avoidance and self-/non-self discrimination, allowing neurons to take up distinct molecular identities. The swathe of putatively syntactic constraints noted here may form the backdrop of what Narita (2014a, 26) identifies as a core aspect of minimal computation, the 'Minimal Workspace' through which the construction and transferring of syntactic structures takes place. To put it more concretely, syntax-external systems (interfaces) may only be able to sustain a single rhythm (or rhythm cluster) from the γ and β bands due to the small size of localised regions, and would hence be incapable of interpreting multiple category-identical elements in a single cycle. The phase/non-phase rhythm of syntactic computation would thus arise from the limits of oscillatory sustainability, and the connection between syntactic phases and oscillatory phases becomes more than purely orthographic: $[C [T \nu[V D/n [N]]]]$ emerges from $[\beta [\gamma \beta[\gamma \beta [\gamma]]]]$ given the labelling role attributed to β earlier, which in turn explains *XX violations.

In recent work, Leivada (2017) goes considerably beyond these initial observations and proposes a comprehensive account of *XX violations. She traces the origins and manifestations of 'identity avoidance' in language and cognition and argues that the forms these take support the existence of a general processing principle, termed *Novel Information Bias*:

Novel Information Bias
Subjects avoid tokenizing multiple, adjacent occurrences of the same type, because of a general bias in the cognitive system to provide more attentional resources to novel information, enhancing perception and production processes accordingly.

Hence, 'in situations where no new information is supposed to be conveyed, Identity Avoidance can be flouted to a greater degree'. Leivada (2017) notes that *XX is not a hard constraint but rather a flexible bias, pointing to a number of cases flouting *XX in both spoken and signed languages. Leivada therefore correctly notes that the background assumptions in Murphy (2015b) seem 'too

2.4. Globularity and Cortico-centrism

strong' given the existence of grammatically licit counter-examples to *XX (see Leivada 2017 for examples). Leivada's proposed processing principle captures how the brain decodes types and tokens and explains why adjacent occurrences of syntactically or phonologically identical tokens is highly restricted. Leivada claims that the aforementioned supposedly linguistic constraints on identity avoidance stem from 'a general, cognitive bias that filters out multiple tokens of the same type when these occur in adjacent positions' (Leivada 2017), shifting the explanation from a derivational crash to a more general cognitive bias.

Along with permitting a broader level of descriptive adequacy across multiple cognitive domains (with identity avoidance also occurring in visual perception; Buffat et al. 2013), this route leads to certain questions about the evolutionary origins of the *Novel Information Bias* and its implementation in other primates. A clear example of humans avoiding repetitions in a non-linguistic domain include the 'apparent motion' illusion, through which identical stimuli flashed in different locations are typically seen as a single stimulus (Vetter et al. 2013). This plainly involves no linguistic procedures, indicating that this pre-existing cognitive bias constrained what form the language faculty ultimately evolved into. But what of the implications for the present oscillatory model? One might simply reframe the above-mentioned oscillatory constraints as module-general, while acknowledging that such constraints may be more widespread across the brain.

One final constraint is worth mentioning. Narita's (2014b) *$\{t,t\}$ constraint, which prohibits the transfer of syntactic objects whose two members are both traces/copies of movement, strikes me as amenable to a similar, if not identical, explanation to the one given earlier for the Distinctness Condition. Objects of the $\{t,t,\}$ kind cannot be labelled, as in (3), and are hence illicit (Moro 2006, 15). These structures involve two elements being moved from the same embedded location:

(3)   *[which picture of the wall]$_i$ do you think that [the cause of the riot]$_j$ was $\{t_i,$ $t_j\}$?

One of the consequences of this approach is that language needs to be reconceptualised as not just a system of thought, planning and interpretation, but also a system of oscillatory information synchronisation. The computational constraints briefly outlined here can direct enquiry into empirically testing neurolinguistic models of oscillatory behaviour.

2.4   Globularity and Cortico-centrism

A general theme I have been developing so far in this chapter is that linguists should pay more direct attention to intrinsic properties of the brain (in particular, its oscillatory properties) as a means of building their computational models of language, rather than purely imposing these models on the data acquired from available experimental techniques. In this section, I will continue to develop this theme by focusing on brain shape and brain networks.

Recent developments in systems neuroscience have identified large-scale distributed brain networks, typically explored through fMRI and MEG (Brookes et al. 2012). Data from fMRI suggests that the implication of a functionally specific set of neurons in any given computation is assisted by a backdrop of large-scale neural assembly intercommunication. These networks are composed of subnetworks with correlating and anti-correlating patterns, leading to a situation in which a single large-scale network may operate through overlapping but distinct neural subnetworks.

While human brains are considerably larger than those of non-human primates and a strong correlation exists between cranial size and cognitive capacities (Benson-Amram et al. 2015), brain size alone cannot account for language evolution, and not even cortical size seems to be responsible (Miller et al. 2019 found that the human neocortex is not exceptionally large relative to other structures); rather, brain shape and organisation may be responsible. The wider cortical minicolumns seen in cytoarchitechtonic subparts of Broca's and Wernicke's regions in humans (Schenker et al. 2008), along with the greater number of arcuate fasciculus projections connecting both regions with association cortex in the middle and inferior temporal cortex, suggests that the memory buffer/stack available to humans during representation construction and maintenance is greater than in other primates.

Genomic investigations of the language faculty are also increasingly focusing their attention on the brain. Consider briefly the genes *RUNX2*, the *DLX* suite and the *BMP* family, involved in skull and brain development (Perdomo-Sabotal et al. 2014). In a series of ongoing research (Benítez-Burraco & Boeckx 2015; Murphy & Benítez-Burraco 2016, 2018), it has been hypothesised that a modification in this gene network gave rise to a more 'globular' head shape (relative to Neanderthals/Denisovans; Bruner 2004; Gunz et al. 2012; Theofanopoulou 2015) – approaching a level of sphericity unseen in our closest ancestors – and the consequent rewiring of cortical and subcortical structures, permitting the construction of the forms of cross-modular representations well established in psychological, philosophical and semantic theories of concepts (Spelke 2010; Pietroski 2018). Globularity may also have contributed, as some have suggested, to an increase in wiring efficiency across the brain (Chklovskii et al. 2002; Murphy 2017b, 2018a, 2018b). Globularity is mainly related to the volume of the frontal cortex, differing from the enlarged occipital bun of Neanderthals, although parietal reorganisation in humans also contributed to this general reshape. It is of great interest to biolinguistics that functional links of this kind are beginning to be drawn between genes and their cellular consequences for the human cognitive phenotype. This task becomes even clearer when we recognise the clear limits of other hypotheses about the origins of human-specific cranial features. For instance, Cornélio et al. (2016) review archaeological data and a range of experimental work and suggest that there is no evidence (contrary to much popular speculation) that human brain expansion was caused by fire control and cooking.

An evaluation of these observations can also be made alongside a consideration of what Piattelli-Palmarini and Uriagereka (2008) see as the optimising role language has in building syntactic and phonological structures, which proceeds via minimal search and related principles of computational efficiency (Larson 2015). This minimalist perspective leads to a separation of optimality from language's proposed 'function' of mapping structures to the interfaces, since similar optimising principles are found elsewhere in the natural world, leading Piattelli-Palmarini and Uriagereka (2008, 209) to 'suspect that the process behind the abstract form follow[s] from physico-chemical invariants'. But lacking a theory of brain dynamics, the authors are unable to ground these general proposals within any neurobiological framework. We can here suggest that the microcellular level and the oscillome, operating within some general physical laws of neural organisation such as free energy, can provide a potential substrate of such 'physico-chemical invariants'. The only human-unique aspect of the model pursued here, then, is the *context* in which the conserved and universal rhythms discussed earlier perform their operations of coupling and decoupling, namely a globular brain case, which would have led to a decrease in 'spatial inequalities' (Salami et al. 2003) between cortical and subcortical regions which prohibit long-distance coupling. This would imply that the numerous centuries-long approaches to human-uniqueness, ranging from philosophy to medicine, have approached the matter from the wrong perspective. Instead of asking what it is about humans which allows us to form complex systems of symbolic interpretation, we should instead ask what it is about other animals which *prohibits* them from doing so (with Salami et al.'s 'spatial inequalities' being a major factor).

Globularity may also have led to the expansion of the neocortex and the pulvinar, spurred on by the reduction of the large Neanderthal visual system (Pearce et al. 2013). As Benítez-Burraco and Boeckx (2015) point out, cross-modular concepts likely employ thalamic nuclei such as the pulvinar and the medio-dorsal nucleus, not least because of the thalamus's role in modulating fronto-parietal activity, regulating cortical oscillations (Saalmann et al. 2012) and enhancing the rhythmic range of different frequency bands (Singer 2013). There are also reasons to believe that human-specific parietal expansions strengthened the connections between Broca's and Wernicke's areas; while the arcuate fasciculus directly connects these areas, the parietal lobe also seems to serve as a point of connection (Catani & Bambini 2014). Indeed, the part of the middle temporal gyrus which the arcuate fasciculus projects to has been called an 'epicenter for lexical-semantic processing' (Turken & Dronkers 2011). In addition, it is highly plausible that globularity is responsible for the features required for language evolution put forward by Rauschecker (2018, 202): namely, 'the existence of longer memory spans, involving feedback loops from auditory to premotor regions, as well as feedback from somatosensory receptors informing internal models of the speech and vocal apparatus'.

The language system also appears to be sensitive to neural retuning, with German speakers exhibiting a stronger arcuate fasciculus than English speakers, and English speakers exhibiting stronger white matter tracks along the temporal lobe (Goucha et al. 2015). It is likely that the freer word order and richer over morphology demands greater working memory loads than English.

More recent work points to other human-specific brain features which could shed some light on language evolution. Li et al. (2018) examined the brains of 223 humans and 70 chimpanzees, focusing on hemispheric symmetry. They found human-specific deviations from symmetric in a Torque pattern comprising right-frontal and left-occipital 'petalia' along with downward and rightward occipital 'bending', and in addition left-ward displacement of the anterior temporal lobe and segments of the superior temporal sulcus (with the posterior superior temporal sulcus likely being part of the labelling network and interpreting hierarchically organised structures; Goucha et al. 2017), and finally a clockwise rotation of the left Sylvian Fissure around the left-right axis. The human left hemisphere was also found to be longer and of less height but equal in width compared to the right hemisphere. These somewhat peculiar asymmetries likely explain how the brain was reorganised such that parts of the Sylvian Fissure and temporal lobe were able to achieve new connections to the subcortical structures documented here as seemingly relevant for language processing. Relatedly, the evolutionary changes underlying the emergence of language may not be due to brain size as such, but more specifically the expansion of certain regions relative to others (Kaas & Stepniewska 2015), such as the prefrontal cortex (Neubert et al. 2015), the expansion of which likely explains our enhanced phonological loop (or lexical memory buffer). Moreover, an expanded frontal lobe (responsible for cognitive control) likely aided in the suppression of associative tendencies, thereby granting an easier route to the establishment of an advanced notion of arbitrary symbolism (as opposed to simple, one-to-one associations between signs and external stimuli or internal cognitive/hormonal states). It was also demonstrated in a meta-analysis that the anatomical asymmetry of the posterior temporal cortex is required for optimal verbal performance (Tzourio-Mazoyer & Mazoyer 2017). But what of other, more frontal areas typically implicated in language processing? Hickok et al. (2014) assessed short-term verbal memory and speech articulation deficits in a group of early-stage stroke patients. They found that articulatory deficits were related to damage in posterior Broca's area, motor areas, along with the insula and somatosensory area. Verbal working memory was related to posterior Broca's area and motor areas. This suggests that a close overlap exists in sensorimotor systems implicated in speech production and verbal working memory, perhaps indicating that the emergence of an expanded phonological loop was causally related to the evolution of speech production.

Recent work indicates that small and medium-sized carnivorans share with non-primates, including artiodactyls, the same relationship between cortical mass and number of neurons, suggesting that 'carnivorans are subject to the same evolutionary scaling rules as other non-primate clades' (Jardim-Messeder et al. 2017). Yet these rules do not apply to larger-bodied carnivorans, with Jardim-Messeder et al. (2017) showing that the golden retriever dog has more cortical neurons than the African lion or the brown bear. The authors invoke metabolic constraints, imposing a trade-off between body size and number of cortical neurons, to explain these results. Even more pertinent is their comparison between domesticated and wild species, which shows that the neuronal composition of carnivoran brains is not affected by domestication, suggesting that whatever domestication processes influenced human brain evolution likely altered cortical and subcortical composition rather than the number of neurons.

Perhaps more fundamentally (and something which has not been addressed in the neurolinguistics literature), functional cortico-cortical connections are realised by cortico-thalamic loops supporting oscillatory coordination, in particular α and θ (Malekmohammadi et al. 2015). Controlling rhythmic behaviour is also a function attributed to *RUNX2* (Reale et al. 2013; see also van der Lely & Pinker 2014 for genetic discussion relating to phonological computations). A literature review leads Theofanopoulou and Boeckx (2016) to claim that the thalamus is 'the part of the brain assigned to tune the oscillations of the other subcortical structures'. Other research points to three thalamic subregions responsible for coordinating oscillatory activity and facilitating memory-related processes (presumably essential for accessing lexical representations), each of which is modulated by frontal cognitive control: the medial dorsal nucleus is implicated in β synchrony (connectivity with parahippocampal/rhinal cortex generates the rhythm), the pulvinar in α synchrony (connectivity with early/visual parietal cortex generates the rhythm), and the anterior thalamus in θ synchrony (connectivity with the hippocampus generates the rhythm; see the 'three circuit model' in Ketz et al. 2015). Thalamo-cortical interactions are increasingly being seen as central to facilitating higher cognitive processes (Pratt et al. 2017), and the earlier-cited evidence for pulvinar expansion in humans would resonate with its presently purported role in language. Together with the earlier proposed code for phrase structure building, this leads to a conception of oscillatory linguistic computation which goes beyond the model in Theofanopoulou and Boeckx (2016, 2018), which relies on one-to-one associations between rhythms and complex operations, and the following pages will add further complexity.

2.4.1   Striatal Disorders

It reasonable to conclude that the thalamus behaves as a relay centre during language processing, in particular with respect to the interface between syntax and semantics (Wahl et al. 2008; David et al. 2011). With respect to these corticosubcortical motor loops, early stages of idiopathic Parkinson's disease have been considered a typical paradigm of striatal dysfunction. The characteristic motor signs (e.g. akinesia, bradykinesia and hypokinesia) are the result of presynaptic dopamine depletion within striatal target structures. Identical pathomechanisms are believed to act on the vocal-tract muscles, and so the speech motor deficits in Parkinson's disease are referred to as hypokinetic/rigid dysarthria. Damage to thalamic relay stations of the basal ganlia loops may also result in the typical constellation of monopitch, reduced stress and imprecise consonants (Duffy 2005; Ackermann & Ziegler 2013). Along with Parkinson's disease, Huntington's chorea represents another example of a striatal disorder. This is an autosomal-dominant hereditary disease; however, the speech motor deficits of this disease have not been extensively explored (Ackermann & Ziegler 2010).

2.4.2   Thalamic and Temporal Combinatorics

Maintaining our subcortical focus for the moment, top-down-induced shifts in α phase between two cortical areas have also been shown to strongly effect interregional γ coherence (Quax et al. 2017). In turn, it has additionally been shown that this higher γ coherence between these cortical regions also led to more efficient transmissions of spiking information. These results point to 'the feasibility of a … realistic mechanism for routing information in the brain based on coupled oscillations' (Quax et al. 2017). Given its prominent inter-areal α, the pulvinar would be able to carry out these combinatorial processes with great efficiency, allowing the brain to 'enhance processing of uncued stimuli' (Quax et al. 2017), with the importance of the final two words of this quote for neurolinguistics being clear given the – as classically formulated – spontaneous creativity of grammar.

   Interestingly, optogenetic approaches suggest that subgroups of the thalamic reticular nucleus facilitate attention switching from external stimuli to internal monitoring (Halassa et al. 2014); a capacity possibly employed during speech comprehension. Saalmann (2014) demonstrated that the envelope of cortical γ power in areas V4 and TEO of the visual pathway was coupled to the phase of cortical α generated in higher-order thalamic nuclei, suggesting that the thalamus plays a major role in the creation of cortical γ rhythms known to be implicated in a variety of cognitive capacities. Since they have been shown to be involved in both local and global oscillatory control (Fogerson & Huguenard 2016), the apparent flexibility of thalamic cellular and synaptic mechanisms could be readily exploited by a global language system.

Deepening our understanding of these regions, Deco et al. (2017) point out that the reason why certain regions can oscillate at very low frequencies and sustain these rhythms is due to internal connectivity along with external thalamo-cortical connectivity, seemingly strengthening the ties between the thalamus and cortical language-relevant regions.

The thalamus is consequently at the centre (both spatially and operationally) of coordinating the dynamic brain activity which gives rise to phrase structure building under the model developed in this book. These thalamic pathways crucially give rise to oscillatory interactions between the prefrontal cortex and medial temporal lobe, two structures widely implicated in language comprehension. The importance of the thalamus for higher cognition was also speculated in work by Campion and Elliot-Smith (1934), rejecting the dominant cortico-centrism and suggesting that cortico-thalamic impulse circulation was responsible for 'thought'. Cortico-subcortical circuits have been implicated in a range of cognitive and motor functions (Bell & Shine 2016). If Klostermann et al. (2013) are correct to suggest that the major thalamic functions with respect to language are 'the control and adaptation of corticocortical connectivity and bandwidth for informational exchange' (a process the authors refer to as 'transthalamic network orchestration'), then it is likely that this region plays a crucial role in regulating other parts of the brain which are responsible for constructing and interpreting syntactic structures, through a fine-tuning of subcortical oscillations.

An additional reason for expecting research into subcortical language processing to be illuminating comes from the recent finding that human prefrontal cortex has the same relative volume of grey and white matter neurons as other primates, challenging the standard account that uniquely human cognitive capacities arose due to an expansion of the prefrontal cortex (Gabi et al. 2016). Cyrus Martin (2016), in a careful review, documents evidence suggesting that the classical view of the cortex as being exclusive to mammals is outdated, and that a number of vertebrates have cortex-like features, boosting the impetus for neurolinguistic research to examine the role of subcortical structures.

Relatedly, due to the few protein differences between humans and chimpanzees, the individuating computational factors may be attributed to cis-regulatory and trans-regulatory genes (Somel et al. 2013). Features which may have led to the higher mental faculties of humans include novel neuronal cell types and the duplication of developmental proteins such as SRGAP2 leading to unique dendritic spine density and form (Geschwind & Rakic 2013). Synaptic and dendritic maturation also occurs in humans for a considerably longer time than in non-humans (Bianchi et al. 2013). If we also consider the conclusions of Harris's review of cortical computation in mammals and birds, that the 'human cortex appears to contain the same cell types, and their patterns of wiring and gene expression appear basically similar to well-studied model systems' (2015, 3184), the importance of subcortical investigations into linguistic computation becomes even clearer.

While subcortical structures have often been derided as the *reptilian brain*, responsible for only primitive drives, far removed from the neocortex's higher echelons of thought, the perspective of oscillomics developed here resituates subcortical regions like the thalamus and the basal ganglia as the core areas responsible for linguistic phrase structure building (see also Johnson & Knight 2015 for evidence that the thalamus plays a key role in neocortical oscillations involved in memory processes). The classical physician Galen held that the seat of the mind was in the ventricles, since donkeys also had highly convoluted brains. Through examining the crucial role of subcortical structures like the thalamus and basal ganglia in language, hopefully the Broca-Wernicke-Lichtheim model will go the way of the ventricular doctrine and the reptilian brain model, paving the way for more comprehensive accounts. And although neocortical expansion is the major focus in studies concerning the evolution of human intelligence, the basal ganglia, cerebellum and hippocampus are two to three times larger in humans than in great apes (Gibson & Jessee 1999). During the process of domestication, limbic structures are typically reduced, yet in humans limbic structures appear larger, not smaller (Bruner & Gleeson 2019), and so it seems somewhat odd to sideline them when discussing human-specific higher cognitive capacities.

To demonstrate the potential of this direction, recent work by Matchin et al. (2017) considers the finding that damage to the inferior frontal gyrus does not impair basic structure-building processes and suggests that increased activity in this area during phrase structure building reflects the generation of top-down structural predictions. The inferior frontal gyrus and posterior superior temporal sulcus did not show increased activity for simple phrases in their fMRI experiment, in contrast for sentences, most likely because the simple phrases used did not trigger structural predictions (see also Mohr et al. 1978 for evidence that Broca's area damage does not significantly impair language function). If the left inferior frontal gyrus did not show increased activation for two-word phrases relative to non-word lists, then it cannot be maintained – as it currently is by most researchers and textbooks – that this region is crucial

for syntactic combinatorics. Rather, it must be involved in prediction generation and/or memory buffer maintenance – admittedly crucial for the interpretation of phrase structures, but not necessarily their construction (Fiebach et al.
2005). As Matchin and Hickok (2019) discuss, left inferior frontal gyrus is also
likely involved in morpho-syntactic linearisation for production; interestingly,
returning to the classical view that Broca's area is primarily used for production
processes. Studies of picture naming also implicate the pars triangularis and
pars opercularis (Giahi Saravani et al. 2019), consistent with this 'syntax
externalisation' model.

Comparing phrases and sentences to word lists, Zaccarella et al. (2017)
found significant activation in BA 44 for the former but not the latter, concluding that 'merge activates the pars opercularis of the left inferior frontal gyrus'
(see also Kang et al. 1999 for similar findings). While it seems true to say that
certain processes involved in interpreting phrases implicates BA 44, this is
quite different from claiming that the Merge operation itself is localised here,
since a number of other processes (prediction, maintenance, comparison, etc.)
need to take place for successful comprehension to take place – processes
ranging far beyond simple concatenation and labelling. Other illuminating
work in this connection includes Uddén et al.'s (2017) transcranial magnetic
stimulation study which showed that Broca's area is causally implicated in
processing non-adjacent syntactic dependencies, since the ability to discriminate between grammatical and ungrammatical sequences in a learned artificial
grammar was impaired when this region, but not other regions, were targeted
by magnetic stimulation. This does not license the conclusion that Broca's area
is crucial for the *construction* of hierarchical linguistic structures, and indeed
Uddén et al. (2017) conclude that their findings 'support a role for Broca's
region in general structured sequence processing, rather than a specific role for
the processing of hierarchically organized sentence structure'. An advantage of
transcranial magnetic stimulation is its ability to target specific brain regions at
specific rhythms, making it highly suited to testing these forms of causality
hypotheses in oscillatory behaviour. In related, follow-up work, Uddén et al.
(2019) use a large cohort (>200) of fMRI subjects to show activity increases in
left inferior frontal gyrus and left posterior middle temporal gyrus when
processing words towards the end of a sentence, relative to processing earlier
words.

Mayberry et al. (2018) also investigated the brain of an individual who
experienced minimal linguistic input until young adulthood, showing that
during language processing the dorsal pathway in the right hemisphere was
primarily active rather than the classical perisylvian network, again bringing
into question the role of Broca's area in language. In this connection, Martins
and Villringer (2018) discuss how structured sequences that are difficult to
process implicate left inferior frontal gyrus, and not hierarchical structures

specifically. This supports the claim that parts of the inferior frontal gyrus provide not the seat of syntax, but rather a crucial maintenance memory buffer interfacing with a construction memory stack in superior posterior temporal regions (both of which are connected with the arcuate fasciculus). The fact that the inferior frontal gyrus is active always during the processing of unexpected stimuli suggests that its role is memory related, not specifically hierarchy related. In addition, the fact that non-sequential hierarchies such as spatial and social hierarchies are processed outside the inferior frontal gyrus also speaks to this model.

As such, the model being proposed in this book is sympathetic to Matchin and Hickok's (2019) approach: These authors do not propose a specific anatomical correlate of syntactic operations, but rather 'speculate that minimal operations such as Merge or Unify are instantiated by subtler biophysical properties within the pMTG [posterior middle temporal gyrus] such as network connectivity patterns or cortical oscillations'.

Clarifying these positions considerably, consider also Sheng et al.'s (2019) MEG mapping of words, phrases and sentences. Distinct ensembles of cortical loci were sensitive to different linguistic structures: superior temporal gyrus was sensitive to all three, and left anterior temporal lobe and left inferior frontal gyrus were sensitive to phrases and sentences (anterior temporal lobe likely due to the semantic combinatorics effect, and left inferior frontal gyrus likely due to the syntactic memory buffer it provides). This broad picture is well supported by much recent literature; for instance, Wu et al. (2019) found a very similar fronto-temporal language network for phrasal construction.

While the left anterior temporal lobe is activated early (~200ms) in two-word phrasal composition, the ventromedial prefrontal cortex is activated later (~450ms); Pylkkänen (2019) suggests that left anterior temporal regions are involved in conceptual and logical processing, and ventromedial prefrontal regions likely contribute to late-stage composition, interfacing the phrasal output with external systems such as episodic memory and social cognition. If the left anterior temporal lobe is damaged, however, single-word processing is impaired but not phrase composition (Wilson et al. 2014). Pylkkänen (2019, 64) addresses this issue with considerable clarity, with her explanation supporting the network-based architecture of phrasal processing assumed in this book:

If many different subroutines carry a roughly similar function (i.e., building a phrase), then this system may be difficult to break. The function of an impaired subroutine could be compensated for by the others, at least to some degree. In contrast, feature binding within a word may not have similar redundancy. This would make single-word processing more fragile than basic combinatory processing. Indeed, focal brain damage hardly ever results in the inability to form simple phrases, whereas problems in single-word access and more complex syntactic processing are classic patient profiles.

In another recent fMRI study by Pattamadilok et al. (2016), which supports these ideas, subjects were presented with sentences of differing levels of syntactic complexity (adjunct and centre-embedded structures), followed by comprehension probes requiring subjects to correctly parse the sentence to give correct answers. Complexity effects were found in the inferior frontal gyrus, posterior superior temporal sulcus and the insula bilaterally at the probe sentences but not the initial sentences, suggesting either that the increased activity found resulted from the deployment of prediction processes triggered by the experimental task, or that subjects engaged in 'shallow parsing' at the initial sentence and only properly parsed the sentence when they were forced to rehearse it (with the latter option being unlikely, given that participants frequently had to focus on certain initial sentences and so would likely parse each of them to ensure maximum task efficiency).

Given the likelihood that the left inferior frontal gyrus is not in fact crucial to elementary linguistic combinatorics, recent work by Wilson et al. (2017) can be more easily integrated into this rapidly maturing neurolinguistic model. These authors synthesised current research into sequence processing in primate frontal cortex and propose a 'ventrodorsal gradient model' of frontal cortical function in sequencing operations. Reviewing comparative fMRI studies led them to propose the existence of a 'conserved, bilateral, ventral frontal and opercular subsystem within frontal cortex that supports the evaluation of adjacent sequencing dependencies'. The literature suggests that in both monkeys and humans ventral regions of frontal cortex conduct processing of adjacent sequence dependencies. This leaves open the possibility that more temporal (e.g. pMTG) and subcortical (e.g. thalamus) regions are responsible for language-specific computational processes, as suggested here.

2.5   Learn to Code: Implementing Hierarchical Phrase Structure

The prominent neuropsychologist Nikolai Axmacher begins an assessment of cognitive neuroscience with the following thoughtful, succinct summary of the field (2016, 1276):

In contrast to other codes, representations in the brain do not only need to provide reliable information about things in the world. They must also deliver this information in a way that allows the brain to usefully guide behavior. Thus, unraveling the code of the brain does not merely imply mapping individual object features onto spike rates in single cells or onto functional magnetic resonance imaging responses in specific brain areas. To unravel the code, it is not even sufficient to determine whether a certain item is encoded by the magnitude of cellular or network activity or by its specific timing (that is, whether a rate code or a phase code is employed). Instead, truly understanding the neural code involves finding out how brain representations of a given experience recruit those neural functions that are conducive to goal-directed behavior.

My intention in this final section of the present chapter is to expand on the aforementioned hypotheses regarding the neurobiological implementation of language and relate some of the proposed ideas back to earlier themes. To set the scene for what follows, it is useful to consider the framework in Boeckx and Theofanopoulou (2015), which highlights the inadequacy of standard cladistic thinking so prevalent in much of contemporary biolinguistics, most notably in the Narrow/Broad Faculty of Language distinction, under which recursion was simply added 'on top' of faculties shared with other species, as if no reciprocal causation had occurred. Boeckx and Theofanopoulou 'very much doubt that cognition can be studied independently of the basic neurophysiological principles that produce it', going against the many who claim that the three Marrian levels (computation, algorithm, implementation) need to be studied in a segregated fashion, privileging the computational level. For instance, while computationally distinct, music and language share a number of important algorithmic properties such as prediction, synchronisation, turn-taking, and oscillatory entrainment (Doelling & Poeppel 2015). This seems to emerge from cell assembly specialisations and distinct rhythmic profiles; language and music have different hierarchical processing networks but shared working memory and cognitive control systems (Rogalsky et al. 2011). As Fitch (2014a, 333) puts it, 'The traditional notion that we can study cognition with little or no attention to its mechanistic, neural basis is misleading, both theoretically and practically.'

If Horgan (2017) is right to claim that '"[n]eural code" is by far the most under-appreciated term, and concept, in science', then it should be of little surprise that this concept has not been applied to one of the most under-appreciated concepts in neuroscience – hierarchical phrase structure. As assumed in this book, a major tradition in contemporary linguistics, generative grammar, argues that humans are endowed with a recursive computational system that can generate an unbounded array of hierarchical expressions. This system interfaces with conceptual systems (for interpretation) and articulatory systems (for expression). Human language is a system of structures, not strings (Everaert et al. 2015), such that the same sequence of words can be parsed to yield distinct meanings depending on the underlying structure:

(4)   a. Jesse [said [Walt lied] again].
       b. Jesse [said [Walt lied again]].
       c. We [watched [a movie with Jim Carrey]].
       d. We [watched a movie [with Jim Carrey]].
       e. John [said [Bill left yesterday]].
       f. John [[said Bill left] yesterday].

Following on from the discussion of labelling and hierarchy in Chapter 1, natural language syntax is sensitive to structural/hierarchical distance as well as the simpler notion of linear/sequential distance, where the former refers to the number of intervening superior nodes in the path from one terminal to another in a tree structure, and the latter refers to the number of terminals in a given output. Leaving aside the intricate and well-developed syntactic explanations, and keeping to the core observations, the structural nature of language can be shown through certain unexpected contrasts, which are due to differences in how specific words are hierarchically merged and subsequently associated with one another, rather than being due to a linear computation over strings (with 'obvious' in the structures below resulting in a reading which purely identifies the individual, and 'stupid' resulting in a reading which adds a description to the individual).

(5)   a. Who left for this reason is obvious/stupid.
        b. Who left and for what reason is obvious/*stupid.

(6)   a. [$_{CP/DP}$ Who$_{DP}$ read this] is **obvious**/*stupid*.
        b. [$_{CP/*DP}$ Who$_{DP}$ read what] is **obvious**/**stupid*.

Other cases show how processes such as contraction are also sensitive to hierarchical structure, and cannot simply be carried out over any chosen word boundary.

(7)   a. Kim's taller than [Tim is] / [*Tim's].

Verb phrase 'ellipsis' (essentially, omission/deletion at externalisation) is also common in natural language, but there are places where it is unacceptable, again due to reasons invoking hierarchical structure. The elided verb phrase in (9b) is the complement of *had*, and if it is not the complement of an adjacent overt head, then the syntax 'crashes' (where '*e*' denotes the elided verb phrase *read it*).

(8)   a. They all had left.
        b. They had all left.

(9)   a. They denied reading it, although they all had [*e*].
        b. *They denied reading it, although they had all [*e*].

Even human focal stress (as in *No, John went to PARIS* in response to *John went to London*) seems to operate within hierarchical principles of c-command and precedence, such that the stress typically appears at the first available foci site (Büring 2015). Willer Gold et al. (2017) show that in certain South Slavic languages there are constructions that prefer linear order over hierarchical order, yet these constructions are limited only to coordinate structures and not more complex structures such as relative clauses. Their particular experiments showed that agreement morphology may be computed in a series of discrete steps, one of which is likely independent of hierarchy; yet, as the authors stress, these findings are wholly in line with the predictions of generative grammar, since while linear order may indeed prevail over hierarchy on very rare occasions, this does not undermine the central importance of hierarchy in the Slavic languages the authors explore.

Hagoort (2019) presents another strong case in favour of the fundamentally hierarchical format of syntax: In an experimental scenario, participants are exposed to an image of eight, horizontally organised balls. All the balls are green except the second and third balls. Participants are told 'Point to the second green ball' – typically chunked as (second [green ball]) – and 99 per cent choose the third ball. Yet it is possible that 'second green ball' could refer to the first green ball, i.e. the second ball in the sequence which happens to be green. The fact that participants opt for the third ball suggests that they are not parsing the sentence via a linear rule, but hierarchically.

Somehow the brain is able to construct from the linear speech stream hierarchical relationships between discrete elements, 'extract[ing] semantic meaning from the spectral features represented at the cochlea', as de Heer et al. (2017) put it. Seemingly paradoxically, it would be more effortful and complex for the brain to deal with finiteness than it would for it to be able to comprehend an infinite number of sentences of different structures, since it would require some cognitive function to impose an additional barrier to the computational system. If the Universal Generative Faculty can simply apply freely, being restricted only by external constraints, this would appear to point linguists in a particular direction for developing neuroscientific linking hypotheses: Find a mechanism in the brain which can freely combine and recombine elements in a particular hierarchical fashion. The following discussion, and the following chapter, is an attempt to discover such a mechanism, given what has already been discussed in this chapter about the possible oscillatory basis of linguistic combinatorics and phrase structure building, using what Chomsky et al. (2019) call 'the formal toolkit' supplied by theoretical linguistics (a set of elementary operations and a cognitive architecture within which language is embedded) as a guide in investigating the neural basis of the most remarkable and fundamental human capacity.

2.5.1   Reconstructing Language

Throughout the twentieth century and into the twenty-first, artificial intelligence research has repeatedly moved in and out of synch with biology, at one point being closely aligned with current developments only to diverge slightly at another. Linguistics, on the other hand, has often claimed to be in synch with biology, but has never in fact achieved this goal. Linguists have often made explicit claims about biology, such as the idea that colour perception is influenced by one's native language and its system of nominal categorisation;

a claim in stark contrast to empirical findings that colour categorisation is constrained by the biology of colour vision, rather than linguistic categories (Skelton et al. 2017). Instead of relying purely on language-based intuitions to develop neurolinguistic hypotheses, we will start from the premise that an examination of neural mechanisms can be a robust guide in formulating implementational models of language. Connectome–phenome associations may be a long way off, but we can at least begin to make advances on Matchin's (2016) speculation regarding the neural basis of phrase structure: 'It might be in the connections between cortical areas, perhaps involving subcortical structures, or some property of individual neurons'.

Much of this section will explore the limits of current research into localising linguistic computations and representations. While functional localisation is certainly initially desirable, the field is currently too far removed from biophysics (both theoretically and in terms of technological power; consider the controversial nature of M/EEG source localisation techniques) to observe the neural basis of linguistic representations at the cellular level.

It should first be stressed that the term 'neural code' exhibits a degree of (often unacknowledged) polysemy in the literature. The term has flexibly been applied to both cellular and oscillatory mechanisms, although predominantly the former. For instance, Chang and Tsao (2017) discuss the neural code of facial identity in the primate brain, focusing on inferotemporal neurons, while Lisman and Jensen (2013) discuss the θ-γ neural code for working memory, focusing on oscillatory couplings (see also Dayan & Abbott 2001; Gallistel 2017a; Panzeri et al. 2017). As should be clear, I will be adopting the latter approach.

In the concluding paragraph of his review of some major trends in neurobiology, Stanley (2013, 263) notes that '[t]he anatomical and biophysical constraints across the various circuits in the brain naturally suggest that the synchronization of spiking across neurons is an important element in propagating signals across brain structures'. This leads him to 'question whether a "synchrony code" based on this premise forms a basis of the neural code'. Stanley's *synchrony code* is effectively synonymous with the present oscillatory sense of coding. He concludes by noting that although there is evidence to support this general idea, 'there is still much work to be done to determine how ubiquitous this phenomenon is in different contexts and across brain regions'. It is my hope that much of the present chapter, and also the subsequent one, can provide a convincing case that since the time of Stanley's conclusion in 2013 there has been much promising work supporting the existence of a *synchrony code* for language.

Of what use is the concept of a neural code to the language sciences? In a discussion of the biology and evolution of language, Friederici (2016) points solely to neuroanatomical studies of functional correlations between linguistic manipulations and BOLD responses on fMRI scans. These correlational studies are doubtless informative, but are couched in a necessarily delimited, restrictive conceptual framework. Top-down perspectives on neurolinguistics are useful up until the point that sufficiently decomposed and generic sub-operations and processes have been discovered. But insisting on a top-down perspective 'all the way down' is inconsistent with both Darwinian and Thompsonian thinking. The early developers of generative grammar in the 1950s and 1960s made important strides in their approach to language as an innate mental computational system, but it is also something of a mystery how anyone took seriously their highly specific, construction-oriented syntactic transformations, as if 'relative formation' and 'question formation' (instead of more generic computational operations) could ever constitute neurobiologically plausible components. Likewise, the lexicalist framework adopted in recent work in linguistics (see Boeckx 2014a for a comprehensive critique) presents a number of obstacles. Most notably, contemporary neurobiology is far from achieving an understanding of *representations*, and focus should instead be placed on investigating *operations*, with set-formation and labelling having a much greater potential to be grounded in (oscillatory) brain processes than intransitive verbs. Berwick and Chomsky (2016) '(speculatively) posit that the word-like elements, or at least their features as used by Merge, are somehow stored in the middle temporal cortex as the "lexicon"' (2016, 159). This sidelines well-accepted findings that conceptual representations are widely distributed across several regions, even if the middle temporal cortex acts as a (densely interconnected) store for many core representations and a crucial memory buffer in phrase structure building (just as how Broca's area – or more specifically, BA 44v, following the recent subparcellation of BA 44 – is most likely a similar kind of buffer in syntactic computation; see Blank et al. 2016b for evidence of distributed syntactic processing). For instance, Momenian et al.'s (2016) fMRI study demonstrated that nouns and verbs both implicated regions in occipital cortex, temporal cortex and the cerebellum; however, only verb processing implicated broader activation in bilateral middle temporal gyrus and the left fusiform gyrus (see Konopka & Roberts 2016 for the role of the cerebellum in language, in particular phonology, and Lametti et al. 2016 for its role in perceptual decision-making during phonetic tasks). More specifically, BA 44, through its temporal connections via the dorsal pathway, is likely to act as this memory buffer (and not 'the pure syntactic merger', as Wu et al. 2019 claim); or, in the language of computer science, it acts as the stack in a pushdown automaton (Fitch & Martins 2014). Addressing a closely related notion, Matchin (2018) draws a necessary and important distinction by proposing that BA 44 is likely selectively sensitive to linguistic representations but not computations, an idea which matches well with what is proposed here. Matchin (2018) points out that the experimental evidence suggests that parts of the left inferior frontal gyrus can be divided into which linguistic representations they are sensitive to: phonology for the pars opercularis, syntax for the pas triangularis, and semantics for the pars orbitalis (note that while Matchin 2018, 9, claims that 'the computations of adjacent subregions of Broca's area ... are quite possibly the same despite their differences in input-selectivity', we have argued here that phonology does not exhibit a labelling mechanism). While linguistic representations may well have been assigned a special memory buffer (phonological loop) in BA 44, the computations associated with Merge are certainly well distributed. In fact, even this perspective might not be wholly accurate: Along with BA 44 being a memory buffer (see Badre & Wagner 2007 for seminal discussion), it may also serve to select between competing syntactic interpretations, both storing and comparing representations (Novick et al. 2010).

With respect to any apparent human-specific computational properties of the Broca's area memory buffer (i.e. its apparent involvement in processing linear morpho-syntactic relations and complex phonology; Matchin & Hickok 2019), Palomero-Gallagher and Zilles (2019) provide a tentative answer as to its cytoarchitectonic and microstructural uniqueness. These authors quantitatively studied the cytoarchitecture of areas 44 and 45 using layer-specific grey-level indices (volume proportion of neuropil and cell bodies) in serially sectioned and cell body-stained human, bonobo, chimpanzee, gorilla, orangutan and macaque brains (i.e. they studied homologues to areas 44 and 45 in non-human primates). Humans were found to have the largest neuropil volume, indicating greater space for local and interregional connectivity.

Other recent evidence points away from the traditional neurolinguistic model. Moreno et al. (2018) used fMRI to scan the brain of congenitally deaf adults who had acquired French sign language as their first language and written French as a second language while watching a list of signs which corresponded to syntactic constituents of varying sizes. They discovered an effect of constituent structure in the basal ganglia (including the head of the caudate and putamen), and a smaller effect on temporal and frontal regions known to be involved in written language. Then, when the same participants read sentences versus word lists, the former condition resulted in activation in the same region. Quite apart from Friederici's (2017) speculations involving the primacy of BA 44 and its dorsal pathway, this study highlights the importance of the basal ganglia in modality-independent syntactic processing. A core part of the labelling operation must therefore take part in subcortical structures involving and close to the basal ganglia. While the left-lateralised perisylvian network typically implicated in language processing is active as early as two months into a child's life (Dehaene-Lambertz & Spelke 2015), the central role of the basal ganglia in generating hierarchically structured and meaningful labelled representations cannot be ignored.

These suggestions, along with the broader framework emerging in this book, speak against the claims in Friederici (2017). In his Foreword to Friederici's monograph, Chomsky claims that 'it is the ventral part of B44 [sic] in which basic syntactic computations – in the simplest case Merge – are localized' (Friederici 2017, x). The evidence reviewed earlier suggests otherwise; the computations are not localised in BA 44 but involve a widespread cortical-subcortical circuit, even if BA 44 appears sensitive to phrase structure. Chomsky also claims that 'BA 45 is responsible for semantic processes' (Ibid); a considerably general and incomplete assessment of both BA 45 and the brain's semantic network (see also Chomsky 2010). Relatedly, in a recent discussion with Ray Jackendoff, Chomsky (2019b) did not appear to know the difference between 'neural nets' and 'real neurons', confusing networks of brain cells of the one hand, with abstract/computerised neural nets on the other.

In other recent developments, Chen et al. (2019) explicitly set out to test the Labelling Hypothesis I have proposed elsewhere (Murphy 2015a) and am defending here, and their results allow us to properly frame the role of Broca's area in this aspect of language. The authors focused on word category information (WCI: functional, lexical; nominal, verbal, adjectival...), which naturally plays a central role in syntactic labelling. Labelling is, as mentioned, the core *process* of syntax, while categorial information is one of the *objects* under manipulation. While many studies have focused on the neurobiological basis of hierarchical syntax, Chen et al. are somewhat unique in their focus on the categorial objects manipulated by syntax. They conducted an fMRI experiment using a pseudo-Chinese artificial language with structures containing a centre-embedded relative clause. Non-Chinese (Korean) speakers were divided into two groups: one was presented with WCI rules before scanning, and the other did not. Participants were tasked with judging the grammaticality of the testing sentences, with long-distance dependencies between two elements (main verb and relativiser). The WCI group were more accurate and faster in their responses, and the scanning results showed that the left superior temporal gyrus and Broca's area were more strongly activated for the WCI group. As such, connections between lSTG and Broca's area seem critical for the processing of categorial information involved in labelling, supporting ideas discussed earlier about the involvement of specific temporal regions in the labelling network.

Moreover, Ding et al.'s (2016) discovery that phrasal and sentential structures produce γ increases in STG can now be understood within the framework presented here: WCI is likely stored in STG and/or STG retrieves the WCI from various sources before maintaining the information in memory, and these γ increases represent the activation of γ-itemised representations coupled with slower δ and θ rhythms – ideas not incompatible with Hagoort's (2005) suggestion that the lSTG stores syntactic node information, although it is likely that lSTG is a multifunctional component of the language system involved in retrieval and maintenance.

Chen et al. (2019) also found greater activation in left posterior BA 45 for the WCI condition relative to the non-WCI condition, although no differences in BA 44 activation were found. These findings are compatible with the claims in Matchin et al. (2014) and also Santi and Grodzinsky (2012) that BA 45 is involved in syntactic prediction rather than narrow syntax. As such, this leaves little left for Broca's area to do with respect to labelling and hierarchical phrase structure building.

As Matchin (2018, 9) concludes, 'If . . . the [pars triangularis] is the locus of working memory resources rather than structure building operations, new ideas must by explored about the neural localization of syntax.' We will here directly pick up from Matchin's conclusion by exploring a number of promising directions for evolutionary neurolinguistics.

2.5.2   Functional Polyhedra: Localisation of Linguistic Function

As the previous sections have made clear, Broca's area has long been – and to a large extent still is – believed to be the seat of syntax. As mentioned, Wu et al. (2019) state that BA 44 is 'the pure syntactic merger'. But what precisely is Broca's area? It is regulated by the basal ganglia and thalamus via a cortico-basal ganglia-thalamic loop (Haber & Calzavara 2009), an integrative system which is much more likely to be involved in structure-building operations than purely Broca's area alone. If anything, Broca's area seems specialised for executing retrieval operations which operate over constructed sets of linguistic features; hence why, after a lesion to this area, individuals retain the ability to comprehend and produce such feature-sets, albeit with reduced cognitive control over them. Contrary to standard models implicating the basal ganglia purely in physical movement, Haber and Calzavara (2009, 70) explore how it is also involved in 'the processes that lead to movement' such as motivation and planning.

Along with the above-mentioned limitations, an examination of the regions implicated in recent oscillatory studies of language comprehension (see Lam et al. 2016 for a review) shows that the classical Broca-Wernicke model is far from adequate. Language comprehension generates multiple, large-scale oscillatory changes in a number of distant regions, and so limiting the 'language regions' to Broca's and Wernicke's areas is unjustified, and the dynamic functioning of the brain at once suggests that a simple mapping between a given region and a particular linguistic representation or operation is not going to be forthcoming. The fact that certain regions implicated in syntactic, semantic and phonological processes are spatially overlapping suggests that a different system of segregation will be required than standard cartographic approaches: namely, frequency-based segregation (see Fedorenko & Thompson-Schill 2014 for a related proposal that 'Network of Interest' should replace the common concept 'Region of Interest', although a Network of Interest is still, it should be stressed, a purely correlational notion at its core). As Tremblay and Dick (2016) document in a careful and thorough review, the classical Broca-Wernicke model is not only based on outdated neuroanatomy, but is also cortico-centric, language-centric (i.e. it ignores the importance of general cognitive processes contributing to language), it does not take into consideration the widespread connectivity required for language, and is also ill-defined – continuing a major trend in cognitive neuroscience through the use of anatomically ambiguous terms like 'dorsolateral prefrontal cortex' and 'temporo-parietal junction'. 'Syntax' is not to be found in any particular brain *region*; rather, it is to be found in particular brain *operations* which are carried out across distributed regions. The next chapter will also expand on this topic through discussing neural plasticity.

It is worth noting in this connection that due to the frequent overlap in roles attributed to β and α waves, Bressler and Richter (2015, 63) argue for a redefinition of neural oscillations based on functionality, not arbitrary clinical and frequency boundaries. Though this does not currently warrant a reformulation of any oscillomic proposals, it is worth keeping this approach in mind, as a reconceptualisation of the cognome may well simultaneously require a reformulation of the oscillome. Relatedly, when it comes to the spectral analysis of δ rhythms in M/EEG investigations of language, it may be crucial to examine the precise waveforms generated, or risk sidelining important details. For instance, Cole and Voytek (2017, 143) document how the 1-5Hz sawtooth-shaped waves occur in human EEG and are typically associated with rapid eye movement (REM) sleep:

Noting the shape of this rhythm has helped to associate it with distinct behaviors and mechanisms that would not have been possible if it was simply filtered and identified as a 'delta oscillation'. In addition, sleep spindles are characterized as bursts of 8–14 Hz oscillations that are observed during sleep, together with slow oscillations and sawtooth waves. Sleep spindle subtypes can be distinguished by their shape.

Neurolinguistic hypotheses often rely solely on imaging studies which point to regional specialisation for particular language tasks, but this methodological cut-off point, while typically acknowledged by fMRI experimentalists (who can now achieve voxels of $0.8mm^3$), is side-stepped by other researchers who ignore the important language-related activation in non-specialised voxels. No one would claim that the responses to tactile sensation in non-selective regions are somehow not part of the story of how we become acquainted with surfaces, and so a strict focus on, for instance, Broca's area amounts to a severely impoverished neurolinguistic model.

Relatedly, it is widely assumed that human and animal concepts are composed of necessary and sufficient features surrounded by a periphery of ancillary but related features used to 'point' the comprehender in the right conceptual direction (grey feathers may be suggestive of a bird, for instance, but are not necessarily part of one), and any neurolinguistic models informed purely by imaging studies will likely reflect only the implementational regions (and not the neurobiological mechanisms) responsible for these peripheral features.

Localisation studies also impose no constraints on the theory of linguistic or cognitive structure they explore. This point is somewhat more obvious, but also seems to me unappreciated in the literature. A given brain region can potentially be involved in any number of mental functions. Indeed, Genon et al. (2018) claim that since many behavioural functions can be mapped to the same brain region, our knowledge of the functional specialisation of a given region can be thought of as a polyhedron with many behavioural functions ('sides') which can only be appreciated by investigating them from different perspectives. Brain dynamics, in contrast to functional localisation, is by definition far more constrained: A single γ cycle, for instance, cannot be claimed to be responsible for processing a full verb phrase purely because of its narrow temporal window. In addition, claiming that a given portion of Broca's area is responsible for interpreting 'word movement' (as is often done) is inadequate biology, and only serves to give credit to a syntactic/processing theory rather than contribute to an understanding of brain and language function.

A positive future for cognitive neuroscience will only arrive, according to Anderson's (2016, 9) succinct summary, when we adopt the following guideline:

We will represent the functional activity of the brain in a multidimensional manner that captures the underlying functional and dispositional properties, and we will give up the notion that the neural responses we observe and measure must reflect the engagement of a single unified function.

Brain networks do not subserve single functions, let alone single complex linguistic functions like word movement. Pessoa (2016) examines a number of studies in systems neuroscience and presents an anti-modular framework through which brain networks do not have a single, unique function and are highly overlapping. Pessoa presents the example of the amygdala, showing that it simultaneously belongs to at least three networks: namely, visual, autonomic and value networks mediated through connections to anterior temporal cortex, hypothalamus and orbitofrontal cortex.

Adopting a complementary perspective, Shine et al. (2016) review recent findings which suggest that 'brain function is most appropriately categorized according to the computational capacity of each brain system, rather than the specific task states that elicit its activity'. If these computational capacities are in turn mediated through oscillations, as this book contends, then this would have wide-ranging implications for the redefinition of a number of major neurocognitive networks. We should also bear in mind the conclusions of Ojemann (1990), who showed that while distinct features of language propagation are strictly localised, such loci are *temporary* and display great individual variability, with the neuronal functions changing over time, and so we can only ever conclude from neuroimaging experiments that cell assemblies are active in particular tasks *at time T, under condition P*, and can at best be specified for particular functions. Gu et al. (2015, 178) summarise these concerns:

With the exponential increase in neuroimaging studies focusing on the spatial localization of cognition, the field of cognitive neuroscience has accumulated a great deal of evidence concerning the functional role(s) of specific brain areas. In comparison, the temporal/oscillatory components of cognition have been largely ignored.

It is the nature of these oscillatory components to which we will now return.

3   A Neural Code for Language

A range of neurobiological models presented in much neurolinguistic work, tainted by cortico-centrism, are incompatible with what is known about the brain and its principal dynamics. As argued in the previous chapter, neural oscillations provide a suitable framework through which to explore mesoscopic computations across a number of cognitive faculties, as is already being done in domains outside linguistics. Importing standard assumptions from theoretical syntax, we can think of the computational system as imposing its own conditions on interfacing systems. The shift in perspective to oscillatory terms allows us to reformulate this such that, for instance, the neural ensembles responsible for storing representations used to construct phrases require particular phase–amplitude–locking levels in order for the interconnected regions coupled with them to 'read off' their content. Studying the human oscillatory profile may provide an excellent way of experimentally investigating what kind of features can pass through the interfaces, and because each rhythm plays numerous, non-overlapping roles, it is crucial for these studies to be accompanied by biophysical modelling and computationally explicit mesoscopic frameworks of regionally localised cross-frequency coupling (CFC) functionality.

Over the past decade, and as reviewed in the previous chapter, the oscillation literature has shown great promise in exploring some major topics in linguistics. The list of language-relevant findings is rapidly expanding, and these need to be accommodated by neurolinguistic theories – an urgent task demanded by the findings and hypotheses presented in this book. For example, recent studies of α have shown that listeners who show better attention-to-memory capacities show more flexible α power allocation, leading to the suggestion that 'selective attention to a specific object in auditory memory does benefit human performance not by simply reducing memory load, but by actively engaging complementary neural resources to sharpen the precision of the task-relevant object in memory' (Lim et al. 2015, 16094). The absence of a complete dorsal-ventral stream 'loop' in the macaque brain (Frey et al. 2014) appears to be only the briefest sketch of the real underlying puzzle, and could be incorporated well into a larger oscillomic system invoking, among other things, human-specific myelination rates as a way of directly modulating the phase and power of oscillations (Pajevic et al. 2014).

As discussed at length in the previous chapter, Ding et al. (2016) provide evidence that distinct rhythms may entrain to distinct grammatical constructs, from words to phrases to sentences, with slow rhythms in the parietal lobe, superior temporal gyrus and inferior frontal cortex entraining only to phrasal and sentential structures, not syllabic ones. As also mentioned earlier, there have been some objections raised about this and also subsequent studies, and general theoretical proposals about the oscillatory dynamics of reading and listening have been proposed, but the basic computational procedures of language comprehension have been absent from these neurobiological debates. Predictive coding hypotheses about top-down predictions influencing reading are welcome, but more direct, fine-grained computational-implementational linking hypotheses are needed. Simply correlating a given rhythm with a stipulated, higher-level psychological construct like 'lexical access', 'Unification' or 'semantic memory' does not approximate the required degree of interdisciplinary granularity to formulate a genuine neurolinguistic theory. As proposed here, oscillatory *interactions* are likely the fundamental computational component of the generative faculty of language. Much of the recent literature has focused on amplitude increases/decreases to the severe neglect of CFC; both Ding et al. (2016) and a recent, comprehensive review of the neurolinguistics oscillations literature, Prystauka and Lewis (2019), mention CFC only once.

Further, as Meyer (2018) notes, 'in spite of the widespread optimism towards predictive coding, the major issue with the adaptation of the framework to language comprehension is the gross lack of empirical reports of beta-gamma coupling during language comprehension, as well as the even grosser lack of intracranial evidence for the within column or network-level interplay of beta and gamma during language comprehension'. Linguistic prediction rather seems to be implemented via coupling between frontal γ and posterior α, if the recent results reported in Wang et al. (2018) are any indication. Chao et al. (2018) have shown that hierarchical predictive coding is instantiated in the primate brain by asymmetric channelling in the γ and α-β ranges – but, again, any direct link with language remains, at the moment, lacking. As such, despite its popularity, we will not discuss the issue any further here.

Similar criticisms apply to Boeckx's (2017) hypothesis. This maintains that since both the fronto-parietel and fronto-temporal networks process sequences, the strengthened connections between them found in the human brain 'could allow for the processing of sequences of sequences, of the sort attested in grammatical constructions'. How these strengthened connections could lead to recursion is not explained, and no further details – algorithmic or implementational – are presented.

In this chapter, we will attempt to go beyond all of these noted limitations and refine the oscillatory model outlined in the previous chapter. Considerably greater empirical coverage will be presented, but the narrow focus on syntactic and semantic comprehension will be maintained.

3.1 Encoding Feature-Sets

3.1.1 Refining the θ-γ Code

While seminal work on the dynamics of phonological computation (from Giraud & Poeppel 2012 to Poeppel & Assaneo 2020) has explored how the brain interprets the rhythmic nature of speech, what is less well acknowledged is that semantics and syntax also exhibit rhythmic qualities (e.g. in the existence of phrasal embeddings, hierarchies of functional projections and many other features). The current section of model-construction which I will now pursue will follow Lisman and Jensen's (2013) hypothesis that items from working memory are extracted via θ-γ embedding (discussed in the previous chapter, and originating in Lisman & Idiart 1995). It will also follow Kamiński et al.'s (2020) discovery that memoranda-selective (i.e. working memory content-selective) persistently active neurons in the human medial temporal lobe phase-lock to θ oscillations during working memory maintenance. Such phase-locking properties are dependent on memory content and load: 'During high memory loads, the phase of the oscillatory activity to which neurons phase lock provides information about memory content not available in the firing rate of the neurons' (Kamiński et al. 2020, 256). In addition, posterior hippocampal θ correlates with movement speed, whereas anterior hippocampal θ does not (Goyal et al. 2018), and so the following claims made below about (para) hippocampal θ will be assumed to be a result of this anterior portion and its apparent role in non-spatial cognition.

Much of the following discussion will be devoted to developing an oscillatory model for the construction of linguistic feature-sets, which I will attribute the following properties: After inhibition reduces over the θ cycle, the most excitable representations are itemised through low-middle γ, followed sequentially by the other, less-excitable clusters. Phase resetting θ would induce a pause in γ activity and, as a result, a γ phase reset (see Tesche & Karhu 2000). This would determine the feature-set composition, completed after the θ phase resets. Consequently, a 'check list' of items would be sent downstream to regions oscillating at slower rhythms to be interpreted in a strict, linear sequence; a cyclic process of competition and activation similar to 'competitive queuing' models of memory for sequential order (Burgess & Hitch 1992, see also Lever et al. 2014). This model presupposes that a given cluster X (or indeed a given neuron within a cluster) will only fire once during the slow cycle, something which at least approximates neurobiological plausibility in that spikes and bursts are followed by strong after-hyperolarisation currents which are normally a consequence of Ca-activated K currents which last ~100ms, hence reducing the chances of multiple within-cycle firings (Storm 1990).

Aside from hippocampal and parahippocampal θ, which other θ rhythms are candidates for linguistic feature-set construction? Recent work by Beese et al. (2017) demonstrates that θ power related to verbal working memory can be segregated into domain-general and syntax-specific components. The authors show that only syntax-specific verbal working memory modulates θ power in Broca's area, while cognitive control and domain-general memory resources call upon fronto-central sites thought to be activated by midline structures like the anterior cingulate. Hippocampal, parahippocampal and Broca's θ are likely crucial for the present θ-γ code. Moreover, as Covington and Duff (2016) review, it is increasingly being shown that 'the same hippocampal computations used in support of memory are also used for language processing', pointing to a shared neural code for particular computations. Assuming Chomsky et al.'s (2019) definition of syntactic objects as *sets of occurrences*, the notion that sets of linguistic features are sequentially activated and bound together through CFC seems compatible with these more general linguistic concepts.

Meyer (2018) reasonably speculates that CFC may be involved in 'the neural binding of discrete phonological units at different granularity levels, facilitating the establishment of a coherent percept', but, as discussed here, it is also likely that this generic process is implicated in binding and associating other features ranging far beyond phonology. In fact, Meyer's claim does not go beyond what Giraud and Poeppel (2012) already proposed. In a recent proposal, Meyer (2019) suggests that sentence-level chunking 'rests on slow electrophysiological processing cycles', storage 'is supported by the functional inhibition of working memory-related cortex through oscillatory power changes', while retrieval 'is enabled through synchronisation across cortical networks'. Meyer's proposal approaches the bare minimum level of detail which the model in this book relies on (e.g. 'slow electrophysiological processing cycles'), and Meyer's model directly follows and even mirrors earlier proposals in Murphy (2015b, 2016a, 2016c).

One of the major limitations of the Lisman and Jensen-inspired model is that it cannot easily deal with the dynamic characteristics of 'leaky' spiking neurons, and it provides no mechanism which can replace items when the θ-based buffer is complete – something with a robust neurolinguistic theory, dealing with cyclic phrasal construction and interpretation. There are a number of potential ways to deal with this limitation; one elegant approach is outlined by Koene and Hasselmo (2007), who propose a 'first-in-first-out' item replacement model through which 'distinct portions of each theta cycle in a buffer can be synchronized with distinct modes of synaptic encoding and retrieval that alternate in each cycle of a theta rhythm in the recurrent networks that receive spike input from that buffer' (2007, 1766). In contrast, the original model (see Jensen et al. 1996) relied on temporally separated periods of several seconds which are required for associative encoding or retrieval, a neurobiologically unfeasible stipulation.

The high-frequency rhythms in this model which correspond to discrete items do not occur throughout the entire θ cycle, but rather occur during 'duty cycles' of high-level activity; that is, immediately after the slow rhythm's trough as it reaches its peak, what Lakatos et al. (2005, 1907) refer to as the 'bursting phase' of the wave. Between these duty cycles, γ excitability is reduced so as to reduce overlap and interference between the distinct representations being triggered. As discussed later, parieto-occipital α rhythms play a vital role in this process through inhibiting interfering activity, such that constructing and maintaining a longer item list requires a greater reduction in α power over extended periods. It has independently been suggested that the peak of the θ cycle is optimal for memory encoding, while the trough is optimal for memory retrieval (Schapiro et al. 2017), allowing the brain to efficiently evade any interference between these two processes.

Further evidence that the θ-γ code is likely implicated in language comprehension comes from Gorišek et al.'s (2016) study of altered oscillatory activity in patients with Broca's aphasia during a verbal working memory task. Their results indicate that the stroke causing Broca's aphasia resulted in impairments to two working memory networks, each represented by θ and γ activity. Gorišek et al. make the sensible inference that these two networks, respectively, represent executive and phonological processes. They found, for instance, a total disintegration of a left fronto-centroparietal γ network in patients relative to healthy controls, reflecting a damaged phonological loop (see also Riddle et al. 2020 for causal evidence from TMS that θ is involved in control of working memory).

More recent work has also suggested that the two memory systems represented by the kind of θ-γ interactions presented here – namely, hippocampus-dependent episodic memory (θ) and neocortical semantic memory (γ) – are jointly utilised during novel word learning (Takashima et al. 2017). The authors did not analyse CFC since they used fMRI, but it is likely that this is how the two complementary memory mechanisms interfaced; indeed, Attal and Schwartz (2013) discuss an emerging body of magneto-encephalographic (MEG) methods used to achieve subcortical source localisation, with high accuracy in detecting rhythmic signatures from hippocampal, thalamic and other subcortical regions, and so an analysis of this kind could in principle be carried out (although any such advanced source localisation technique remains, as noted earlier, controversial in the literature).

A potentially interesting topic for research surrounds whether each stored γ item/representation within the slower rhythm is maintained with equal accuracy, or whether a degree of decay occurs depending on the circuits involved, and indeed whether this would influence the retrievability and interpretability of a given feature in comparison with its neighbours. Increases in γ, nested within θ, have been found across working memory maintenance tasks, including visual (Roux & Uhlhaas 2014), auditory (Kaiser et al. 2009) and somatosensory (Haegens et al. 2010), suggesting that this general mechanism can be implemented via distinct neural codes triggering domain-specific representations.

The range of potential neural codes for language is considerably broader than one might consider upon initial inspection of the typology of wave bands discussed in the literature (i.e. the δ-γ range). As Singer (2018) notes in a discussion of oscillatory temporal relations:

> The propensity of coupled oscillators to synchronise within a few oscillation cycles can be exploited to establish precise temporal relations between the discharges of the neurons participating in the respective oscillatory circuits and this provides a huge coding space provided that information can be encoded in and read out from temporal relations among the discharges of distributed neurons.

This delivers a capacity for generating precisely timed discharge sequences for controlling speech, movement and presumably many other things.

Returning again to the θ-γ code, using the classical Stroop cognitive control task to explore the neural basis of cognitive control, Verguts (2017) showed that $\{\theta(\gamma)\}$ phase–amplitude coupling is used to increase γ power in posterior processing areas via random frontal θ bursts, enhancing performance on the task. This elegant model, according to Verguts, 'solves a central computational problem for cognitive control (how to allow rapid communication between arbitrary brain areas)'. Verguts rightly objects to the current absence of oscillatory phase coding in models of cognitive control, given that this mechanism has long been known to be computationally useful in executing rapid neural binding. These findings support the present proposal that CFC is the mechanism through which linguistic information is transferred, and also support the general idea proposed by Verguts that $\{\theta(\gamma)\}$ coupling is used by the brain 'for its cognitive bookkeeping'.

The next issue which needs to be addressed concerns the regions involved in γ-itemisation during feature retrieval, a topic requiring some understanding of semantics. The semantic system in the brain could be modular and domain-specific, or interactive and domain-general. Chen et al. (2017) propose a third option, dubbed connectivity-constrained cognition (C^3). This view holds that functional specialisation in the cortex is jointly caused by learning, perceptual, linguistic and motor structures in the environment, and anatomical connectivity. This would predict a typically global response to the θ-driven process of γ-itemisation. Likewise, a number of studies using a range of technologies (electrocorticography, transcranial magnetic stimulation, lesion-symptom mapping, amongst others) have implicated the ventral anterior temporal lobe in domain-general semantic processing, and so it is highly probable that interactions between this region and parahippocampal regions are crucial for the θ-γ code.

While each γ cycle represents an individual item, each θ cycle represents the rehearsal of the set of all γ items. In the context of language, it is reasonable to hypothesise that during internal or external speech processing, the slower rhythms responsible for phonological processing (δ and θ) trigger the synchronisation of rhythms responsible for syntactic and semantic feature-set composition. θ would extract and rehearse a given feature set until another is prompted by the phonological systems; and given the findings discussed in Chapter 2, it is reasonable to assume that this process is marked by phrasal status, such that these items would oscillate at γ until a new phrase is encountered, at which point they would slow to β to be maintained as the current cognitive set (following the model proposed in Chapter 2).

The function of ultrafast γ rhythms (100–250Hz) may provide some insight at this point. While studies of the cognitive relevance of fast–spiking γ ripples are in their infancy, it is known that they are implicated in the transference of memories from the hippocampus to the neocortex for permanent storage (Buzsáki 2010). The relevance of this function for language may arise during post-stimuli lexical storage, as in the case of early language acquisition, and it is possible to imagine a more direct derivational purpose for linguistic phrasal construction and interpretation.

Motivations for assuming that the stored γ-individuated features are widely distributed across the cortex come, most recently, from Keene et al. (2016). This study of object-context associations in rats showed that all task dimensions (object position, identity and context) were encoded in every parahippocampal processing stream they investigated: the medial entorhinal cortex, the lateral entorhinal cortex and the perirhinal cortex. This degree of representational diversity across the hippocampus was present even at the single-cell level; neurons traditionally assumed to be 'spatial' cells (e.g. grid cells) were often involved in object identity, in the same way that the perhaps ill-named 'place cells' can also be involved in object encoding. It is therefore likely that semantic features triggered during sentence comprehension are also widely distributed and not specified to a particular language-relevant cortical or sub-cortical region.

With respect to the distributed, cross-cortical nature of the γ-itemisation process involved in the present θ-γ code, other recent work is highly relevant. Testing a number of congenitally blind individuals during the performance of a property-generation task with concrete nouns, Handjaras et al. (2016) discovered patterns of activity within a large semantic network comprised of parahippocampal, lateral occipital, temporo-parietal-occipital and inferior parietal cortices, which was independent of the presentation modality (visual or auditory). These regions are largely known to be language-relevant with respect to semantic composition. Handjaras et al. (2016, 232) concluded that 'conceptual knowledge in the human brain relies on a distributed, modality-independent cortical representation that integrates the partial category and modality specific information retained at a regional level'.

More recent evidence in support of the model proposed in this book comes from Pu et al. (2020). These authors note that since θ has been implicated in memory and navigation, but also recently in language processing, this suggests 'a shared neurophysiological mechanism between language and memory. However, it remains to be established what specific roles hippocampal theta oscillatons may play in language.' They discovered, as predicted here and in Benítez-Burraco and Murphy (2019), that hippocampal θ indexes specifically lexico-semantic processing, rather than more general sentential processing. Moreover, Pu et al. (2020) found transient θ phase coupling between hippocampus and left superior temporal gyrus both during semantically correct and incorrect sentence endings, which following the model presented here would indicate a general interface between lexico-semantic memory and phrase structure-building processes.

How is this relevant to linguistic theory? Consider Chomsky's (2019b) suggestion that, following much recent work in generative morphology (and also syntax, for instance Adger 2013), many syntactic operations likely take place in the lexicon itself, before any workspaces are even constructed. That is to say, one of the first operations in language comprehension (and also production) is to merge a bare lexical Root (e.g. MAN) with a category, as in <*n*, R>. This suggestion departs quite radically from traditional frameworks for language architecture, such as the tripartite division between *lexicon, generative component* and *representing component* in Lewis (1969, 165). From these observations, we would therefore predict that the CFC properties outlined in this book take place in temporal 'lexicon' areas at very early stages, before progressing anteriorly (see Section 3.7 for a return to these themes). Quian Quiroga (2012) discusses the nature of 'concept cells' (formerly termed 'Jennifer Aniston neurons', which respond to specific persons or objects) in the medial temporal lobe, and argues that the sparse, explicit and abstract representation of these neurons is crucial for declarative memory functions (memories of facts and events), but these features are also likely an explanation for the robust medial temporal activation found during syntactic and semantic processing (in particular, the rhinal cortex and hippocampus). *Jennifer Aniston* is a relatively robust and invariant concept, altering very little with age, but so are lexical Roots like MAN and BOAT. While the medial temporal lobe may store invariant and abstract representational information ('concepts'), other details and features are likely stored cross-cortically, depending on the type of information demanded by the language system for real-time extraction. Medial temporal lobe neurons (with the exception of neurons in parahippo-campal cortex) fire to pictures of persons as well as to their written and spoken names (Quian Quiroga et al. 2009). While the anterior temporal 'hub' appears to be the major site for lexical representations, the same principles likely apply: neurons in the medial temporal lobe receive input from cross-cortical areas supplying specific representational details, linking them to a single concept (aiding, for instance, the learning of people's names, involving the association of two types of data: linguistic and visual).

A useful intervention from Clarke (2015, 416) can set these findings in an appropriate context:

While [we are] beginning to unravel the information processing states associated with transitions and early interplays between perception and semantics, many important aspects of meaningful object recognition remain unclear – such as the role of network connectivity in information transitions and the functional role of different oscillatory frequencies.

3.1.2   Hub, Spoke and Causation

The potential importance of the 'hub and spoke model' of semantic representation should also be addressed here. This model assumes that the multimodel features of objects are extracted from modality-specific 'spokes' across the cortex (in particular, occipital and motor regions) by an anterior temporal lobe 'hub'. Mollo et al.'s (2017) MEG study of manmade and animal concepts supports this model; more specifically, their results suggest that 'conceptual identification emerges from the simultaneous recruitment of hub and spoke sites', rather than extraction preceding identification in the anterior temporal lobe. The rapid flashes of activation throughout the entire hub and spoke system found by Mollo et al. are something of an indication that the language system – relying as it does on the syntax-semantics interface – is also richly dynamic and involves large-scale activations, rather than sequential, localised activation for specific linguistic computations such as merging, moving and chunking lexical features, as in many current, Grodzinsky-inspired models.

$\{\theta(\gamma)\}$ coupling in entorhino-hippocampal regions has been shown to be crucial for memory recall (Schomburg et al. 2014) and what Headley and Paré

(2017) refer to as 'the efficacious encoding and retrieval of declarative and procedural memories'. Moving somewhat beyond this, reasons to believe that the $\{\theta(\gamma)\}$ code is causally implicated in memory retrieval and maintenance (and does not simply correlate with some experimental manipulation) come from Vosskuhl et al.'s (2015) use of transcranial alternating current stimulation (tACS) to decrease participant's θ such that the $\theta{:}\gamma$ ratio changed and an abnormally large number of γ cycles could be nested within θ. This resulted in enhanced short-term memory performance (i.e. the storage of information, but not the manipulation of a memorised set of items); however, working memory operations themselves (i.e. manipulation of items) were not affected, neither during nor after stimulation. This suggests that the CFC documented in memory tasks is not epiphenomenal but is rather representative of a coding scheme and the physical limitations of cognition. Given what has been reviewed earlier, the reason why working memory operations were not affected by θ modulation may be a result of the fact that this process does not influence the structure of γ-itemisation nor does it change the topology of the derived feature-set, it merely expands it. Chuderski and Andrelczyk (2015) have also demonstrated that enhanced coupling of γ and θ rhythms – leading to a maximisation of γ oscillations in a single θ cycle – is related to enhanced performance in fluid intelligence tasks. Lastly, Fernández-Ruiz et al. (2019) looked at the rat brain and showed that learning and correct recall in spatial memory tasks were associated with extended sharp wave ripples; artificially prolonging these ripples improved working memory performance, suggesting again a causal role for these rhythms in representational maintenance.

It should be noted, however, that since tACS is a form of transcranial electric stimulation (tES), it typically only affects 'subthreshold' local field potentials (as opposed to transcranial magnetic stimulation, which can induce action potentials, i.e. 'suprathreshold'). As such, while forms of transcranial magnetic stimulation like repetitive TMS (rTMS) can induce artificial neural activity, forms of tES can only modulate ongoing activity through resonance (Hanslmayr et al. 2019). For instance, Hanslmayr et al. (2014) used simulta- neous electroencephalographic (EEG) recordings to show that 5Hz rTMS enhances θ oscillations during stimulation, with these oscillations persisting for at least a couple of cycles after stimulation ended (what is known as an entrainment echo). Nevertheless, although tES effects are more delicate than TMS, tES allows a clearer test of oscillatory entrainment. An important task for future research is to discover ways to increase the efficacy of tES stimulation approaches.

Following directly on from Vosskuhl et al.'s (2015) seminal study, Wolinski et al. (2018) conducted a visuospatial working memory task, delivering tACS at both slow (4Hz) and fast (7Hz) θ along with a placebo condition. In their task, coloured squares were presented in both visual hemispheres and participants had to retain items either in their left or right field and compared to a probe. As such, left parietal tACS application should have caused effects in trials in which coloured squares in the right visual hemifield (i.e. contralateral to the stimulation) had to be retained. The authors only reported modulation of working memory capacity for the visual hemifield contralateral to stimulation, and compared to placebo, tACS at 4Hz led to increased working memory capacity, while tACS at 7Hz had a detrimental impact on working memory capacity. This provides further evidence that slower θ cycles permit a larger number of nested representations.

In addition, slower θ waves would presumably improve the fidelity of the representations accessed, given the greater number of γ bursts nested. However, a certain trade-off is also at play: There would also be a slower rate of memory re-activation for a sequence of items if the θ waves are long, since slower waves would need more time before all memory items are represented. As such, a careful balancing act needs to be played, whereby the brain selects an appropriate representational fidelity whilst also trying to maximise reactivation speeds. Consequently, it is likely not strictly true that working memory is necessarily limited to a fixed number, but rather that cognitive resources need to be allocated appropriately and responsibly if a sufficient number of sub-features of items are to be retained over successive cycles without decaying rapidly. Therefore, upwards of 10, 15 or a greater number of items could be retained in working memory, but only a small number of features of these items would be retained, and the likelihood of substantial decay would increase over time (see Bays 2015 for a neurobiological model of how these shared cognitive resources are implemented). This also leads to the prediction that slower γ waves represent more fine-grained, complex representations.

Recent work suggests that phase resetting, a mechanism closely related to CFC, is not specifically involved in memory information processing but is rather responsible for 'a more general synchronizing event induced by task relevant stimuli' (Kleen et al. 2016, 11) and is involved in synchronising networks involved in the same task. Phase resetting can also occur at multiple frequencies in the temporal lobe (Rizzuto et al. 2006), with the range of phase resettings available potentially reflecting the extent to which rhythms encoding distinct information from different regions can be synchronised. Since human language is representationally rich enough to combine information from a number of distinct domains (syntax, semantics, phonology, pragmatics), phase resetting in the temporal lobe and other language-relevant regions will likely be fruitful avenues of experimental investigation. In particular, the phasal properties of the left temporal lobe will be of interest given recent fMRI findings that certain areas of this region are implicated in hierarchical syntactic representations – something which is not the case, somewhat surprisingly, for the left inferior frontal gyrus, according to data in Brennan et al. (2016).

Working memory capacity also appears to be strongly limited purely in terms of the number of objects maintained, and is only negligibly modulated by how many features each individual object contains (Cowan et al. 2013). While of great interest to psychologists, this finding also brings with it certain directions for neurolinguists. For instance, it suggests that the CFCs used here to account for basic elements of phrasal construction are governed largely by the slower rhythms responsible for modulating faster rhythms storing language-relevant features, and that the properties of these faster rhythms will present only minor interference effects. It suggests also that the number of faster rhythms entrained to a slower rhythm (with each fast rhythm storing a discrete representation) only weakly affects the more global computations of object construction and maintenance. This form of 'top-down' analysis allows us to use psychological data to generate certain testable predictions for lower-level neural processes.

Having covered earlier some of the basic neurochemistry behind γ clusters, we will now turn to the implementational basis of θ, a clear requirement if a greater understanding of the causal role of oscillations is to develop. Since θ rhythms are generated by an interplay between glutamatergic and GABAergic neurons, they are likely modulated by the septum, which provides cholinergic inputs to GABAergic inputs, therefore acting as a pacemaker of θ oscillations (Pignatelli et al. 2012). This process of serial activation of features may also be involved in object and concept processing, with recent work suggesting that a momentary glance at an object yields a different conceptual representation than a longer, more considered look; different features of the object are activated in the latter scenario as time progresses (Yee & Thompson-Schill 2016; see also Balaban & Luria 2016 for evidence that visual object representations are modified by the context they are presented in). While $\{\theta(\gamma)\}$ coupling is likely the major mechanism responsible for linguistic feature-set composition, both animal and human studies have revealed that γ couples to the phase of α and β (Canolty et al. 2006; Ketz et al. 2015), so it is possible that $\{\alpha(\gamma)\}$ coupling is also involved in some aspects of phrase structure building (perhaps in the initial stages of semantic feature activation as suggested in Chapter 2, due to the role of α in attentional mechanisms). Lastly, further evidence for the current model can be found in Doesburg et al. (2012), whose verb generation experimental task led to increased γ phase-locked to slower cortical θ rhythms.

Overall, there are an increasing number of reasons to reserve a role for γ and θ interactions in language processing.

3.2   Encoding Phrasal Units

I have so far proposed that labelling is initiated via the slowing down of γ to β followed by {δ(β)} coupling. This takes care of the maintenance aspect of labelling (keeping a multi-unit complex in memory), but what of the identity attribution aspect, which assigns to a constructed complex a syntactic identity? Building on the earlier suggestions, this section will move away from the faster oscillatory frequencies and suggest that the amplitude of θ (and possibly also the phase, depending on the region) is in turn coupled with the phase of δ. We will then progress to certain broader implications for the field.

3.2.1   What We Talk About When We Talk About δ

The reasons for assuming a role for slower oscillatory interactions in language range across a number of domains. For instance, although phase–amplitude coupling is most commonly found between θ and γ, recent work suggests that θ can also entrain to δ in the human brain (Miller et al. 2010; Maris et al. 2011) and that there is, in turn, a broader range of CFC relations in the human brain relative to non-human primates, with the cortex exhibiting a species-specific level of richness in its CFCs (Maris et al. 2016). Given experimental findings that these two slow rhythms entrain to the full range of hierarchical linguistic structures from syllables to phrases and sentences (Ding et al. 2016), the discovery of human-specific {δ(θ)} phase–amplitude coupling is potentially of great significance, in particular when trying to ground the present Labelling Hypothesis.

More recently, Mariscal et al. (2019) have documented developmental changes in EEG phase–amplitude coupling over the first three years of life, discovering that frontal and occipital α-γ coupling, θ-γ coupling, θ-β coupling and δ-γ coupling increases with age. Changes in δ-γ coupling were found mostly in frontal sites. The authors found coupling across the whole scalp, suggesting a relatively ubiquitous presence of coupling. The changes in θ-β coupling might index (amongst other things) the maturation of the interface between the workspace and syntax, the changes in θ-γ coupling likely index a maturing working memory capacity, while δ-γ changes may index a maturing combinatorial capacity (based on the findings that δ-γ coupling is involved in fluid intelligence and increases with the number of predicates bound to a word, as reviewed later; Brennan & Martin 2019; Gągol et al. 2018). Given that the basic phrase structure-generating (labelling) capacity is typically assumed to have matured very early on in infancy, this likely explains why across the three-year period δ-θ coupling did not significantly change. Their findings also indicate that feedforward (bottom-up) information is indexed by γ increases at the slow wave *peak* in occipital regions, while feedback (top-down) information is indexed by γ increases at the slow peak *trough* in frontal regions. The implications of this cross-phasal information distribution model should be explored in future electrophysiological analyses of neurolinguistic datasets (i.e. does the brain optimise representational search via cross-phasal distribution of γ-itemisation peaks?).

To my knowledge, Lakatos et al. (2005) were the first to clearly show the existence of δ-θ and θ-γ phase amplitude coupling (in macaque monkeys in auditory cortex), associating them purely with stimulus-related responses in neuronal assemblies. They propose the *oscillatory hierarchy hypothesis*, which simply states that 'the amplitude of the oscillations at each characteristic frequency (gamma, theta, etc.) is modulated by the oscillatory phase of a local lower frequency oscillation' (Lakatos et al. 2005, 1904). This *oscillatory hierarchy hypothesis* naturally forms the backbone of much of what this book explores.

Evidence that $\{\delta(\theta)\}$ coupling is involved in large-scale neuronal network coordination relevant to language comes from findings that $\{\delta(\theta)\}$ phase synchronisation coordinates interactions between deep and superficial cortical layers, modifying learning processes (Carracedo et al. 2013). In addition, while the rat globus pallidus can nest β and γ rhythms within a slower δ rhythm, Dejean et al.'s (2011) electrode recordings of local field potentials indicated that when such nesting did occur, β and γ were negatively correlated and at anti-phase, with the phase positions of both the β and γ clusters being significantly different. The rat oscillome and its intrinsic rhythmic hierarchies may exhibit reduced nesting capabilities relative to the human oscillome – and, indeed, relative to the primate oscillome more generally, given Charvet et al.'s (2016) findings of expanded anterior to posterior cortico-cortical tracts in primates relative to other mammals. These species-specific oscillatory interactions may lay the foundations of Hauser and Watumull's (2017) Universal Generative Faculty common to language, mathematics, morality and music. Greater δ power has also been linked to enhanced subcortical activity (Gray 1982), and given the role of subcortical structures in language, discussed earlier, the importance of δ likely extends beyond its most basic role in modulating global coherence. These proposals are aligned well with Chuderski's (2016, 1) exploration of fluid intelligence and neural oscillations, which concurs that '[c]ross-frequency coupling may serve as the optimal level of description of neurocognitive processes, integrating their genetic, structural, neurochemical, and bioelectrical underlying factors with explanations in terms of cognitive operations driven by neuronal oscillations'.

As mentioned, I am claiming here that the above-cited $\{\theta(\gamma/\beta)\}$ feature-set multiplexing algorithm can itself be embedded within δ cycles originating within regions shown to entrain to hierarchical linguistic structures and which can also oscillate at slow δ frequencies, namely the superior temporal gyrus and left inferior frontal cortex. This additional layer of nesting would then give rise to the additional layer of hierarchy seen in human syntax, which goes beyond both the phonological syntax of birdsong and the semantically atomic structure of primate call systems.

Indeed, phase–amplitude coupling is itself not unique to language, let alone humans, being involved in perception, decision-making and navigation (Lakatos et al. 2005; Kepecs et al. 2006), and so the interactions between distinct types of CFCs and the representations they manipulate are instead the likely source of language-specific combinatorial capacities. There is a growing consensus that phase–amplitude coupling can support the phase coding of neural representations through, for instance, the categorisation of visual objects (Watrous et al. 2015), and given the inherently semantic nature of the categorisation processes documented by Watrous et al. – faces, tools, houses and scenes – it would be somewhat surprising if this form of CFC is not also involved in the interpretation of linguistic structures. As the authors of the study put it, exploring CFC 'may provide new avenues for decoding the human representational system'.

These ideas reflect another trend in the recent literature: δ used to be almost solely implicated in deep sleep, but its function in long-range coordination of neural processing has recently been discovered (Leszczyński et al. 2015). Research into human δ dates back at least to 1985, when its involvement in perception, attention and working memory was shown (Başar & Stampfer 1985), but it appears that we are only just beginning to scratch the surface of the computational properties of δ and its role in higher cognition. It will be important to focus on the regions of oscillatory generation, particular phasal properties, CFCs, and other details of oscillatory dynamics when investigating language, since δ seems to be implicated in a variety of behaviours and cognitive faculties; indeed, {δ(β)} coupling has even been implicated by Najjar and Brooker (2017) in paternal (but not maternal) caregiving behaviours. The multiplicity of functions each oscillatory band appears to have led Karakaş and Barry (2017) to suggest that researchers pay attention to the following parameters: 'enhancement, attenuation, blocking, duration (prolongation), latency, time-locking, phase-locking and frequency-locking of the oscillations'.

Nevertheless, there is little doubt that oscillatory interactions are responsible for a range of memory and attentional processes. Leszczyński et al. (2015) conducted two independent experiments examining working memory maintenance using intracranial EEG. They found that in visual working memory tasks periods of memory activation are correlated with load-dependent α power reductions and low levels of CFC, and that these occurred in an interleaved manner with load-independent high α levels and CFC. Fluctuations between the two periods were a strong predictor of successful performance and were phase-locked to δ. Weaker levels of {δ(α)} CFC and load-dependent hippo-campal disinhibition during extended list construction is moreover consistent with the idea that the hippocampus plays an important role in representing long sequences. One particular question for future research is whether this mechanism is implicated in linguistic phrasal and sentential memory, and is not simply exclusive to the hippocampus.

Are there any other indications that δ may be implicated in phrase structure building? In naturalistic speech, phrase duration appears to be at around two to three seconds (Vollrath et al. 1992) and anything lasting longer usually gets chunked by comprehenders into newly formed phrases (Webman-Shafran & Fodor 2015). Interestingly, this maps onto the phase of δ, suggesting that this rhythm either exploits the periodicity of speech patterns to generate phrasal interpretations or the rhythm itself imposes direct preferences on language processing and phrasal generation. The elementary role attributed in the present model to δ in phrase structure building – regardless of its more complex phase-coupling relations – becomes even more justified through Meyer et al.'s (2017) EEG study of phrasal grouping biases, which demonstrated that units inter-preted as phrases modulated δ activity during auditory language comprehen-sion. Going somewhat beyond other recent findings (e.g. those reported in Ding et al. 2016), Meyer et al. (2017) suggest that δ rhythms provide an 'internal linguistic searchlight' which aids the construction of linguistic phrases. Taking this into account, along with the literature discussed earlier, δ rhythms can at the most general level be described as reflecting top-down processes. But this merely begs the question: What are the neurocomputational roles of such rhythms, and how do these distinct oscillations operate within a more global system of information transmission? (Note that the proposal of an 'internal linguistic searchlight' is of similar theoretical granularity as Bonhage et al.'s (2017) suggestion earlier that δ modulations 'reflect chunking processes'). Perhaps more useful directions in this respect come from Güntekin and Başar's (2016) comprehensive review of evoked and event-related δ responses in humans, which indicates that this rhythm seems to be largely implicated in attentional mechanisms and that a decrease in global δ may even constitute a marker of cognitive dysfunction, with decreased δ being found in mild cogni-tive impairment (MGI), Alzheimer's, schizophrenia and Dipolar disorder in a range of cognitive tasks such as visual and auditory oddball tasks. Decomposing the role of δ into cognitive sub-operations will likely be a more fruitful enterprise than top-down experimental studies when it comes to exposing the oscillatory logic of neural computation.

Coinciding somewhat with these findings, Headley and Paré (2017) con-ducted a large-scale review of the oscillatory memory literature in humans. In order to account for differences in oscillatory activity in memory-relevant regions during sleep (i.e. some forms of memory are sensitive to slow-wave sleep, others REM), they suggest that while θ rhythms seem responsible for consolidating procedural memories during sleep (a proposal supported by Khodagholy et al. 2017, who showed that declarative memory consolidation in rats involves fast γ phase-phase coupling between hippocampal and neocortical regions, in particular medial prefrontal and posterior parietal regions), the literature indicates that δ rhythms during slow-wave sleep additionally promote the consolidation of declarative memories. Given the presently proposed role of δ in phrasal – and, hence, sentential and propositional – construction and interpretation, it is possible that during sleep the language system is active in this declarative consolidation process, what with the crucial role of language in the generation of facts and events, the core of declarative memory. Indeed, the potential role of linguistic computations in declarative consolidation is easy to square with the well-known interactions between the hippocampus and cortical δ rhythms (Hahn et al. 2006). It would be of interest for future research to examine the CFC during declarative consolidation to examine any potential similarities with language processing. I first proposed this idea in Murphy (2018b) (circulated in summer 2017), and the first steps in this direction subsequently came from Cross et al. (2018), who hypothesise that sleep-dependent consolidation of sentence-level combinatorics is implemented via slow neocortical δ modulations, although these ideas are yet to be experimentally tested (the complete model of sentence comprehension presented by Cross et al. 2018 is remarkably close to the one presented in Murphy 2016a, which they cite as a 'similar perspective'). It may well be that once modern humans moved away from sleeping in trees and gradually began to sleep on the ground (a process shown to result in longer, more peaceful periods of sleep), their ability to consolidate the newly evolved combinatorial processes of language were enhanced as a corollary. In addition, recent advances in closed-loop feedback inactivation experiments are making headway in determining the basis of memory consolidation and showing that θ has a causal role in spatial memory 're-play' (Zielinski et al. 2020); shifting the focus of these experiments to linguistic short-term memory and the particular rhythms documented here may well break new ground in improving our understanding of the consolidation of sentential processing.

Considering Ding et al.'s (2016) finding of (possible) 2Hz entrainment to phrases, and 1Hz entrainment to sentences, it is of interest that phase–amplitude coupling increases when the lower-frequency power decreases (Park et al. 2016), suggesting that larger linguistic units (sentences relative to phrases, and phrases relative to words) may require increased coupling with the faster rhythms they are paired with, likely as a function of the number of linguistic features/representations being constructed and maintained. When subjects were asked to ignore an upcoming visual item, Park et al. (2016) found stronger α power in visual cortex compared to when subjects were asked to remember it.

In their 'Remember' condition, during low α, phase–amplitude coupling was stronger.

More recently, and following on from themes in the previous chapter, Tavano et al. (2020) have further dissociated entrainment from internal synchrony. While low δ rhythms likely index a combination of grammatical knowledge and more generic speech tracking, the authors found that repetition of abstract syntactic categories generated a harmonic structure of their periodic appearance unconnected to stimulus rate, separating endogenous from exogenous rhythms in the δ band. The strength of harmonic structures predicted the degree to which their native German-speaking participants were sensitive to word order violations, and so their δ responses importantly indexed the final point of linguistic parsing, but not the real-time temporal unfolding of syntactic structure building and lexico-semantic combinatorics. For these latter processes, it may be that the mechanisms explored in this book (e.g. CFC; see also Section 3.2.3 and 3.7.1) will be of more direct relevance than entrainment or structure-aligned synchrony, as I have argued here. For an excellent, recent review of the electrophysiology of sentence processing which also discusses some more traditional issues pertaining to the relation between oscillations and event-related potentials (which seem to be organised by oscillatory phase; e.g. the N400 is seen as reflecting δ phase-resetting; van Petten & Luka 2006), see Martorell et al. (2020).

The literature on the role of δ in language processing is also rapidly expanding. In a recent study of acoustic periodicity and intelligibility in speech, Steinmetzger and Rosen (2017) found global increases in δ in response to periodic intelligible speech (sentences such as 'Say it slowly but make it ring clear') and conclude that 'delta oscillations are an indicator of successful speech understanding'. They provide no mechanistic basis for this but provide a psychoacoustic explanation, although their findings can be incorporated into the present model, with δ increases being responsible for constructing extended phrases and additional neurocomputational resources being recruited to interpret forms of speech which sound less natural than aperiodic speech. Interestingly, Steinmetzger and Rosen found these δ responses only at around 1000ms after the onset of intelligible periodic sentences (with average sentences being 2000ms), an expected result if a full phrasal status had not been constructed until around this half-way point in the sentence. This δ rhythm was found at a number of electrode sites, but only reached statistical significance at the frontal scalp region. Furthermore, δ power increases in the latter half of the stimulus window were also observed in the other two intelligible experimental conditions (aperiodic speech, and mixed periodic and aperiodic). The authors conclude that 'this [δ power] effect is not confined to the unnatural sounding periodic condition' (2017, 180). But we can add a further conclusion: the present δ-based phrase structure building multiplexing algorithm gains further experimental support from these commonly found δ power increases.

In a similar connection, Assaneo and Poeppel (2018) show that the temporal patterns of speech likely emerge as a direct consequence of the intrinsic oscillatory rhythms of cortical areas (namely, auditory and speech-motor brain regions). They measured oscillatory synchronisation between auditory and speech-motor regions while participants listened to syllables of various rates. Synchronisation was only significant over a restricted range and was enhanced at ~4.5Hz, a value compatible with the mean syllable rate across languages. This suggests that oscillations directly impact speech patterns.

Are there any other indications that δ is involved in the more complex syntactic and semantic processes involved in language comprehension? Returning to a study mentioned earlier, Di Liberto et al. (2018) showed that speech envelope tracking was more enhanced due to prior knowledge (i.e. when semantic context is presented) in the δ band compared to the θ band, with δ covering the slower modulations of meaningful phrases and sentences. This supports the idea proposed here that θ plays a more mechanistic role in constructing linguistic feature-sets while δ indexes interpretative processes.

Other recent experimental work can enrich our understanding of the importance of δ. Ohki et al. (2016) acquired MEG data from fifteen healthy subjects performing an audiovisual speech matching task, in which they were exposed either to sounds matching or differing from particular lip movements. They applied phase–amplitude coupling and imaginary coherence measurements to their regions of interest in the temporal pole, and found prominent δ power and strong {δ(β)} phase–amplitude coupling, suggesting that the integration of linguistic and non-linguistic sensory information is mediated through δ-phase coherence. The detection of this oscillatory coupling may result in part from the role of β in storing linguistic structures in memory, which may need to be paired with visual representations through CFC. It is likely that δ is also involved in other aspects of multisensory linguistic processing due to its ability to manipulate global coherence, an intuition awaiting further experimental work.

For now, we can tentatively conclude that Ghirlanda et al.'s (2017) suggestion – that the major species-defining feature of humans is a particular way of executing 'the coding of information' – is not only justifiable, but may also be most clearly exhibited in the construction of hierarchical phrase structure through the oscillatory interactions proposed here. Indeed, these authors tested a mathematical model of non-human sequence discrimination, collating the results of 108 experiments. Their model suggested that 'animals represent sequences as unstructured collections of memory traces', and the results of the model predicted non-human performance with only 5.9 per cent mean absolute error. If the enhanced coding of sequential memory is a human-specific trait, and if the construction of hierarchical phrase structure yields numerous core features of event semantics (Pietroski 2018), then it is likely that the emergence of the neural underpinnings of labelling aided the maintenance and categorisation not simply of linguistic sequences, but of sequences more generally, including mathematical, musical and other elements interfacing with the Universal Generative Faculty. For instance, the output of many mathematical computations depends on the order of operations executed – one cannot simply divide, multiply and subtract in any order and generate the same outcome – and the order of musical notes also influences aesthetic quality.

To summarise, empirical and conceptual motivations have been presented to defend the idea that δ-θ interregional phase–amplitude coupling (ir-PAC) constructs multiple sets of linguistic syntactic and semantic features. This occurs when the phase of δ is synchronised with the amplitude of θ. Causal directionality remains an open issue, and while the phase typically influences the amplitude in standardly documented PAC, certain cases of θ-γ coupling appear to exhibit unidirectional prefrontal-hippocampal cortex coupling from γ activity to θ activity (Nandi et al. 2019; relatedly, Fellner et al. 2019 also discovered that in memory encoding γ increases are found to occur significantly earlier than paired θ power decreases). Nandi et al. (2019, 8) summarise their findings about ir-PAC as follows: 'Assuming that high-gamma reflect population spiking [...] and that low frequency oscillations (e.g., theta) reflect somatic/dendritic processing [...] we conclude that ir-PAC [...] connects the output of a driver and the input of a receiver network.' These dynamics also rely on distinct neurochemical substrates: δ is generated in the thalamus and neocortex by synaptically coupled bursting neurons operating in networks controlled by $GABA_B$ receptor-mediated synaptic inhibition; θ is generated by fast-slow interactions of $GABA_A$ receptor-mediated inhibitory synaptic inputs to principal cells (see Adams et al. 2019 for review). Lastly, the full computational power of the present model is achieved via distinct β and γ sources also being coupled with θ (e.g. θ-γ phase–amplitude coupling) for, respectively, syntactic prediction and conceptual binding. Figure 3.1 outlines the basic structure of this oscillatory model. Note that θ in Figure 3.1 could also be conceived as θ/α (specifically 7–13Hz) due to Bahramisharif et al.'s (2018) findings about the cortical phase code for working memory, but the strict θ range is the more commonly supported band. Due to the complexity of cortical layers, modulations in γ amplitude could emerge from many different cell types with distinct memory-related functions during retrieval and maintenance; while this book is primarily concerned with the oscillatory basis of language, these lower-level concerns will be picked up in subsequent sections. In addition, while the role of β in linguistic prediction has been documented quite robustly (e.g. Armeni et al. 2019), this is not an uncontroversial stance (e.g. Terporten et al. 2019), and it currently remains an open question how linguistic prediction can be implemented.

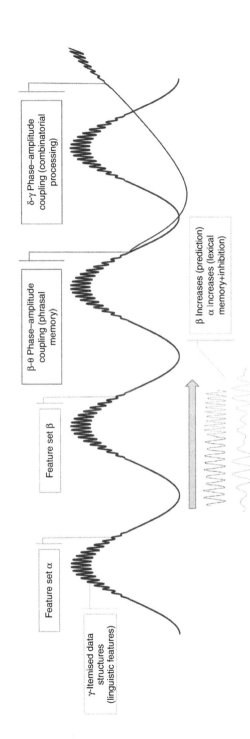

Figure 3.1 A neural code for language, representing the various cross-frequency coupling interactions proposed here to implement hierarchical phrase structure building. To contrast this with the initial development of the current model, compare with Murphy (2016c, 11, fig. 1)

3.2.2   The Evolution of Language

Returning to some earlier concerns, given the close similarity in 'semantics' exhibited between humans and other primates, it is likely that no substantial changes needed to occur in this domain in order for language to emerge and the human-specific computational properties of δ outlined earlier to develop, forming a core part of the present Labelling Hypothesis. It is more likely that slight genetic changes reorganising features of the regions oscillating at δ and those coupled to it were responsible for the emergence of language. Likewise, the research in Moore (2017, 2018) concerning intentional communication, which decomposes traditional Gricean notions into less complex versions and demonstrates that these simpler concepts can provide the same level of explanatory adequacy whilst also bridging the gap between human and non-human primate communication. Considering the consensus from biology, 'phenotypic novelty is largely reorganisational rather than a product of innovative genes' (West-Eberhard 2003), and so it is highly probable that only minor genome-oscillome modifications were required to reorganise the brain in such a way to permit the emergence of hierarchical phrase structures.

Following the present oscillatory model, it seems reasonable to hypothesise that the $\{\theta(\gamma)\}$ feature-sets invoked here ultimately shift to $\{\delta\{\theta(\beta/\gamma)\}\}$ phrasal/labelled units. An important question, which must be addressed in future experimental work, is how this shift occurs. There appear to be two options: Either the γ-itemised clusters first slow to β before the $\{\theta(\beta)\}$ complex is nested within δ or the multiplexed $\{\theta(\gamma)\}$ units are embedded first and the items slowed to β at a later point. Fewer β-itemised clusters would be able to phase-lock to θ due to the size of each β cycle (around three β cycles per θ cycle), potentially accounting for the unequal ratio between feature-sets responsible for determining phrasal status and feature-sets which perform other roles with respect to syntactic function (e.g. Tense features) and content (e.g. lexical features). Indeed, both routes may be taken under different scenarios. In the case of an ambiguously labelled phrase, it may be that γ is not slowed to β until after phase-entrainment to δ has taken place when the precise interpretation is fixed.

Alternatively, it may be that only some γ-itemised clusters slow to β, namely those clusters responsible for storing the features determining the phrasal/labelled status of a given δ-entrained set. Generative grammar has long suggested that what determines the label of a given set of lexical items is only a subset of the entire feature complex, and so it is possible that the language system is composed of two simultaneously entrained δ and θ complexes; β labelling features and γ non-labelling features. Pefkou et al. (2017) found that both θ and γ were sensitive to syllable rate, but only β power was modulated by comprehension rates and was insensitive to syllabic structure. This suggests that θ and γ play a more mechanistic role in feature-set construction while β does indeed appear to be involved in the tracking or prediction of semantic or phrasal identity.

This labelling/non-labelling distinction can also be supported by more traditional psycholinguistic studies. Parsing research by Momma (2016) investigating the time course of syntactic priming effects has even suggested that structure-building units during production are very small (facilitation as a result of priming localises to the primed constituent), going against much of the production literature which claims that pre-formed templates are large. The aforementioned basic oscillomic schema (accounting only for labelled units) may therefore carry considerable explanatory reach both in terms of production and comprehension.

θ power has also been found to increase after the presentation of each word in a sentence, and more specifically θ power is modulated by the position of a word within a sentence, indicating that θ power during sentence comprehension is somehow linked to higher-order processes such as phrase formation (Bastiaansen et al. 2002), with the model proposed here answering the 'somehow' with {δ(θ)} coupling. Further reasons to believe that δ-θ interactions are involved in phrase structure building come from Roehm et al. (2007), who showed that syntactic word order reanalysis resulted in δ and θ increases (see also Brilmayer et al. 2017). Meyer and Gumbert (2018) also performed an auditory EEG study utilising uniformly distributed morphosyntactic violations across natural sentences, with their results providing evidence that the synchronisation of electrophysiological responses at δ to speech implicitly aligns neural excitability with syntactic information. A topic for future research concerns the physiological properties of {δ(θ)} and {θ(γ)} coupling, their developmental profile, and whether their emergence can be explained within the frameworks presented here (e.g. the globularity hypothesis and empirically motivated claims about human-specific CFCs). Hunt et al. (2016) probed the relationship between grey matter myelination and neural oscillations and demonstrated a significant correlation, with this being strong for networks mediated by β, becoming even stronger during CFC. Given the primary role of coupling in the present model, it seems that myeloarchitecture and its support for cross-frequency connectivity should be a major focal point for future neurochemical enquiry. In addition, glial cells have been shown to produce slow oscillations (Amzica 2002) while long-lasting hyperpolarisations generated by pyramidal neurons have been shown to generate δ rhythms (Steriade 1993), but our understanding of the neurophysiological basis of these rhythms remains fairly imprecise.

Other indications that human-specific neural features are relevant to language evolution come from a review conducted by Lucas and Hardin (2017) exploring Slit-Robo GTPase-activating proteins (srGAPs) and their ability to influence membrane dynamics. They explain how '[g]ene duplication of the human-specific paralog of srGAP2 has resulted in srGAP2 family proteins that may have increased the density of dendritic spines and promoted neoteny of the human brain during crucial periods of human evolution'. The functional role of these particular forms of spine density increases in higher cognition may illuminate some questions regarding the evolution of neural dynamics.

Halgren et al. (2017) also revealed that in the human brain cortical δ phase 'robustly modulates theta power, with an increase in theta-band power during the falling phase of the ongoing delta rhythm'. Interestingly, both δ and θ rhythms in upper, superficial cortical layers modulated α, β and γ during wakefulness and sleep, suggesting a maximal capacity for the human cortex to modulate the full roster of brain rhythms relevant for language. The presently proposed neural code for language is also consistent with a circuit model of cortical integration in which deep fast activity regulates superficial slow rhythms (of the kind proposed in Jiang et al. 2015).

Further reasons to assume that the regional oscillatory properties reviewed here are accurate comes from Vidaurre et al. (2018), who used MEG to examine the power and phase-coupling connectivity of brain-wide networks during rest in humans. The brain states for higher-order cognitive networks were documented and divided into anterior and posterior networks. Both networks exhibited high power and coherence in the α range (posterior) and δ/θ range (anterior), findings which map on to the rhythmic profiles presented here. In particular, the extent of δ/θ phase-coupling in the anterior brain network included a clear range from anterior temporal regions to inferior frontal regions, which provides strong evidence for the relevance of δ-θ coupling for higher cognition. More recently, Wang et al. (2019) have shown that δ and θ increases both specifically index intelligibility increases in speech processing, further motivating a role for these slower frequencies in language comprehension.

The emergence of these species-specific oscillatory nestings would constitute the exclusive content of species-specific aspects of linguistic computation, the neural alterations required to bring about modern *homo sapiens* and 'narrow syntax', the basis of Tattersall's (2017) symbolic capacity. The Labelling Hypothesis defended in this book is therefore given renewed support. Given that the rhythmic interactions explored in this section reflect endogenous brain activity, and are not simply triggered by external input, this leads to a possible evolutionary scenario in which the processes of phrase structure building emerge directly from biophysical constraints, perhaps ultimately fulfilling some recent claims in generative grammar that syntax is a system of minimal/efficient computation.

Lastly, it should be noted that although it appears to have great potential explanatory power, the evolution of certain linguistic interfaces likely cannot

be reduced simply to CFC. For instance, Park et al. (2018) explore the oscillatory basis of audiovisual speech integration and show that this is very clearly
implemented by two independent computational mechanisms. θ rhythms in the
posterior superior temporal gyrus/sulcus code speech information common to
auditory and visual inputs, while θ rhythms in left motor and inferior temporal
regions code synergistic inputs between both modalities. It may be that information integrated via CFC and information integrated via simultaneous and
independent processes yield qualitatively distinct cognitive events and conscious experiences.

3.2.3   Phase-Phase Coupling and Other Approaches to Neural Computation

The limitations of traditional cartographic neuroimaging have been dealt with
in some detail already, but a more challenging issue to address is how precisely
the newly emerging oscillatory perspectives on language can be reconciled
with this literature. Reconciliation could take a number of forms, but it seems to
me that the most parsimonious and empirically adequate direction would be to
assume that after a phrase has been constructed via CFC feature-set construction (implicating temporal regions of the ventral stream like the medial temporal lobe), regions along the dorsal stream firing at β (likely regions closer
towards the inferior frontal gyrus) would be able to synchronise with the
cortico-basal ganglia-thalamic loop via phase-phase coupling and transfer the
categorised set to be maintained through an increasing β rhythm. This model
acquires some indirect support from the suggestion that the desynchronisation
(in the case of language, after the cognitive set is built and maintained via β
increases) of induced β may reflect memory formation (Hanslmayr & Staudigl
2014), with the semantic content of a given phrasal construction constituting a
form of memory. These β increases during phrasal maintenance may also
spread to the left planum temporale, which has been implicated in long-
distance lexical storage (Kuhnke et al. 2017). Indeed, phase-phase coupling
involving approximately identical rhythms may have a number of interesting
computational roles relevant for language, and may be responsible for transferring or comparing representations of equal type or hierarchical complexity
(hence, of comparable phasal dimensions). For instance, consider the notion of
agreement discussed in Chapter 1, involving the establishment of relations
between multiple lexical features. Chomsky et al. (2019) note that '[a]greement
phenomena indicate that there is an algorithm that relates *features* of syntactic
objects, called AGREE'. Associating as it does mental representations of equal
featural complexity and type, this algorithm appears well suited to being
implemented via phase-phase coupling over the regions implicated in storing
the relevant features. Long-range neural synchronisation and directionality,
involving coherence-based detection of interconnected nodes, will also likely

play a vital role in developing a more mature model of the language system (as Kujala et al. 2007 discuss in a seminal study of phase coupling during reading).

Some recent support for these hypotheses comes from Rimmele et al. (2019). Using MEG, these authors had participants listen to disyllabic words presented at a rate of four syllables per second. They found that lexical content (as opposed to mere syllable-transition information) activated a left-lateralised frontal and superior and middle temporal network, and also increased the interaction between left middle temporal areas and auditory cortex at 2Hz via phase-phase coupling. This particular phase-phase coupling likely acts as a sound-meaning interface between auditory and linguistic representations, mapping acoustic-phonemic processing to lexical processing. The authors also discovered phase–amplitude coupling between 2Hz and 4Hz in middle temporal gyrus and superior temporal gyrus in conditions with lexical and transitional and syllable information, but not with only-syllable information, suggesting that syllable information is exploited for lexical-level processing. Rimmele et al. found a decreased tracking of syllables (cerebro-acoustic coherence) at 4Hz in superior temporal gyrus when lexical content was presented, suggesting that syllabic information was used largely in the service of lexical interpretation. This suggests, as predicted here, that CFC implements the coordination of distinct linguistic information, such that it aids the construction of lexical items out of smaller syllabic units.

Taking into consideration much of the working memory oscillation literature (Lundqvist et al. 2016, for instance, show that working memory information is linked to brief γ bursts while β bursting reflects a default network state interrupted by γ), it seems reasonable to suggest that features are associated in some form (e.g. 'valued'/'checked') by distinct ensembles being phase-locked, 'agreeing' in both rhythmic and representational senses (see also Ward 2003 for the crucial role of γ in long-term memory processing). Working memory and linguistic phrase structure building are therefore likely implemented not via sustained neuronal activity (as much contemporary neuroimaging work tries to suggest), but rather via discretised, rhythmic pulses of coordinated neuronal firing.

These proposals are in line with Mai et al.'s (2016) finding of γ-related modulations during semantic and syntactic processing. A general computational operation (feature valuation) can therefore approach a degree of alignment with a general oscillatory mechanism (CFC). The question of whether these computations are achieved through increasing or decreasing phase–amplitude coupling is an open one, and should not be assumed a priori, with distinct cognitive systems likely employing oscillomic processes in different ways. For instance, Esghaei et al. (2015) show that visual attention in macaque monkeys decreases phase–amplitude coupling, seemingly to increase neuronal discriminability for attended stimuli. Visual cortex appears to use phase–amplitude coupling to regulate interneuronal correlations and enhance the discrimination of visual stimuli, selecting the appropriate representations. Relatedly, Mai et al. (2016) found decreased $\{\theta(\gamma)\}$ coupling for speech relative to non-speech, along with increased θ power for speech and increased γ power for real words relative to pseudo-words (as predicted by the present model). They suggest that the reasons for decreased coupling in speech may be due to the higher difficulty of sound matching in non-speech sounds which result in higher psychoacoustic working memory demands (with a greater load placed on working memory resulting in increased $\{\theta(\gamma)\}$ coupling), yet their findings may also be due to a similar neuronal discrimination process as the one proposed by Esghaei et al. (2015). Phase–amplitude coupling increases (as in a range of studies reviewed earlier) and decreases (as in Esghaei et al. 2015) consequently play a number of distinct functional roles, although the underlying physiological mechanisms which give rise to them are still not well understood (see also Asano & Gotman 2016 for the emerging potential of electrocorticography to monitor the oscillatory dynamics of language). A more serious and linguistically realistic level of engagement with syntactic, semantic and phonological computations will also be required of future oscillatory experiments, with Mai et al. (2016) claiming that γ increases are representative of 'lexical memory retrieval' and 'processing grammatical word categories', highly multifaceted processes, far from generic.

Other research has contributed to an understanding of the dynamics of auditory processing. In particular, Keitel et al.'s (2017) MEG study of auditory cortical δ-entrainment, and its interactions with fronto-parietal networks, provide support for the present oscillomic model and also contribute important, previously unknown details about the reach and influence of language-relevant δ manipulations. Keitel, Ince et al. discovered that during intelligible speech (a natural speech narrative) δ entrained with three networks: $\{\delta(\beta)\}$ coupling occurred between δ in the left anterior superior temporal gyrus and β in left-lateralised medial orbitofrontal areas, which the authors claim reflected predictive top-down modulations of auditory encoding (however, this finding is also compatible with the present proposal that δ-β coupling constitutes the final stage of the Merge-labelling algorithm). $\{\delta(\alpha)\}$ coupling occurred between δ in left Heschl's Gyrus and α in anterior superior temporal gyrus. Finally, δ in right posterior superior temporal gyrus coupled with predominantly right-lateralised parietal θ (specifically, in the cuneus, precuneus and superior/inferior parietal areas), which likely reflected semantic memory engagement (note that support for this comes from Bhattasali et al. 2018, who looked at multi-word expression processing and found the precuneus to be involved in memory retrieval during naturalistic sentence comprehension, while anterior temporal regions were called upon for phrase structure building). Unlike these rich δ interactions, θ rhythms in auditory cortex were not significantly entrained to any fronto-parietal structures, even though auditory θ has been implicated in processing a range of acoustic features (Ding & Simon 2013). Since the stimuli used by Keitel, Ince et al. were extended narratives constructed out of continuous, natural speech, it may be that this study has further exposed the role of δ-entrained computations in processing higher levels of linguistic complexity like phrasal categories and semantic intelligibility, rather than lower-level acoustic properties. Notice that, under the present model, Keitel et al.'s (2017) data concerning {δ(β)} and {δ(θ)} coupling can also be explained by invoking successful phrase structure building computations implemented via the hierarchical nesting of the β and θ complexes within δ, along the lines discussed earlier. Gross et al. (2013) also discovered {δ (θ)} phase-phase coupling during speech perception and that θ also controlled the amplitude of γ, suggesting that δ phase likely modulates both the phase and amplitude of θ depending on the computation. As mentioned earlier, δ-δ phase-phase coupling likely indexes the mapping of acoustic-phonemic processing to lexical processing, and so the δ-θ phase-phase coupling reported in Gross et al. (2013) may index the mapping of acoustic-phonemic processing to more specific morphosyntactic features. As Molinaro and Lizarazu (2018) note, '[h]ow this cross-frequency interaction develops and through which cortical networks must be better evaluated in the future'.

At a minimum, then, auditory δ entrainment is influenced by left orbito-frontal β and parietal θ and interacts with central α. This model appears to map onto the oscillomic predictions presented earlier, namely that β, θ and α, in approximately the regions discussed by Keitel et al. (2017), all play distinct roles in phrase structure building, feature-set construction, and functional inhibition. The finding that the orbital gyrus is involved in phrasal processing (Grodzinsky & Friederici 2006) adds further credence to this model.

Palva and Palva (2018) also review evidence suggesting that phase-phase synchronisation of two distinct frequency bands serves to integrate and regulate separate processes being carried out in different brain regions, and enhancing the efficiency and scope of this process may have contributed to a number of cognitive functions. The authors also discuss how this form of cross-frequency phase synchrony (CFS) is the only form of CFC that could be associated with consistent neuronal spike-time relationships: 'While related neuronal processes could be CF-synchronized and associated with coincident neuronal spiking [...] unrelated neuronal processing in two distinct neuronal assemblies would not be associated with CFS and their spiking activity would be unrelated.' The information represented in spectrally distributed assemblies could thus be related via CFS. CFS would be well positioned to connect the most central cortical (and subcortical) hubs of a given within-frequency network, positioning CFS as 'a putative mechanism for coordinating processing and communication across fast and slow oscillatory networks carrying out functionally distinct computational functions'. Although to my knowledge (and as reviewed here) there is currently limited evidence of important examples of phase-phase synchrony in language comprehension (it is found consistently in various memory tasks, however, as when Akiyama et al. 2017 document θ-α phase-phase coupling during working memory), this mechanism should be the target of future experimental research. Lastly, the mechanism of phase precession also seems at play during speech segmentation when listeners predict upcoming speech, whereby the neural phase advances faster after listeners acquire knowledge of incoming speech, 'skipping ahead' of incoming stimuli (Teng et al. 2020). The full explanatory scope of phase precession with respect to other linguistic predictive processes (e.g. semantic or syntactic prediction) is yet to be settled.

3.2.4   Linear Grammar

It is clear from the fairly disparate collection of recent studies reviewed earlier that δ plays an important role in a number of cognitive faculties relevant for language, such as phrasal comprehension. This motivated its inclusion into the present oscillatory model of language, and a seminal study by Raghavachari et al. (2001) can add some further enhancements. They made EEG recordings while subjects that participated performed the Sternberg working memory task, and found that at a number of electrode sites θ amplitude increased substantially at the beginning of the trial, was maintained throughout, and dropped at the end. This phenomenon, termed 'gating' by the authors, seems to play a role in organising multi-item sequences. Given these findings, and others reported earlier concerning δ-driven phrasal sensitivity, it is likely that an equivalent 'δ gating' phenomenon occurs during sentence comprehension.

The algorithm outlined here, if it is responsible for elementary phrase structures, might also form the basis of what Jackendoff (2017) calls 'linear grammar'; a meaningful, compositional grammar lacking complex morphosyntax of the kind found across modern languages. Instead of generating 'If you shoot a cop then you go to jail', linear grammar would simply generate 'You shoot a cop, you go to jail', which still relies on phrases. While this can generate a fairly extensive compositional semantics and communication system, it is likely that the reason why complex morphosyntax developed across, for instance, Indo-European languages over the past millennia is because it adds certain levels of communicative precision to the simple structures generated by linear grammar. There are also reasons to believe that there was a period without morphology, as argued by Comrie (1992), a period with no affixes and no morphological alternations (see Carstairs-McCarthy 2010). Relatedly, there was almost certainly a period after syntax but before rigorous, systematic categorisation of lexical items, when there was an emerging distinction between nouns and verbs without morphology (Heine & Kuteva 2002).

If the structures generated by linear grammars rely on the above-mentioned δ-θ-γ interactions, then presumably the additional morphosyntactic elements added do not require a novel phase code but rather the recruitment of the multiple demand system to access structures stored in long-term memory. This would help us localise the likely species-specific elements of the language system.

There also appears to be some fairly compelling diachronic evidence supporting this model. The generation of bare, basic nominal structures (e.g. 'sheep') was exhibited in Proto-Indo-European languages. Later, Proto-Germanic languages exhibited a slot for adjectives ('black sheep'): [NP A [N]]. Thereafter, Old English exhibited a slot for determiners ('the black sheep'): [NP D [A [N]]]. Finally, early modern English exhibited a slot for peripheral modifiers ('only the black sheep'): [NP M [D [A [N]]]]. To take one of many interesting examples, in a seminal paper van de Velde (2011) showed that elements existing at the sentence level are progressively incorporated as part of the noun phrase. This suggests that the elementary mechanisms for phrasal construction were certainly in place from the time of Proto-Indo-European languages, and that only some extra information derived at the syntax-semantics interface was incorporated as part of the extended projection. It is likely that this extra information was constituted via conceptual features stored cross-cortically. Indeed, van de Velde summarises that '[t]he whole 'growth' process is a result of a series of reanalyses and analogical extensions' (2011, 387). In neurobiological terms, the 'analogy' may well be a reapplication of the δ-θ-γ code to different cortical regions.

3.3   A Bridge to Biology

Having outlined the core computational system of language and its likely oscillatory basis, I will now turn to the broader architecture within which this system operates. I will present a number of ways that an oscillatory model of language can make further explanatory connections with the biological sciences.

3.3.1   Dual Workspaces

An emerging consensus in generative syntax is that the language system needs to exploit not one, but two memory workspaces in order to generate and maintain/interpret non-local syntactic relations. One workspace is used to *construct* syntactic phrases, and the other is used to *maintain* these units once they have been transferred (in the terminology of Adger 2017, these workspaces are, respectively, the Operating space and the Resource space), yielding a simple pushdown stack. The distinction between these two memory systems (with an expanded phonological loop housing at least one of them), and the conflicts between global and local memory they often lead to, can be illustrated well by the existence of syntactic illusions, such as in the sentence 'More people have been to Russia than I have', which speakers initially parse as acceptable even though the sentence lacks a coherent interpretation (Montalbetti 1984) (British writer and comedian Stephen Fry uttered a similar type of sentence on the BBC programme *QI*, which is also meaningless: 'It so happens that more people in the world are bitten by New Yorkers every year than they are by sharks'). More broadly, human memory seems to be composed of a number of long-term systems and a separate, but interacting system 'recording' recent events which lasts a few seconds. The peculiar interaction between what we remember briefly through this latter memory system and long-term storage gives rise to the aspect of consciousness Edelman (1989) refers to as the *Remembered Present*.

I would like to suggest that the initial $\{\theta(\gamma)\}$ code discussed earlier constitutes the first workspace, and the subsequent $\{\delta(\theta)\}$ code constitutes the second. This would explain why left-inferior regions seem sensitive to syntactic violations in fMRI and M/EEG paradigms, and why anterior temporal regions seem to be implicated in semantic composition operations. If the particular $\{\delta(\theta)\}$ interactions predicted here are indeed human-specific, this would go some way to derive the apparent uniqueness of the dual workspace model proposed by Adger (2017) and others (as well as motivating the more general Labelling Hypothesis I am defending here). As we have seen, many studies point to the importance of δ in language comprehension, but from a neurocomputational perspective CFC involving δ may also play a vital role in the online construction of phrases, instead of purely entraining to phrasal units (as in the Ding et al. 2016 model). In brief, the present proposal amounts to the claim that the initial $\{\theta(\gamma)\}$ generates serial order, but since language requires hierarchical order, an additional step – namely, a $\{\delta(\theta)\}$ code through which syntactic complexes are maintained in memory and thereby generating *complexes of complexes* – may be required. When Adger (2017) recommends that syntacticians 'aim for an architecture that embodies the constraints rather than representing them explicitly', neurolinguists should respond by invoking the aforementioned phase codes as evidence that the physical limitations of cognition arise from the coupling possibilities inherent in oscillatory behaviour and are not externally imposed from some independent source in the overall neurocomputational architecture.

There is also reason to believe that the cross-cortical γ rhythms triggering the ensembles responsible for storing language-relevant features are widely distributed across the brain, and are not confined to the classical areas. Huth et al.'s

(2016) fMRI study of the brain's semantic maps not only revealed extreme lateralisation (contrary to the left-lateralisation hypotheses regarding semantic representations), it also revealed that across twelve semantic categories (including 'visual', 'violent', 'emotional', 'locational' and 'numeric') a large number of cortical areas were systematically activated when a word belonging to each category was processed. Nevertheless, studies of phase–amplitude coupling during working memory tasks using decomposition techniques have demonstrated that the spatial reach of the phase-providing slow rhythm is typically more widespread than the faster rhythm (Maris et al. 2011), a generalisation which makes sense if the particular features extracted during phrase structure-building are narrowly stored in specific cortical regions in contrast to the source of slower rhythms, which can extend across full brain structures like the thalamus and large portions of the hippocampus.

Taking a step back, the more general conclusion of recent literature on the cognitive neuroscience of memory is that successful memory formation (in contrast to unsuccessful formation, i.e. forgetting) is reflected in decreases in low-frequency power (below 30Hz) occurring alongside increases in high-frequency power (typically >40Hz). A comprehensive, dual MEG-iEEG (intracranial EEG) investigation by Fellner et al. (2019) tried to dissociate distinct memory formation processes. The authors discovered that decreases in α/β power (8–20Hz) predicted the encoding of words but not faces, while increases in γ power followed by decreases in θ power predicted memory formation for both words and faces. Furthermore, these distinct relations could be tracked to distinct brain regions, with α/β power decreases for words occurring at left sensor sites including the inferior and middle frontal gyrus, the supramarginal gyrus, and middle and superior temporal gyrus. Meanwhile, α/β decreases for faces occurred at posterior sensor sites including lingual, occipital middle and inferior gyrus in the right hemisphere.

These results also align with Beese et al.'s (2017) study of successful linguistic memory formation across different age groups. Since processing resources decline with age, Beese et al. recorded the electroencephalogram from three age groups (twenty-four, forty-three and sixty-five years) during a sentence comprehension task. Previous work has shown that syntactic but not semantic processing is compromised in older adults (Poulisse et al. 2019). Successful encoding in younger subjects resulted in α decreases, but as subjects increased in age the strength of α decreases lessened to the point that, amongst the oldest subjects, α increases were found. These results point to a change in cortical inhibition-disinhibition balance across age groups, impacting verbal working memory.

For our purposes, since power decreases (indicating a decrease in local synchronisation) have often been found to co-occur with increases in long-range phase synchronisation (Solomon et al. 2017), power decreases might therefore be something of a prerequisite for the formation of large-scale, fine-grained connectivity needed for distributed representations. As such, the relationship between local power decreases and CFC is ripe for future research. Fellner et al. draw the well-motivated conclusion that broadband shifts and spectral tilts have limited explanatory value in terms of explaining the neural dynamics of cognition, and a more fine-grained perspective dissociating memory processes (linguistic, visual, etc.) and power increases/decreases across brain regions is needed.

Lastly, turning back again to linguistic theory, in the most recent model of the generative enterprise Chomsky et al. (2019) and Chomsky (2019b) discuss a fundamental question: When MERGE takes X and Y from a workspace (WS) [X,Y] and forms the set {X,Y}, does it add this new object to WS, yielding WS' = [X,Y,{X,Y}], or does it instead replace X and Y with the newly formed object, yielding WS' = [{X,Y}]? Considerations of computational efficiency lead Chomsky et al. (2019) to reasonably opt for the latter option. The fact that the oscillatory model presented here holds that γ clusters slow to β for maintenance is potentially compatible with this position on workspace architecture, such that WS = [X,Y] (individual feature-sets itemised through cross-cortical γ) is indeed 'replaced' with WS' = {[X,Y]} by slower β-generated representations (or, alternatively, the same γ-itemised units but positioned at different points of the slower cycle), rather than newly formed β-itemisation processes taking place alongside the maintained γ clusters. Indeed, as Chomsky (2019b) discusses, recursion for language is different to recursion for other cognitive modules: It involves what he terms Resource Restriction, whereby a workspace is cleared and objects are deleted from it. This limits computational accessibility, making syntactic computation more efficient such that there are fewer objects possible to manipulate. Likewise, a core function of CFC is to delimit the number of phase-synchronised representations (e.g. limitations on the number of γ items within θ), making rehearsal of the slower cycle a more straightforward process than if the phase were to frequently shift. As such, MERGE effectively becomes what Chomsky (2019b) terms 'Replace' (an operation rooted in the original definition of Merge in Chomsky 1995) whereby objects are not sustained across the derivation but are replaced in the workspace. Limiting accessibility is also computationally efficient, such that MERGE/Replace can only operate on a limited number of representational types, like syntactic features but not certain semantic features or workspaces. In fact, with sensory systems more generally, one of the brain's main functions is to *limit* what information it takes in, immediately dispensing with the majority of data it receives. Oscillations, by targeting and triggering very specific cell populations, in particular sequences across the phase of slow rhythms, can implement part of this filtering process.

In recent syntactic work which embraces this framework, Murphy and Shim (2020) propose that the labelling algorithm can only operate over categorial labels, such that non-categorial elements (e.g. Q, φ) cannot serve as phrasal identifiers. The authors also discuss how labelling can be situated within the syntactic workspace, and one might extend such a discussion and defend an *Economy of Labelling* theorem, that if two workspaces have distinct numbers of copies, the workspace with fewer copies is labelled (an idea within the traditional Minimalist framework of the Merge-over-Move debate, which also invoked competing derivations being assessed by the grammar, where 'derivations' are now seen as workspace histories). This extends Chomsky's concern of Resource Restriction to the domain of labelling, whereby the syntax is limited to labelling workspaces with the fewest number of copies able to generate a legal interpretation at the semantics interface. When syntactic representations are merged ('replaced'), they appear to do so across the smallest possible search space (Larson 2015, 60):

General Restriction on Merge
Merge can only apply to an object in a given space if there is no possible Merge with an object in a more constrained search space.

This notion is closely related to the 'strong hypothesis' entertained in Chomsky et al. (2019, fn. 17) that 'operations never extend [the workspace]'. These proposals are all in line with moves already made in the literature to make the derivation more cognitively oriented, taking into consideration memory and search processes. Complementing Adger's (2017) dual workspace model of syntax, Ke (2017, 11) proposes the following:

Two-Phase Workspace Hypothesis
Narrow Syntax is able to keep two active phases, and no more, in the workspace at a time. A phase is active in the workspace if it is not Transferred.

There are a number of instances where two separate workspaces are needed, as when the lower phase contains unvalued features, such as in v*P-internal subjects (where the external argument contains uF[-CASE]) or long-distance *wh*-movement (the *wh*-phrase hosts uF[-Q]). Experimental stimuli involving these workspace-intensive processes would allow researchers to uncover the oscillatory signatures of language's dual workspace architecture.

By implementing a form of Resource Restriction, both labelling and the currently proposed workspace model can be seen as arising from 'third factor' considerations. As such, this in turn motivates a neurobiological model of these phenomena which is also grounded in (electro-)physiological constraints, such as processes seeking minimal CFC distances and efficient 'packaging' of γ-itemised representational data structures within the phase of slower rhythms (and, in turn, packaging them at the most efficient point of the phase, such as the activity-intensive peak as opposed to the less-intensive trough period). As reviewed earlier, it is becoming increasingly possible to motivate such an account (e.g. the θ-γ code for working memory). Consider also the generative thesis that MERGE is unconstrained and issues of labelling and ordering only arise at the interfaces between syntax and interpretation/externalisation. This is effectively analogous to the claim from theoretical neurobiology that representational identity and sequence ordering is only put in place via neurocomputational algorithms such as the θ-γ code; that is to say, the third factors of language design emerge from the biophysical design of oscillatory couplings.

Lastly, pertaining to these and some other concerns raised throughout this book, a major form of evidence supporting the hypothesis that the language system is optimised for computation (and not, say, communication) comes through the observation that computational efficiency appears to be a feature of biological organisation. Working on computational neuroanatomy, Cherniak (1994) applied combinatorial network optimisation theory (Garey & Johnson 1979) to neural organisation and showed that 'when anatomical positioning is treated like a microchip layout wire-minimisation problem, the 'best of all possible brains' hypothesis predicts actual placement of brains, their ganglia, and even their nerve cells' (1994, 89). Wire-minimisation therefore appears to be a fundamental structuring principle of neural organisation, going far beyond 'good-enough' criteria. Likewise, Rieke et al. (1997, 267) note that while there is no a priori 'reason to think that [...] physical limits are relevant to real brains' and that 'the design of the nervous system could be driven by completely independent criteria', they discuss a range of evidence for 'performance close to physical limits' set by spike train entropy for the brain's neurons, putting this forward as 'a general principle from which many aspects of neural coding and computation can be understood'.

Overall, by minimising the language system's phrase structure building architecture, and by also minimising its reliance on (and the size of) memory workspaces, contemporary labelling theory is gradually developing points of possible contact with neurobiological models of memory and attention.

3.3.2   γ-Itemisation

I have assumed since the previous chapter that individual language-relevant features are represented by γ cycles. These presumably exhibit a degree of feature selectivity, in which a cell's response depends strongly on a small number of parameters and is maximal at some optimum value of these parameters (Rieke et al. 1997). But what precisely are these cycles? Regarding the cellular mechanisms behind cross-cortical γ generation, the standard view is that they are produced by single cells such as fast-bursting neocortical neurons (Cardin et al. 2005) and neurons in the central lateral nucleus of the thalamus

(Steriade et al. 1993). A more common mechanism of production is the reciprocal interaction between excitatory glutamatergic and inhibitory GABAergic neurons (Welle & Contreras 2017). More interestingly, these oscillations are typically grouped into *broadband* γ (exhibiting a range of spectral peaks) and *narrowband* γ (exhibiting little variation in frequency). Welle and Contreras (2017, 247) note that while recent experimental work has made some headway, '[t]he conditions in which these two types of gamma oscillations are generated and their functional significance are largely unknown'. Given the generic chunking and gating role of oscillations reviewed here, I would like to suggest that narrowband and broadband γ parcellate representations of distinct complexity during coupling with θ, such that broadband γ extracts complex linguistic features and narrowband γ extracts more elementary representations. This matches the proposals made earlier concerning slower γ cycles representing more complex features than fast γ cycles. An experiment involving different types of syntactic and semantic features of varying complexity would be an ideal way to test this working hypothesis.

Research by Saleem et al. (2017) and Storchi et al. (2017) appears consistent with these ideas. For instance, these authors demonstrate that increases in *luminance* (computing the amount of light in a single area) modulate narrowband γ, while the more complex notion of *contrast* (computing the difference in luminance across two areas) involves broadband increases. In particular, Saleem et al. suggest that narrowband and broadband γ represent distinct channels of information transfer for distinct types of visual information. Given that one of the major themes of recent neurobiology is the transformation of domain-specificity into domain-generality, it is not unreasonable to suggest that this distinction can be extended to the linguistic and other conceptual domains, with these two major γ bands being responsible for transferring distinct types of information of varying complexity.

Indeed, Artoni et al. (2019) have recently shed some light on this issue. These authors constructed homophonous phrases with the same acoustic content but are interpreted as either NPs or VPs depending of their syntactic context. After performing stereo-EEG (SEEG) recordings in epileptic patients, they showed that VPs – which are more semantically complex than NPs – elicited greater activity in the high γ (150-300Hz) range than NPs across language-relevant areas. This reinforces a core proposal in this book concerning the role of γ-itemisation in semantic processing.

Having explored what appears to be a legitimate, empirically motivated neural code for hierarchical phrase structure, it seems reasonable to address the broader topic of linking this code to findings in neurobiology ranging outside language. A fruitful area to start this process is spatial navigation. Constantinescu et al. (2016) have shown that the neural code which has long been implicated in spatial navigation may also be implicated through the recruitment of grid cells in navigating more abstract representations, such as conceptual space (see also Kriegeskorte & Storrs 2016). Recent work also points to the same code being implicated in navigating auditory space. Aronov et al. (2017) found that neurons involved in a task in which rats changed the frequency of sound in their environment overlapped with spatial cell types in the hippocampal-entorhinal circuit, such as place and grid cells, which, as the authors conclude, may be involved in 'supporting cognitive processes beyond spatial navigation' (2017, 719). Moreover, '[s]patially localized place and grid codes might therefore be a manifestation of a general circuit mechanism for encoding sequential relationships between behaviourally relevant events'. If these and other domain-specific barriers are seemingly being broken – and broken rapidly – in a manner which opens up considerable scope for investigation into the neural basis of conceptual representations, then the language sciences should adapt flexibly to these emerging paradigms (see also Morton et al. 2017). As we will see, this is not currently the case in major domains of neurolinguistics, where many studies have embraced the 'cartographic imperative' (Poeppel 2008) of confusing localisation for explanation.

Other related research indicates that the hippocampal-entorhinal complex can encode spaces demarcated on the basis of transitions between discrete items (Garvert et al. 2017). Epstein, Patai et al. (2017) note that each of the navigation functions of parahippocampal regions involves a core distinction between context retrieval and orientation. While these processes are clear to adjudicate in the case of spatial navigation, it is currently unclear how they might apply to semantic navigation. The authors plausibly speculate that context retrieval in the case of semantics might involve 'bringing up knowledge related to a given topic' (2017, 1510–1511), while orientation might involve 'alignment to salient prototypes and axes in the corresponding semantic similarity space' (2017, 1511). As a result, hippocampal-entorhinal grid cells could feasibly code for major features of the semantics-pragmatics interface, and their evolution and development could contribute to an understanding of certain conceptual and social cognitive capacities, while damage to this system could result in an impairment of these functions. The importance of the hippocampus does not end here. 'Concept cells' have been shown to fire in the hippocampus when participants think about famous buildings or people irrespective of the type of stimulus used to evoke these thoughts (Quian Quiroga et al. 2005).

A study by Kaiser et al. (2008) showed that different γ rhythms of distinct amplitudes code for different working memory items, and so it is likely that different linguistic features are represented at distinct amplitudes (e.g. Number features vs. Person features). Agreement or feature-checking (e.g. φ-feature agreement followed by Q-feature agreement within the same syntactic cycle/ phase) may arise from the particular sequence of items extracted within a given oscillatory cycle, alongside the other mechanisms mentioned earlier for these computations. Related work suggests that if the working memory load shifts from sequentially ordered items to discrete visuo-spatial information, then {θ (γ)} coupling is replaced by {α(γ)} coupling (Sauseng et al. 2005; see also Nevins 2016 for a discussion of feature composition and motivations for assuming that Number and Person features do not combine via symmetric conjunction but rather through specific orders, possibly grounded in these oscillatory mechanisms). The success of the human language system may depend on how flexibly it can shift from one form of CFC to another, and how the representations built by one coupling can be manipulated or enriched by subsequent couplings. Fell and Axmacher (2011) point out that a major overlapping region between working memory and long-term memory systems is the medial temporal lobe, with a number of studies suggesting that phase synchronisation in this region permits distinct memory systems to interact and feed information between each other. Since this region is also crucial for lexical memory, it is likely that phase synchronisation also permits lexicalised representations to interface with external memory systems, allowing – amongst other things – syntactic and semantic information about a given lexical feature set to trigger particular memories.

Research by Sternberg (1966) suggested that short-term memory items are recalled at a rate of one per 30ms, and this appears to be the approximate temporal separation of γ cycles – possibly placing constraints on the number of linguistic features able to be retrieved. Given that top-down, higher-level processes involved in language comprehension begin to occur around 200–600ms post-utterance (Skeide & Friederici 2016), this presumably presents these γ rhythms with enough time to extract a number of features before top-down processes (such as lexical-semantic categorisation and phrase structure reconstruction, coordinated by slower rhythms) end and bind them into feature-sets. This permits a natural transition to the well-established findings of the cartographic literature, which has shown that 200–400ms post-stimulus lexical information is sent from the left anterior superior temporal gyrus and superior temporal sulcus to BA 45 and BA 47 via the fronto-occipital fasciculus, at which point semantic relations between lexical feature-sets is determined via interactions with the inferior parietal cortex (Binder et al. 2009). This is also in line with Goucha et al.'s (2017) suggestion that posterior superior temporal sulcus is involved in labelling, transforming a tree structure into a rooted tree after syntactic categorisation.

It is also possible that clusters of features are recalled from memory at a faster rate after a number of features have been activated together a number of times (a process recently found to influence memory recall in mice; Cai et al. 2016), increasing neuronal excitability and biasing γ cycles such that the triggering of one feature increases the likelihood of another being triggered.

For instance, this process of increased excitability would ensure that clusters of φ-features were activated in a successive sequence of γ cycles during phase-locking with slower θ or β rhythms. As with the mouse brain (Cai et al. 2016), it is conceivable that certain features share overlapping ensembles, with the degree of overlap being based on frequency of activation or similarity of formal properties (syntactic, semantic, phonological), increasing the efficiency of linguistic computation.

Importantly, evidence that spike phase-locking during working memory maintenance occurs often without increases in firing rates suggests that it is the temporal coordination and ordering of ensemble firing which the most fundamental feature of representation manipulation, and not spike firing rate (Lee et al. 2005). Since only a small number of faster rhythms can be embedded within a θ or β cycle, there is naturally less variance in ensemble ordering than in firing rate, which can vary widely across cortical regions, and so the stable (relatively) 'fixed' nature of semantic representations likely arises from the stability seen in ensemble orderings rather than the contrastive variability exhibited by firing rates.

The 'lexicon' may consequently amount to stored time-frequency profiles, with each item being composed of particular, sequentially excited and bound feature-sets. To invoke standard set-theoretic notations, oscillatory embeddings under the present model would permit the transformation of stored sets of representations – $\{R_1, R_2,...,R_n\}$ – into ordered sequences – $<R_4, R_7, R_3>$. Neural oscillations under this model act as a timing mechanism for controlling the serial processing of linguistic features. There will certainly still be a need to invoke processes such as cultural evolution to account for the ultimate complexity of the grammatical system acquired by speakers, but this algorithmic model can act as the foundation of this linguistic knowledge.

Along with novel cell structures, external constraints would also influence the temporal serialisation of feature extraction: Ray and Maunsell (2015) note that the coordination of γ phases across multiple, distant areas is difficult due to conduction delays, mediated by myelin thickness and nodal structure. For instance, a conduction delay of only 5ms could change the interactions of coupled γ oscillators from constructive to deconstructive interference (Pajevic et al. 2014).

Before moving on, it should be noted that while I have made the distinction between broadband and narrowband γ, it is also necessary to consider the different types of γ rhythms in cognition, rather than viewing γ as a monolithic unit of cortical computation. The integration between broadband and slow (30-50Hz) γ is an interesting case in this respect. Broadband γ correlates with neuronal spiking; spiking is phase-locked to slow γ; and, in turn, fast γ exhibits CFC with slow γ (Bahramisharif et al. 2016). The fact that recent studies of the oscillatory basis of linguistic semantics and reading result in high γ responses (with Bahramasharif et al. 2018 showing high γ responding in an item-specific way to certain letters) suggests that it reflects the spiking of cells that represents specific items. Slow γ does not seem to be triggered in such an item-specific way, and so slow γ power likely does not carry information via amplitude but is rather responsible for temporally organising other signals (Bahramasharif et al. 2018). The rich degree of synchronisation between slow and fast γ also points towards the possibility of multiple sites of representational coordination, rather than purely slow δ-α coordinating cross-cortical representational extraction. It is possible that the sites of slow γ rhythms act as relay stations between the sites of slow rhythms and the ultimate representational content stored in broadband γ clusters, necessitated and structured by specific projections. This proposal can also be reconciled with recent findings that sites in frontal cortex that have mnemonic activity exhibit brief and sporadic bursts of activity, rather than long and sustained bursts. If information is encoded in synaptic weights (Lundqvist et al. 2011) coordinated via γ(slow)-γ(fast) coupling, rather than specific durations of bursts, then persistent firing would not be necessary to maintain item-specific representations.

Lastly, there is the more fundamental issue of what, precisely, γ oscillations (and oscillations more generally) are arising from at the neurochemical level. Since this topic goes beyond the neurocomputational and psycholinguistic focus of this book, I will address it only briefly here. While Chapter 2 discussed some of the apparent biophysics underlying oscillations, Leszczynski et al. (2019) challenge some common assumptions by revealing that suprathreshold but also subthreshold neural activity can contribute to broadband high γ (70–150Hz) oscillatory signatures in primary visual and auditory cortex using laminar multielectrode data in monkeys. As such, high γ origins 'include a mixture of the neuronal action potential firing and dendritic processes separable from this firing' (Leszczynski et al. 2019). Therefore, the neurochemical basis for the present oscillatory code for language should not be assumed to be strictly tied to neural firing patterns (i.e. multiunit activity).

3.4   Refining the Model

So far, we have implicitly assumed a rather simplistic model under which each rhythm involved in language comprehension is generated in a macroscopic brain region. The neurobiological validity of this assumption needs to be questioned, and a potentially more realistic revision to the present oscillomic model should be devised if it is found to be empirically indefensible.

3.4.1   Frequency Generators

The topic of single versus multi-frequency generators has only recently been addressed in the literature, but it has been addressed comprehensively enough to permit a brief discussion of it here. Deco et al. (2017) reviewed a host of resting-state studies and used them to compare two possible models of the brain: one model stipulates that each brain area generates oscillations in a single frequency, while a second model stipulates that brain areas can generate oscillations in multiple frequency bands. Deco et al. obtained a best fit with the resting-state MEG data they reviewed when multiple frequency generators were placed at each local brain area in their computer model, indicating that the brain most probably oscillates more dynamically during rest than has typically been assumed. One immediate implication of this finding in the present context is that the θ-γ feature-set combination procedure will likely be able to extract much more local features in parahippocampal regions without the threat of interference effects, with multiple regions within the hippocampus, for instance, being able to oscillate at both frequency bands.

There also appears to be recent evidence that the present phrase-sensitive oscillatory structures (slow δ rhythms) are constructed via a level of conscious attention significantly degraded relative to the oscillatory structures responsible for constructing smaller linguistic structures such as syllables (faster β and γ rhythms). In an MEG study, Kösem and van Wassenhove (2016) contrasted acoustic and linguistic parsing using bistable speech sequences. Their participants were asked to volitionally maintain one of the two possible speech percepts. Oscillatory entrainment tracked not only acoustic properties, but also the participant's conscious percept. Their results suggest that low-frequency modulations are compatible with the encoding of pre-lexical segmentation cues, while high-frequency modulations specifically informed conscious speech percepts. We can additionally conclude that the oscillations responsible for constructing larger lexical and phrasal units are distinct from those responsible for linguistic attention.

3.4.2   Basic Arithmetic

The oscillatory model defended in this book is an inherently 'additive' one: It purely involves the generation of cross-cortical language-relevant features and their combination into larger structures. Gallistel and Matzel (2013, 194) pose a fundamental question which has not yet been addressed: 'Complex computations reduce to sequences of the basic arithmetic operations. How are these operations implemented and at what level of neural structure (circuit, cellular, molecular)?' The emerging picture I am developing here would suggest that basic arithmetic operations over elementary representations generated by neural clusters would occur through interacting, coupling rhythms. This is a highly evolutionarily preserved series of computations; witness Howard et al.'s (2019) discovery that the numerical cognition in honeybees enables addition and subtraction, with the bees being able to use blue and yellow as symbolic representations for addition and subtraction. The derivational operations of contemporary linguistic theory – word movement, feature copying and valuation, agreement relations, semantic conjunction, feature deletion, and so forth – can be summarised as implementations of basic addition and subtraction processes operating over these generated feature sets. Section 3.7.1 will return to this topic.

3.4.3   Coupling Concerns

There is also an emerging consensus that phase resetting of ongoing oscillatory activity to endogenous or exogenous cues enables information transfer within neural circuits and between distinct regions. Phase-resetting mechanisms that facilitate CFC may even represent the construction of a cell assembly. The phases of multiple oscillators can be reset via a burst of dopaminergic input from the ventral tegmental area (see Gu et al. 2015). As Voloh and Womelsdorf (2016) claim after reviewing the existing literature, 'phase-resets can drive changes in neural excitability, ensemble organisation, functional networks, and ultimately, overt behavior'. Phase resetting permits '(1) the proper readout of stimuli encoded in the phase; (2) the transmission of multiplexed information over large anatomical distances; and (3) nesting of high frequency activity in low frequency phase that increases the informational content of neural signals'.

The final point is potentially critical: One of the human-unique aspects of language is its featurally rich lexical representations, which cannot be reduced to simplex or binary structures and are rather composed of a cluster of distinct syntactic, semantic and phonological features. This level of representational complexity could possibly and feasibly be generated by more widespread CFC yielding greater levels of representational information than that permitted in the brains of other primates. As already mentioned, phase-aligned oscillatory activity also permits multiplexing, or the encoding and decoding of multiple information streams (Akam & Kullmann 2014) – precisely what is required to bind the representationally distinct syntactic, semantic and phonological streams of information which constitute any given lexical item. Multiplexing allows the reconfiguration of connectivity and information types stored and extracted from a given neural network (Akam & Kullmann 2014).

Moreover, and as briefly discussed earlier, there appears to be a human-unique level of CFC diversity in the neocortex (Maris et al. 2016), with both phase and frequency being modulated to transfer information stored in local ensembles across distributed networks. Language evolution therefore almost certainly involved some form of CFC tuning. More broadly, the encoding of relations between events can be executed through oscillatory temporal relations and their discharge sequences, such that organisms can learn that event X systematically occurs after event Y due to the particular discharges responsible for each event (Singer 2018). These learning mechanisms likely involved in establishing semantic relations between conceptual representations – simulation studies attest that chains of conventional integrate-and-fire neurons are able to transmit temporal information with great precision (Mainen & Sejnowski 1995) – although how this is done in the human brain remains at the horizons of current enquiry. What we can hypothesise with confidence is the following: Since much of semantic structure appears to be innate in humans, the responses of conjunction-specific neurons (labelled line codes) storing the representations of such structures must be genetically determined, such that it is determined which line codes are established, and hence which representations are associated prior to experience. Recent findings have also suggested that, although oscillatory synchronisation is often highly volatile and chaotic (non-stationary, frequency variability, short duration etc.), whatever short bouts of coherent synchronisation emerge they are nevertheless sufficient to contain information about the contents of working memory and the direction of information flow (Singer 2018).

In this sense, the computational properties of brain rhythms appear able to implement some (perhaps all) of the core syntactic and semantic operations of language. For example, the underlying physiology thought to generate γ rhythms seems suited to forming cell assemblies and expediting neural communication via rhythmic coherence (see Cannon et al. 2014 for a review). It is possible that the human-unique levels of CFC diversity documented by Maris et al. (2016) emerge out of what Lourenço and Bacci (2017) discovered to be 'human-specific, very powerful excitatory connections between principal pyramidal neurons and inhibitory neurons', which they found to be highly plastic. In particular, given the crucial role of these cells in generating brain rhythms, this indicates that human-specific levels of plasticity seen in certain microcircuits might result in novel oscillatory couplings, and hence novel forms of information transfer between brain regions. The precise forms of oscillatory behaviour generated by these forms of plasticity remains an open question, and one ripe for future experimental research. As mentioned, it seemingly only takes brief bouts of phase synchronisation to execute complex computations relevant for higher cognition, which indeed makes the experimental task of finding, say, language-relevant δ-θ coupling more difficult, but it nevertheless makes the challenge all the more legitimate. These dynamical concerns not only provide a more comprehensive picture of the language system than classical models, but they also chime well with recent developments in neurophysiology, which indicate that a single brain function (with the exception of basic reflexes) cannot be performed with a small number of cells or an individual brain structure. Instead, several areas are activated at once, coordinated by oscillatory dynamics, in particular during higher cognitive processes (Yener et al. 2016).

3.4.4   Plasticity

This issue of plasticity brings with it other implications for neurolinguistics. Higher order cognitive functions develop idiosyncratically across individual brains, and so neurolinguists should look for a more generalisable neural code for language than one tied strictly to one fixed region, a code able to be executed independently of where core steps in the processing of recursively embedded syntax may be implemented. Certain changes in the brain throughout development are known to be genetically determined and are experience-independent, whereas others are experience-dependent, which require the reception of certain input from the environment. Developmental data in neurotypical and impaired brains indicate that the neural organisation for language is neither predetermined nor strictly domain-specific (Kiran & Thompson 2019). Reallocation of distinct hemispheric resources, strengthened anatomical connections via increased white matter density, increased coherence among regions, and increases and decreases in neural activation can all occur during major periods of phonetic learning (Zhang & Wang 2007), and though there is currently a poverty of data, it is likely that other linguistic developmental processes are established via these processes. There is also evidence in favour of *pluripotentiality*, the notion that cortical tissue is able to undertake a wide range of representations depending on the timing of development and length of exposure (Bates 1999). The possible neuroanatomical centres of higher language development (i.e. areas involved in phrase structure generation) may differ between individuals, but in line with the data reviewed in this book it is likely that the candidate areas will nevertheless be restricted to temporal and inferior frontal sites. Under the form of emergentist perspective on domain-specific cognitive function adopted in this book (i.e. that ancient neural mechanisms were recruited in the service of new, domain-specific tasks, rather than all domain-specific features of language having genetically dedicated subcircuits), domain-general neural mechanisms used by higher linguistic processes like phrase structure building are still nevertheless recruited in the service of their earlier cognitive functions (memory, motor planning, prediction, etc.) and have thereby 'kept their day jobs', as Bates (1999) would put. Plasticity is not some form of emergency procedure which is only called upon in times of crisis (e.g. lesions), but is part of normal, healthy brain function.

Perhaps the most dramatic form of evidence in favour of the present neural code thesis (as opposed to standard functional localisation theses) comes from the finding that the visual cortex of congenitally blind individuals is called upon for processing syntactically complex sentences (involving movement operations) but not for a sequence memory task involving pseudowords or for processing complex mathematical equations, indicating that this region can support the computation of sentence-level syntax (Lane et al. 2015). The so-called 'visual' cortex therefore seems able to execute the appropriate oscillatory code for constructing and maintaining complex phrasal units.

Given all this, and considering broader implications from neuropsychology and neurorehabilitation, I believe it less defensible to claim that region X is a 'syntax region' or a 'semantics region' than it is to claim that certain brain areas appear *more likely and are more susceptible* to have circuits set during maturity which code for certain functions. There is no species-universal, fixed syntax area (although each individual will likely, by maturity, have a fixed network dedicated to it), contrary to virtually all models in current neurolinguistics. Many such models are based on fMRI findings, which are averaged over group databases, indicating which regions are the *most common, likely areas* of syntax-specificity. But since this is not generalisable across all neurotypical subjects, let alone all brain types, we need a different account for language in the brain: a more abstract, generalisable neural code which can be implemented via different circuits across different regions. There will presumably be many factors determining where in the brain higher language functions are set, including intrinsic anatomical connectivity and cell type, but these factors are currently on the horizons of exploration. For example, Saygin et al. (2016) showed that the fixation of the so-called visual word form area in children at age eight was not based on functional responses they found at age five, but could rather be predicted by connectivity fingerprints. This possibly reflects a more general mechanism of development, whereby reading acquisition piggybacks off pre-existing circuitry.

Gomez et al. (2019) also provide a Pokémon-themed exploration of this topic, and they effectively come to the same conclusion about recently emerged stimuli (i.e. both written words and Pokémon are, in evolutionary time, extremely recent) piggybacking off pre-existing circuitry through development. Subjects who had extensively played the GameBoy masterpiece as children tended to have a specific part of occipitotemporal sulcus which was sensitive to images of Pokémon, while subjects who were sadly deprived of this experience did not show this sensitivity. Hence, there was no innate 'Pokémon region' but rather an innate ability to coordinate and fix circuitry to the specific task of identifying Pokémon. More generally, the further away we move from direct primary sensory regions and towards higher cognitive processes, the less rigidly fixed the neuroanatomical basis appears to be, varying considerably across individuals based on their history and independent genetic factors influencing neural organisation.

3.4.5 *Ironic α Decreases*

The oscillatory model for language developed in this book maintains that CFC can coordinate activity across distant cortical areas as a way of integrating information from different representational domains, giving rise to the combinatorial power of human cognition and, in particular, linguistic computation. The role of the α band is crucial in this model, but I have so far not dedicated much attention specifically to the computational properties of this rhythm – having focused on δ, θ, β and γ – and so this section will briefly address this.

Due to the inherently inhibitory nature of α, it is likely that this rhythm (generated, for instance, via pulvinar connectivity with early/visual parietal cortex) inhibits a given region permitting only the most excitable representations to be triggered. This α inhibition and information gating could contribute to the efficient coordination of the present {θ(γ)} coupling model. The α band would therefore act to shield the ongoing concatenation of features from irrelevant information, which are otherwise excitable; a form of 'protection', for Roux and Uhlhaas (2014). Effectively, increased parieto-occipital α is thought to reflect functional inhibition of certain processing streams, e.g. the dorsal visual stream would be inhibited during visual working memory tasks, preventing the processing of irrelevant information. Hence, as demands placed on verbal working memory increase, so too does occipital α activity (Proskovec et al. 2019). Noguchi and Kakigi (2020) also report that fronto-parietal α (and also β) activity increases with visual working memory load. This would constitute a particular implementation of the 'inhibition-timing hypothesis' of Klimesch et al. (2007), according to which α can inhibit task-irrelevant neural circuits, increasing in amplitude over irrelevant regions. For instance, Friese et al. (2013) discovered that successful memory encoding not only yielded enhanced {θ(γ)} phase–amplitude coupling, but also decreased prefrontal and occipital α (see also Kaplan et al. 2014 for evidence of the role of {θ(γ)} coupling in spatial memory retrieval, with their θ source being the medial temporal lobe, and also Tamura et al. 2017 for evidence that hippocampal-prefrontal {θ(γ)} coupling reflects a compensatory mechanism to maintain spatial working memory performance during environments of increased difficulty). Likewise, Michelmann et al. (2016) found that when subjects mentally replayed a short sound or video clip, α decreases were found in sensory-specific regions. Pursuing a similar research agenda, and using simulated neural networks, Gips et al. (2016) also showed that inhibitory α modulation coupled to γ serves to temporally segment visual information, preventing an overload of information. Finally, α decreases at right fronto-temporal sites were also found when clear syllables were temporally expected, with a longer foreperiod duration (Wilsch et al. 2015); these expectancy effects also appear in language, with increased semantic predictability leading to reduced parieto-occipital α (Wöstmann et al. 2015).

The role of α seems well suited, then, to Headley and Paré's (2017) description of certain generic oscillatory mechanisms, which may play something of an administrative role: 'They may serve as general-purpose mechanisms that enable the efficacious encoding and propagation of activities within and between networks, while at the same time being blind to their information content' (see also Meyer et al. 2013).

Explorations of discourse processing have also shed some light on the likely computational roles of α. Regel et al. (2014) contrasted literal and ironic target sentences which followed a particular context; in turn, the literal contexts were either grammatical or contained a syntactic violation. They discovered α decreases and θ increases in response to ironic sentences and syntactic violations, in comparison to grammatical literal sentences. Akimoto et al. (2017) also discovered greater α desynchronisation in the right anterior temporal lobe in response to ironic relative to literal sentences. As a result, α desynchronisation might index greater processing demands (intention of others, theory of mind, etc.), or at least a 'broader' processing network, for irony comprehension.

Wianda and Ross (2019) also provide evidence for distinct functional roles for α which can be executed in parallel, with α desynchronisation being found during memory encoding in a Sternberg memory task, and α power increases during memory retention in the same task. The authors found that α-γ phase–amplitude coupling (in the upper α band) also revealed centres of local computation involved in encoding and retention. This phase–amplitude coupling depicted a hierarchy of information flow from frontal to temporal and occipital brain areas. Recent findings about α in language processing can likely be subsumed to an extent by this multi-function model of encoding and retention in higher cognition.

The finding that α is generated in the thalamus and hippocampus (Buffalo et al. 2011) lends further support to the roles defended in this book for subcortical structures in language comprehension, and the spatial proximity of thalamic and hippocampal rhythms suggests that the above-mentioned oscillomic model of feature-set composition could be implemented highly efficiently, with minimal conduction delays (see also Kleen et al. 2016). The susceptibility of particular circuits to synchronise with α is modulated by cholinergic and serotonergic mechanisms alongside glutamatergic afferents acting via metabotropic receptors (Uhlhaas et al. 2008). Both metabotropic glutamate receptors (mGluR) and muscarinic acetylcholyn receptors (mAchR) generate thalamo-cortical α, with this distinction being of particular functional relevance: Vijayan and Kopell (2012) tested a conductance-based thalamic model of awake α which demonstrated that mAChr-generated α supports information processing during tasks, while mGluR-generated α performs the role discussed earlier of shutting out interfering information. Thalamic α has also been implicated in modulating cortical γ power, and is also suited to synchronise distinct cortical regions oscillating at α (Gips et al. 2016), increasing the likelihood that it plays an important role in phrase structure building and semantic composition.

Thalamic, hippocampal and frontal α and θ rhythms may consequently act as, respectively, inhibitory and control processes which modulate γ-related processes involved in the retrieval and activation of language-relevant features, with β then being employed in the maintenance of existing feature-sets in memory (see also Crandall et al. 2015 for evidence of neocortical control of thalamic gating, enhancing the role of the thalamus in higher cognitive functions). Whether θ or α are involved in synchronising γ would likely depend on which γ-itemised regions are implicated and the 'size' of the feature-set needed to be constructed.

Altogether, this suggests that linguistic communication and the interpretation of speech/gesture/sign results in multiple brains being coupled together, their oscillatory activity in some degree of synchrony. Taken with the more established findings that β desynchronisation is involved in the execution and processing of active and passive movements (Neuper et al. 2006) and the observation of another person's movements (Babiloni et al. 2002), and considering also Hickok's (2014) convincing rejection of the supposed centrality of mirror neurons in social cognition, we could conclude that a more appropriate metaphor for how the brain interprets other minds might be 'mirror rhythms'.

One final study sheds some further light on the computational properties of α. Piai et al. (2016) used EEG to explore context-driven word retrieval in patients with a left-temporal stroke (100 per cent overlap between patients in the middle temporal gyrus) and healthy controls. Retrieving an appropriate word from memory resulted in α-β desynchronisation at left temporal and inferior parietal lobe sites in healthy controls, but the brains of patients recruited identical right-hemispheric sites to perform this task (there being no significant difference with respect to task performance between patients and controls). Piai et al. also found hippocampal θ to be modulated by the amount of contextual linguistic information provided by their experimental sentences, which again indicates that parahippocampal θ is involved in the presently proposed θ-γ code. This points oscillatory investigations in a particular direction for lexical retrieval during sentence comprehension, and it also suggests a potential role for posterior transcallosal white matter connections via the splenium in right-hemisphere language comprehension. Indeed, the role of the right hemisphere in language comprehension is becoming much clearer with recent MEG forays into natural speech processing (Alexandrou et al. 2017).

Overall, while there is likely a specific role for α in certain brain regions in early-stage phrase structure building, the fact that α responses (in the form of (de)synchronisation, but also coupling) are found across such a wide range of linguistic processes suggests that it acts as a general information and attentional mechanism, e.g. with the magnitude of α desynchronisation being proportional to the degree of cortical activation.

3.5   Further Topics in Memory, Attention and Combinatoriality

The question of how the neural code for language interfaces with other cognitive systems will likely be the central topic of future research in neurolinguistics. An emerging theme in this book is that research into non-linguistic systems can help improve our understanding of the oscillatory dynamics employed by the language system. This will involve an engagement with the literature on memory, attention and combinatoriality, working out how best to incorporate these findings within a coherent oscillatory model of language.

3.5.1   Hippocampal Binding

As one of the leading research groups exploring the computational properties of θ, Hanslmayr et al. (2016) review the experimental literature from rodents and humans and suggest a general trend: While hippocampal $\{\theta(\gamma)\}$ phase–amplitude coupling mediates the binding of distinct episodic memory representations, the desynchronisation of slower neocortical rhythms (α and β) also appears to mediate the encoding of episodic memories, exposing the inhibitory role of α in aiding successful memory encoding and retrieval by other regions of the brain. The hippocampal synchronisation system therefore appears to *bind* information, while the neocortical desynchronisation system *stores* the representational content. Both episodic memory and language involve the binding of discontiguous representations such as distinct memories and unrelated semantic features (a hallmark of linguistic creativity exhibited in, for instance, polysemy). This crucial computational similarity may imply that both systems recruit the same hippocampal-neocortical system for aspects of their representational triggering and storage.

There are also interesting comparative directions opening up with respect to explorations of the neurobiological basis of episodic memory: Panoz-Brown et al. (2016) report for the first time that rats can remember multiple episodic memories encoded in different contexts, suggesting that this capacity is not unique to humans, and that the well-known oscillatory basis of memory in rats could inform discussions of human memory.

More generally, since it is situated at the terminus of the processing pathway, the hippocampus is assumed by Hanslmayr et al. (2016) to be involved in learning and interpreting complex conjunctive representations, whereas more atomic representations are interpreted in regions further towards and including the neocortex. A fascinating, unanswered question surrounds the mechanistic interaction between these two systems: At the neural level, how do slower hippocampal rhythms (and indeed other closely situated subcortical slow rhythms) relate to faster neocortical ones? Further research is required in order to address this question.

The role of the hippocampus in language may also range beyond what has presently been described and speculated. For example, recent work by Ellamil et al. (2016) points in very promising directions, demonstrating the central role of the hippocampus in spontaneous thought generation (often termed 'mind-wandering', which putatively takes up 20–50 per cent of daily life; Killingsworth & Gilbert 2010), with a large portion of the region's neurons being equally involved in short-distance and long-distance connections (see also Kucyi 2018). This may also explain some of the qualities of spontaneous thought, such as the fact that they often contain semantic representations 'of wild diversity and content', as the authors put it, since these hippocampal long-range connections interface with numerous cortical regions responsible for storing a variety of representations. If spontaneous thought were generated in another, less densely connected region, it would likely exhibit a greater degree of semantic regularity. It may also be the case – as argued in Teyler and DiScenna's (1986) hippocampal memory indexing theory – that through retaining indexes of neocortical representations, these hippocampal 'memory traces' achieve an archetypal role of word meaning as typically conceived by semanticists, namely that individual lexical items are *instructions to build concepts* (Pietroski 2018), and instructions for the language system to employ distinct cognitive systems to construct a larger, richer representation.

The hippocampus, then, could not only explain core features of what Ellamil et al. (2016, 195) call 'the restless nature of our minds', but it could also more specifically shed some light on lexical semantics (see also Mišić et al. 2014 for evidence that the hippocampus is a crucial convergence zone for information flow). Above all else, these observations reinforce the central position subcortical structures should occupy in any neurolinguistic model.

3.5.2   Cartographic Reconciliation

We have so far covered much ground with respect to brain dynamics and brain shape. Some attempts have also been made to reconcile traditional cartographic neurolinguistic models with the one emerging in this book. However, some issues concerning functional neuroimaging remain to be addressed before this chapter can progress to a number of final refinements to our understanding of the oscillatory nature of language. This will allow us to properly situate the literature on memory, attention and combinatoriality within the context of linguistics.

Biophysiological research has conclusively shown that the cortex operates via interactions between 'feedforward' and 'feedback' information, projecting between deep and superficial layers (Larkum 2013). The set of feedforward γ rhythms employed in the present oscillatory model of language would be mostly generated in supragranular cortical layers (L2/3) (Maier et al. 2010), while hippocampal θ would be generated via slow pulses of GABAergic inhibition as a result of medial septum input, part of a brainstem-dienceph-alo-septohippocampal θ-gene rating system (Vertes & Kocsis 1997). The interactions between the hippocampus and medial prefrontal cortex necessary to focus attention on language-relevant features (considering the conclusions of Lara & Wallis 2015 on the role of prefrontal cortex in working memory, which stressed the centrality of attention rather than storage, and also the conclusions in Morton et al. 2017 regarding the role of the medial prefrontal cortex and hippocampus in memory integration) may be mediated through an indirect pathway passing through midline thalamic nucleus reuniens (Jin & Maren 2015). Empirically speaking, this model is compatible with the finding that sentences containing licit lexical categories result in increased γ relative to sentences involving violations of word category (Bastiaansen et al. 2010). Differences in θ power are known to exist for function words versus content words (Bastiaansen et al. 2005; a finding incorrectly reported in Friederici et al. 2017, 131 as differences in γ power, despite Bastiaansen et al. 2005, 535 stating that 'we were not able to analyse activity in the gamma frequency range'), indicating at least some role for θ pockets of distinct sizes (or memory traces) in accommodating different types of linguistic representations.

Friederici's (2016) claim that BA 44 and its dorsal fibre connections to the temporal cortex 'support the processing of structural hierarchy in humans' is therefore not incorrect, but is rather a piece of a larger system found in the language-ready brain (see also Zaccarella & Friederici 2015, and also Bulut et al. 2017 for evidence that the familiar left inferior frontal and anterior temporal regions are implicated in processing Chinese sentences, stretching beyond the usual list of Indo-European languages tested, and finally Bradley et al. 2017 for evidence that BA 44 is sensitive not just to hierarchically organised Noun Phrases – as in Zaccarella & Friederici 2015 – but also Verbs Phrases, Adjective Phrases and Preposition Phrases). Indeed, structural hypotheses regarding language comprehension and production are necessarily limited by technology: fMRI may (and in fact appears to) implicate distinct structures from, for instance, MEG. Relying solely on fMRI to build a cartographic model of the language system will lead to hypotheses ignoring the dynamical nature of the brain's activity.

If there is no specialisation in the brain for complex syntax, but there is for lexical-semantic processing (as is shown in Siegelman et al. 2017), why is there so much focus on BA 44 and dorsal stream activity in the literature? The reason may be that the dorsal stream corresponds fairly well to domain-general regions, which suggests that the domain-general executive system is responsible for interpreting complex morphosyntax. The fact that there is specialisation for lexical information simply supports the present γ-itemisation model, in which distinct regions are specialised for certain representations and semantic categories.

Zaccarella and Friederici (2017) review the neuroimaging literature and suggest (in contrast to Friederici 2016) that the most ventral anterior portion of BA 44 may be the seat of 'the Merge computation'. Although there are a number of reasons to believe this model to be highly reductive and neurobiologically implausible (as discussed earlier), this fMRI literature nevertheless needs to be reconciled somehow with the oscillatory framework developed here. I would like to suggest, building on earlier observations, that the language system exploits BA 44 as part of its external memory during phrase structure building; while the oscillatory phase code outlined in this book is responsible for structure building operations, circuits in BA 44 are used to maintain sets of feature-sets; and given what has been discussed here, the prediction which follows from this is that this region would exhibit β increases during this process. In newborns, the dorsal pathway connecting BA 44 to the posterior temporal cortex is not fully formed with respect to its myelination (Perani et al. 2011), presumably barring the development of this phylogenetically young (relative to most cortical structures) memory buffer. Crucially, the development of this pathway throughout childhood correlates with performance on hierarchically structured sentences (Skeide et al. 2016), suggesting that while the pathway is indeed important for external syntactic memory (the more mature the pathway, the more complex the structures it is able to 'send' to the inferior frontal memory workspace), it is not essential for structure building computations (although further evidence is needed to elucidate the precise role of the dorsal pathway in syntactic processing). Furthermore, minimal linguistic hierarchies such as two-word phrases seem to trigger no significant activation in subcortical regions in fMRI experiments, suggesting either that these regions become more sensitive to maintaining and (re)analysing larger structures, or that fMRI itself is not sensitive to tracking the dynamic activation in these regions during minimal phrasal construction.

Due to a recent subparcellation of BA 44 into five subregions (Clos et al. 2013), each of which likely contributes functionally distinct processes to linguistic computation, Zaccarella et al. (2017) close their fMRI study of simple phrasal constructions by commenting that '[f]uture investigations on merge may want to use highly detailed parcellation maps to allow for a finer grained structure-to-function cortical mapping'. But this cartographic research programme will lead to a conceptual dead end. Even if particular syntactic and semantic sub-operations could be correlated with particular subregions of BA 44, this would be of limited theoretical value. Functional studies can only take us so far; oscillatory investigations have the potential to build far stronger bridges between linguistic theory and neurobiology.

Nevertheless, what the cartographic programme can say with confidence is that cortical regions relevant for language in the left hemisphere share a similar multireceptor organisation. Zilles et al. (2014) constructed a receptoarchitectonic 'fingerprint' of areas shown to be involved in syntactic processing, and demonstrated a remarkable similarity between BA 44 (both ventral or dorsal parts, BA 44v and BA 44d), the inferior frontal sulcus, the posterior temporal gyrus and sulcus, and the posterior superior temporal gyrus. This common molecular structure for the cortical syntax network is likely an evolutionary novelty, although further receptoarchitectonic studies with non-human primates will be required to explore this topic in greater detail.

3.5.3   Grounding Memory and Attention

Oscillatory research into the development of attentional mechanisms will be crucial for language scientists attempting to explain fundamental features of linguistic behaviour. Recent work shows a direct correlation between the emergence of endogenous attentional mechanisms (mind-internal directed attention, in contrast to exogenous attention, directed at the environment) and the ability to track non-adjacent morphosyntactic dependencies, both emerging at around twelve to fifteen months (de Diego-Balaguer et al. 2016). Infants also display a bias such that words featuring adjacent reduplications (such as *neenee*) are easier to learn than non-reduplicated words (Ota & Skarabela 2016). This occurs due to exogenous attentional mechanisms maturing earlier than endogenous ones. Ota and Skarabela (2018) more recently suggested that register-specific reduplications of the kind found in infant-directed speech evolved as a response to a predisposition in infants to parse words featuring adjacent reduplications better than words without such reduplications.

Recent work suggests that spatio-temporal patterns of processing syntactically complex, memory-demanding sentences result in left parietal α increases, while higher β is found for long- relative to short-distance dependencies (β is more generally implicated in the maintenance of existing cognitive sets; see Engel & Fries 2010; Sheng et al. 2019). A possible reason for this is that the greater working memory load needed to resolve long-distance dependencies requires a higher frequency band to synchronise the cell assemblies implicated in the feature-sets of the filler and gap; certain assemblies would be preactivated by the filler (since dependents share a subset of their features). As Grimaldi (2019) summarises, 'beta synchronization serves to bind distributed sets of neurons into a coherent representation of (memorised) contents during language processing'.

Elaborating on the earlier discussion concerning the presently proposed oscillatory code for language, because γ is modulated by cloze probability (Wang, Zhu et al. 2012) $\{\theta(\gamma/\beta)\}$ synchronisation may be the central mechanism of feature-set binding within phrase structures, with γ being responsible for semantic prediction and feature-binding (compositional meaning) and β being responsible for syntactic object maintenance (monotonic labelling) and possibly also feature-binding, depending on the format of the feature. Much recent work has shown that β is sensitive to syntactic violations (Kielar et al. 2014, 2015) along with semantic incongruities (Wang, Jensen et al. 2012), with β power decreasing when such anomalies occur. An interesting part of these findings is that such β decreases were found not just in standard perisylvian 'language' regions, but also large areas of occipital cortex and parts of the superior frontal gyrus. Supporting the present assumptions about the role of β in labelling, recent work has also correlated cortico-basal ganglia-thalamic loop β with working memory (Parnaudeau et al. 2013). Lastly, memory formation of verbal material has been linked with β power decreases in the left inferior frontal gyrus. Suggestions that this link is a causal one come from an rTMS study revealing that synchronising the left inferior prefrontal cortex at β (~18.5Hz) impaired verbal memory formation (Hanslmayr et al. 2014). The entrained β oscillations also persisted for ~1.5s after stimulation, leading to an 'entrainment echo'.

A recent study concerning episodic memory also made a small step towards the goals for neurolinguistics outlined here. Heusser et al. (2016) showed that episodic sequence memory is supported by a θ-γ phase code, such that 'elements within an experience are represented by neural cell assemblies firing at higher frequencies (gamma) and sequential order is encoded by the specific timing of firing with respect to a lower frequency oscillation (theta)'. This should surely boost the confidence of language scientists trying to show that some form of phase–amplitude coupling is responsible for basic aspects of syntactic and semantic feature composition. Given that baboons have recently been shown to be capable of accurately storing the linear position of single episodes (Noser & Byrne 2015), a comparative neuroethological approach to episodic memory could easily be adopted. Interestingly, Heusser et al. found phase–amplitude decreases over items in a sequence in left lateralised and left posterior MEG clusters, not increases. This was due to the broadening of the γ distribution over a θ cycle. This finding also closely matches the work of Vaz et al. (2017), who discovered that successful memory formation resulted in phase–amplitude coupling decreases in left temporal lobe (θ coupled to low γ), left and right inferior frontal gyri (θ coupled to high γ), and medial temporal lobes along the parahippocampal gyri and the right orbitofrontal cortex (α coupled to low γ). This suggests that these two anatomically distinct sites of coupling were responsible for two different memory processes which are ultimately responsible for successful episodic memory encoding. Over-coupling may therefore place certain limits on cortical processing flexibility. Alternatively, as argued by Vaz et al. (2017), phase–amplitude decreases may be due to the fact that γ cycles are distributed over a greater number of phase bins of the slower rhythm.

In more recent work, Bahramisharif et al. (2018) asked participants to retain a sequence of three letters for several seconds, and showed that γ representations of the individual letters peaked at distinct phases of the θ/α (7-13Hz) cycle: γ representations of the first letter peaked earlier in the θ/α cycle than the second letter, and the second letter earlier than the third. Thus, the θ/α cycle appears to organise the sequence, dictating the order of representational encoding. The γ rhythms ensure that cell populations putatively coding for individual elements fire approximately 20ms after the preceding cell population fires. Given the cluster of syntactic and semantic features attributed to individual lexical items during comprehension, this ~20ms time course can readily be exploited by the language system to activate and rehearse word-internal representations. For example, the cortical phase code supported by Bahramisharif et al. (2018) – or an analogous one – could ground the serial representation of items in language processing. Mapping this neural code onto linguistic representations and real-time language processing, as proposed here, can take a number of potential experimental routes.

These mechanisms can also shed potential light on the implementational basis of the syntactic notion of multidimensionality. Consider a structure such as 'The young, eager, happy, either going to Oxford or Cambridge, pleasant man'. These forms of modificational structures are unbounded and unstructured, can involve coordination involving disjunction ('either X or Y...'), and are highly complex semantic structures. CFC could implement the 'Pair-Merge' operation typically invoked in the linguistics literature (a form of adjunction, not modifying the hierarchical structure of the element it adjoins to, which can be reduced to a set-forming process, Oseki 2015) to yield multidimensional structures, with multiple points of phase-synchronised contact between γ-itemised units representing each item. More specifically, consider the proposal in Griffiths and Fuentemilla (2020) for how θ-γ coupling can construct episodic memories interrupted by event boundaries (e.g. a conversation interrupted by a disruption, and then continuing afterwards). These authors suggest that during the course of the first event (i.e. the first part of the conversation), each element of the ongoing event is coded for by a unique hippocampal cell population locked to a discrete phase of the θ cycle. The event model is maintained as a θ-γ code for the event's duration. These are by now standard assumptions; however, Griffiths and Fuentemilla propose an innovation, such that as the event unfolds and becomes more complex, new cell populations coding for new elements of the event are added to the end of the existing θ-γ code (along the lines of the system in Heusser et al. 2016 discussed earlier). This procedure could readily map to elements in the multidimensional structure ('young, eager, happy…') which make the structure increasingly complex. When an event boundary is encountered in Griffiths and Fuentemilla's system – or, for us, when an interruption occurs in the multi-dimensional structure such as a shift in categorial format to, for example, disjunction – the θ-γ code is rapidly replayed to facilitate additional retroactive encoding of the finalised event representation, most likely reflected in a spike in hippocampal activity after the boundary. Through this process, the current event/structure becomes conjoined (Pair-Merged) with the original event/struc-ture. As proposed earlier, slower δ interactions with this θ-γ complex would also be needed to index and monitor the phrase structure identity of the units constructed, unlike in the case of Griffiths and Fuentemilla's (2020) episodic memories, which involve no such hierarchical structure.

To again briefly elaborate on proposals made earlier, in the model I am pursuing here α is assumed to play an important inhibitory role, but I would additionally like to suggest that it is closely related to θ cycles such that α can coordinate feature-sets organised by θ. Since α is a crucial part of domain-general attentional mechanisms, I will adopt the claim in Jensen et al. (2014) that direct attention is allocated only to the first items in a given θ- or α-constructed sequence, and that the final (and hence least excitable) items are processed pre-attentively. Along with explaining a number of visual phenom-ena (see Jensen et al. 2014), it is possible that this mechanism is responsible for certain facts about language, such that, quite often, only certain features of a given word or phrase come to attention during sentence comprehension and are made 'prominent'. The firing of particular neural clusters representing a given feature X could also engage fast GABAergic inhibition (a result of γ activity) and inhibit the firing of clusters representing feature Y. Indeed, it has been found that patients with attention deficit hyperactivity disorder exhibit impaired control of posterior α (Mazaheri et al. 2010), and it is possible that these sorts of oscillatory connectomopathies could explain deficits in cognitive functions reliant to some extent on attention.

A recent thesis by Heinz (2016) includes novel experimental work confirm-ing some of these proposals. Heinz asked participants to perform two tasks demanding short-term retention of visual working memory items. EEG results suggested that α oscillations reflect the implementation of an attentionally selective executive control process which inhibits task-irrelevant processes and supports the stability of active item retention.

The assumptions of the present oscillatory model are also supported by a self-paced reading study which monitored oscillatory dynamics. Vignali et al. (2016) had participants read syntactically and semantically well-formed sen-tences, sentences containing a semantic violation, and word lists. Fixations at semantically unrelated words elicited lower β desynchronisation, while γ power increased as well-formed sentences were processed. This γ effect was not found with word lists. In addition, θ power increased in the 300–800ms window after sentence onset in well-formed sentences, but not during word lists, lending support to the present hypothesised role of θ in memory retrieval and syntactic 'chunking' operations. A further advantage of the present model is that it points to the compatibility between dynamical systems approaches to the brain and more traditional computational models which treat the brain as a digital computer. These perspectives are not incommensurable if we assume that particular discrete computational operations are executed via dynamical properties of neural oscillations.

This account, if accurate, would serve as part of a model for the neural formatting of human thought. Human-specific diverse phase relations (Maris et al. 2016) would permit a greater degree of featural 'size' via the range of cross-coupling information gating. Similar approaches (accompanied by hodological research into the pathways responsible for a given CFC relation) could be taken to the oscillatory behaviour of non-human ape brains (a topic returned to later).

In the present model, bottom-up γ would rapidly shift the ongoing set of featural representations through a standard feedforward mechanism, updating hippocampal θ and the widely distributed inter-areal β. The responsibility for linking distinct cortical areas into *neurocognitive networks* (NCNs; Bressler & Richter 2015; otherwise known as coordinative structures; Kelso et al. 2013), or large-scale, self-organising cortical networks, likely falls to β. Bressler and Richter (2015) claim that this rhythm plays dual roles, being implicated in NCN maintenance and transferring top-down signals to lower levels in the cortical hierarchy, e.g. the γ range (see Lewis & Bastiaansen 2015, Lewis et al. 2015). Supporting evidence comes, for instance, from seminal work by Klimesch et al. (2001) which demonstrated that interpreting pseudowords resulted in decreased β power over left frontal and left parietal regions relative to real words. This model is compatible with the need for phrases to be labelled via two (domain-general) sub-processes, mentioned earlier: object maintenance (keeping the constructed set in memory) and property attribution (affording the set an independent computational identity), since β would be able to simultaneously maintain an object as a cognitive set (via its steady or increasing amplitude) and attribute a specific representational property to it (via top-down feed-back and transferring prediction signals).

Work by Fedorenko et al. (2016) using intracranial recordings has also revealed monotonic γ increases over the course of sentence processing during both reading and listening, a finding absent during the reading of nonword-lists. Since nonword-lists result in higher cognitive demand, the γ increases during sentence comprehension are most likely due to an underlying neurocomputational procedure which derives the structure of the sentence, constituting support for the model proposed here. Interestingly, Fedorenko et al. found distributed γ increases across the fronto-temporal language network, rather than narrowly localised activation, going against more classical models and, again, supporting the notion that cross-cortical γ clusters are implicated in sentential feature-set construction. This study underscores the need for neuro-linguists to explore possible algorithmic models to explain their data, rather than redescribing their results through embedding them in rhetorical constructions in the manner of Fedorenko et al. (e.g. associating dynamic processes like 'γ increases' with higher-order, complex, multifaceted cognitive processes like 'successful comprehension').

EEG experiments conducted by Lewis, Lemhöfer et al. (2016) indicate that when gender features are mismatched, β immediately decreases relative to gender agreement. This effect is present in L2 speakers only when they are explicitly asked to focus on the ungrammaticality of the gender violation; normal reading does not yield this β decrease. These results at once suggest (contrary to the actual conclusions drawn by Lewis, Lemhöfer et al. 2016) that focusing purely on individual rhythms will not deliver a comprehensive model of phrase structure building and feature-set construction, since β in this instance seems to be modulated more by attentional load than any necessary structure-building operations: Phrases are constructed whether the L2 speakers are consciously focusing on ungrammaticalities or not, and yet a β difference is found. Indeed, number agreement violations seem to not modulate β at all (Davidson & Indefrey 2007), although the evidence here is mixed since Pérez et al. (2012) found α and (exclusively) low β decreases after subject-verb number agreement violations ('The cook$_{3sg}$ *cooked$_{2sg}$ ...'). These decreases after agreement violations typically occur alongside θ increases, pointing to the recruitment of additional lexical access resources (e.g. Kielar et al. 2015).

Yet the present oscillatory model also crucially diverges from an NCN account. To claim that β fluctuations denote NCN revisions is to restrict one's theory of neural computation to the most general, psychological level of analysis, and the operations and sub-processes of representation construction remain at a distance. The few current oscillatory models of sentence comprehension that exist (Lewis & Bastiaansen 2015; Vignali et al. 2016) all rely on basic notions such as rhythmic increases and decreases, and little else besides. Attempting to construct serious linking hypotheses by keeping solely to experimental constructs like β desynchronisation, without exploring the processes that give rise to such effects, is to commit the same mistake correlational, functional imaging studies have done for decades, limiting theory construction purely to immediate empirical observables.

Other recent work suggests that rhythmic modulation is far from a baroque procedure, occurring not only between cortical micro-columns but also within them. A study of human temporal neocortex detected γ in superficial layers and also θ in supra- and infragranular layers (Florez et al. 2013). The γ phase lagged behind the θ phase, pointing to an influence on θ from deep to superficial layers. It is noteworthy for our purposes that γ was strongly modulated by the θ phase. If emerging research suggests that temporal cortical regions are saturated with phase-modulating oscillatory activity, this should point neurolinguists in new directions for exploring the implementation of linguistic computation.

3.5.4   *Reservoir Computing, Discrete Results and the Syntax of Silence*

At this point, concerns will naturally arise about the explanatory scope of the oscillome. To what extent can this model of neural dynamics – informed as it is so deeply by findings from research into non-linguistic cognitive domains – suffice with respect to linguistic computation? Exploring a branch of recurrent neural networks – reservoir computing – may provide additional neurocomputational power to the present oscillomic model. Enel et al. (2016) discuss how mixed selectivity in cortical neurons is generated by randomly connected recurrent networks, with this mixed selectivity contributing to the representation of diverse situations which an organism can then use to respond appropriately in novel contexts. With reservoir computing, the recurrent networks are fixed, and learning only changes the connections these fixed neurons have to output neurons, not the networks themselves. Enel et al. (2016) summarise that '[t]he fixed recurrent connections provide the network with an inherent high dimensional dynamics that creates essentially all possible spatial and temporal combinations of the inputs which can then be selected, by learning, to perform the desired task'. The ability to recombine past and present sensory inputs allows reservoir networks to generate mixed selectivity in order to deliver what Enel et al. (2016) call 'pre-coded representations of an essentially universal set of contexts'.

Reservoir computing involves the arbitrary combination of present and past sensory inputs via circuit loops, something of potentially great use to a language system which exhibits novel combinations of seemingly discrete and fixed representations. It would be worth investigating whether language-relevant regions of the left inferior frontal cortex such as Broca's area, along with middle temporal regions and subcortical structures implicated in language, exhibit reservoir computing capacities, with recurrent networks of the kind explored by Enel et al. potentially generating stored (neurally fixed) lexical representations which can be accessed and deployed in novel situations, acting as a particular perspective the brain imposes on the world of sensory experience. In other words, since learning only changes the connections that fixed neurons have to output neurons and not the actual networks, this combination of representational persistence alongside implementational dynamism is precisely the kind of granularity that models of the lexicon could be formulated at.

Related research has shown that the output cells of reservoir networks can feed back into these networks and act as working memory via an input-driven attractor which can maintain this information (Pascanu & Jaeger 2011).

These ideas have been implemented by Hinaut and Dominey's (2013) reservoir network, through which BA 47 receives recurrent online input related to word categories with plastic cortico-striatal connections. Hinaut and Dominey exploit the homology between the cortico-striatal system and reservoir computing, with recurrent frontal cortical networks being the reservoir and plastic cortico-striatal synapses being the readout. The authors showed that this network can successfully decode grammatical structure from sentences through generating parallel sets of predictions about sentence meaning, which are confirmed or updated during processing. Szalisznyó et al. (2016) followed up on this work to show that cortico-striatal language pathways utilise this reservoir logic to dynamically adjust for syntactic complexity during online processing and assign thematic roles, suggesting that this is a neurobiologically realistic model of language comprehension.

In tandem with reservoir logic, another potential way to ground basic features of linguistic computation is via sequences of 'Discrete Results', or discrete spatio-temporal functional units formed by fast-spiking interneurons, which is the name Castejon and Nuñez (2016) give to the cortical mechanism of extracting, coding and memorising neural information. The authors discuss how a synchronised network of fast-spiking inhibitory cells can control a spatially distributed set of excitatory pyramidal cells, forming an ensemble. Fast-spiking interneurons limit the temporal window during which action potentials can be created, and so pyramidal cells are more likely to fire at precise temporal points. As a result, there will also be a cycle of no spiking, creating what Castejon and Nuñez call 'Silent Gaps', and this cyclic nature of pyramidal firing within ensembles defines Discrete Results. As the authors put it, '[i]nformation is encoded in the precise relations between temporal structured discharges'. They add that 'discrete cortical processing can be dynamically adjusted to meet the finest processing resolution depending on perceptual, task or attentional demands'. Evidence for this view includes data showing that perceptual coding and discrimination are enhanced by increasing fast spiking (Lee et al. 2012). It may be that this cyclic process of forming Discrete Results produces the emergent phenomenon of neural oscillations at the population level of ensembles. The Discrete Results model also permits the same cells to be implicated in multiple representations, with only modulations in Silent Gaps being needed.

While Merchant (2001) can point theoretical syntacticians in the direction of a 'syntax of silence' for 'omitted' or 'elided' structures like in ellipsis and sluicing (e.g. 'Someone called but I can't say who <called>', where the lower copy is not pronounced), this issue of spiking gaps can also lead neurolinguists to a discussion of the (neural) syntax of (spike) silence. Li and Tsien (2017) propose a *Neural Self-Information Theory*, according to which neural coding operates via the self-information principle under which variability in the time durations of inter-spike-intervals is self-tagged with discrete information. As such, different periods of spiking inactivity would carry different information, depending on the variability-probability distribution of the inter-spike-interval. Inter-spike-intervals which have a high probability (e.g. the balanced excitation-inhibition 'ground state' is the most highly predictable) would therefore carry minimal information, while extremely transient or prolonged silence would carry more information. The ways in which patterns of spike silence can influence larger-scale forms of synchronised oscillatory behaviour is a topic for future research.

3.5.5   Modelling Phrase Structure Generation via Phase–Amplitude Coupling

Phase–amplitude coupling is a diverse phenomenon, as this book has demonstrated. Yet, if our understanding of the neurochemical basis of oscillations appears opaque, then our understanding of the biophysical basis of phase–amplitude coupling is even more so. Theoretical neurobiologists disagree on how precisely to mathematically capture this phenomenon. This section aims to embed the present oscillatory model of language more directly within these nascent frameworks, although a more concerted effort to comprehensively describe the properties of various coupling processes will be left for future work.

Theoretical neuroscience is based on the proposal that methods from mathematics and physics can provide insight into nervous system function (Dayan & Abbott 2001). Embracing this proposal, consider first how a core tenet of signal processing is that a linear output from an input-state-output system will have a frequency profile identical to its input. For nonlinear systems, energy at a given frequency in the inputs appears at different frequencies in the outputs. This results in CFC between two sources, when the output of one source provides an input to another (Chen et al. 2008; Kramer & Eden 2013; Sotero 2015). Pyramidal cells can produce a range of intrinsic dynamics based purely on the type and localisation of conductances, such that a combination of sodium, potassium and calcium conductances yield simultaneous γ and θ signatures on tonic depolarisation. We have already suggested that CFC, supposedly generated by these neurochemical dynamics, plays a role in neural computation. There are currently two main schools of thought with respect to modelling these neural population dynamics, each of which can potentially provide insights into the nature of oscillatory coupling (see the seminal review in Sotero 2015, from which much of this discussion is adapted). One approach involves neuronal networks where individual cells are described by Hodgkin-Huxley-type equations (using multiple compartments for the soma, axon and dendrites, or alternatively single compartments for computational simplicity; White et al. 2000), and the other approach involves neural mass models (NMMs) where only the average activity of neuronal populations are entertained, putting aside second-order statistics (i.e. variance and covariances) (Jansen & Rit 1995). Both of these provide a potential means of studying phase–amplitude coupling.

One way to construct an NMM is to suppose that each neural population executes two mathematical operations, following Jansen and Rit (1995): (1) conversion of postsynaptic potentials into the average density of action potentials, modelled via a sigmoid function; (2) conversion of action potentials into postsynaptic potentials via a linear convolution with an impulse response function (which describes the evolution of a variable along a time horizon after a given moment, a concept used in signal processing and economics; Hamilton 1994, 318–320). The Jansen-Rit model is achieved when the impulse response function has the following form:

$$g(t) = Gkte^{-kt}$$

This yields a system of second-order differential equations describing the dynamics of postsynaptic potentials across neural populations. This model invokes pyramidal cells, excitatory interneurons and inhibitory interneurons, and is described by a system of second-order differential equations:

$$\frac{d^2x_0(t)}{dt^2} = -2a\frac{dx_0(t)}{dt} - a^2x_0(t)$$
$$+ AaS(x_1(t) - x_2(t)),$$
$$\frac{d^2x_1(t)}{d^2} = -2a\frac{dx_1(t)}{dt} - a^2x_1(t)$$
$$+ AaS(p + \Gamma_2S(\Gamma_1x_0(t))),$$
$$\frac{d^2x_2(t)}{dt^2} = -2b\frac{dx_2(t)}{dt} - b^2x_2(t) + Bb\Gamma_4S(\Gamma_3x_0(t))$$

x_0 is the excitatory postsynaptic potential feeding into the two populations of interneurons, and x_1 and x_2 are, respectively, excitatory and inhibitory postsynaptic potentials entering into the pyramidal population. Γ_{1-4} are the connection strengths between populations, and the EEG signal is assumed to be proportional to $x_1(t) - x_2(t)$ (see Sotero 2015 for details of how this model can be realised through δ-α phase–amplitude coupling)

As indicated, models of phase–amplitude coupling generation consist of inhibitory networks (White et al. 2000) or networks with both inhibitory and excitatory cells (Spaak, Zeitler et al. 2012). For example, considering the former (Inhibitory-Inhibitory networks, or *I-I* networks) White et al. (2000) provided a simulated hippocampal inhibitory network with fast and slow interneurons which generated θ-γ phase–amplitude coupling under certain fixed conditions. Their network was comprised of single compartment neurons modelled with the Hodgkin-Huxley formalism, where $i = 1,..., N$ counts the number of cells in the network, I_i is the applied current, and η is normally distributed noise:

$$C\frac{dV_i}{dt} = I_i = I_{Na} = I_K = I_L = I_S + \eta$$

Sodium (I_{Na}), potassium (I_K), leak (I_L) and synaptic (I_S) currents are given as:

$$I_{Na} = g_{Na}m_{\infty}^3 h(V_i - V_{Na})$$

$$I_K = g_K n^4(V_i - V_K)$$

$$I_L = g_{lN}(V_i - V_L)$$

$$I_S = \sum_{j=1} \frac{g_{s,j}}{N} s_j(V_i - V_s)$$

In White et al. (2000), synaptic conductances $g_{s,j}$ were valued as fast to fast cells, fast to slow cells, slow to slow cells or slow to fast cells (further equations for the gating variables h, n and s are in White et al.; see also Sotero 2015 for discussion). Phase–amplitude coupling was achieved when there were strong connections between the same populations, or weaker connections between populations (in particular, from fast to slow populations). Modelling the coupling dynamics of the language network should therefore follow these insights, such that the forms of phase–amplitude coupling proposed in this book as being responsible for generating phrase structure building would be predicted to occur as a consequence of either strong within-population connections or weak between-population connections where the directionality of coupling is from γ to δ, or γ to θ, or γ to α. Hülsemann et al. (2019) also provide evidence that of all the methods of computing coupling, only the generalised linear model cross-frequency coupling (GLM-CFC) method and the modulation index (MI) can detect biphasic coupling.

Continuing with this particular form of coupling, and shifting focus from *I-I* to Excitatory-Inhibitory (*E-I*) networks, consider how the hippocampus is also composed of pyramidal cells. Kopell, Börgers et al. (2010) develop a model comprised of pyramidal cells, fast-spiking basket cells and oriens lacunosum-moleculare (O-LM) interneurons. The outputs of these O-LM neurons are projected as slow inhibitory postsynaptic potentials onto the distal apical dendrites of pyramidal cells. Basket cells and O-LM cells were modelled with a single compartment, while pyramidal cells were modelled by five compartments (one for basal dendrites, one for soma, three for apical dendrites). Along with sodium, potassium, leak and synaptic current (as mentioned earlier), Kopell, Börgers et al. (2010) also considered two additional currents: the h-current and the A current (see Tort et al. 2007 for further details and equations for each compartment). The results indicated that O-LM cells alone can coordinate cell assemblies, and that a single θ rhythm can coordinate different cell assemblies with distinct γ frequencies.

Applying these insights to the present model, it seems neurobiologically plausible to suggest that the hypothesised δ-θ, δ-γ and θ-γ interactions claimed here to form the core component of phrase structure building rely on an additional dynamic mechanism: modulation of γ-itemisation via amplitude coordination by slower rhythms, and hence a phase–amplitude coupling-based manipulation of representational format and complexity.

More recently, Sotero et al. (2019) investigated the interactions between different temporal scales of information flow in complex networks to better understand the basis of phase–amplitude coupling. They looked at two types of networks, Erdős-Rényi networks and scale-free networks. The former type is a random graph where each possible edge has the same probability p of existing, and the degree of a node $i(k_i)$ is defined as the number of connections it has to other nodes. The degree distribution $P(k)$ of the network is a binomial distribution, decaying exponentially for large degrees k, permitting only small degree fluctuations. The other type of network, scale-free networks, is constructed on the assumption that new nodes in a network are not connected at random but with high probability to those which possess a large number of connections (i.e. hubs). In these networks, $P(k)$ decays as a power law, yielding scale-invariance, permitting large degree fluctuations.

Sotero et al. found that scale-free networks facilitate phase–amplitude coupling between slow and fast frequency components, while Erdős-Rényi networks facilitated coupling between slow frequency components. As such, it is likely that regions of the brain hosting forms of slower couplings responsible for phrase structure building in the present model (e.g. δ-θ and δ-β couplings, in addition to slow phase-phase coupling) host certain properties of simulated Erdős-Rényi networks.

The final part of Sotero et al.'s (2019) analysis involved comparing phase–amplitude coupling between Alzheimer's disease patients and healthy controls. They found that the strongest form of phase–amplitude coupling in both of these populations was across a particular pathway, a right superior frontal-right medial orbitofrontal-left superior frontal pathway. The phase–amplitude coupling pathway that increased the most for Alzheimer's disease patients was left insula-left pars opercularis-left superior temporal, suggesting a hyperactive level of coupling strength relative to healthy controls. This issue of over-coupling has been discussed elsewhere (Murphy & Benítez-Burraco 2016), and appears to relate to perturbations in information flow and may also be caused by white matter degradation (Wang et al. 2015), but this finding is also potentially relatable to the existence of certain language deficits in Alzheimer's disease, since this pathway cuts across major portions of language-relevant cortex. For instance, naming disorders, impaired auditory and written comprehension, fluent but empty speech, and semantic paraphasia have all been documented as typical deficits in Alzheimer's disease (see Szatloczki et al. 2015 and references therein). This issue, along with the others addressed in this brief section, are ripe for future experimental and modelling work.

3.6   Implications and Qualifications

The remainder of this book will attempt to make some final qualifications with respect to the implications of assuming an oscillatory perspective of language. For instance, what are the implications for language development, philosophy and other neighbouring domains? Afterwards, the final section of this chapter (3.7) will discuss how to further extend the neural code presented here.

3.6.1   *Language Acquisition and its Implications for the Oscillome*

Although I have so far paid little attention to the topic, electrophysiological studies of infant and child language processing will be crucial in furthering our understanding of the growth and development of the oscillome, since the developmental characteristics of human oscillatory behaviour are far from well understood. To take one of the very few current examples of this, Schneider et al. (2016) recently showed θ and β power decreases in adults at, respectively, left frontal and parietal sites and right parietal sites during the processing of ungrammatical sentences. These results were not replicated in children, despite similar abilities to detect ungrammatical construction. The children instead displayed an N400 effect at ungrammatical words while adults showed a greater P600 effect (see also Schneider & Maguire 2019). These results suggest that syntactic neurocomputational mechanisms go through various, dynamically marked developmental stages.

Continuing this line of research, Leong et al. (2017) used EEG to show that infants not only entrain to the speech rhythm, but appear better prepared for this than adults. Examining gaze-directed speech in which an adult spoke to an infant, partial directed coherence (PDC) was computed for all pairwise connections at all EEG frequencies. PDC is a directed measure of statistical causality (*How much does i predict j, independent of j's history*). Leong et al. showed that phase coupling was weaker when the adult speaker shifted their gaze away during speech in θ, α and β (see also Schoch et al. 2017, who explore across-night dynamics of slow oscillations in children).

A study of γ synchronisation in children also revealed greater synchronisation when a representation of two objects was held in memory during occlusion relative to one object, reflecting object maintenance demands rather than sensory processing and lending support to the present claim that γ power reflects the generation of item sequences from across cognitive domains (Leung et al. 2016). Medial temporal lobe θ rhythms increased when participants successfully linked two distinct memories. These rhythms were synchronised with the medial prefrontal cortex, an area involved in storing knowledge networks. Increased hippocampal-medial prefrontal cortex θ coupling appears to be causally implicated in memory integration (Backus et al. 2016).

What is also needed is a more extensive investigation of the oscillatory activity of infants during complex thought, before they acquire language. Much of the language neural network is already in place (left-lateralised) before birth, suggesting that exposure to speech is not necessary for the oscillatory basis of elementary syntax to develop (Dehaene-Lambertz 2017). Moreover, Winkler et al. (2018) explored the ontogenesis of embedding through implementing nested relations in tone sequences, hence minimising perceptual and memory demands. They examined five-month-olds' brain responses in two auditory oddball paradigms, presenting sequences with one or two levels of embedding, interspersed with deviant sequences violating embedding rules. Event-related potentials indicated that the infants were sensitive to the embedding violations. The study which most closely approximates an extension of these interests is Brookes et al. (2018), who used MEG to investigate stationary (i.e. time averaged) and rapidly modulating (dynamic) electrophysiological connectivity in participants aged nine to twenty-five years. They found that stationary functional connectivity (gauged via interregional coordination of neural oscillations) increased with age in α and β bands, particularly in bilateral parietal and temporo-parietal connections.

The topic of bilingualism is of great relevance to oscillatory studies of language, given its potential to refine (and falsify) hypotheses about the role of certain bands and frequency interactions in language processing. To take a recent example, Burgaleta et al.'s (2016) study of bilingual brains revealed significantly expanded subcortical structures relative to monolinguals, localised in bilateral putamen, thalamus, left globus pallidus and right caudate nucleus. The caudate has also been implicated in lexico-morphological processing (Fiebach et al. 2004) and has been argued to support syntactic operations (Kotz et al. 2009) – pushing the language system even further beyond the classical regions.

These global (and indeed globular), dynamic concerns also speak to Gallistel and Matzel's (2013) assessment that, as a fundamental mechanism of synaptic transmission, the properties of long-term potentiation cannot explain the properties of associative learning and memory. As Fitch (2014b, 392) writes, we should be 'under no illusions that the theory of computation, with its stacks and queues and rewrite rules, provides anything even close to a final model of biological computation'. Along with being able to describe how the brain performs large-scale interregional computations (potentially moving towards alleviating Fitch's anxiety), oscillatory phase hierarchies may support the extraction of morphological representations (see Leong & Goswami 2015 for related discussion). These considerations, and the experimental oscillatory literature reviewed here, suggest that there is a genetically specified computational mechanism in the human brain for hierarchically organising feature sets and for allowing the transference of information from distinct memory and perceptual systems to the system responsible for constructing and holding in memory such feature sets (broadly, the 'language system').

Fitch also favours a single-neuron model of representational storage, through which single neurons carry discrete representational information and may even be responsible for individual representations. Indeed, there are a number of reasons to be wary of any model which places the synapse at the centre of representation/memory formation (for excellent discussion, see Trettenbrcin 2016), and so single neurons may be a more fruitful place for investigation (even if synaptic plasticity itself is likely not wholly irrelevant for learning and memory). As Trettenbrein (2016) summarises the literature: '[M]emory persists despite synapses having been destroyed and synapses are turning over at very high rates even when nothing is being learned.' Pursuing this intuition, Ryan et al. (2015) suggest that synapses should be understood as providing 'access points' to information already stored within cells. Linked memories furthermore appear to share synaptic clusters within the dendrites of overlapping neural populations, and the locus of protein synthesis shapes the structure of the memory trace (Kastellakis et al. 2016). Explorations of single neuron-based representations (though, as argued earlier, likely not computations, which require larger dynamic systems) will be an important venture in the coming years; yet as Kristan Jr. (2016, R950) notes, this task faces a number of obstacles:

[S]ome perfectly good neurons have no processes, some vertebrate neurons do not generate action potentials, and some small (less than a millimeter in any dimension) invertebrate animals get along just fine without fast action potentials in any of their neurons.

3.6.2   *Processes and Processors*

It seems from what has been reviewed that memories and representations are (somehow) stored within cells, and that synaptic connectivity simply provides ways of accessing them. It also appears that the neural basis of representations is getting gradually smaller (i.e. the cellular and subcellular level), while the neural basis of computations is getting larger (i.e. systems level oscillatory interactions). Verguts (2017), for instance, can note that different neural populations which have their spiking patterns modulated by γ rhythms are, 'presumably, cognitive representations'. For now, exploring the neural basis of computations and their oscillatory basis seems like a more manageable task than investigating representations. Despite leaving representations at a safe distance, this approach permits a renewed understanding of the classical software/hardware distinction, which Sternberg (2011, 158) succinctly defines as 'the distinction between processors and the processes that they implement' (see also Jirenhed et al. 2017).

Be that as it may, Gallistel (2017b) also points out that computational operations necessarily operate over the objects that carry the information about which they are computing. In the design of a computing machine, he argues that it is vital to place the computing part as close to the information-carrying part as possible. As Sterling and Laughlin (2015) summarise: 'Compute with chemistry; it's cheaper.' This puts neurolinguistics and computational neuroscience into a major conflict: As noted, while the source of representations is getting smaller, the putative source of operations is getting larger. Therefore, part of the computational operations themselves must be carried out also at the cellular level. Relatedly, the proposed γ pockets responsible for processing language-specific features constitute only the beginning of a full neurophysiological account, which will ultimately extend to lower-level biophysics. For now, experimental work investigating the localised oscillatory basis of particular linguistic features can help distinguish the role of different cell types in language, much like how oscillatory research into spatial memory has helped elucidate the role of place cells.

Returning to the hardware theme, in modern humans there is increased fronto-cortical connectivity and a more developed role for the subplate in achieving this, which likely altered the structural and functional role of cortical γ oscillations. The evolution of the subplate additionally aids language network interconnectedness, which relies not only on axon pathways but on the synchronous firing of cortical cell assemblies transmitting information between each other (although in what format this 'information' is stored remains unclear). This gives rise to γ, essential for higher cognition. Relatedly, fast-spiking interneurons such as chandelier cells play an enhanced role in humans relative to other species, aiding the cortex in transmitting longer sequences of information (Molnár et al. 2008). Different interneurons can compete to generate the same γ rhythm, as Clowry (2014, 227) summarises:

The degree of involvement of each cell type dictates the frequency of the network rhythm within the gamma band. This ability to switch between frequencies opens up the possibility for a group of neurons to bind with different neuronal assemblies depending on which frequency channel was in operation.

As previous sections have shown, there is a dense literature on the functional role of brain rhythms in a number of cognitive domains, which could inform major debates in the field of linguistics. For instance, Jensen et al.'s (2012) approach to the visual system's prioritisation of salient unattended stimuli claims that γ rhythms phase-lock to posterior α- and β-oscillating regions to form a clocking mechanism sequentially activating particular visual representations, such that object X in a given scene is interpreted before object Y, imposing general cognitive set-constructing rules of efficiency. At oscillatory peaks, α or β inhibition would prevent neural firing and only the most excitable clusters would be able to fire, with less excitable ones firing at later stages of the slow cycle (see also Jensen et al. 2014). CFC may consequently be able to connect segmentation/parsing with representation decoding/interpretation, with oscillations (implementation) being the mechanism to address segmentation (computation) via coupling and phase resetting (algorithm). This type of multidimensional perspective on language can already be found in Bechtel's (1994) model of *mechanistic explanation*, in which different levels of description are composed of discrete entities with causal-explanatory force between each level. Instead of coming up with new names for the Language/Logic of Thought (*à la* Hauser 2016) or tweaking and revising models of the Italian left periphery and addressing other computational concerns, it may be more beneficial (both to linguistics and neurolinguists) if efforts were instead made to discard as much of the 'attendant logico-philosophico-mathematical baggage' (Tomalin 2006, 188) carried by modern linguistics and retranslating or re-embedding only the bare minimum required for hierarchical phrase structure building into the biological and neurophysiological sciences (returning to an original goal of the minimalist programme).

It is also well understood within the linguistics literature that there exists a 'lexical' layer (composed of 'content' words like *John, likes* and *Mary*) which interacts with a 'functional' layer (composed of question and tense words like *did* and *what*). A more globular brain may have resulted in richer interactions between the neocortical regions storing conceptual representations and subcortical structures responsible for building feature-sets, introducing the duality of semantics (Chomsky 2000) through which content and function items interact via hierarchical relations. Interestingly, as noted by Miyagawa et al. (2013), the lexical layer seems capable of recursive embedding, whereas the functional layer seems more restricted; for instance, no language can generate structures like $\{CP\{TP\{CP\{TP...\}\}\}\}$. Since this functional layer shares other similarities with birdsong syntax, and since songbirds share a number of homologous neural structures putatively responsible for their 'phonological syntax', the possibility arises that the oscillomic code responsible for depth-one hierarchical structures is also shared across humans and songbirds, and it would follow from this that the feature-set algorithm proposed earlier is responsible for the recursion exhibited not simply by the lexical layer, but rather by the *interaction* of the two layers: Lexical elements alone cannot generate unbounded hierarchical structures (e.g. 'book want', 'Sam watch'), and it is only with the introduction of functional items or morphological elements that the novelty of human language syntax arises. There is a notable component of rhythmicity to this interaction: Lexical and functional elements are often combined in sequence, as in the following phrase:

(10)   {L ate {F the {L pie {F that John ate}}}}

It is possible that some of the unique aspects of language exist purely to generate an interaction between these two layers. Displacement and agreement, for instance, connect items from across the two layers:

(11)   What did you eat __?

In this instance, a lexical item has been displaced to the functional layer, facilitating novel conceptual combinations and hierarchical relations. Cross-frequency interactions between the structures responsible for storing representations from each layer (presumably facilitated, amongst other things, by a more globular braincase and calvaria) may give rise to this L-F-L-F pattern. Indeed, Singer (2018) even claims that 'as common in evolution, properties like the unavoidable oscillations of networks with recurrent inhibition, that initially were at best functionally neutral attributes, may have acquired functional relevance once embedded in a novel context', namely a more globular context. If this is the case, then evolutionary neurolinguists would be justified in speculating that the forms of oscillatory interactions reviewed in this book can be exploited for computations ranging far beyond feature-binding, assembly formation and the encoding of relations.

As Rizzi (2012) notes, functional elements trigger language's fundamental computational Merge operations, and are consequently 'the locus of much of the syntactic action' (2012, 491). They also express basic syntactic parameters and are consequently responsible for most cross-linguistic variation. It may be that lexical/content structures are derived from pre-existing conceptual representations while functional elements may have been the result of *reciprocal causation* (Lewontin 1983), birthed by the novel interfacing of the Universal Generative Faculty with other, distinct representational domains. In line with this perspective, content and functional words appear to have a distinct neural grounding, with content words eliciting greater activation in middle and anterior temporal cortex, a subregion of the orbital frontal cortex and the parahippocampal region (Diaz & McCarthy 2009). In addition, due to the close, reciprocal anatomical connections between subcortical structures (e.g. thalamus, hippocampus) and the cortex, the default perspective should be that any human-specific morphological change in the cortex (e.g. the left inferior frontal regions) would naturally impact – and likely functionally implicate – the organisation of subcortical structures. Bohsali et al. (2015) document substantial structural connectivity between Broca's area and the thalamus, in particular the pulvinar (which receives extra GABAergic cells migrating from the ganglionic eminence in humans; Letinic & Rakic 2001). It is highly probable that the well-documented expansion of Broca's area in humans resulted in thalamic expansions, likely enhancing its ability to act as the (cartographically) central oscillatory modulator in the binding of distant cortical representations. Indeed, the only sensory system which does not include a thalamic nucleus receiving sensory signals and transferring them to primary cortical regions is the olfactory system, and unless it is discovered that the sense of smell plays an unprecedentedly important role in language processing, it seems safe to assume that the thalamus is central to the coordination and integration of cross-modular representations, required for typical sentence comprehension involving distinct conceptual domains.

Are there any other electrophysiological findings relevant to this discussion of linguistic rhythm, and which might help ground the aforementioned observations about L-F-L-F patterning? Not much is currently known; however, Li et al. (2019) conducted an EEG study in which participants listened to Mandarin Chinese sentences that had a regular or irregular rhythm context preceding a critical noun. Although other details of their study will not concern us, it is notable that during the regular-rhythm context they found amplitude increases in β relative to the irregular-rhythm context. This likely relates to prediction satisfaction and the ease with which the existing cognitive set could be maintained (which is more difficult when stimuli are irregularly structured). We would therefore predict β increases in standardly structured L-F-L-F syntax relative to non-standardly structured syntax.

The reciprocal connections between these cortical and subcortical structures, newly enhanced and reshaped by modern human evolution, is in some ways parallel to the notion that labelling is needed by the conceptual system in order for syntax to transfer objects to it (Shim 2018). Broca's area and the cortico-basal ganglia-thalamo-cortical loop are in many anatomical respects independent, but they both need to coordinate their oscillatory activity if they are to go beyond their individual functions – of large-scale representational segregation (thalamus) and acting as a memory buffer and executive system (Broca's area) – in order to reach a level of computational complexity neither would be able to in isolation. Cyclically concatenating objects (via cortical-subcortical loops) permits certain cognitive processes, and maintaining established hierarchical relationships permits certain others, but it is only when structures are cyclically transferred into hierarchical units that 'narrow syntax' can emerge (the conclusion drawn in Chapter 1).

Matchin and Hickok (2016) provided further evidence against the classical Broca-Wernicke model of neurolinguistics, with syntactic perturbation (involving the cued, mid-utterance restructuring of the planned syntax of a sentence) being shown to not involve Broca's area or the anterior temporal lobe, but rather a cortical-subcortical network involving the right inferior frontal gyrus (Lam et al. 2016 also provide an oscillation-based rejection of the classical Broca-Wernicke model). More broadly, the response profile for Broca's area during sentence processing seems to reflect domain-general functions such as working memory or cognitive control, rather than exclusively syntactic operations (Matchin & Hickok 2016).

Finlay et al. (2001, 278) discuss the evolutionary implications of these kinds of proposals: '[T]here is no reason to presume selection pressures for cortically based functions drove brain expansion at all. […] [T]he brain grows as a covarying whole, increasing in size according to a fairly straightforward log function. It is just as likely, therefore, that pressures for enhanced archicortical, corticoid, or subcortical processing could have triggered the adjustment of global timing constraints that led, incidentally, to much bigger isocortices.' They add that '[s]uch demands on subcortical processing could have had little or nothing to do with the suite of cognitive traits (language, advanced tool-making) we prefer to think of as distinctly human', which points to some form of exaptation for the evolution of linguistic computation at least with regards to subcortical-cortical reciprocal connectivity (see also Kolodny & Edelman 2018 for an alternative perspective that the exaptation yielding language evolution is related to sequential processing and motor execution – a less likely scenario under the framework presented in this book). This perspective is commensurable with the idea that labels are not part of syntax itself, but are rather convenient ways of marking the effects of syntax on the interfaces – 'and hence (informally speaking) "don't exist"', as Epstein et al. (2017b, 25) put it – since the brain's implementation of phrase structure building arises from this mutual interplay between cortical and subcortical structures and is not explicitly marked by any immutable neural cluster.

3.6.3   The Physics of Language: Finding a 'Perfect' Solution

> Perfection is achieved, not when there is nothing more to add, but when there is nothing left to take away.   Antoine de Saint-Exupéry, *Airman's Odyssey*

Studies of the human oscillome (and the remarkable symmetry exhibited by human neural networks; de Lange et al. 2016) could provide an elegant way of grounding some recent proposals about third factors in language design. We will here briefly review some of these emerging avenues.

Using Laplacian Eigenmodes to analyse MRI and DTI data, Atasoy et al. (2016) demonstrate that resting brain function is related to brain shape. They argue that 'the critical relation between the neural field patterns and the delicate excitation-inhibition balance fits the neurophysiological changes observed during the loss and recovery of consciousness'. The eigendecomposition of the Laplace operator may provide fundamental principles permitting a direct macroscopic description of collective cortico-cortical and thalamo-cortical dynamics. The spatial harmonic waves they observed seem to predict resting state networks and obey the same physical principles as other self-organising phenomena (such as tiger and zebra stripes or the patterns of vibrating sand), lending support to Descartes's original intuition that the brain is organised through principles of 'efficient causation', and not being incompatible with recent work in generative grammar suggesting that syntactic computation operates via principles of efficient computation (Narita 2014a). As Torday and Miller (2016) put it, 'Life must adhere to basic physics, and then too, cognition must as well.'

What is the relevance of this to language? Consider how, as was discussed earlier (Section 1.6.2), the syntactic operation AGREE might be formed through a process of symmetry-formation (Narita et al. 2017), and it may well be the case that the CFC of neural oscillations can achieve a similar level of symmetry (such as how the phase/amplitude of distinct rhythms can be symmetrically related) to derive these effects. Syntactic derivations seem to be a cyclic process of symmetry-breaking and symmetry-formation, with the ultimate state typically being one of symmetry (phases are formed and transferred, new objects are merged and their features are valued, featural symmetry is established etc.). The standard distinctions between External Merge and Internal Merge, and the lexical relations (predicate-argument structure, selection etc.) and discourse relations (quantificational information, topic-focus etc.) they each derive, can also be seen, respectively, as exhibiting asymmetric and symmetric relations. Narita et al. (2017) even extend the symmetry-forming tendencies found in AGREE operations to formal syntactic features more generally.

Another way to approach language evolution through third factors is to construct a *physics of language*. Though this is currently the most speculative subfield of biolinguistics, some concrete and fairly comprehensive proposals have been made. At the most general level, the materialisation of physical principles of optimisation and 'least effort' can be found in the structure of the genetic code (Itzkovitz & Alon 2007), the evolution of insect wings (Kingsolver & Koehl 1985) respiratory patterns in birdsongs (Trevisan et al. 2006), and brain wiring (Cherniak 2010). The instantiation of Fibonacci patterns in language has been documented by Medeiros (2008) and Piattelli-Palmarini and Vitiello (2017). Medeiros, for instance, has argued that the Fibonacci numbers govern syntactic tree structures such that the construction of a higher node in a tree is only forced when the number of syntactically licensed words reached a Fibonacci number, with these elementary physical principles supposedly governing the labelling mechanism. Piattelli-Palmarini (2017) discusses recent work showing that 'in identifying sequences of tones or syllables, [and] in predicting their continuation and in remembering them, humans have a special facility when the sequences are Fibonacci sequences, even with respect to superficially similar sequences'. Since Fibonacci sequences cannot be easily guessed by probabilistic expectations, a Bayesian explanation is likely to be inadequate (as it likely is for other aspects of language), and lower-level physical principles may exhibit more explanatory power. As Fitch (2010a, 110) correctly notes of Bayesian models and information theory: 'The main difficulty with such approaches is that, at the computational ("automaton") level, they are *too* powerful: they can do virtually anything. We need more fine-grained analyses of simple, less powerful systems if we are to understand the limitations of real brains.' If these ideas carry any weight, then they must ultimately be related to the oscillatory model of language developed here – how exactly one might do this will be a topic for future research.

3.6.4   The Representation Problem

The various extensions from working memory and other neural codes to a linguistic neural code seen in the model presented in this book is similar to Gu et al.'s (2015) coupled excitatory-inhibitory model, which they claim explains 'how interval timing and working memory can originate from the same oscillatory processes, but differ in terms of which dimension of the neural oscillation is utilized for the extraction of item, temporal order, and duration information'. In this respect, I think it is sensible to assume with Postle (2006) that working memory should be regarded as an emergent property of neural systems representing distinct pieces of information, such that 'if the brain can represent it, the brain can also demonstrate working memory for it' (2006, 29; indeed, there may also be something to the claim that working memory can be reduced to a form of attention). Though we have so far touched on the algorithmic phase-locking/resetting properties of language – the backbone of the working memory/syntax interface – there still remains the problem of how the brain evolved the ability to create linguistic representations to begin with, a problem we will not attempt to solve here. Indeed, Poeppel (2017, 172) correctly notes that 'we do not have even the foggiest idea of how information of *any* type is actually stored in the brain (notwithstanding descriptive and largely metaphorical statements on patterns of synaptic connectivity, which begs the question)'.

Nevertheless, there are some potential avenues one might pursue to explore the representation problem. Concerning the topic of what type of grammatical representations are manipulated by the brain, Greenhill et al. (2017) used a Dirichlet process mixture model (a probability distribution whose range is itself a set of probability distributions) to explore the rates of change in lexical and grammatical data from eighty-one Austronesian languages, showing that while many features change rapidly, there exists 'a core of grammatical and lexical features that are highly stable' (2017, E8822), and hence are strong candidates for being central components in the dynamics of language evolution. These stable features include inclusive vs. exclusive distinctions, gender distinctions, the existence of tense auxiliaries, prepositions, clause chaining and the presence of animacy features on the noun/class gender system (see Dataset S2 in Greenhill et al. 2017). Recent work has revealed that different cortical regions appear responsible for storing distinct representational formats, with γ rhythms in the ventrolateral prefrontal cortex signalling low-level, stimulus-based category abstraction (e.g. *dog*) and β rhythms in the dorsolateral prefrontal cortex signalling high-level, rule-based category abstraction (e.g. *animal*; Wutz et al. 2018). A slight reorganisation in the shape of the prefrontal cortex (of the kind discussed in Neubauer et al. 2018) may have permitted the brains of anatomically modern humans to generate oscillatory migrations and phrase synchronisations such that these two major ontological representational bases could interact more efficiently, potentially allowing the generation of a greater number and broader range of low-level categories to be stored within a given high-level node.

While the aforementioned Wutz et al. (2018) study found increased β during high-level abstraction, Antzoulatos and Miller (2016) found increased β and δ synchrony between and within prefrontal cortex and posterior parietal cortex, with β being selective to task-relevant dimensions and δ additionally responding to task-irrelevant dimensions of stimuli. Finding a link between these results, Riddle et al. (2019) used tACS during a cognitive control task to show that by artificially increasing δ-β phase–amplitude coupling, participants were more accurate in tasks involving greater abstraction (relative to sham trials). This might indicate that δ-coordinated β rhythms indexing motor control inhibited motor initiation and slowed down evidence accumulation (whereby β increases index the current cognitive set in memory), hence improving task accuracy. Meanwhile, Riddle et al. also artificially increased θ-γ phase–amplitude coupling, and found that this also improved task accuracy *when the set size increased* (i.e. when in their match/non-match task the number of on-screen objects participants needed to make judgements about increased). This maps directly onto the present assumptions about θ-γ coupling indexing (cross-modular and cross-domain) representational concatenation and maintenance. While Riddle et al.'s (2019) seminal study attributes causal power to coupling in cognitive control, for our purposes it should also be noted that cognitive control involves a certain degree of selecting among potential, already-activated cortical representations. That δ-β and θ-γ phase–amplitude coupling are involved in this suggests that phase–amplitude coupling can in fact be used as a neurocomputational algorithm for feature extraction and association.

Likewise, understanding of how the brain processes adjective-noun combinations is still in its infancy, but could also contribute to our understanding of the representational basis of language in the brain. A recent MEG study by Fyshe et al. (2016) revealed that the neural representations of adjective semantics entrain to α – yet, they explain their results with the conclusion that, 'during semantic composition, oscillatory activity is used to coordinate brain areas, to retain and to recall information as it is needed'. A more refined picture could certainly be generated given the model presented in this book. For instance, the semantic operation of Function Application has not properly been exposed via neuroimaging (see Pylkkänen 2019 for discussion); at best, left anterior temporal lobe seems sensitive to combinatorial processes sensitive to conceptual relations between words, but the real-time neural implementation of Function Applications remains in obscurity. Nevertheless, Frankland and Greene (2020) have recently provided evidence that left-mid superior temporal cortex (lmSTC) and anterior medial prefrontal cortex (amPFC, specifically BA 10) play distinct roles in computing thematic relations and compositional event structure in natural language; for example, lmSTC encodes broad thematic roles (like *woman-as-agent*) while the amPFC (BA 10) seems to encode narrow roles (*woman-as-chaser* in 'The man chased the dog'). I think oscillatory interactions of the kind discussed in this book can direct future enquiry here, in particular given that Function Application is guided by syntax. Of course, semantic composition should be computationally tractable, or a subset of polynomial-time computable functions, in addition to super-polynomial-time computable functions for which one or more input parameters are small in practice (van Rooij 2008).

Perhaps the most promising work in this direction comes from Sun et al. (2020). These authors identified hippocampal CA1 neurons in mice whose activity is modulated not only by spatial location in a maze, but also by the number of laps completed around the maze. They term these 'event-specific rate remapping' (ESR) cells, and show that they remain lap-specific even when the maze length is unpredictable. 'Laps' are therefore treated as fundamental computational units. As such, ESR cells may form parts of an independent hippocampal code: 'an "event code" dedicated to organizing experience by events as discrete and transferable units' (Sun et al. 2020, 651). This hippocampal event code is possibly connected in humans to natural language event semantics, only the units of eventive computation would scale beyond 'laps' and include thematic roles and their associated event structures (Pietroski 2018), forming part of the broader neural code for language outlined in this book.

Still, this discussion brings with it certain foundational (or philosophical) concerns, such as the 'aboutness' of things like β-generated categorial representations. Without going into too much terminological depth, there are reasons to assume that linguistic and, more specifically, syntactic representations lack intentionality, and do not exhibit an aboutness relation with the external world. Instead, they are mind-internal configurations imposed on the data of sense, certain aspects of which are 'transduced' from language-external cognitive systems (following Adger 2019b; Pylyshyn 1984). Indeed, similar brain regions are selectively activated when evaluating whether scenarios involving fictional characters could occur in our reality (e.g. 'Is it possible to speak to Cinderella?') compared with those involving real entities (e.g. 'Is it possible to speak to Bernie Sanders?') (Abraham et al. 2008), very much supporting a form of internalism according to which mental representations are *imposed* on the data of sense for interpretation, as opposed to properties of the world being extracted (somehow) by neural mechanisms.

The representation problem becomes more vivid when we consider how the type of phonological representations explored in Giraud and Poeppel's(2012) dynamical model of the human auditory system crucially rely on perceptual events. Syntactic representations, in contrast, are internally self-generated. Nevertheless, if γ waves, for instance, reflect a fundamental unit of linguistic interpretation, as proposed earlier, then analysing the time course of γ embedded within slower rhythms would likely be a fruitful direction for experimental research in humans, even if the semantic content manipulated by such rhythms remains 'invisible' – as, indeed, it may remain, given our cognitive 'scope and limits' (Russell 1948), 'bounds of sense' (Strawson 1966) and other such constraints (contra the claims in Ravignani et al. 2018, for whom the existence of progress in the study of language evolution disproves *mysterianism*, or the view that human scientific enquiry necessarily has limits; see also Ravignani et al. 2014; Buzsáki 2010).

There is one last avenue I would like to pursue, and it relates to a topic already briefly mentioned earlier in this chapter and has bearing on the potential neural basis of representations, namely the potential for grid cells to implement not just spatial navigation, but conceptual navigation. Examining these hippocampal-entorhinal processing mechanisms involved in spatial navigation (place cells and grid cells), I would like to argue that certain cognitive representations can be implemented in the same fashion. Place cells in the hippocampus preferentially fire when an animal occupies certain environmental positions, while grid cells in the medial entorhinal cortex exhibit multiple firing fields located at the vertices of equilateral triangles tiling the environment (providing a 'grid') (Bellmund et al. 2018). Cognitive spaces, if we assume a connection to place and grid cells, must to some extent be spanned and delimited by dimensions satisfying geometric constraints such as betweenness and equidistance. This enables concepts to be represented via grid and place cells as convex regions of cognitive space. For example, along a simple axis based on *speed* and *weight*, different types of vehicles can be plotted (fast but light, slow but heavy etc.), which place cells can implement through modulating the size of firing fields in a given hippocampal region, while entorhinal grid cells can implement these concepts through providing a continuous code and having different cells activate across the dimensions of the grid, yielding relations like *larger than* once we consider the temporal, oscillatory dynamics of the system. More generally, grid cells would produce nearby positions on the grid for similar stimuli, and larger distances between positions for dissimilar stimuli.

On the notion of convexity, Bellmund et al. (2018) assume that for all points x and y in a given grid region, the points between x and y also fall into the region. Bellmund et al. (2018) further note that considering properties or concepts as convex regions enables a form of generalisation (and, hence, learnability), in that a property of stimuli x and y can be inferred to be shared by stimulus z falling between x and y. A general concept can be mapped between multiple nodes, while a more specific instantiation of a concept will occupy a specific place in the grid. What are the implications of this? Most prominently, for any given concept p falling into a specific region of the entorhinal grid, relations can automatically be derived based on the proximity of its node to other parts of the grid. In these newly understood cognitive spaces, 'stimuli can be located based on their values along the feature dimensions mapped by place and grid cells' (Bellmund et al. 2018, 8; for the most recent form of evidence in favour of this hippocampal concept memory model, under which the hippocampus encodes domain-general cognitive maps, see Theves et al. 2019).

For our purposes, we can propose that encountering a series of stimuli will result in a trajectory being mapped along this space, triggered and coordinated by oscillations coupled with distinct brain regions, depending on the faculty involved in the interpretation of experience, e.g. a linguistic interpretation of a series of stimuli would involve – under the model presented in this book – CFC between the particular linguistic subdomain (compositional semantics in anterior temporal regions, etc.) and the hippocampal-entorhinal complex.

In this way, given what is known about the computational scope of entorhinal grid cells, spatial navigation can therefore serve as a model system for the constraints and neurocomputational principles of cognition. Any semantic concept which can be implemented via interacting and neighbouring nodes on an axis could be implemented via place and grid cells, e.g. *larger than, next to, more, climb* (including its Boolean operator requirements). Even concepts like *justice*, involving some representation of valuation between distinct levels as a means of calculating a place on a continuous spectrum, might be amenable to this explanation.

Overall, spatial codes for place and grid cells could provide an initial format for cognitive representations, which the language system likely exploits – a picture consistent with the evolutionarily preserved circuitry of the hippocampal-entorhinal circuit (in this connection, see also Bush & Burgess 2019 for a discussion of recent evidence that the phase code for location exhibited by place and grid cells is preserved across species). Certain basic properties of cognitive map navigation, such as spatial coding, landmark anchoring and route planning, might therefore be recruited by nonspatial domains, like language, to form fundamental elements of thought (Epstein, Patai et al. 2017).

It may appear that we are moving somewhat beyond our initial authority by discussing these issues. Yet consider the following: Maidenbaum et al. (2018) examined oscillatory patterns in entorhinal cortex using intracranial EEG (iEEG) while neurosurgical patients navigated a virtual world and showed that the power of entorhinal θ bilaterally exhibited a distinctive six-way symmetric directional modulation (peaking at 6.1Hz). This matches the properties of grid cells, which are activated when one crosses a series of locations arranged in a hexagonal lattice tiling the environment – six primary axes which correspond to the underlying structure of the cells themselves, which have a hexadirectional structure. Maidenbaum et al.'s findings indicate that these oscillations correlated with grid representations (i.e. the oscillatory behaviour detected was a signature of grid cells), and that the signal correlated with spatial memory performance. As such, researchers are beginning to 'reconstruct' (or at least confirm) the cellular basis of cognition based on the type of oscillatory signatures detected. It will be of considerable interest to the language sciences to push this research direction towards language comprehension. Not only could this be used to test the present grid cell hypothesis of conceptual navigation, but it could also be used to detect other likely candidates for the cellular basis of language-relevant oscillatory signatures.

3.6.5   *Philosophical Reflections*

In this section, I will address some broader issues which often hover in the background during discussions of neural computation and language evolution. Developing a comprehensive, falsifiable oscillatory model of linguistic computation has been the primary objective of this chapter and the previous one, yet it is also important to occasionally take a step back and attempt to situate these concrete proposals within a proper historical and theoretical context, in particular given that philosophical biases are difficult to avoid and should be 'called out' and scrutinised (Anderson et al. 2019).

Having developed an oscillatory model of the language system through establishing significant isomorphisms between linguistic structure and oscillatory behaviour, there remain unaddressed tensions between the Darwinian thinking of descent, evo-devo perspectives on the organic form-function divide, and the generic computational properties of the language faculty. As a way of addressing these tensions, it is useful to first draw attention to the inadequacy of traditional linear cladograms, 'according to which every seemingly new or more sophisticated feature of a cognitive mechanism, viewed as a novelty, is represented as a node on top of the old and shared elements' (Boeckx & Theofanopoulou 2015). The lack of non-human models for language has often been used to discourage biological enquiry into language, with linguists focusing purely on computational issues (Chomsky's 2018b, 37, decision to discuss the nature of consciousness and language by 'excluding here Marr's "hardware level"' is typical of the field). But evolutionary homologues to language should be sought not just in the animal world, but also within the human brain.

A general defence of a highly interdisciplinary comparative biolinguistics was made by Hall (2012), who noted that a biolinguistic approach to phonology would lead to an expansion of the concerns of phonologists (embracing particular aspects of biology), but would also simultaneously lead to a narrowing of other particular concerns, since '[i]f some of phonology is really syntax, and some of it is really phonetics, then relatively little of phonology is phonology'. The point is well directed: By translating linguistic theory into non-syntactic terms (i.e. neurobiological and biophysical terms), notions such as *language* and *cyclicity* can be resituated and potentially given a biologically plausible level of explanation, as was attempted in the previous chapter. The range of available biophysical discussion has by now expanded sufficiently to permit the construction of a science of language which can exploit the full interdisciplinary range seen in the cognitive, biological and natural sciences.

A notable justification for an interdisciplinary study of language is found in Miłkowski's (2012, 81) assessment of the limits of computational explanations of cognition, which notes that '[s]ome really basic cognitive systems, such as sponges or plants, may be explained in terms of simpler computation models, whereas more complex processes require interlevel explanations to give meaningful, idealized explanations and predictions'. The biological study of language should be concerned with presenting generic computational operations that, in Poeppel's (2012, 52) words, 'could be implemented quite straightforwardly in neural circuits'. There are doubtless certain domains which have regularly exploited the findings of modern neuroscience and, more often, quantum physics and other fields, in particular, certain strands of psychology and neo-spiritualism (see Burnett 2016 for the pitfalls of 'neuro-nonsense'). Care must be taken, then, to decompose the language faculty into the kinds of constituent computational parts which could be deemed neurobiologically plausible. The right level of granularity must be sought after at all levels of biological and cognitive analysis. As already discussed, linguists approaching the biology of language who keep to discussions of *syntax* and *semantics* do so from purely atheoretical grounds. There is nothing in the principles of theta-role assignment, agreement relations or the labelling algorithm which prohibits the formation of multidisciplinary perspectives on language evolution and language processing. Just as classical concepts like *mind* and *motion* are now understood to be too coarse-grained and vague to be of any empirical use, so too should linguists begin to see *labels* and *movement* as inadequate to the task of constructing cognitive phylogenies.

One of the core advantages of a multidisciplinary approach to language is that it permits the combination of constraints from distinct disciplines to narrow the hypothesis scope. Matsunaga and Okanoya (2014), for instance, discuss what they call 'potential regulators in the faculty of language', a superfamily of proteins (cadherins) identified as cell adhesion molecules and which may play a role in vocal behaviour. This biolinguistic perspective is to be welcomed, but the target of this discovery is the sensorimotor faculty, not the syntactic faculty – a conclusion not attainable through sticking to intuitive, E-language concepts and not differentiating between language, communication, speech, and so forth.

Relatedly, the concept of third factors is often ridiculed for being 'vague', as if it supposedly constitutes a uniform neurobiological mechanism. Similarly, in 1734 Bishop Berkeley criticised the intuitive notion of infinitesimals as 'Ghosts of departed Quantities' (1992, 199), and it was not until 1966 that Abraham Robinson provided a firm mathematical foundation for them through his Non-Standard Analysis. This should encourage us not to rule out a forthcoming formulation of specific third factor constraints within the domain of, for instance, molecular biology or neurobiology (see Johansson 2013 for an insightful critical review of the third factor literature and its goals and limitations). As mentioned earlier, neural oscillations may well be what is needed to explain the minimal search principles of labelling, departing from the neo-Darwinian adaptationism of contemporary neurolinguistics (e.g. Schoenemann 2012). As already discussed, and as Lightfoot (2011, 313) puts it, there are certain properties about the mind that 'are not selected for and are not accidental by-products, but they emerge because of deep, physical principles that affect much of life'. Following up on this, he notes that '[t]he fundamental properties of physical systems limit the mutations that organisms and specific organs might undergo' (2011, 314). Gould (1997) concurred with this perspective and criticised what Lightfoot terms 'natural selection-it is' by inventing the concept of the 'singularist', namely somebody who only invokes a single evolutionary force (typically natural selection) to explain a given trait. As Lightfoot correctly concludes, the functions of the brain are 'specified by precise, interconnected regional circuits and all this is constrained by physical and biochemical laws' (2011, 314), with the efficiency displayed by oscillatory interactions being formed through these laws. Ultimately, Lightfoot concludes, 'natural selection is just one force and it operates only at the level of behaviour; the physical and biochemical constraints on the brain system are other forces that define possibilities' (2011, 317).

One final philosophical issue to address relates to the existence of computational efficiency. Considering the present demands of a multidisciplinary approach to language evolution, it may be useful here to distinguish between laws of physics and laws of nature. The former laws are found in the physical sciences, such as Newton's laws of motion, while the latter are underlying principles which have parametric application via distinct mechanisms (e.g. neural, entomological) across various domains ranging from insect navigation to subatomic particles. Likely candidates for natural laws include least effort (Zipf 1965/1949) and last resort principles, implemented within the context of a specific explanatory theory (linguistics, neurophysiology, chemistry, etc.). The labelling operation in theoretical linguistics utilises notions of least effort, a law of nature, but would not apply to the motion of planetary bodies, which would implement this natural law through different mechanisms. Similarly, brain rhythms are a manifestation of a natural law of 'periodicity' (the term used in the earth sciences) or 'oscillation' (physics) or 'cyclicity' (engineering and linguistics), which all refer to the steady recurrence of a particular theoretical structure (see Tass 1999 for a discussion of dynamic synchronisation in physics which may be responsible for the oscillations of the dynome, in a similar way that oscillomic operations may be responsible for the cyclicity of the cognome; see also Rodrigues et al. 2016). As argued here, the neural mechanisms which construct the human computational system are likely not unique to language, being instead domain-general and operative in other cognitive faculties (see the hierarchical processing found in vision (Ursini 2011) and motor planning (Fujita 2009)), and indeed other species (Schlenker et al. 2014). Higher cognitive functions implicated in γ, for instance, have their origin in 'a limited set of circuit motifs which are found universally across species and brain structures' (Bosman et al. 2014, 1982). These considerations have direct theoretical and experimental implications for linguistics, neuroscience and anthropogeny. While it could be said that the present oscillomic approach to language amounts to a special kind of localisation, understanding brain rhythms could on the contrary shed light on why language is restricted to its particular computational properties, and not some other imaginable operations which fall outside neurophysiological constraints.

3.7   Extending the Model

In this final section, I will propose a number of possible extensions to the model
of linguistic computation proposed in this book. Taking stock, it will be
suggested that these revisions provide the most satisfying way to ground
generative frameworks of language within the brain sciences, implementing
in neural dynamics not only linguistic operations, but also the broader architecture of the language faculty.

To briefly summarise our current position before approaching new terrain:
We have proposed an oscillatory framework for phrase structure building,
involving, at a minimum, $\{\delta(\theta)\}$ phase–amplitude coupling to construct multiple sets of linguistic syntactic and semantic features, with distinct β and γ
sources also being embedded within θ for, respectively, syntactic prediction
and conceptual binding. This provides a specific neural code for *recursive
hierarchical phrase structure* (reapplying the set-forming operation to its
own output), with α being involved in the early stages of binding (Pina et al.
2018) to synchronise distant cross-cortical γ sites needed for the θ-γ code of
working memory and to modulate attentional resources. True recursion defines
its output value in terms of the values of all of its previous applications,
grounded in the initial application (Lobina 2017), and this self-referential
quality of recursion can be implemented via repeated nestings of θ within
successive δ rhythms. As mentioned, the θ-γ code is a generic mechanism
utilised for visual, auditory, somatosensory and even vibrotactile working
memory (von Lautz et al. 2017), and is also involved in interregional communication (Solomon et al. 2017), and so it is likely recruited by the language
system. θ-γ phase-phase coupling in the human hippocampus has also been
shown to be involved in multi-item working memory maintenance (Chaieb et
al. 2015), and different cognitive domains may construct representational
stacks via different types of couplings. Given the rich interfaces between
language and other cognitive and perceptual domains, it is likely that language
processing is implemented via a range of CFCs, as argued here.

3.7.1   *Travelling Oscillations*

Building on a large body of work into the nature of oscillations (Le Van Quyen
& Bragin 2007; Patten et al. 2012; Kopell et al. 2014), Zhang et al. (2018)
present novel insights into a relatively new mechanism for large-scale neural
coordination in the form of *travelling oscillations* which cycle cross-cortically
at a speed of ~0.27–0.75 metres per second. These form spatially coherent
waves that move across the cortex. In purely physical terms, a travelling wave
is a disturbance travelling through a medium such as water, air or a cellular
network. Instead of involving precise zero-lag synchrony (involving perfect

temporal alignment between synchronied oscillations), Zhang et al. show how a range of phase offsets can be achieved (whereby the phase of multiple oscillations differs), producing travelling waves of various shapes such as plane, radial and spiral waves. The propagation of travelling oscillations was found in 96 per cent of neurosurgical patients (through electrocorticography) and was consistent with good performance on the Sternberg working memory task (Sternberg 1969). Zhang et al. (2018, 1269) conclude that 'human behaviour is supported by travelling waves'. These waves have recently been implicated in multiple sensory, motor and cognitive systems, and Muller et al. (2018, 1) recently speculated that 'travelling waves may serve a variety of functions, from long-term memory consolidation to processing of dynamic visual stimuli'. Summarising recent literature, Muller et al. (2018, 8) suggest that hippocampal CA1 travelling waves in the θ band exhibit a particular computational role ('patterning pyramidal spiking from small to large place fields in each theta cycle') which can be contrasted with the putative role of travelling fast γ waves in the same region ('pattering spiking in either direction of the dorsoventral axis in hippocampus'). More broadly, it seems clear that travelling waves serve to organise spike timing along a particular behaviourally relevant axis.

It is clear from Muller et al. (2018, table 1) that only visual, sensorimotor, motor, hippocampal and macroscopic computational principles of travelling waves can be proposed with any certainty, with the development of large-scale, high-precision recording technologies being able to expand current understanding. What precisely constitutes the range and influence of travelling waves over the rest of cognition is a topic for future study, and Muller et al.'s project should readily be expanded to language processing such that neurolinguists should investigate the computational role of travelling waves across various regions. For now, we can begin to sketch possible directions and explanations for these discoveries.

Zhang et al. (2018) discovered what they define as travelling *theta and alpha oscillations*, although their analysis reveals that the full range of migrating waves stretched from 2Hz to 15Hz, therefore implicating mid-δ. Mid-δ is involved in phrasal chunking, though not sentential chunking (which low-δ seems responsible for). This could potentially lead to a refined neural code for language processing: δ waves cycle across the cortex, building up the syntactic representation phrase-by-phrase and being endogenously reset by a newly constructed phrase, either travelling to parts of the cortex responsible for storing the required semantic representations or being coupled to travelling θ waves which perform the same function. The second option seems more likely, given what is known about where δ seems to be localised during language comprehension (Ding et al. 2016). The limitations of semantic processing could be derived either from the physical limitations placed on the speed of travelling cycles as they move from station to station (~0.25–0.75 m/s) or the width of the propagating waves (median: ~2.4–4.8cm) which might limit the range of conceptual structures manipulated. What exactly the precise wave structure is for the neural code for syntactic composition remains open, and ripe for future empirical work.

As discussed in previous chapters, the brain was reshaped in our lineage via globularisation, through which our braincase adopted a more globular shape, and so I would like to hypothesise that this granted oscillations the ability to travel across new areas of the cortex and subcortex whilst also being coupled to a number of other regions. This would have opened up new interfaces for conceptual representations (in particular, it may have helped pair the entity and event semantics networks in, respectively, the anterior temporal lobe and angular gyrus with networks in inferior frontal gyrus responsible for morpho-syntactic linearisation and externalisation), and in combination with the present neural code would also have derived Gärtner and Sauerland's (2007) equation 'Interfaces + Recursion = Language'. Further, Zhang et al.'s findings support a model of travelling waves as a network of *weakly coupled oscillators* (WCO), according to which the travelling wave is a result of phase coupling. According to the WCO model, oscillators are arranged in a linear array and are weakly coupled with their neighbours. The model also assumes that there is a spatial gradient in intrinsic frequency across the oscillators. Since the travelling wave is assumed to be the result of phase coupling, these assumptions conspire to yield the prediction – fulfilled by Zhang et al.'s (2018) data – that faster waves would travel in the direction of slower waves. The language model proposed in this book complements these findings, since Zhang et al. found that waves typically travelled in a posterior-to-anterior direction. It is assumed here that elementary syntactic combinatorics involves a parahippocampal and cortico-basal ganglia-thalamo-cortical loop (concatenation and semantic conjunction) coupled with posterior superior temporal gyrus, which is later coupled with left inferior frontal regions such as BA 44 and BA 45 which act as crucial memory buffers for the maintenance of hierarchically organised syntactic objects.

It should be noted that Zhang et al. only analysed grid electrodes in neuro-surgical patients (which are placed on the cortical surface) and not intracranial, subdural electrodes which penetrate portions of grey matter. As such. Zhang et al.'s data only pertains to gyri, not sulci, and further analyses of sEEG sites are needed to validate the general picture presented in Zhang et al. and discussed here in relation to language comprehension.

Both this model and the WCO travelling wave model predict posterior-to-anterior directionality as the language system proceeds from selecting linguis-tic features (parahippocampal, thalamic and basal ganglia regions), to combin-ing them (posterior temporal regions), to attributing to them a labelled identity (cortico-basal ganglia-thalamo-cortical loop) and, finally, to storing them in working memory (left inferior frontal regions, in particular pars opercularis). This directionality also notably correlates with the rhythms hypothesised to be responsible for these operations, with faster γ and β rhythms in posterior and central regions being coupled with slower central θ and α rhythms, which in turn travel towards slow left inferior frontal δ regions they are coupled with. While faster γ and β rhythms have currently not been shown to migrate, we can assume that this reinforces the neuroanatomically fixed nature of conceptual representations as being stored in typically resilient neural clusters (= *representations*), which can nevertheless be coupled to slower, travelling rhythms (= *computations*).

More pertinently, Zhang et al. (2018, 1276–1277) conclude that '[w]hen phase coupling is absent, there are no travelling waves because intrinsic oscillation frequencies differ between electrodes'. This suggests a strong degree of co-dependence between the phenomenon of CFC and travelling waves. If certain findings reviewed in this book are accurate – in particular, the finding of human-specific phase coupling diversity, hypothesised here to have occurred due to cranial reshaping – then the language system likely evolved as a direct outcome of a broader range of oscillatory migration routes which resulted from new interregional phase couplings. One of language's hallmark characteristics of breaking modular boundaries and combining representations from distinct domains to be stored cyclically in an expanded memory buffer (or phonological loop; Aboitiz, 2017), would arise immediately from this – as would the language system's ability to interface with conceptual and articulatory apparatuses. Though we have explored how the core oscillatory architecture of particular cross-frequency interactions can generate phrase structure building, the work of deriving the mechanism of syntactic combinatorics was previously left simply to phase–amplitude coupling. We can now add to this basic mechanism the understanding that language-relevant representations can be accessed cross-cortically through a process of posterior-to-anterior wave propagation.

Since the posterior-to-anterior propagations documented in the literature are involved in feedforward processes, it is possible that instances of anterior-to-posterior migration (a phenomenon documented in Zhang et al. 2018, and which was extremely rare compared to the reverse migration pattern) have a distinct functional role such as supporting feedback or top-down processes. It would be of interest to explore in future work whether δ waves propagate in an anterior-to-posterior direction at particular points of syntactic processing, perhaps accessing distinct loops of a memory buffer stretching from pars opercularis to posterior regions of Broca's area as the number of syntactic labels/nodes increases. Moreover, these findings should encourage neurolinguists to reconsider some core assumptions considering event-related potentials, which might (under the present framework) result from travelling waves transiently organising at a given time point and phase. The general anterior-to-posterior directionality is preliminarily supported by Pylkkänen's (2019, 65) review of the time course of syntactic and semantic processing, which proceeds as follows (see also Fromont et al. 2020 for event-related potential evidence that syntactic and semantic information may be processed in parallel, which is not incompatible with the overlap between the 200-250ms and 200-260ms windows below):

> 180–220ms: Angular gyrus shows sensitivity to argument structure.
> 200–250ms: Posterior temporal lobe shows combinatory effects.
> 200–260ms: Left anterior temporal lobe shows conceptual combinatory effects.
> 300–450ms: Left inferior frontal gyrus shows sensitivity to long-distance dependencies.
> 350–460ms: Ventromedial prefrontal cortex shows combinatory effects.

If δ rhythms are shown to migrate during phrase structure building, it would be possible to attribute particular computational roles to these oscillations in the way Muller et al. (2018) have done for spatial navigation. For instance, travelling δ waves could be responsible for patterning spiking from single- to multiunit lexical structures in each δ cycle.

In my view, these observations speak against the idea that linguistic computation is based on *regional stasis* (e.g. the common claim that BA 44 and its temporal dorsal pathway constitutes the basis of natural language syntax) and is rather implemented via a cortical circuit even more dynamic than previously assumed (for perspective: Zhang & Jacobs 2015 discovered for the first time travelling θ waves, but only throughout the human hippocampus; see also Patten et al. 2012). Indeed, Muller et al. (2018, 12) note that 'the existence of stimulus-evoked travelling waves in the sensory cortex presents a challenge to the orderly topographic arrangement of selectivity first described by Hubel and Wiesel at the trial-averaged level'. Likewise, the existence of weakly coupled travelling oscillators presents quite a dramatic challenge to the language sciences, and it has been my intention here to sketch out possible directions for reconciling the cortical language circuit with these emerging discoveries and principles.

Current neurolinguistic work on oscillations provides simple associative oscillation-computation models mapped to strict brain regions, as when Meyer (2018) claims that β is strictly involved in prediction, or when Ding et al. (2016) propose that δ entrainment to phrasal and sentential structures is a core feature of language comprehension, or when Bastiaansen and Hagoort (2015) claim that γ is involved in semantic unification and β is involved in processing syntactically coherent structures. All of these studies doubtless shed some light on the dynamics of the cortical language circuit, but they should be understood to be only a partial take, with the existence of travelling oscillations potentially forcing a more elaborate set of models to emerge.

It may not simply be oscillations, then, but more specifically travelling oscillations that could provide the optimal way to bridge neuroanatomy and brain dynamics. Travelling wave cycles represent spatially discrete pulses of neural activity corresponding to distinct behavioural states, and the future task for the language sciences is to investigate how travelling waves might serve as a general mechanism for transmitting discrete pockets of neural activity in ways which map onto the functions of semantic, phonological and syntactic combinatorics. Muller et al. (2018, 1) document 'the generality of their role in cortical processing' but their role in language processing remains unknown. Indeed, in their original discovery of travelling waves, Patten et al. (2012, 7) speculate that 'the thalamus may exert an important influence on cortico-cortical propagation via thalamocortical reentrant loops', and since travelling waves appear to propagate along corticocortical fibres, the role of the thalamus may be crucial. Touching briefly on a related lower-level issue, in a recent seminal study Guo et al. (2017) used extensive sampling and optogenetic dissection to show that corticofugal (thalamic projecting) neurons in layer 6 can mediate δ and θ phase resetting. As such, corticofugal neurons seem capable of influencing the entrainment of a syntax-relevant frequency band, and these cells should therefore be the subject of further enquiry into the neurobiological basis of the language oscillome.

Travelling oscillations may also be able to account for certain language disorders and aphasias, since in the literature there are often cases documenting damage to brain areas not typically seen as language areas and yet which negatively impact language processing (Papathanasiou et al. 2017). It is possible that the migration of oscillations is disturbed by lesions and other forms of brain damage, which may serve to block them. Likewise, there are an even greater number of documented cases regarding the survival of key language skills after a supposedly core language region is damaged (see Ardila et al. 2016). Under the present perspective, this could simply imply that only part of the migration route was taken, impairing some representations from being accessed but nevertheless leaving much intact, or indeed that only part of the migration route was damaged. It is well known, for instance, that Broca's aphasia can be caused by damage to a number of areas outside Broca's area, such as the superior longitudinal fasciculus (see papers collected in Bastiaanse & Thompson 2012). Lesions to the precentral gyrus, anterior insula, and even the basal ganglia and anterior temporal lobe have been implicated in Broca's aphasia (Abutalebi & Cappa 2008); see also Woolnough et al. (2020) for a comprehensive examination of the role of the insula in language. Crucially, notice that these structures lie along the broader language circuit implicated in the model developed in this book, suggesting that damage to different stations

of the path taken by language-relevant travelling oscillations (mediated necessarily by connecting neural streams) can result in aphasias just as severe as
those resulting from damage from more classically core language regions.
Disruption of the anterior head of the caudate and putamen results in verbal
aphasias (Lieberman 2000), which may be due not simply to damage to white
matter fibres projecting from the cortex to the striatum (*à la* Nadeau & Crosson
1997) but more specifically because oscillations responsible for constructing
necessary speech signals are blocked from travelling across the full network
responsible for vocal production, extending far beyond the thalamus (it should
be noted that transmission speed in cortical grey matter is estimated to be
approximately 1,000 times slower compared to white matter, pointing us
towards likely sources of linguistic computational efficiency; Kurth et al.
2017). A similar explanation might account for the various verbal communication deficits resulting from lesions to the globus pallidus (Strub 1989). A
possible way to provide some criteria of falsification for these hypotheses
would be to conduct MEG or EEG scans of participants with various aphasias
alongside neurotypicals during basic semantic and syntactic processing tasks,
determining whether particular oscillations migrate as a function of a linguistic
manipulation and whether they do so in ways which significantly differ
between these groups.

Turning briefly to another area where travelling oscillations may provide
novel insights, Gągol et al. (2018) discovered that *fluid intelligence* level (*gf*),
or the ability to solve novel problems via abstract reasoning regardless of prior
knowledge, depends on the precise synchronisation of fast rhythms to the phase
of slow rhythms. In particular, {δ(γ)} phase–amplitude coupling was found to
be indicative of *gf* (more precisely, low γ at ~36Hz and δ at ~3Hz), suggesting
under the model proposed in this book that δ coordinates the extraction of
various cortical representations (Chacko et al. 2018 also showed {δ(γ)} phase–
amplitude coupling to be crucial for spatial attention). No intervening rhythms
are involved in this form of phase–amplitude coupling, unlike in linguistic
computation, which involves hierarchical structures and hence coupling
between δ, θ, β and γ of differing combinations. Buzsáki et al. (2013) discuss
that the propagation of low-frequency oscillations across the cortex is considerably faster in the human brain than in the smaller rat brain, likely explaining
the origins of *gf*. Mechanical morphogenesis – or 'the process through which
simple mechanical forces can lead to instabilities that [contribute] to the
emergence of complex shapes' (Foubet et al. 2019, 3) – may also play a role
in the development of complex neocortical organisation, further motivating the
idea that core features of the cortical language network are a third factor effect.

Further, the close rhythmic similarities between the oscillatory basis of fluid
intelligence and language processing support the notion discussed earlier that
the computational basis of memory and certain language processes – *Load*,

Maintain, Spell-Out, Concatenate and so forth – is shared (with the exception of labelling and cyclicity). Billeke et al. (2017) provide related evidence from EEG that the coupling of the amplitude of slow γ ripples (90–110Hz) to the phase of cortical δ differs as a function of cognitive task, ranging from memory recall to directed attention, supporting the role of δ-γ interactions in fluid intelligence.

Duncan (2013) discusses his fronto-parietal Multiple Demand system and regards it as the basis of fluid intelligence, with this system more broadly implicating subcortical structures like the thalamus and basal ganglia. It seems to follow from this model and the findings in Gągol et al. (2018) that {δ(γ)} coupling ranges over this fronto-parietal circuit, with the general processes of fluid intelligence possibly being enhanced by elementary forms of linguistic computation involving *Search* and *Concatenate* processes. While general forms of intelligence are coordinated by {δ(γ)} coupling, more complex, hierarchical syntax arrives only through a broader range of CFCs. This likely explains why fluid intelligence is also at risk of impairment in the event of brain lesions, with either the paths of the travelling δ waves across the fronto-parietal Multiple Demand circuit either being limited, or the cortical γ clusters they are typically coupled with being unable to synchronise. Flanagan and Goswami (2018) also present evidence that changes in the magnitude of the phase synchronisation index (ΔPSI) of slow amplitude modulations in the δ-θ range accompanies both phoneme deletion and plural elicitation – basic morphophonological tasks – suggesting that sensitivity to slow rhythms in speech forms is a major aspect of morphophonological knowledge.

Another potential avenue for oscillatory theories of language is to implement logical operators like NOT, AND, NAND, XOR, NOT and Neg-AND. For instance, the first could be rooted in phase asynchrony. Merging/synchronising two oscillations might implement an AND operation, an increase in amplitude of a long-range wave relative to the stable signature of a local travelling wave might serve to represent a NOT function, the rapid de-synchronisation or phase-resetting of multiple waves could execute a NOR computation, and the annihilation of two oscillations might implement a XOR logic gate. The localisation of these operations would vary as a function of which representations were involved (shapes, numbers etc.). Empirically, these hypotheses would be readily falsifiable given the use of an experimental paradigm which permitted a careful execution of these basic semantic operations, such as in a setting where participants were tasked with implementing these operations over a range of auditory, linguistic and visual objects (see Baggio et al. 2016 for initial attempts to map the neuroanatomical basis of logical connectives, which implicate left pIFG and left aIFG). In addition, Zhang and Pylkkänen (2018) used MEG to look at neural correlates of conceptual negation, and showed that left anterior temporal lobe was involved in both conceptual and logical processing, suggesting that it is not entirely unreasonable to suppose that semantic combinatorics and logical operators call upon analogous neural codes.

While there are currently no electrophysiological reports pertaining to this issue, Coetzee et al. (2019) conducted a related study. Although the issue of the oscillatory code is not touched on, these authors provide evidence that logical and linguistic processes are implemented in distinct brain areas. Using continuous theta burst stimulation (cTBS), a form of TMS, they demonstrated that inhibition of Broca's area impairs accuracy on a linguistic task but not on a matched logic task. Inhibition of fronto-medial cortex (media BA 8), an area implicated in deduction, produced the opposite performance pattern. Deductive reasoning may not be parasitic on language, then, but as mentioned there may be a common oscillatory code implementing these lower-level computations in distinct brain areas.

What else can be said of the potential function of travelling waves? According to Wexler's (1998) *Unique Checking Constraint* (UCC), a child's linguistic system is limited to checking only one syntactic property per linguistic environment. For instance, in the clausal domain Agreement and Tense features cannot both be checked, and so only one is eliminated (producing the Optional Infinite stage of language acquisition). Since we are beginning to understand the oscillatory differences between child and adult language comprehension (Leong & Goswami 2015), this constraint may be due to particular limitations on travelling θ oscillations across cortical areas responsible for coupling with γ pockets storing Agreement-relevant and Tense-relevant features, with maturity likely providing the brain with a broader and more extensive travelling path. Recent work from Kurth et al. (2017) examined slow oscillations in sleep in a group of children ($n = 23$; two to thirteen years) and showed that with increasing age, slow oscillations propagated across longer distances, with an average growth of 0.2 cm per year. The speed of the travelling waves remains unchanged across childhood, suggesting that the *interface* component of the language system is subject to greater developmental changes than the core neural code for phrase structure building. Since this area of neurobiological research is a recent development, further studies of child language processing within these frameworks will be needed to elaborate on these hypotheses any further.

The psycholinguistic possibilities of testing the morphology of travelling oscillations using MEG seem highly promising. An interesting question for future research concerns the relevance of travelling subcortical oscillations (e.g. parahippocampal migrations) and the morphology of travelling waves in non-human primates. As Alexander et al. (2016) also point out, the existence of travelling waves suggests that many MEG studies that analysed only standing waves are missing a large chunk of the puzzle. Relatedly, the fact that the lateralised location of oscillatory entrainment displays substantial individual variability (as Lam et al. 2018 show in a sample of 102 MEG participants) emphasises the need for travelling waves to be taken seriously as part of any analysis of sentence comprehension, since while the location may differ, the underlying neural code (of specific CFCs) appears to be robust.

3.7.2   Neuroethological Perspectives on the Neural Code for Language

> Contrary to popular opinion, imposing our mind on non-human animals is not a sign of our respect for them: perhaps it is the opposite, to colonize a territory that we cannot chart.
>
> Hinzen & Sheehan (2013, 58)

Extending the insights presented in this book further, we will here attempt to assimilate much of the aforementioned in order to explore the evolution of the neural code for hierarchical phrase structure. The core insights presented from ethology, animal communication, brain dynamics and philosophy of biology will be used to address the differences in oscillatory profiles between humans and our closest relatives.

There have so far been conducted no neuroethological experiments using the kind of stimuli which would allow researchers to compare the oscillatory basis of putatively human-specific computations (like phrase structure building) to the neural responses of non-human primates attempting to interpret or parse identical structures (see Murphy 2016b). For instance, Kikuchi et al. (2017) expose humans and monkeys to artificial grammars. Not only does this not guarantee that the human subjects would recruit their language systems, but even if it did, Kikuchi et al.'s data analysis did not investigate the kind of CFCs over the particular regions and rhythms claimed here to be responsible for phrase structure building. The authors only examine coupling between low frequencies and γ (see their Figure 2), and not coupling between low frequencies such as δ, θ and β (or indeed phase-phase coupling). The authors found that 'learned ordering relationships modulate the observed form of neural oscillatory coupling in [humans and monkeys]', but this is a far cry from interpreting or generating hierarchically structured expressions.

Contextualising this somewhat, Franz Mesmer was likely the first to discuss what he referred to as 'animal magnetism', an idea mocked during his time and which claimed that all living organisms have electrical fields which they can manipulate to change their behaviours (see Pearson 1790). But the existence of oscillatory dynamics influencing cognition and behaviour is not too far distant, even if the electric fields are brain-internal rather than features of the environment. This has been shown to be relevant to human cognition in this chapter, but what about non-human primates? As Chapter 1 explored, there are many differences between language and non-human primate call systems, but the continuities that do exist become more obvious when we consider the neural mechanisms underlying call perception, which include (but are not limited to) the following: mechanisms for facial recognition (Freiwald et al. 2009), vocal perception (Petkov et al. 2008), perceiving auditory sequences (Wilson, Kikuchi et al. 2015) and the integration of multisensory stimuli such as voices and facial movements (Ghazanfar & Eliades 2014). These common mechanisms lead to the possibility that apes and early hominins were placed in communicative scenarios with a substantial number of overlapping features, and evolved similar mechanisms as a response (an instance where adaptationism certainly has a place).

When the neural code for language later emerged, it would have been built into these mechanisms, naturally interfacing with many of the pragmatic features already in place, hence the existence of what linguists term the syntax-pragmatics and semantics-pragmatics interfaces. Non-human primate communication, though syntactically simple, is nevertheless accurately characterised as a discrete, rule-governed computational system operating over semantically complex representations, and so the idea that the human brain developed a cyclic labelling mechanism on top of this already-existing system to yield language seems well motivated. Evidence reviewed in Seyfarth and Cheney (2017) helps us elaborate on what *discrete* refers to in *discrete computational system*: When a baboon hears a call, they form a representation of the meaning by making a number of pragmatic inferences about discrete elements relevant to the 'conversation': '[T]he type of call, the caller's identity, recent events, and the caller's dominance rank and kinship affiliation'. With respect to the receivers, 'the discrete elements of call type, caller identity, and kin group are combined according to the rules of call delivery to create a message whose meaning is more than just the sum of the meanings of its constituent elements' (Seyfarth & Cheney 2017, 82).

This general claim that there are common, pre-existing mechanisms for the language system to interface with is not without other sources of evidence. Räsänen et al. (2017) show that prelinguistic speech segmentation into syllable-like units (a process common to all infants acquiring language) can be accurately achieved through attending simply to sonority fluctuations, which they show are 'highly informative of syllable and word boundaries' (2018, 130). The question for future research is whether infants use sonority-based rhythmic units as discrete perceptual chunks or probabilistic cues to linguistic structure, and how this seemingly domain-general chunking/probabilistic procedure was recruited by the language faculty during the course of human evolution.

As Chapter 1 reviewed, non-human primate syntax generally seems limited to single-instance concatenation and a form of adjunction, itself a form of concatenation. The communication systems of non-human primates (prosimians, monkeys and apes) appear to have a fully specified semantics related to basic, non-complex concepts.

Reboul (2015) presents related, convincing arguments against the common idea that human language is a communication system; indeed, *communication* is not a natural class and so any putative human communication system cannot have been subject to the laws of evolution, and is rather a collection of distinct processes like intention, reference, imitation, etc. (see also Reboul 2017). In fact, the term *communication* will always need considerable unpacking, no matter what theoretical context it appears in. As Chomsky (2018b, 34) notes, 'probably 99% of our use of language' involves 'talking to ourselves, something that we do constantly, night and day, and can only be prevented by a dedicated act of will'. Chomsky notes that while internal speech is 'conscious' in its phonology, everything else about it is unconscious (syntax and semantics). Dor (2017, 44) even argues that the evolution of language aided our ability to lie possibly more than it aided our ability to communicate: 'We evolved *for* lying, and *because* of lying, just as much as we evolved for and because of honest communication.' He adds: 'Language would be much simpler had it evolved just for honest communication, and we would be much less imaginative, suspicious and inquisitive, and emotionally controlled. We would probably have very little symbolic culture, no myths, no propaganda, and we would also probably insult each other much more often' (Dor 2017, 57).

Returning to syntax, Schlenker, Chemla, Schel et al. (2016) review studies of Putty-nosed monkeys, Campbell's monkeys, King Colobus monkeys and New World monkeys, and conclude that all are capable of morphologically simple calls, but that Campbell's monkeys may be additionally capable of producing finite-state root-suffix structures (*-oo*) with an independent meaning generated by a simple conjunctivist semantics (contra Tallerman 2016). These call systems seem capable of concatenation (to what end, such as compositional semantics, remains open for debate), but not hierarchical phrase structure-building. This may be a consequence of their lack of a labelling mechanism, likely human-unique, which would also explain why basic call pairs do not appear to form even the simplest of labelled structures such as compounds like 'apron string' (subordinate), 'sword fish' (attributive) or 'bitter sweet' (coordinate).

Monkeys appear unable to, firstly, construct nested and cross-serial dependencies, which are plausibly defined as dependencies between phrasal labels, not terminal strings (Fukui 2015). Secondly – and following directly from this – they are unable to construct a categorial identity for a multi-set object and maintain this object in memory. These two processes (property attribution and object permanence), though not species-specific, appear to function in humans in two unique ways: they are executed unboundedly, not being limited to *n* applications, and they interface with a large number of other cognitive systems, not being confined to a small subset of representations. This system becomes more dynamic with the attribution of exocentric categorial labels which are distinct from either of the objects in a compound, such as the Brazilian Portuguese 'quebra-quebra' ('break-break', or 'riot'), in which two verbs conjoin to be labelled N, not V.

If primate calls are non-compositional, then it may be that the lexical atoms/ roots used in human language are partly derived from such calls, since neither primate calls nor roots can be combined together to form new calls/words, being feature-less. Roots need to merge with categorial labels and other morphological elements to enter the derivation (Panagiotidis 2014, 2015). If labelling is human-unique, then we would expect that a degree of variation in language change – indeed, perhaps a substantial degree – would result from labelling choices. This is precisely what van Gelderen (2018) found, with labelling failures in [XP, YP] structures (typically leading to movement) accounting for a number of syntactic phenomena cross-linguistically. It would be of interest to see if any primates have call systems involving multiple cases of conjunction, involving either whole units or morphemes, as in 'interest-ing-ly' (though likely nothing as complex as 'edit-or-ial-ize').

As we have seen, monkey calls have a highly constrained syntax, with, for instance, Black-and-White Colobus monkey calls being limited to *snort-roar* patterns. The generative power of concatenated *-oo* morphemes would not go beyond the finite-state, and would require only a concatenation operation and a memory buffer capable of maintaining two objects in memory (see Veselinovic et al.'s 2014 analysis of Diana monkey calls and their 'merged associations'). It follows that keeping to computational concerns, though such investigations are necessary, will provide impoverished and biologically inadequate evolutionary scenarios.

In a combinatorial system like human language, in which roots appear to be underspecified for meaning and need to be conjoined with grammatical feature complexes in order to be interpreted, 'fewer elements are required to express the same number of possible messages, and so it allows for more efficient communication than a system in which each signal has a distinct form' (Scott-Phillips & Blythe 2013, 1). Bonobos, our closest living primate relative, exhibit a degree of functional flexibility in their *peep* calls (Clay et al. 2015), and so presumably it did not take a particularly drastic neurological reorganisation to arrive at the flexibility of human language. Recent evidence points to the precuneus (a central hub of brain organisation) as being prominently expanded in modern humans (Bruner et al. 2017), and given its role in visuospatial integration and consciousness, it may also be involved in linguistic and non-linguistic combinatoric systems.

Attaheri et al. (2015) documented a P500 effect in macaques in response to mixed complexity grammars, homologous to the human P600, a late positivity relating to complex syntactic processing. The type of processing reflected in such late positivities in macaques may be a dormant faculty, not actively used by them but exposed in artificial circumstances, and when placed in a new domesticated environment and skull size may have adopted a novel function.

If non-human primate brains are restricted in their cross-cortical and sub-cortical rhythmic coupling profile and they are limited to extracting a reduced sequence of features, this may explain why monkey calls convey limited information, not interfacing with conceptual systems responsible for actions, agents, patients and so forth. The finding that Campbell's monkeys are limited to the deployment of the roots *boom*, *hok* and *krak* and a bound affix *–oo* would follow naturally from this oscillatory profile. The primate electrophysiological and oscillatory literature is comprehensive enough to permit a tentative reconstruction of call comprehension from the perspective of brain dynamics. For example, Brincat and Miller (2015) found functional differences and frequency-specific interactions between the Rhesus hippocampus (HPC) and prefrontal cortex (PFC) when the monkeys were learning object pair associations, with θ synchrony being stronger after errors and decreasing with learning, while correct associations promoted β-α synchrony which was stronger in the HPC-PFC direction.

Interestingly, when the homologue of Broca's region in the monkey brain is lesioned, call vocalisations are not impaired, suggesting other regions are involved, such as the limbic system and brainstem (Sage et al. 2006). On the interpretation side, macaques share similar call comprehension substrates with human language comprehension in the left posterior temporal gyrus (Heffner & Heffner 1986). The superior temporal gyrus is implicated in the interpretation of species-specific vocalisations in macaques (Hackett et al. 2001). However, the density of white matter connections between Broca's and Wernicke's regions is also greater in humans than in monkeys (Petrides & Pandya 2009), and the human arcuate fasciculus connecting the two regions substantially projects to expanded temporal association cortex implicated in semantic processing. It is possible that these structural changes partly yielded the increased rate of information transfer between conceptual and articulatory systems in humans, restricting monkey calls to their limited hormone- and alarm-related content. Moreover, Wilson, Kikuchi et al.'s (2015) fMRI study of humans and macaques during nonsense word and rule-based sequence processing revealed that areas specified for sequence comprehension in the ventral frontal and opercular cortex, adjacent to BA 44 and 45, have functional counterparts in the monkey brain. This leads to the possibility that 'language-related processes in modern humans are functionally integrated with highly conserved, originally non-linguistic processes shared with our extant primate relatives' (Wilson, Kikuchi et al. 2015, 10), the basis of which are likely oscillatory in nature (both humans and macaques also appear to use similar auditory sequence learning strategies when processing artificial grammars; Wilson, Smith et al. 2015). Hage and Nieder (2016) also claim that complex behaviours such as sequence planning and strategy formation are encoded by neurons in the monkey lateral prefrontal cortex, which may constitute a precursor to elements of the human neural code for syntax. The authors summarise that there are two neural circuits for controlling speech. The first is a volitional motor network reliant on the prefrontal cortex (in particular, Broca's area) and a phylogeneti-cally more ancient vocal motor network reliant on limbic areas and the brain-stem, implicated respectively in initiating and controlling motor output. While the volitional circuit is present in monkeys, its links to the vocal motor network are extremely weak, such that monkeys can only control the *initiation* of stereotyped vocalisations, and not subsequent muscle movements.

Returning to the oscillome, consider also the findings of Esghaei et al. (2015), who documented the phase–amplitude coupling of local field potentials from extra-striate area MT of macaque monkeys, a region specialising in processing visual motion. They discovered that directing spatial attention into the receptive field of MT neurons decreased the phase–amplitude coupling between the low-frequency phase (1–8Hz) and higher power (30–100 Hz) of local field potentials, suggesting that CFC is suppressed as a function of visual attention (see also Lowet et al. 2016). Esghaei et al. (2015) suggested that the macaque visual cortex uses phase–amplitude coupling to regulate inter-neuro-nal correlations, coding relevant stimuli more efficiently. β-γ phase–amplitude coupling also appears to be involved in visual stimulus routing and attentional control of stimulus activation in the macaque brain (Richter et al. 2017). Further investigations of phase–amplitude coupling during complex cognitive tasks in monkeys such as call interpretation and production would allow for comparative models of the functional role of dynamic brain activity to be constructed. It should be stressed that rhythms have distinct, non-overlapping roles varying by regional source, such that pulvinar γ can be involved both in feedforward processing for snake images and in cortico-pulvinar-cortical inte-gration for face images (van Le et al. 2016). Care should be taken to differ-entiate between distinct oscillatory roles in studies of monkey call systems. Relatedly, other primate studies have revealed that phase resetting of slow oscillations in the anterior temporal lobe during face stimuli presentation increases the probability of voice cell firing (Perrodin et al. 2015), and so cross-modal input integration appears to be a feasible role for low-frequency oscillations.

Since increased γ correlates with greater working memory load and main-tenance and is primarily involved in local operations as a result of conduction delays, this rhythm may be involved in the generation of the roots which constitute morphologically basic call units (such as *krak* and *boom*). Upon the conjunction of an *-oo* unit (also generated by γ), a complex object such as *krak-oo* would be held by the β band, with this rhythm being implicated in maintaining existing cognitive sets, as discussed earlier. A recent study of Rhesus monkeys revealed that during the internally monitored continuation phase of a synchronisation-continuation task β increased relative to the amplitude found in reaction-time tasks, with the basal ganglia likely being responsible for generating the initiation signal before it spreads across portions of the striatum (Bartolo & Merchant 2015). These observations would speak to Honkanen et al.'s (2015) findings that more complex objects are represented with β rather than γ. Koziol et al. (2009) present evidence suggesting that disinhibiting a basal ganglia loop leads to the maintenance of a particular representation to the exclusion of others, while the dependence on inhibitory rebound documented in β1 (slow β) permits it to 'continue in the absence of continuing input' (Kopell, Kramer et al. 2010, 3). In humans, this might allow a labelled object to be held in memory beyond the perception of its constituent elements, while in non-human primates it may allow the maintenance of a call pair.

Keeping with these frequency bands, consider Lewis, Schoffelen et al.'s (2016) MEG study of Dutch subject- and object-relative clauses, which revealed that β is an index of the maintenance/change of the ongoing sentential structure (or under the present model, the constructed feature-sets), and so an investigation into the role of β in primate call sequences may shed light on the mechanisms responsible for representation retrieval and maintenance. β additionally seems to be implicated in the maintenance of muscle synergy representations in the primary motor cortex (Aumann & Prut 2015), in contrast to Watanabe et al.'s (2015) findings that β is 'related more to the attentive state and external cues as opposed to detailed muscle activities' in Japanese monkeys (*Macaca fuscata*) and Hosaka et al.'s (2016) findings that β suppression reflects erroneous action sequence updating in the same species. These comparisons will lead to precisely the kind of explanatory granularity linguists and ethologists should be seeking in their investigations of the structure and evolution of cognitive combinatorics. For instance, the correct updating of action sequences in Japanese monkeys is achieved via increases in γ (Hosaka et al. 2016), an oscillatory profile similar to that involved in the chunking of linguistic feature-sets, which also involves γ power increases, though doubtless ones of distinct phasal properties.

This leads to direct predictions for the monkey oscillome given what is known about the combinatorial capacities of monkeys. Schlenker, Chemla, Schel et al. (2016), for instance, show that monkeys can combine two word-like elements, but cannot then combine this set with another atomic element. This would require a concatenation operation, a representational base ('lexicon') and, finally, a temporary workspace where the combined set can be stored in memory. Rizzi (2016) calls this a two-merge system (word–phrase merger), while monkeys seem limited to one-merge systems (word–word) – although they may be capable of two-merge systems if one defines a *krak-oo* conjunction followed by another distinct call as a type of phrase–word combination. Human language, in contrast, is a three-merge system, permitting not just word–phrase merger, but phrase–phrase merger, requiring a secondary workspace in addition to the temporary workspace required by two-merge systems. Nested rhythmic activity of the kind discussed earlier might act as the foundation of this secondary workspace, with a greater number of nested couplings seemingly available to the human oscillome yielding the greater number of stored representations in memory (see Section 3.3.1). Interestingly, monkey vocal tracts have been shown to be structurally adequate to produce the full range of human language (Fitch et al. 2016), and it rather appears that neural changes were instead responsible for the emergence of language – conclusions which readily lend new urgency to oscillatory investigations. More recently, a monkey homolog for the arcuate fasciculus (central to many models of language evolution) was discovered by Balezeau et al. (2020) originating in auditory cortex, which is also line with the idea that human language evolution was not due to one important brain area, but was rather more likely due to the implementation (via a widespread network) of a more abstract generalizable neural code for mapping semantic representations to sets of larger syntactic units, as proposed here.

Additional insights come from Ramirez-Villegas et al.'s (2015) study of sharp wave-ripples in the macaque hippocampal CA3-CA1 network, which attributed a role for γ rhythms in memory reactivation, transfer and consolidation (findings echoed in Kaplan et al. 2016). Each γ-generated item would couple with hippocampal θ (see Lee et al. 2005 and Jutras et al. 2013 for the role of this rhythm in monkey working memory) in order to achieve the binding of morphological elements ('*krak-oo*') before coupling with basal ganglia-initiated and striatal β, which would in turn increase in amplitude until the event of either an erroneous action sequence (call production) or the termination of the call series. This hypothesis is supported by studies claiming that β activity operates as a general coupling mechanism of assembly activity across brain structures (Fujioka et al. 2012).

It appears, then, that in humans and monkeys construction of an internal sequence leads to β increases, maintenance failure/disruption leads to β decreases, and the execution of the sequence is achieved via subsequent γ increases (these findings about the role of β in language and motor control may speak to Llinás's 2001 intuition that thinking amounts to a form of 'internal movement'). It is the execution of a cyclic labelling mechanism that the human oscillome alone can implement.

4   Conclusions and Future Directions

We fill pre-existing forms and when we fill them we change them and are changed.
                                         Frank Bidart, *Borges and I*

As discussed throughout this book, information extracted from oscillatory entrainment seems to be utilised by processes that are not phase-synchronised to any given external stimuli. The discussion in Chapters 2 and 3, though ranging across a broad number of topics, gradually conspired to yield the conclusion that it will be at this crucial divide – the interface between exogenous oscillatory entrainment and endogenous rhythmic activity – that the neural code for phrase structure will be implemented. This is the juncture where evolutionary neurolinguists should focus their attention, not vocal learning nor imitation nor theory of mind, but the implementation of the recursive computational system. As the empirical and theoretical considerations discussed earlier suggest, studies of the computational properties of neural oscillations have the potential to achieve what Poeppel (2012, 35) terms 'theoretically well-motivated, computationally explicit, and biologically realistic characterizations of function'. I take this approach to be part of a line of research starting with Lisman and Idiart's (1995, 1512) seminal suggestion that 'brain oscillations are a timing mechanism for controlling the serial processing of short-term memories' (although the conceptual roots of these ideas can be traced further back, as noted). While Ravignani and Norton (2017, 16) suggest that ethologists should construct 'rhythmic phylogenies' of birdsong, this book has proposed a parallel aim for the neurocomputational basis of language. The explanatory reach of oscillatory processes still remains fairly modest, but experimental advances in tandem with developments in theoretical neurobiology along the lines I have suggested may well prove conducive to grounding linguistic computation in the brain.

    All in all, it may be that the richer levels of hierarchy seen in human language result from the broader range of cross-frequency couplings available. Upon its emergence, the human-specific oscillatory profile would have interfaced with more ancient systems shared with other primates, in turn influencing and modifying the internal organisation of such systems through a process of reciprocal causation (Lewontin 1983; Walsh 2015), with the characteristics of an organism arising through interacting cascades of selection and construction. This idea is supported by Hoshi's (2019, 8) claim that the emergence of Merge 'made a significant contribution to diversifying a variety of concepts (both simplex and complex)'. Reciprocal causation effectively ensures that causal relationships are bi-directional, since a given cause could later become an effect (and vice versa). Hence, the 'gene-centrism' of the neo-Darwinian Synthesis requires some modification (see Svensson 2018), with evolutionary neurolinguists needing to expand their scope of concerns beyond natural selection. Indeed, Levins and Lewontin (1985, 104) noted over three decades ago how one cannot simply analyse an organism's genes in isolation from its environment, and that both factors reciprocally influence each other. Bacteria, the authors note, 'are largely outside the influence of gravity as a consequence of their size, that is, as a consequence of their genes. On the other hand, they are subject to another universal force, the Brownian motion of molecules, which [humans] are protected from by our large size, again a consequence of our genes'.

As a result of reciprocal causation, the neural code for language, with its cyclic labelling mechanism, would likely have reshaped the representations of the conceptual systems it interfaced with. This may explain why primate call units appear to be lacking in the diverse array of, for instance, Tense and φ-features. There also exists a close alignment between certain grammatical structures and neo-Davidsonian event representations, possibly emerging through reciprocal causation: The Complementiser domain corresponds to the point of existential closure; 'little verbs' (v) to internal/external thematic role assignment; 'little prepositions' (p) to adjunct insertion. Exactly how this and other forms of representational diversity emerged from the combination of the oscillatory mechanisms responsible for labelling and cyclicity remains a mystery, and presupposes a neural model of representations, which, as Chapter 3 discussed, we are currently lacking, having only various claims about synchronously activated call assemblies acting as informational sources. But regardless of the model of neural representation one adopts, it is clear that the present oscillatory model of language yields a serious degree of biological engagement not present in standard generative descriptions of 'the rich expressive and open-ended power of human language, the creative aspect of normal language use in the Cartesian sense' (Everaert et al. 2015, 740). It is the task of future research to deepen these biological connections.

An answer to what Embick and Poeppel (2015, 363) term the second specialisation question was presented in Chapter 1: 'Are there particular parts of the [computational-representational] theory that are more likely to be candidates for explanatory neurolinguistic explanation than others?' Labelling and cyclic transfer were suggested as candidates. These are the operations which attribute to a given set a syntactic identity and maintain it in memory whilst transferring these structures to the conceptual and sensorimotor interfaces in 'chunks' of a given size, determined by the coupling properties of distinct waves. As Collins (2020) argues, labelling remains the core, fundamental component of natural language syntactic and semantic interpretation processes that cannot be dispensed with, essential for generating the asymmetry between distinct units of a syntactic structure – 'cultural evolution' and other such notions will not be of use here. Repeating ideas presented earlier, Collins (2020, 232) notes: '*Brown cow* applies to animals of a certain colour, not to a colour that is manifest in certain animals. *Chase a cow* applies to an event that has a cow as its target, not to a cow that is being chased'. As Moltmann (Forthcoming) stresses, complex semantics (and ontology more generally) is intimately tied to natural language syntax; 'language-driven ontology is super-imposed on the ontology of ordinary objects', for Moltmann (Forthcoming), and is part of the generative component that produces such an ontology. That is, our conception of the world of ordinary objects and their part-whole relations is influenced by language, and so the neural components of asymmetrical syntactic interpretation will ultimately have extensive cognitive implications.

But what about the opposite problem of neurobiological specificity? This is posed by Embick and Poeppel's first specialisation question: 'Are there particular levels of [neurobiological] organisation that are to be privileged as candidates for [computational-representational] specialisation?' I have argued that brain dynamics, in particular neural oscillations, are likely candidates to be privileged in such a way. Embick and Poeppel (2015) also make a useful distinction between *correlational, integrated* and *explanatory* neurolinguistics. The first occurs when neurobiological computation is correlated with a computational/representational theory, the second when neurobiological data provides a way of selecting between computational/representational theories, and the third when properties of neurobiology explain why a computational/representational theory is the way it is. As the authors explain, 'Although cognitive theories and [neurobiological] theories are advancing in their own terms, there are few (if any) substantive linking hypotheses connecting these domains' (Embick & Poeppel 2015, 357). The translation project undertaken in this book – converting parts of the cognome into the oscillome – is only one step towards explanatory neurolinguistics, concerned as it is primarily with *correlational* investigations, although some suggestions have also been made concerning how properties of the computational system can emerge directly from properties of oscillatory behaviour.

As emphasised a number of times in this book, top-down perspectives on evolutionary neurolinguistics can be highly instructive up until the point that sufficiently decomposed and generic operations and processes have been discovered. But insisting on a wholly top-down perspective is inconsistent with both Darwinian and Thompsonian thinking (see Balari & Lorenzo 2013). The goal should be to unite, and not divide, information from different computational and implementational levels through generic brain mechanisms. The timeless urge to impose on nature human-specific concepts crops up in neurolinguistics all too often; as Buzsáki (2006) puts it, 'we take a man-created word or concept . . . and search for brain mechanisms that may be responsible for the generation of this conceived behaviour'. Some degree of compromise must naturally be sought. The best we can do, to my mind, is to stick to those atomic, domain-general operations which could conceivably be implemented in the brain and reconstruct our knowledge of language from the bottom-up. Every theory of language will therefore sit somewhere on this spectrum ranging from fully anthropomorphic models to fully naturalistic ones; indeed, 'for a system as complex as a brain, a pure bottom up approach appears to be a non-starter' (Gomez-Marin & Mainen 2016, 86).

As explored by Balari and Lorenzo (2013), evolution 'tinkers' existing mechanisms (e.g. slight changes in oscillatory operations like selective inhibition via lower-level connectome-based modifications) to yield novel higher-level operations like set-formation. Richer collaboration between linguists, systems neuroscientists, computer scientists and geneticists consequently needs to take place. For instance, the glymphatic system (responsible for 'cleaning' the brain of protein aggregates) is also responsible for delivering glucose to neurons, and possibly also to white matter (Jessen et al. 2015). Its potential role in brain function, and consequently cognition, is only just beginning to be researched. Other recent work has shown that electrical signalling is present in bacterial communication (Prindle et al. 2015), suggesting with fascinating and timely clarity that the oscillatory properties of the language-ready brain arise from ancient, generic mechanisms.

It is also worth noting in this connection that simply because there may be no brain region specialised for complex syntax, it does not follow that syntax is not genetically built into human brain function, since there are other cognitive capacities which are distributed across the brain but are still derived from innate mechanisms. Indeed, Zador (2019) provides a robust critique of artificial neural networks and argues, contrary to many recent proposals, that animals are born with highly structured brain connectivity, enabling them to learn very rapidly: 'Because the wiring diagram is far too complex to be specified explicitly in the genome, it must be compressed through a 'genomic bottleneck" (Zador 2019). More generally, brains are built with a rich amount of preconfigured connectivity and dynamically switching cortical states (Kenet et al. 2003; Dragoi & Tonegawa 2013), which grounds its oscillatory coding schemes.

As discussed in Chapter 3, there is an emerging consensus that the neural code used for spatial navigation is implicated in navigating more abstract representations. Conceptual space has been shown to be interpreted and explored using a grid-like code comparable to the grid cells standardly proposed to navigate space, and auditory space also appears to rely on mechanisms involved in spatial navigation. Indeed, it is becoming something of a general theme in the neurobiology of cognition that cellular and oscillatory mechanisms once believed to be highly domain-specific are in fact recruited in the service of computationally analogous processes operating over distinct representational domains (see also Murphy 2016d). This book has attempted to apply this insight to language.

Moreover, a recurrent proposal in this book that has been that future research should be geared less towards functional neuroanatomy (e.g. the localisation of syntactic functions) and more towards an oscillatory coding scheme. Support for this proposal has been presented from a range of domains; consider, for example, Genç et al.'s (2018) discovery that diffusion markers of dendritic density and arborisation in grey matter predict differences in intelligence. The authors note: 'These results suggest that the neuronal circuitry associated with higher intelligence is organized in a sparse and efficient manner, fostering more directed information processing and less cortical activity during reasoning.' If these conclusions about 'higher intelligence' between language-speaking human subjects generalise across cognitive capacity (and across species) more generally, this would motivate an increased emphasis on a generalisable neural code of the kind proposed in this book, as opposed to a focus on lower-level neuroanatomical connectivity.

The experimental obstacles towards a comprehensive oscillatory account of language are numerous, imposing serious limits on investigation. Most notably, speech contains no markers for the hierarchical structure of language, and so some measure of internal marking needs to be employed instead. Following the careful and broad literature review in VanRullen (2016), the linguistic rhythmicity documented earlier appears to be crucially distinct from the more general forms of perceptual cyclicity, which can be decomposed into sensory cycles (~10Hz) and attentional cycles (~7Hz), suggesting that hierarchical phrase structure building is a more complex operation invoking richer levels of oscillatory interactions. At the same time, it has also been shown that attention is a central modulatory variable for neural entrainment, of the kind needed for interpreting the rhythmic nature of speech (Zoefel et al. 2017). The (likely rich) oscillatory interactions between attentional mechanisms and phrase structure building remain a promising topic for future study.

Addressing now the issue of testability, due to its high temporal and spatial resolution and signal-to-noise ratio, electrocorticography (ECoG) is highly applicable to testing some claims made here, having been used to investigate speech production (Bouchard & Chang 2014) and language comprehension (Cervenka et al. 2011) and being flexibly deployed both in humans and animals. In addition, it not difficult to think of a range of experimental possibilities which open up at this point. Focusing on the human oscillome, MEG could be used to record the brains of subjects tasked with memorising or attending to distinct lexical feature-sets ('You' and 'She' share a Number φ-feature in common, for instance), with the strength and load-dependence of particular oscillations being tracked to determine if any permit the differentiation, or contribute to the maintenance of, these features.

As a way of summarising, Figure 4.1 contrasts the classical 'language areas' with the model we are proposing, revealing a considerably greater degree of complexity. For instance, depicting certain proposals in Chapters 2–3, in Figure 4.1 δ waves cycle across left inferior frontal parts of the cortex, building up the syntactic workspace phrase-by-phrase and potentially being endogenously reset by a newly constructed phrase, and being coupled to travelling θ waves which perform the same function. δ would coordinate phrasal construction while θ-γ interactions would support the representational construction of linguistic feature-sets. It has also been proposed that δ-γ coupling may be a generic combinatorial process, combining representations from within and across domains, and the cerebellum has also been shown to play a role in processing linguistic rhythmicity and hence aids phrasal processing in fronto-temporal regions (Murphy 2019). Meanwhile, linguistic prediction seems to be implemented via coupling between frontal γ amplitude and posterior α phase

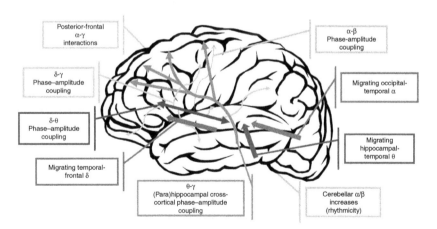

Figure 4.1 A connectome of the hypothesised neural code for recursive hierarchical phrase structure building. The large number of specific regions implicated in this connectome are discussed throughout the main text

(Wang et al. 2018) and prefrontal predictions facilitate δ-entrained speech tracking in anterior superior temporal gyrus (Keitel et al. 2017). Lastly, event representations (thematic relations between entities) in the angular gyrus (and also entity/object category representations in the anterior temporal lobe; Binder & Desai 2011) serve as an interface to the processing of hierarchical lexical-syntactic information in the posterior middle temporal gyrus, a major node in migrating δ and also δ-θ phase-amplitude coupling. Of course, entities and events are not the only forms of representations manipulated by syntactic structures. White matter tracts to other loci of conceptual representations (in the presently proposed system: γ-itemised units) will likely be needed; a topic ripe for future neuroimaging research.

How could this model map onto articulation/externalisation, a topic we intentionally put to one side in order to focus on comprehension? Consider the findings reviewed in Goswami (2019). Goswami's lab has shown that stressed syllables in children's nursery rhymes, during perception, entrain to δ ('LON-DON'), individual syllables entrain to θ ('LON') and the onset-rime structure entrains to β ('L', 'ON'. . .). Meanwhile, the adult brain exploits amplitude rise times to discover the temporal rates of perceived speech, and subsequently phase resets the activity of particular cortical cell networks in order to ensure that their activity is aligned with this new, incoming information. Alongside this, there exists *motor prediction* of speech, through which δ phase in auditory cortex couples with β power in motor cortex (Arnal et al. 2014). This {δ(β)} phase–amplitude coupling could support the rhythmic synchronisation of movement to certain positions within an external rhythmic input (speech, music, etc.) but could also facilitate the coordination of externalising prosodic information, ensuring motor commands adhere to the internally generated phonological structures being mapped onto articulatory pathways. Thus, we would expect two types of {δ(β)} phase–amplitude coupling across distinct regions: one for comprehension, the other for production.

There is also increasing support for the oscillatory model presented in this book, alongside the evidence discussed in Chapter 2 and 3. For instance, Brennan and Martin (2019) analysed a naturalistic story-listening EEG dataset (twelve minutes of the first chapter of *Alice's Adventures in Wonderland*) and showed that δ-γ phase-amplitude coupling increases with the number of predicates bound on a given word (the authors analysed only the Cz electrode – central, top scalp site – so further analyses are needed to flesh out the picture). They also discovered an increasing scale of δ-θ coupling beginning at the point of a word completing a single phrase, through to words completing two and three phrases. As such, δ-γ and δ-θ coupling increases with predication.

The specific computational roles attributed here to α are also supported by Chapeton et al.'s (2019) findings. These authors looked at intracranial EEG in the human temporal lobe and discovered that pairs of EEG sensor regions with correlated broadband activity are also α coherent (specifically in the 6–13Hz range, so technically also θ and low β, varying between participants). The phase delays of the coherent α oscillations also matched the time delays of the correlated components, suggesting that large-scale correlations and spiking activity are modulated by the phase of α. Interestingly, when the authors examined δ coherence, they found the phase delays between δ rhythms do not appear to be well suited to large-scale communication through coherence, suggesting that the migrating δ temporal (and frontal) rhythms postulated in the model defended in Chapter 3 do indeed play a more specific computational function.

Other recent work reveals further exciting prospects for testing the model I have developed here. Using MEG, Adams et al. (2019) discovered phase-amplitude coupling between δ and θ in subjects performing a semantic decision task, involving the reading of word pairs. The presentation of the second word was not time-locked to either δ or θ, and Adams et al.'s results were from all of the δ/θ periods from the point of stimulus presentation to the subject's decision. This particular form of phase-amplitude coupling forms the core component of the model I have developed here (and in Murphy 2016a, 2018b), lending specific computational advantages responsible for higher linguistic computation. Of course, δ-θ alone is only part of the computational machinery, with further coupling with γ, cross-cortical migrations, and other hypothesised low-frequency couplings providing further resources, as argued here (see Figure 4.1). Further modelling by Adams et al. (2019) revealed that local, interlaminar neocortical δ-θ phase-amplitude coupling 'may serve to coordinate both cortico-cortical and cortico-subcortical computations during distributed network activity' (2019, 1150). Specifically, regular spiking neurons (θ) project purely cortico-cortically, while intrinsic bursting neurons (δ) in layer 5 project subcortically. Given the proposed cortico-cortical and cortico-subcortical interactions in the model I have developed, this provides additional motivations for exploring the role of δ-θ coupling in language (see also Harmony 2013 for evidence that frontal δ activity increases during a range of general cognitive tasks). Pushing past disciplinary boundaries will be essential here; Adams et al.'s (2019) work appeared in the *Journal of Neurophysiology*, not known as a hotspot for linguists.

There is also a particular objection to oscillatory investigations of language which is worth addressing at this point, having presented all hypotheses and proposals. This objection states that inner linguistic cognition, loosely shackled to inner speech, is too rapidly constructed on the fly to be implemented by anything as slow as a δ wave, let alone multiple successive δ waves (Chomsky 2019b reproduces the same argument in the context of neural firing more generally). But, as made clear in Chapters 2–3, δ and also θ are merely the coordinators of the much more rapidly oscillating γ-itemised linguistic representations. Furthermore, with the shorter phase duration from peak-to-trough (and not peak-to-peak, or trough-to-trough) being the period when the most excitable representations will be phase-locked, we only have to invoke the peak-to-trough δ and θ periods. For instance, keeping with conservative timings (and not discussing faster δ at 3.5Hz or 4Hz), 1–3Hz peak-to-trough δ would permit two to six sets of θ-directed γ ripples per second. In turn, when we factor in the issue of γ ripple size (which can range from 30 Hz to over 100Hz) the combinatorial power of oscillatory synchronisation becomes clear.

More generally, and related to these issues, one of the more efficient ways to test the importance of oscillatory interactions in language processing would be to reanalyse existing (and often publicly accessible) EEG, MEG and ECoG datasets. As noted, there is a large variety of such datasets already in existence, which previous investigators have often used to simply look at amplitude fluctuations or general patterns of neural activity. Making use of these datasets, in particular those involving naturalistic dialogue or narratives, would permit neurolinguists to map out the most prominent forms of cross-frequency coupling apparent at certain stages of interpretation and would boost the ecological validity of oscillatory models.

With respect to testing the broad range of oscillatory interactions centred in the model proposed here, while it is possible to explore general band interactions, especially in the slower ranges, it is currently difficult to acquire γ activity with a high signal-to-noise ratio non-invasively. As such, a finer-grained perspective on precise δ-γ, θ-γ and α-γ interactions will require intracranial patient recordings using implanted electrodes. Still, this electrocorticographic (ECoG) method is limited in its cortical range, differing on a patient-by-patient basis, and many current studies only include five to twenty patients per experiment. Relatedly, while intracranial EEG (iEEG) involves electrodes implanted directly in brain tissue and provides high spatial resolution, iEEG data is naturally recorded in non-healthy brains, and is possibly confounded with changes in frequency spectra, epileptogenic changes and artefacts (Fellner et al. 2019). Meanwhile, MEG provides whole-head coverage and permits recordings of healthy subjects. As such, future work should aim to combine these methods, as in Fellner et al.'s (2019) dual iEEG-MEG study involving large sample sizes. Measuring magnetic dependencies in MEG can also be done in a number of ways, and strong sensor connections can imply a strong local neural connection or a strong non-local connection across large neural pathways; ECoG does not have this limitation

Moreover, most current analyses of coarse-grained brain activity, such as that measured by ECoG, are based on *linearity* assumptions (e.g. structural equation modelling and Granger causality). Linear models cannot describe flexible time-dependent or context-dependent interactions, of the kind exhibited by language comprehension and production. In an effort to move beyond these limits, Giahi Saravani et al. (2019) explore switching linear dynamics, where the switch determines which linear dynamical system currently best describes observed neural dynamics. The authors use an autoregressive Hidden Markov Model to identify dynamical network states exhibited by ECoG signals recorded from human neurosurgical patients, allowing them to characterise individual network states according to the patterns of directional information flow between cortical regions of interest, focusing on broadband γ. They found that these network states occur consistently and in specific, interpretable sequences across trials and subjects, such that the brain seems to exhibit a particular, fixed-length state of visual processing, then a variable-length language state, followed by a terminal articulation state. The dynamics of this second state should be of outstanding interest to future neurolinguistics work; in particular, exploring beyond the broadband γ range would be imperative to testing (parts of) the presently proposed neural code for language.

The theories we have presented here, concerning the interactions of oscillations, are also currently limited mathematically. Basic amplitude and phasal fluctuations can readily be captured, but the mathematical properties of cross-frequency coupling (and its various manifestations) are more difficult to capture. Moving forward, word-level theories will naturally be insufficient; mathematical theories are needed. Mathematical theories of learning and computation by neural systems, employing concepts from dynamical systems (attractors, oscillations, chaos) and statistics (information, uncertainty, inference) should be used to relate the dynamics and functions of neural behaviour.

From what was discussed in Chapter 1, a number of questions remain unanswered and unaddressed in much of the literature. For instance, how are third factors implemented in the brain (e.g. via principles such as Friston's free energy) and how do they impact the language architecture? Which subdomains of linguistics have the potential to make greater contact with the life sciences (e.g. pragmatics)? Which elements of the language system seem amenable to explanations invoking natural selection (as opposed to other accounts)? The extensive range of experimental approaches discussed in Chapter 1 also leads one to wonder how it is possible to further assess the auditory-vocal working memory capacity of non-human primates and songbirds. Yet other questions arise: Which linguistic structures (e.g. exocentric VN compounds) are candidates for being some of the earliest forms of syntactic objects? What possible evolutionary route did the pragmatics system of language take, given what is known about certain shared competences in this domain?

The conclusions in Chapter 2 result in (at least) the following, central questions for future research: What are the anatomical similarities and differences regarding human and non-human temporal processing networks? How do prediction and binding processes – seemingly implemented via distinct oscillatory codes – interface? What are the boundary conditions determining

when features of overlapping lexical items are integrated into a single representation rather than separated? What is the relationship between local power
decreases and cross-frequency coupling (and network connectivity more
broadly)?

Lastly, Chapter 3 presented a number of hypotheses about emerging areas of
inquiry in the cognitive neurosciences, with the research questions carrying the
most urgent relevance for linguistics being the following: How does the notion
of a travelling weakly coupled oscillator tie in with existing findings concerning the supposedly fixed, regionalised oscillatory activity found in existing
research into language processing? At what point does entrainment end and
endogenous neurocomputation begin? How might single-neuron models of
mental representations account for well-known features of the lexicon? How
might one test the hypothesis that non-human primates exhibit a differently
organised array of cortical cross-frequency couplings? Lastly, it is known from
intracellular recordings in vitro that cortical layer 5 pyramidal cells play an
important role in organising slow oscillations (Sanchez-Vives & McCormick
2000), but the more specific cellular and neurochemical basis of slow rhythms
(of the kind – and in the neuroanatomical locations – discussed here) remains in
relative obscurity.

While many of the topics related to language processing and evolution do
indeed remain difficult to approach, I hope to have shown that some – given the
right multidisciplinary perspective – are becoming increasingly tractable. If
feature-set binding, object maintenance, property attribution, featural comparisons, and cross-modular searches are experimentally found to be implemented
via generic oscillatory subroutines and various cross-frequency coupling interactions, this would be a substantial step towards understanding the biological
basis of language. Research into the neurochemical and genetic basis of the
human oscillatory profile is rapidly expanding, widening the scope for interdisciplinary investigations into its lower-level implementation and origins.
Although this work is not typically described as language evolution literature,
given the promising directions open to oscillatory experimental and theoretical
work, it may not be all that long until studies of thalamic α and frontal γ are
considered contributions to the implementational basis of phrase structure
building.

To conclude, my intention here has been to explore the potential causal-
explanatory power of neural oscillations with respect to the generation of
hierarchical phrase structure. This process has led to a number of new suggested directions for educing latent proposals by a number of researchers
concerning the various roles oscillations have in parsing grammatical phrases.
What are the implications for the neuroscience of language? The studies
reviewed above reflect a more general current trend in neurobiology, such
that processes and structures which were once deemed highly domain-

specific are now being understood to implement more generic computations, and the only domain-specific entities left are the representations these processes operate over. Further examples are increasingly reported in the literature, such as the discovery that domain-general preparation and control mechanisms implemented via θ and α modulations are recruited by the language system when generating predictions during sentence comprehension (Rommers et al. 2017). This opens up new avenues for investigating the biological basis of language and its emergence in our lineage. Along with a broader reach into domains which were not long ago believed to be irrelevant to the language sciences, this enterprise requires what the novelist John Cowper Powys (1951, 697) described as an 'insanely intense and incorruptible concentration on the mystery of words'.

Glossary

Agreement: When the form of a word/morpheme covaries with that of another word or phrase. Compare *John runs to the park* with *We run to the park*, where the form of the verb is conditioned by whether the noun is singular or plural.

Artificial grammar learning: A class of experimental paradigms employing invented rules to produce meaningless grammars.

Axon: A nerve fibre that conducts electrical impulses away from the neuronal cell body.

Binding theory: A set of principles accounting for the distribution of anaphoric elements (e.g. pronouns). A pronoun, or 'bindee', typically has an antecedent, or 'binder', as in *John said he was happy*, where the pronoun can successfully refer to the noun, unlike in **He said John was happy*.

Brodmann area (BA): A region of the cortex defined by its cytoarchitectonics, or cell structure.

C-command: An expression of the relationship between nodes on a hierarchically organised syntactic tree. If a node has any 'sibling' nodes (nodes which are dominated by the same node), then it c-commands them, and if not, then it c-commands every node its dominating 'parent' node c-commands.

Cell assembly: A network of functionally connected neurons that is activated by a particular mental process.

Clade: A natural grouping of organisms linked via descent from a common ancestor.

Content word: Words which name objects and their qualities. These are typically nouns but can also be verbs, adjectives and adverbs.

Cross-frequency coupling: When interactions between discrete frequency bands give rise to more complex regulatory structures. For instance, phase–amplitude coupling denotes the statistical dependence between the phase of a low-frequency band and the amplitude of a high-frequency band.

Displacement: A core concept in generative grammar whereby syntactic objects are displaced from the position where certain of their features are interpreted.

Embedding: The ability for a linguistic unit to host within it another linguistic unit.

Ethology: The study of animal behaviour with particular focus on the wild.

Evo-devo: Evolutionary-developmental biology; the recent synthesis of neo-Darwinianism and embryology and molecular developmental biology.

Exaptation: An evolutionary process through which mechanisms change their function before being tuned to a new function.

Function word: Words denoting grammatical relationships between content words, such as prepositions, pronouns and conjunctions.

Generative grammar: The branch of linguistics which assumes that natural language is a mental computational system of rules generating an unbounded array of hierarchically structured expressions, with varying degrees of acceptability.

Home sign: A communication system based on gestures developed by a deaf child lacking any linguistic input.

Homologous trait: A characteristic shared in a set of species as a result of inheritance from a common ancestor.

Label: The basic unit of structural identity in syntax.

Markedness: A method of designating regular versus irregular linguistic forms, where a regular form is regarded as 'unmarked' and an irregular form is regarded as 'marked'.

Merge: The computational operation which selects two lexical items, α and β, and forms a set, $\{\alpha,\beta\}$, in a workspace.

Oscillation: The unfolding of repeated events in terms of frequency; in brains, these are caused by excitatory and inhibitory cycles in cell assemblies.

Passivisation: The transformation of a sentence from an active form to a passive form, such as when *John ate the sandwich* is transformed into *The sandwich was eaten by John*.

Phi-feature (φ): Linguistic features of Person, Number and Gender.

Phenotype: Fixed morphological or behavioural features of an organism.

Phonology: The system of sound, or a set of sound-related features and rules stipulating how these features interact in a given language.

Pragmatics: The study of language use, action, and linguistic context.

Question formation: A common type of inversion where constituents switch their order of appearance, such as when *John will arrive* transforms into *Will John arrive?*

Recursion: The hallmark of natural language syntax; when a linguistic rule can be applied to the result of the application of the same rule, creating, for instance, 'nested' structures like *John, who likes Sarah, will come to the party* from *John will come to the party*.

Select: The computational operation which selects a lexical item (or feature, or a set of features, depending on one's assumptions) from long-term memory, or the 'lexicon'.

Spell-Out: The cyclic computational operation which transfers syntactic objects (sets of linguistic features, typically hierarchically organised) to the sensorimotor and conceptual interfaces for production and interpretation. Once Spell-Out has applied, a standard assumption is that these objects are inaccessible to the rest of the derivation (and hence the active construction workspace).

Syntax: Informally termed the 'grammar', this is the set of principles governing the structure of sentences.

Theta phase precession: When place cells fire at increasingly earlier phases of the underlying theta oscillation when approaching the place field.

References

Abe, K. & Watanabe, D. (2011). Songbirds possess the spontaneous ability to discriminate syntactic rules. *Nature Neuroscience* 14(8): 1067–1074.

Abel, T. J., Rhone, A. E., Nourski, K. V., Ando, T. K., Oya, H., Kovach, C. K., Kawasaki, H., Howard III, M. A., & Tranel, D. (2016). Beta modulation reflects name retrieval in the human anterior temporal lobe: an intracranial recording study. *Journal of Neurophysiology* 115(6): 3052–3061.

Abels, K. (2013). Comments on Hornstein. *Mind & Language* 28(4): 421–429.

Aboitiz, F. (2012). Gestures, vocalizations, and memory in language origins. *Frontiers in Evolutionary Neuroscience* 4: 2.

Aboitiz, F. (2017). *A Brain for Speech: A View from Evolutionary Neuroanatomy*. London: Palgrave Macmillan.

Abraham, A., von Cramon, D. Y., & Schubotz, R. I. (2008). Meeting George Bush versus meeting Cinderella: the neural response when telling apart what is real from what is fictional in the context of our reality. *Journal of Cognitive Neuroscience* 20: 965–976.

Abutalebi, J. & Cappa, S. F. (2008). Language disorders. In Cappa, S. F., Abutalebi, J., Démonet, J.-F., Fletcher, P. C., & Garrard, P. (eds.). *Cognitive Neurology: A Clinical Textbook*. Oxford: Oxford University Press. 43–66.

Ackermann, H. & Ziegler, W. (2010). Brain mechanisms underlying speech motor control. In Hardcastle, W. J., Laver, J., & Gibbon, F. E. (eds.). *The Handbook of Phonetic Sciences*. 2nd ed. Malden, MA: Wiley-Blackwell. 202–250.

Ackermann, H. & Ziegler, W. (2013). A 'birdsong perspective' on human speech production. In Bolhuis, J. J. & Everaert, M. (eds.). *Birdsong, Speech, and Language: Exploring the Evolution of Mind and Brain*. Cambridge, MA: MIT Press. 331–352.

Acsády, L. (2017). The thalamic paradox. *Nature Neuroscience* 20: 901–902.

Adams, N. E., Teige, C., Mollo, G., Karapanagiotidis, T., Cornelissen, P. L., Smallwood, J., Traub, R. D., Jefferies, E., & Whittington, M. A. (2019). Theta/delta coupling across cortical laminae contributes to semantic cognition. *Journal of Neurophysiology* 121(4): 1150–1161.

Adger, D. (2013). *A Syntax of Substance*. Cambridge, MA: MIT Press.

Adger, D. (2017). A Memory Architecture for Merge. Ms. Queen Mary University of London. ling.auf.net/lingbuzz/003440.

Adger, D. (2019a). *Language Unlimited: The Science behind Our Most Creative Power*. Oxford: Oxford University Press.

Adger, D. (2019b). Linguistic Representations: A Note on Terminology vs. Ontology. Ms. Queen Mary University of London. ling.auf.net/lingbuzz/004616.

Adger, D. & Svenonius, P. (2011). Features in minimalist syntax. In Boeckx, C. (ed.). *The Handbook of Linguistic Minimalism*. Oxford: Blackwell. 27–51.

Ainsworth, M., Lee, S., Cunningham, M. O., Roopun, A. K., Traub, R. D., Kopell, N. J., & Whittington, M. A. (2011). Dual gamma rhythm generators control interlaminar synchrony in auditory cortex. *Journal of Neuroscience* 31: 17040–17051.

Akam, T. & Kullmann, D. M. 2014. Oscillatory multiplexing of population codes for selective communication in the mammalian brain. *Nature Reviews Neuroscience* 15: 111–122.

Akimoto, Y., Takahashi, H., Gunji, A., Kaneko, Y., Asano, M., Matsuo, J. et al. (2017). Alpha band event related desynchronization underlying social situational context processing during irony comprehension: a magnetoencephalography source localization study. *Brain and Language* 175: 42–46.

Akiyama, M., Tero, A., Kawasaki, M., Nishiura, Y., & Yamaguchi, Y. (2017). Theta-alpha EEG phase distributions in the frontal area for dissociation of visual and auditory working memory. *Scientific Reports* 7: 42776.

Alcalá-López, D., Smallwood, J., Jefferies, E., Van Overwalle, F., Vogeley, K., Mars, R. B., Turetsky, B. I., Laird, A. R., Fox, P.T., Eickhoff, S.B., & Bzdok, D. (2018). Computing the social brain connectome across systems and states. *Cerebral Cortex* 28(7): 2207–2232.

Alexander, D. M., Nikolaev, A. R., Jurica, P., Zvyagintsev, M., Mathiak, K., & van Leeuwen, C. (2016). Global neuromagnetic cortical fields have non-zero velocity. *PloS ONE* 11(3): e0148413.

Alexandrou, A. M., Saarinen, T., Mäkelä, S., Kujala, J., & Salmelin, R. (2017). The right hemisphere is highlighted in connected natural speech production and perception. *NeuroImage* 152: 623–638.

Allen, K. & Monyer, H. (2015). Interneuron control of hippocampal oscillations. *Current Opinion in Neurobiology*, 31: 81–87.

Amalric, M. & Dehaene, S. (2018). Cortical circuits for mathematical knowledge: evidence for a major subdivision within the brain's semantic networks. *Philosophical Transactions of the Royal Society B* 373: 20160515.

Amalric, M. & Dehaene, S. (2019). A distinct cortical network for mathematical knowledge in the human brain. *NeuroImage* 189: 19–31.

Amundson, R. (1998). Typology reconsidered: two doctrines on the history of evolutionary biology. *Biology and Philosophy* 13: 153–177.

Amundson, R. (2006). EvoDevo as cognitive psychology. *Biological Theory* 1(1): 10–11.

Amzica, F. (2002). In vivo electrophysiological evidences for cortical neuron-glia interactions during slow (<1 Hz) and paroxysmal sleep oscillations. *Journal of Physiology Paris* 96(3–4): 209–219.

Anderson, F., Anjum, R. L., & Rocca, E. (2019). Philosophical bias is the one bias that science cannot avoid. *eLife* 8: e44929.

Anderson, M. L. (2016). Précis of *After Phrenology: Neural Reuse and the Interactive Brain*. *Behavioral and Brain Sciences* 39: e120.

Andics, A. & Miklósi, Á. (2018). Neural processes of vocal social perception: dog-human comparative fMRI studies. *Neuroscience and Biobehavioral Reviews* 85: 54–64.

Antzoulatos, E. G. & Miller, E. K. (2016). Synchronous beta rhythms of fronto-parietal networks support only behaviorally relevant representations. *eLife* 5: e17822.

Arbib, M. A. (ed.). (2006). *From Action to Language via the Mirror Neuron System*. Cambridge: Cambridge University Press.

Ardila, A., Bernal, B., & Rosselli, M. (2016). Why Broca's area damage does not result in classical Broca's aphasia. *Frontiers in Human Neuroscience* 10: 249.

Armeni, K., Willems, R. M., van den Bosch, A., & Schoffelen, J.-M. (2019). Frequency-specific brain dynamics related to prediction during language comprehension. *NeuroImage* 198: 283–295.

Arnal, L. H., Doelling, K. B., & Poeppel, D. (2014). Delta-beta coupled oscillations underlie temporal prediction accuracy. *Cerebral Cortex* 25: 3077–3085.

Aronov, D., Nevers, R., & Tank, D. W. (2017). Mapping of a non-spatial dimension by the hippocampal-entorhinal circuit. *Nature* 543: 719–722.

Artoni, F., d'Orio, P., Catricalà, E., Conca, F., Bottoni, F., Pelliccia, V., Sartori, I., Lo Russo, G., Cappa, S. F., Micera, S., & Moro, A. (2019). Electrophysiological correlates of syntactic structures. *bioRxiv*. http://dx.doi.org/10.1101/660415

Aru, J., Aru, J., Priesemann, V., Wibral, M., Lana, L., Pipa, G., Singer, W., & Vicente, R. (2015). Untangling cross-frequency coupling in neuroscience. *Current Opinion in Neurobiology* 31: 51–61.

Asano, E. & Gotman, J. (2016). Is electrocorticography-based language mapping ready to replace stimulation? *Neurology* 86(13): 1174–1176.

Assaneo, M. F. & Poeppel, D. (2018). The coupling between auditory and motor cortices is rate-restricted: evidence for an intrinsic speech-motor rhythm. *Science Advances* 4: eaao3842.

Atasoy, S., Donnelly, I., & Pearson, J. (2016). Human brain networks function in connectome-specific harmonic waves. *Nature Communications* 7: 10340.

Attaheri, A., Kikuchi, Y., Milne, A. E., Wilson, B., Alter, K., & Petkov, C. I. (2015). EEG potentials associated with artificial grammar learning in the primate brain. *Brain & Language* 148: 74–80.

Attal, Y. & Schwartz, D. (2013). Assessment of subcortical source localization using deep brain activity imaging model with minimum norm operators: a MEG study. *PLoS ONE* 8(3): e59856.

Aumann, T. D. & Prut, Y. (2015). Do sensorimotor β-oscillations maintain muscle synergy representations in primary motor cortex? *Trends in Neuroscience* 38(2): 77–85.

Axmacher, N. (2016). A useful code for sequences. *Nature Neuroscience* 19(10): 1276–1277.

Axmacher, N., Henseler, M. M., Jensen, O., Weinreich, I., Elger, C. E., & Fell, J. (2010). Cross-frequency coupling supports multi-item working memory in the human hippocampus. *PNAC* 107: 3228–3233.

Babiloni, C., Babiloni, F., Carducci, F., Cincotti, F., Cocozza, G., Del Percio, C., Moretti, D. V., & Rossini, P. M. (2002). Human cortical electroencephalography (EEG) rhythms during the observation of simple aimless movements: a high-resolution EEG study. *NeuroImage* 17: 559–572.

Backus, A. R., Schoffelen, J.-M., Szebényi, S., Hanslmayr, S., & Doeller, C. F. (2016). Hippocampal-prefrontal theta oscillations support memory integration. *Current Biology* 26(4): 450–457.

Baddeley, A., Eysenck, M. W., & Anderson, A. C. (2014). *Memory*. 2nd ed. Abingdon, Psychology Press.

Badin, A-S., Fermani, F., & Greenfield, S. A. (2017). The features and functions of neuronal assemblies: possible dependency on mechanisms beyond synaptic transmission. *Frontiers in Neural Circuits* 10: 114.

Badre, D. & Wagner, A. D. (2007). Left ventrolateral prefrontal cortex and the cognitive control of memory. *Neuropsychologia* 45(13): 2883–2901.

Baggio, G., Cherubini, P., Pischedda, D., Blumenthal, A., Haynes, J-D., & Reverberi, C. (2016). Multiple neural representations of elementary logical connectives. *NeuroImage* 135: 300–310.

Bahramisharif, A., Jensen, O., Jacobs, J., & Lisman, J. (2018). Serial representation of items during working memory maintenance at letter-selective cortical sites. *PLoS Biology* 16(8): e2003805.

Bahramisharif, A., Mazaheri, A., Levar, N., Schuurman, P. R., Figee, M., & Denys, D. (2016). Deep brain stimulation diminishes cross-frequency coupling in obsessive-compulsive disorder. *Biological Psychiatry* 80(7): e57–58.

Baillet, S. (2017). Magnetoencephalography for brain electrophysiology and imaging. *Nature Neuroscience* 20: 327–333.

Bakker, I., MacGregor, L. J., Pulvermüller, F., & Shtyrov, Y. (2013). Past tense in the brain's time: neurophysiological evidence for dual-route processing of past-tense verbs. *NeuroImage* 71: 187–195.

Balaban, H. & Luria, R. (2016). Object representations in visual working memory change according to the task context. *Cortex* 81: 1–13.

Balari, S. & Lorenzo, G. (2013). *Computational Phenotypes: Towards an Evolutionary Developmental Biolinguistics*. Oxford: Oxford University Press.

Balari, S., Boeckx, C., & Lorenzo, G. (2012). On the feasibility of biolinguistics: Koster's word-based challenge and our 'natural computation' alternative. *Biolinguistics* 6(2): 205–21.

Balezeau, F., Wilson, B., Gallardo, G., Dick, F., Hopkins, W., Anwander, A., Friederici, A. D., Griffiths, T. D., & Petkov, C. I. (2020). Primate auditory prototype in the evolution of the arcuate fasciculus. *Nature Neuroscience* 23: 611–614.

Bartolo, R., Prado, L., & Merchant, H. (2014). Information processing in the primate basal ganglia during sensory-guided and internally driven rhythmic tapping. *Journal of Neuroscience* 34: 3910–3923.

Bartolo, R. & Merchant, H. (2015). β oscillations are linked to the initiation of sensory-cued movement sequences and the internal guidance of regular tapping in the monkey. *The Journal of Neuroscience* 35(11): 4635–4640.

Bartos, M., Vida, I., & Jonas, P. (2007). Synaptic mechanisms of synchronized gamma oscillations in inhibitory interneuron networks. *Nature Reviews Neuroscience* 8: 45–56.

Başar, E. (2006). The theory of the whole-brain-network. *International Journal of Psychophysiology* 60: 133–138.

Başar, E. & Stampfer, H. G. (1985). Important associations among EEG-dynamics, event related potentials, short-term memory and learning. *International Journal of Neuroscience* 26: 161–180.

Bassett, D. S. & Sporns, O. (2017). Network neuroscience. *Nature Neuroscience* 20(3): 353–364.

Bastiaanse, R. & Thompson, C. K. (eds.) (2012). *Perspectives on Agrammatism*. London: Psychology Press.

Bastiaansen, M. & Hagoort, P. (2015). Frequency-based segregation of syntactic and semantic unification during online sentence level language comprehension. *Journal of Cognitive Neuroscience* 27(11): 2095–2107.

Bastiaansen, M., Van Berkum, J. J., & Hagoort, P. (2002). Event-related theta power increases in the human EEG during online sentence processing. *Neuroscience Letters* 323: 13–16.

Bastiaansen, M. C. M., Magyari, L., & Hagoort, P. (2010). Syntactic unification operations are reflected in oscillatory dynamics during on-line sentence comprehension. *Journal of Cognitive Neuroscience* 22: 1333–1347.

Bastiaansen, M. C. M., van der Linden, Marieke., ter Keurs, M., Dijkstra, T., & Hagoort, P. (2005). Theta responses are involved in lexical-semantic retrieval during language processing. *Journal of Cognitive Neuroscience* 17(3): 530–541.

Bastos, A. M., Martin Usrey, W., Adams, R. A., Mangun, G. R., Fries, P., Friston, K. J. (2012). Canonical microcircuits for predictive coding. *Neuron* 76: 695–711.

Bastos, A. M., Vezoli, J., & Fries, P. (2015). Communication through coherence with inter-areal delays. *Current Opinion in Neurobiology* 31: 173–180.

Bates, E. (1999). Plasticity, localization and language development. Broman, S.H., & Fletcher, J.M. (Eds.). *The Changing Nervous System: Neurobehavioral Consequences of Early Brain Disorders*. Oxford: Oxford University Press. 214–253.

Bates, E., Benigni, L., Bretherton, I., Camaioni, L., & Volterra, V. (1979). *The Emergence of Symbols: Cognition and Communication in Infancy*. New York: Academic Press.

Bauer, A.-K. R., Bleichner, M. G., Jaeger, M., Thorne, J. D., & Debener, S. (2018). Dynamic phase alignment of ongoing auditory cortex oscillations. *NeuroImage* 167: 396–407.

Bays, P. M. (2015). Spikes not slots: noise in neural populations limits working memory. *Trends in Cognitive Sciences* 19: 431–438.

Bechtel, W. (1994). Levels of description and explanation in cognitive science. *Minds and Machines* 4: 1–25.

Beese, C., Meyer, L., Vassileiou, B., Friederici, A. D. (2017). Temporally and spatially distinct theta oscillations dissociate a language-specific from a domain-general processing mechanism across the age trajectory. *Scientific Reports* 7(1): 11202.

Bell, P. T. & Shine, J. M. (2016). Subcortical contributions to large-scale network communication. *Neuroscience and Biobehavioral Reviews* 71: 313–322.

Bellmund, J. L. S., Gärdenfors, P., Moser, E. I., & Doeller, C. F. (2018). Navigating cognition: spatial codes for human thinking. *Science* 362: eaat6766.

Belluscio, M. A., Mizuseki, K., Schmidt, R., Kempter, R., & Buzsáki, G. (2012). Cross-frequency phase-phase coupling between θ and γ oscillations in the hippocampus. *Journal of Neuroscience* 32: 423–435.

Bemis, D. K. & Pylkkänen, L. (2013). Basic linguistic composition recruits the left anterior temporal lobe and left angular gyrus during both listening and reading. *Cerebral Cortex* 23: 1859–1873.

Benítez-Burraco, A. & Boeckx, C. (2015). Possible functional links among brain- and skull-related genes selected in modern humans. *Frontiers in Psychology* 6: 794. DOI:10.3389/fpsyg.2015.00794

Benítez-Burraco, A., Mineiro, A., & Castro-Caldas, A. (2014). The emergence of modern communication in primates: a computational approach. In Pina, M., & Gontier, N. (eds.). *The Evolution of Social Communication in Primates: A Multidisciplinary Approach*. Cham: Springer. 289–311.

Benítez-Burraco, A. & Murphy, E. (2016). The oscillopathic nature of language deficits in autism: from genes to language evolution. *Frontiers in Human Neuroscience* 10: 120.

Benítez-Burraco, A., & Murphy, E. (2019). Why brain oscillations are improving our understanding of language. *Frontiers in Behavioral Neuroscience* 13: 190.

Benson-Amram, S., Dantzer, B., Stricker, G., Swanson, E. M., & Holekamp, K. E. (2015). Brain size predicts problem-solving ability in mammalian carnivores. *PNAS* 113(9): 2532–2537.

Berger, H. (1929). Uber das elektrenephalogramm des menschen. *Archiv für Psychiatrie und Nervenkrankheiten* 87: 527–570.

Berger, J. I., Gander, P. E., Kumar, S., Banks, M. I., Nourski, K. V., Oya, H., Kawasaki, H., Howard III, M. A., & Griffiths, T. D. (2019). Oscillatory correlates of auditory working memory in human intracranial EEG. Poster presented at the 49th Meeting of the Society for Neuroscience, Chicago, 19–23 October.

Bergmann, T. O. & Born, J. (2017). Phase-amplitude coupling: a general mechanism for memory processing and synaptic plasticity? *Neuron* 97: 10–13.

Bergson, H. (1911). *Creative Evolution*. London: H. Holt.

Berkeley, G. (1992). *"The Analyst"*. 1734. Reprinted in Jesseph, D. M. *"De Motu and The Analyst: A Modern Edition, with Introductions and Commentary"*. London: Kluwer Academic Publishers Dordrecht.

Bertossa, R. (2011). Morphology and behaviour: functional links in development and evolution. *Philosophical Transactions of the Royal Society B* 366: 2056–68.

Berwick, R. C. (2017). A feeling for the phenotype. In McGilvray, J. (ed.). *The Cambridge Companion to Chomsky*. 2nd ed. Cambridge: Cambridge University Press. 87–109.

Berwick, R. C. & Chomsky, N. (2016). *Why Only Us: Language and Evolution*. Cambridge, MA: MIT Press.

Beukema, P. & Verstynen, T. (2018). Predicting and binding: interacting algorithms supporting the consolidation of sequential motor skills. *Current Opinion in Behavioral Sciences* 20: 98–103.

Bhattasali, S., Hale, J., Pallier, C., Brennan, J. R., Luh, W-M., & Spreng, R. N. (2018). Differentiating phrase structure parsing and memory retrieval in the brain. *Proceedings of the Society for Computation in Linguistics (SCiL) 2018* 74–80.

Bianchi, S., Stimpson, C. D., Duka, T., Larsen, M. D., Janssen, W. G., Collins, Z., Bauernfeind, A. L., Schapiro, S. J., Baze, W. B., McArthur, M. J., Hopkins, W. D., Wildman, D. E., Lipovich, L., Kazuwa, C. W., Jacobs, B., Hof, P. R., &

Sherwood, C. C. (2013). Synaptogenesis and development of pyramidal neuron dendritic morphology in the chimpanzee neocortex resembles humans. *PNAS* 110 (Supplement 2): 10395–10401.

Biasiucci, A., Franceschiello, B., & Murray, M. M. (2019). Electroencephalography. *Current Biology* 29: R80-R85.

Bichakjian, B. H. (2017). Language evolution: how language was built and made to evolve. *Language Sciences* 63: 119–129.

Billeke, P., Ossandon, T., Stockle, M., Perrone-Bertolotti, M., Kahane, P., Lachaux, J.-P., & Fuentealba, P. (2017). Brain state-dependent recruitment of high-frequency oscillations in the human hippocampus. *Cortex* 94: 87–99.

Binder, J. R. & Desai, R. H. (2011). The neurobiology of semantic memory. *Trends in Cognitive Sciences* 15: 527–536.

Binder, J. R., Desai, R. H., Graves, W. W., & Conant, L. L. (2009). Where is the semantic system? A critical review and meta-analysis of 120 functional neuroimaging studies. *Cerebral Cortex* 19: 2767–2796.

Binney, R. J., Embleton, K. V., Jefferies, E., Parker, G. J., & Ralph, M. A., (2010). The ventral and inferolateral aspects of the anterior temporal lobe are crucial in semantic memory: evidence from a novel direct comparison of distortion-corrected fMRI, rTMS, and semantic dementia. *Cerebral Cortex* 20: 2728–2738.

Bitar, M. & Barry, G. (2018). Multiple innovations in genetic and epigenetic mechanisms cooperate to underpin human brain evolution. *Molecular Biology and Evolution* 35(2): 263–268.

Blank, I., Duff, M. C., Brown-Schmidt, S., & Fedorenko, E. (2016a). Expanding the language network: domain-specific hippocampal recruitment during high-level linguistic processing. *bioRxiv.* https://doi.org/10.1101/091900

Blank, I., Balewski, Z., Mahowald, K., & Fedorenko, E. (2016b). Syntactic processing is distributed across the language system. *NeuroImage* 127: 307–323.

Bloom, H. (1997). *The Anxiety of Influence: A Theory of Poetry.* 2nd ed. Oxford: Oxford University Press.

Blümel, A. (2017). Exocentric root declaratives: evidence from V2. In Bauke, L. & Blümel, A. (eds.). *Labels and Roots.* Berlin: Walter de Gruyter. 263–289.

Boeckx, C. (2011). Approaching paramaters from below. In Di Sciullo, A. M. & Boeckx, C. (eds.). *The Biolinguistic Enterprise: New Perspectives on the Evolution and Nature of the Human Language Faculty.* Oxford: Oxford University Press. 205–221.

Boeckx, C. (2013). Merge: biolinguistic considerations. *English Linguistics* 30(2): 463–484.

Boeckx, C. (2014a). *Elementary Syntactic Structures: Prospects of a Feature-Free Syntax.* Cambridge: Cambridge University Press.

Boeckx, C. (2014b). Our brain's language-readiness. *El País.* 7 February.

Boeckx, C. (2017). A conjecture about the neural basis of recursion in light of descent with modification. *Journal of Neurolinguistics* 43(B): 193–198.

Boeckx, C. & Benítez -Burraco, A. (2014a). The shape of the human language-ready brain. *Frontiers in Psychology* 5: 282.

Boeckx, C. & Benítez-Burraco, A. (2014b). Globularity and language-readiness: generating new predictions by expanding the set of genes of interest. *Frontiers in Psychology* 5: 1324.

Boeckx, C. & Fujita, K. (2014). Syntax, actions, comparative cognitive science, and Darwinian thinking. *Frontiers in Psychology* 5: 627.

Boeckx, C. & Grohmann, K. K. (2007). The *Biolinguistics* manifesto. *Biolinguistics* 1: 1–8.

Boeckx, C. & Theofanopoulou, C. (2015). Cognitive phylogenies, the Darwinian logic of descent, and the inadequacy of cladistic thinking. *Frontiers in Cell and Developmental Biology* 3: 64.

Bohsali, A. A., Triplett, W., Sudhyadhom, A., Gullett, J. M., McGregor, K., FitzGerald, D. B., Mareci, T., White, K., & Crosson, B. (2015). Broca's area – thalamic connectivity. *Brain and Language* 141: 80–88.

Bolhuis, J. & Wynne, C. D. L. (2009). Can evolution explain how minds work? *Nature* 458(7240): 832–833.

Bolhuis, J. J., Beckers, G. J. L., Huybregts, M. A. C., Berwick, R. C., & Everaert, M. B. H. (2018) Meaningful syntactic structure in songbird vocalizations? *PLoS Biology* 16(6): e2005157.

Bolhuis, J. J. & Gahr, M. (2006). Neural mechanisms of birdsong memory. *Nature Reviews Neuroscience* 7: 347–357.

Bolhuis, J. J. Tattersall, I., Chomsky, N., & Berwick, R. C. (2014). How could language have evolved? *PLoS ONE* 12: e1001934.

Bolker, J. A. (2008). Developing a history of evo-devo. *BioScience* 58: 461–463.

Bonhage, C. E., Meyer, L., Gruber, T., Friederici, A. D., & Mueller, J. L. (2017). Oscillatory EEG dynamics underlying automatic chunking during sentence processing. *NeuroImage* 152: 647–657.

Bornkessel, I., Zysset, S., Friederici, A. D., von Cramon, D., & Schlesewsky, M. (2005). Who did what to whom? The neural basis of argument hierarchies during language comprehension. *NeuroImage* 26(1): 221–233.

Bornkessel-Schlesewsky, I., Schlesewsky, M., & Small, S. L. (2014). Implementation is crucial but must be neurobiologically grounded. Comment on 'Toward a computational framework for cognitive biology: Unifying approaches from cognitive neuroscience and comparative cognition' by W. Tecumseh Fitch. *Physics of Life Reviews* 11: 365–366.

Bosman, C. A., Lansink, C. S., & Pennartz, C. M. A. (2014). Functions of gamma-band synchronization in cognition: from single circuits to functional diversity across cortical and subcortical systems. *European Journal of Neuroscience* 39: 1982–1999.

Bosman, C. A., Womelsdorf, T., Desimone, R., & Fries, P. (2009). A microsaccadic rhythm modulates gamma-band synchronization and behavior. *Journal of Neuroscience* 29: 9471–9480.

Bota, M., Sporns, O., & Swanson, LW. (2015). Architecture of the cerebral cortical association connectome underlying cognition. *PNAS* 112: E2093-101.

Bouchard, K .E. & Chang, E. F. (2014). Neural decoding of spoken vowels from human sensory-motor cortex with high-density electrocorticography. *Conf Proc IEEE Eng Med Biol Soc* 6782–6785.

Boucher, V. J., Gilbert, A. C., & Jemel, B. (2019). The role of low-frequency neural oscillations in speech processing: revisiting delta entrainment. *Journal of Cognitive Neuroscience* 31(8): 1205–1215.

Bradley, C. R., Siskind, J. M., & Wilbur, R. B. (2017). Neural representation of minimal syntactic units. Annual Conference on Cognitive Computational Neuroscience (CCN), New York. 6–8 September.

Bradshaw, A. R., Thompson, P. A., Wilson, A. C., Bishop, D. V. M., & Woodhead, Z. V. J. (2017). Measuring language lateralisation with different language tasks: a systematic review. *PeerJ* 5: e3929.

Bragin, A., Jando, G., Nadasdy, Z., Hetke, J., Wise, K., & Buzsáki, G. (1995). Gamma (40–100 Hz) oscillation in the hippocampus of the behaving rat. *Journal of Neuroscience* 15: 47–60.

Brandon, M. P., Koenig, J., Leutgeb, J. K., & Leutgeb, S. (2014). New and distinct hippocampal place codes are generated in a new environment during septal inactivation. *Neuron* 82: 789–796.

Brennan, J. R. & Martin, A. E. (2019). Delta-gamma phase-locking indexes composition of predicates. Poster presented at 23rd Annual Meeting of the Cognitive Neuroscience Society, San Fransisco, 23–26 March.

Brennan, J. R. & Pylkkänen, L. (2017). MEG evidence for incremental sentence composition in the anterior temporal lobe. *Cognitive Science* 41(S6): 1515–1531.

Brennan, J. R., Stabler, E. P., Van Wagenen, S. E., Luh, W.-M., & Hale, J. T. (2016). Abstract linguistic structure correlates with temporal activity during naturalistic comprehension. *Brain & Language* 157–158: 81–94.

Bressler, S. L. & Menon, V. (2010). Large-scale brain networks in cognition: emerging methods and principles. *Trends in Cognitive Sciences* 14: 277–290.

Bressler, S. L. & Richter, C. G. (2015). Interareal oscillatory synchronization in top-down neocortical processing. *Current Opinion in Neurobiology* 31: 62–66.

Brilmayer, I., Sassenhagen, J., Bornkessel-Schlesewsky, I., & Schlesewsky, M. (2017). Domain-general neural correlates of dependency formation: using complex tones to simulate language. *Cortex* 93: 50–67.

Brincat, S. L. & Miller, E. K. (2015). Frequency-specific hippocampal-prefrontal interactions during associative learning. *Nature Neuroscience* 18(4): 576–581.

Brodbeck, C., Gwilliams, L., & Pylkkänen, L. (2016). Language in context: MEG evidence for modality-general and -specific responses to reference resolution. *eNeuro* 3(6): e0145–16.2016.

Brookes, M. J., Groom, M. J., Liuzzi, L., Hill, R. M., Smith, H. J. F., Briley, P. M., Hall, E. L., Hunt, B. A. E. et al. (2018). Altered temporal stability in dynamic neural networks underlies connectivity changes in neurodevelopment. *NeuroImage* 174: 563–575.

Brookes, M. J., Liddle, E. B., Hale, J. R., Woolrich, M. W., Luckhoo, H., Liddle, P. F., & Morris, P. G. (2012). Task induced modulation of neural oscillations in electrophysiological brain networks. *NeuroImage* 63: 1918–1930.

Brookshire, G., Lu, J., Nusbaum, H. C., Goldin-Meadow, S., & Casasanto, D. (2017). Visual cortex entrains to sign language. *PNAS* 114(24): 6352–6357.

Brown, J. W. (2014). The tale of the neuroscientists and the computer: why mechanistic theory matters. *Frontiers in Neuroscience* 8: 349.

Bruner, E. (2004). Geometric morphometrics and paleoneurology: brain shape evolution in the genus homo. *Journal of Human Evolution* 47(5): 279–303.

Bruner, E. & Gleeson, B. T. (2019). Body cognition and self-domestication in human evolution. *Frontiers in Psychology* 10: 1111.

Bruner, E., Preuss, T. M., Chen, X., & Rilling, J. K. (2017). Evidence for expansion of the precuneus in human evolution. *Brain Structure and Function* 222 (2):1053–1060.

Brunetti, E., Maldonado, P. E., & Aboitiz, F. (2013). Phase synchronization of delta and theta oscillations increase during the detection of relevant lexical information. *Frontiers in Psychology* 4: 308.

Bryant, K. L. & Preuss, T. M. (2018). A comparative perspective on the human temporal lobe. In Bruner, E., Ogihara, N., & Tanabe, H. (eds.). *Digital Endocasts: From Skulls to Brains*. Replacement of Neanderthals by Modern Humans Series. Tokyo: Springer.

Buffalo, E. A., Fries, P., Landman, R., Buschman, T. J., & Desimone, R. (2011). Laminar differences in gamma and alpha coherence in the ventral stream. *PNAS* 108: 11262–11267.

Buffat, S., Plantier, J., Roumes, C., & Lorenceau, J. (2013). Repetition blindness for natural images of objects with viewpoint changes. *Frontiers in Psychology* 3: 622.

Bufill, E. & Carbonell, E. (2004). Are symbolic behavior and neuroplasticity an example of gene-culture evolution? *Revista de Neurologia* 39: 48–55.

Bulut, T., Hung, Y. H., Tzeng, O., & Wu, D. H. (2017). Neural correlates of processing sentences and compound words in Chinese. *PLoS ONE* 12(12): e0188526.

Burgaleta, M., Sanjuán, A., Ventura-Campos, N., Sebastian-Galles, N., & Ávila, C. (2016). Bilingualism at the core of the brain. Structural differences between bilinguals and monolinguals revealed by subcortical shape analysis. *NeuroImage* 125: 437–445.

Burgess, N. & Hitch, G. J. (1992). Towards a network model of the articulatory loop. *Journal of Memory and Language* 31(4): 429–460.

Büring, D. (2015). Unalternative semantics. *Proceedings of SALT* 25: 550–575.

Burkhardt, P. & Sprecher, S. G. (2017). Evolutionary origin of synapses and neurons – bridging the gap. *Bioessays* 39: 1700024.

Burnett, D. (2016). *The Idiot Brain*. London: Faber & Faber.

Buschman, T. J. & Miller, E. K. (2007). Top-down versus bottom-up control of attention in the prefrontal and posterior parietal cortices. *Science* 315: 1860–1862.

Bush, D. & Burgess, N. (2019). Neural oscillations: phase coding in the absence of rhythmicity. *Current Biology* 29: R50–R70.

Buzsáki, G. (2006). *Rhythms of the Brain*. Oxford: Oxford University Press.

Buzsáki, G. (2010). Neural syntax: cell assemblies, synapsembles, and readers. *Neuron* 68: 362–385.

Buzsáki, G. & Draguhn, A. (2004). Neuronal oscillations in cortical networks. *Science* 304: 1926–1929.

Buzsáki, G. & Freeman, W. (2015). Editorial overview: brain rhythms and dynamic coordination. *Current Opinion in Neurobiology* 31: v–ix.

Buzsáki, G. & Llinás, R. (2017). Space and time in the brain. *Science* 358: 482–485.

Buzsáki, G. & Wang, W.-J. (2012). Mechanisms of gamma oscillations. *Annual Review of Neuroscience* 35: 203–225.

Buzsáki, G., Logothetis, N., & Singer, W. (2013). Scaling brain size, keeping timing: evolutionary preservation of brain rhythms. *Neuron* 80: 751–764.

Bybee, J. L. (2011). Domain-general processes as the basis for grammar. In Gibson, K. R. & Tallerman, M. (eds.). *The Oxford Handbook of Language Evolution*. Oxford: Oxford University Press. 528–536.

Byrne, R. W. & Russon, A. E. (1998). Learning by imitation: a hierarchical approach. *Behavioral and Brain Sciences* 21: 667–721.

Cai, D. J., Aharoni, D., Shuman, T., Shobe, J., Biane, J., Song, W., Wei, B. et al. (2016). A shared neural ensemble links distinct memories encoded close in time. *Nature* 534: 115–118.

Calabrese, A. & Woolley, S. M. N. (2015). Coding principles of the canonical cortical microcircuit in the avian brain. *PNAS* 112(11): 3517–3522.

Campion, G. & Elliot-Smith, G. (1934). *The Neural Basis of Thought*. New York: Harcourt Brace Jovanovich.

Cannon, J., McCarthy, M. M., Lee, S., Lee, J., Börgers, C., Whittington, M. A., & Kopell, N. (2014). Neurosystems: brain rhythms and cognitive processing. *European Journal of Neuroscience* 39(5): 705–719.

Canolty, R. T. & Knight, R. T. (2010). The functional role of cross-frequency coupling. *Trends in Cognitive Sciences* 14: 506–515.

Canolty, R. T., Edwards, E., Dalal, S. S., Soltani, M., Nagarajan, S. S., Kirsch, H. E., Berger, M. S., Barbaro, N. M., & Knight, R. T. (2006). High gamma power is phase-locked to theta oscillations in human neocortex. *Science* 313: 1626–1628.

Canolty, R. T., Ganguly, K., Kennerley, S. W., Cadieu, C. F., Koepsell, K., Wallis, J. D., & Carmena, J. M. (2010). Oscillatory phase coupling coordinates anatomically dispersed functional cell assemblies. *PNAS* 107(40): 17356–17361.

Cao, H., Dixson, L., Meyer-Lindenberg, A., & Tost, H. (2016). Functional connectivity measures as schizophrenia intermediate phenotypes: advances, limitations, and future directions. *Current Opinion in Neurobiology* 36: 7–14.

Cardin, J. A., Palmer, L. A., & Contreras, D. (2005). Stimulus-dependent γ (30–50 Hz) oscillations in simple and complex fast rhythmic bursting cells in primary visual cortex. *Journal of Neuroscience* 25: 5339–5350.

Carracedo, L. M., Kjeldsen, H., Cunnington, L., Jenkins, A., Schofield, I., Cunningham, M. O. et al. (2013). A neocortical delta rhythm facilitates reciprocal interlaminar interactions via nested theta rhythms. *Journal of Neuroscience* 33: 10750–10761.

Carroll, S. B. (2006). *The Making of the Fittest: DNA and the Ultimate Forensic Record of Evolution*. New York: W.W. Norton.

Carstairs-McCarthy, A. (2010). *The Evolution of Morphology*. Oxford: Oxford University Press.

Castejon, C. & Nuñez, A. (2016). Cortical neural computation by discrete results hypothesis. *Frontiers in Neural Circuits* 10: 81.

Catani, M. & Bambini, V. (2014). Amodel for social communication and language evolution and development (SCALED). *Current Opinion in Neurobiology* 28: 165–171.

Catani, M., Mesulam, M. M., Jakobsen, E., Malik, F., Martersteck, A., Wieneke, C., Thompson, C. K., Thiebaut de Schotten, M., Dell'Acqua, F., Weintraub, S., & Rogalski, E. (2013). A novel frontal pathway underlies verbal fluency in primary progressive aphasia. *Brain* 136: 2619–2628.

Catchpole, C. K., & Slater, P. J. B. (2008). *Bird Song: Biological Themes and Variations*. Cambridge: Cambridge University Press.

Caton, R. (1875). The electric currents of the brain. *British Medical Journal* 2: 278.

Cecchetto, C. & Donati, C. (2015). *(Re)labeling*. Cambridge, MA: MIT Press.

Cervenka, M. C., Boatman-Reich, D. F., Ward, J., Franaszczuk, P. J., & Crone, N. E. (2011). Language mapping in multilingual patients: electrocorticography and cortical stimulation during naming. *Frontiers in Human Neuroscience* 5: 13.

Chacko, R. V., Kim, B., Woo Jung, S., Daitch, A. L., Roland, J. L., Metcalf, N. V., Corbetta, M., Shulman, G. L., & Leuthardt, E. C. (2018). Distinct phase-amplitude couplings distinguish cognitive processes in human attention. *NeuroImage* 175: 111–121.

Chaieb, L., Leszczynski, M., Axmacher, N., Höhne, M., Elger, C. E., & Fell, J. (2015). Theta-gamma phase-phase coupling during working memory maintenance in the human hippocampus. *Cognitive Neuroscience* 6: 149–157.

Chaitin, G. (1977). Algorithmic information theory. *IBM Journal of Research and Development* 21: 350–359.

Chang, A., Bosnyak, D. J., & Trainor, L. J. (2016). Unpredicted pitch modulates beta oscillatory power during rhythmic entrainment to a tone sequence. *Frontiers in Psychology* 7: 327.

Chang, Le. & Tsao, D. Y. (2017). The code for facial identity in the primate brain. *Cell* 169: 1013–1028.

Chao, Z. C., Takaura, K., Wang, L., Fujii, N., & Dehaene, S. (2018). Large-scale cortical networks for hierarchical prediction and prediction error in the primate brain. *Neuron* 100: 1252–1266.

Chapeton, J. I., Haque, R., Wittig Jr., J. H., Inati, S. K., & Zaghloul, K. A. (2019). Large-scale communication in the human brain is rhythmically modulated through alpha coherence. *Current Biology* 29: 1–11.

Charvet, C. J., Hof, P. R., Raghanti, M. A., van der Kouwe, A. J., Sherwood, C. C., & Takahashi, E. (2016). Combining diffusion magnetic resonance tractography with stereology highlights increased cross-cortical integration in primates. *Journal of Comparative Neurology* 525(5): 1075–1093.

Chen, C. C., Kiebel, S. J., & Friston, K. J. (2008). Dynamic causal modelling of induced responses. *NeuroImage* 41(4): 1293–1312.

Chen, L., Junjie, W., Yongben, F., Kang, H., & Feng, L. (2019). Neural substrates of word category information as the basis of syntactic processing. *Human Brain Mapping* 40(2): 451–464.

Chen, L., Lambon Ralph, M. A., & Rogers, T. T. (2017). A unified model of human semantic knowledge and its disorders. *Nature Human Behaviour* 1: 39.

Cherniak, C. (1994). Philosophy and computational neuroanatomy. *Philosophical Studies* 73: 89–107.

Cherniak. C. (2010). Brain wiring optimization and non-genomic nativism. In Piattelli-Palmarini, M., Salaburu, P., & Uriagereka, J. (eds.). *Of Minds and Language: A Dialogue with Noam Chomsky in the Basque Country.* Oxford: Oxford University Press. 108–119.

Chiarello, C. (2003). Parallel systems for processing language: hemispheric complementarity in the normal brain. In Banich, M. T. & Mack, M. (eds.). *Mind, Brain, and Language: Multidisciplinary Perspectives.* Mahwah, NJ: Lawrence Erlbaum Associates. 229–47.

Chklovskii, D. B., Schikorski, T., & Stevens, C. F. (2002). Wiring optimization in cortical circuits. *Neuron* 34: 341–347.

Chomsky, N. (1956a). On the limits of finite-state description. *Quarterly Progress Report* 42: 65–65.

Chomsky, N. (1956b). Three models for the description of language. *IRE Transactions on Information Theory* 2: 113–124.

Chomsky, N. (1957). *Syntactic Structures.* The Hague: Mouton.

Chomsky, N. (1959). On certain formal properties of grammars. *Information and Control* 2: 137–167.

Chomsky, N. (1963). Formal properties of grammars. In Luce, R. D., Bush, R. R., & Galanter, E. (eds.). *Handbook of Mathematical Psychology.* Vol. 2. New York: Wiley. 323–418.

Chomsky, N. (1965). *Aspects of the Theory of Syntax.* Cambridge, MA: MIT Press.

Chomsky, N. (1968). Quine's empirical assumptions. *Synthese* 19(1): 53–68.

Chomsky, N. (1995). *The Minimalist Program.* Cambridge, MA: MIT Press.

Chomsky, N. (1998). Comments: Galen Strawson, *Mental Reality. Philosophy and Phenomenological Research* 58(2): 437–441.

Chomsky, N. (2000). *New Horizons in the Study of Language and Mind.* Cambridge: Cambridge University Press.

Chomsky, N. (2001a). Derivation by phase. Kenstowicz, M. (ed.). *Ken Hale: A Life in Language.* Cambridge, MA: MIT Press. 1–52.

Chomsky, N. (2001b). Beyond explanatory adequacy. *MIT Occasional Papers in Linguistics* 20: 1–28.

Chomsky, N. (2005). Three factors in language design. *Linguistic Inquiry* 36(1): 1–22.

Chomsky, N. (2008). On phases. Freidin, R., Otero, C. P., & Zubizarreta, M. L. (eds.). *Foundational Issues in Linguistic Theory: Essays in Honor of Jean-Roger Vergnaud.* Cambridge, MA: MIT Press. 133–166.

Chomsky, N. (2010). Some simple evo devo theses: how true might they be for language? In Larson, R. K., Déprez, V., & Yamakido, H. (eds.). *The Evolution of Human Language: Biolinguistic Perspectives.* Cambridge: Cambridge University Press. 45–62.

Chomsky, N. (2012). *The Science of Language: Interviews with James McGilvray.* Cambridge: Cambridge University Press.

Chomsky, N. (2013). Problems of projection. *Lingua* 130: 33–49.

Chomsky, N. (2014). Minimal recursion: exploring the prospects. In Roeper, T. & Speas, M. (eds.). Studies in Theoretical Psycholinguistics 43. *Recursion: Complexity in Cognition.* London: Springer. 1–15.

Chomsky, N. (2015a). Problems of projection: extensions. Di Domenico, E., Hamann, C., & Matteini, S. (eds.). *Structures, Strategies and Beyond: Studies in Honour of Adriana Belletti.* Amsterdam: John Benjamins. 1–16.

Chomsky, N. (2015b). Some core contested concepts. *Journal of Psycholinguistic Research* 44(1): 91–104.

Chomsky, N. (2018a). Science, mind, and limits of understanding. In Gallego, Á. J. & Martin, R. (eds.). *Language, Syntax, and the Natural Sciences.* Cambridge: Cambridge University Press.

Chomsky, N. (2018b). Mentality beyond consciousness. Caruso, G. (ed.). *Ted Honderich on Consciousness, Determinism, and Humanity.* London: Palgrave Macmillan. 33–46.

Chomsky, N. (2019a). Puzzles about phases. Franco, L. & Belliuci, G. (eds.). *Linguistics Variation: Structure and Interpretation – A Feschrift in Honour of M. Rita Manzini.* Berlin: Mouton de Gruyter.

Chomsky, N. (2019b). Lecture at MIT. April 10. http://whamit.mit.edu/2019/05/06/no am-chomskys-lectures-now-online

Chomsky, N., Gallego, Á. J., & Ott, D. (2019). Generative grammar and the faculty of language: insights, questions, and challenges. In Gallego, Á. J. & Ott, D. (eds.). *Generative Syntax: Questions, Crossroads, and Challenges. Special issue of Catalan Journal of Linguistics,* 226–261.

Chow, B. Y., Han, X., Dobry, A. S., Qian, X., Chuong, A. S., Li, M., Henninger, M. A., Belfort, G. M., Lin, Y., Monahan, P. E., & Boyden, E. S. (2010). High-performance genetically targetable optical neural silencing by light-driven proton pumps. *Nature* 463: 98–102.

Christiansen, M. H. & Chater, N. (2016). *Creating Language: Integrating Evolution, Acquisition, and Processing.* Cambridge, MA: MIT Press.

Christiansen, M. H. & Chater, N. (2017). Towards an integrated science of language. *Nature Human Behavior* 1: 0163.

Chuderski, A. & Andrelczyk, K. (2015). From neural oscillations to complex cognition: simulating the effect of the theta-to-gamma cycle length ratio on analogical reasoning. *Cognitive Psychology* 76: 78–102.

Chuderski, A. (2016). Fluid intelligence and the cross-frequency coupling of neuronal oscillations. *Spanish Journal of Psychology* 19(e91): 1–13.

Cinque, G. (1999). *Adverbs and Functional Heads: A Cross-Linguistic Perspective.* Oxford: Oxford University Press.

Citko, B. (2011). *Symmetry in Syntax: Merge, Move, and Labels.* Cambridge: Cambridge University Press.

Clancy, K. J., Baisley, S. K., Albizu, A., Kartvelishvili, N., Ding, M., & Li, W. (2017). Transcranial alternating current stimulation induces long-term augmentation of neural connectivity and sustained anxiety reduction. *bioRxiv.* http://dx.doi.org/10.1101/204222

Clarke, A. (2015). Dynamic information processing states revealed through neurocognitive models of object semantics. *Language, Cognition and Neuroscience* 30(4): 409–419.

Clarke, A. & Tyler, L. K. (2015). Understanding what we see: how we derive meaning from vision. *Trends in Cognitive Sciences* 19(11): 677–687.

Clarke, E., Reichard, U. H., & Zuberbühler, K. (2006). The syntax and meaning of wild gibbon songs. *PLoS ONE* 1(1): e73.

Clay, Z., Archbold, J., & Zuberbühler, K. (2015). Functional flexibility in wild bonobo vocal behaviour. *PeerJ* 3: e1124.

Clos, M., Amunts, K., Laird, A. R., Fox, P. T., & Eickhoff, S. B. (2013). Tackling the multifunctional nature of Broca's region meta-analytically: co-activation-based parcellation of area 44. *NeuroImage* 83: 174–188.

Clouter, A., Shapiro, K. L., & Hanslmayr, S. (2017). Theta phase synchronization is the glue that binds human associative memory. *Current Biology* 27: 1–6.

Clowry, Gavin J. (2014). Seeking clues in brain development to explain the extraordinary evolution of language in humans. *Language Sciences* 46: 220–231.

Cocchi, L., Sale, M. V., Lord, A., Zalesky, A., Breakspear, M., Mattingley, J. B. (2015). Dissociable effects of local inhibitory and excitatory theta-burst stimulation on large-scale brain dynamics. *Journal of Neurophysiology* 113: 3375–3385.

Coetzee, J., Monti, M., Iacoboni, M., Wu, A., & Johnson, M. (2019). Separability of logic and language: a TMS study. *Brain Stimulation* 12(2): 543.

Cole, S. R. & Voytek, B. (2017). Brain oscillations and the importance of waveform shape. *Trends in Cognitive Sciences* 21(2): 137–149.

Colgin, L. L. (2013). Mechanisms and functions of theta rhythms. *Annual Review of Neuroscience* 36: 295–312.

Collins, J. (2015a). Naturalism without metaphysics. In Fischer, E. & Collins, J. (eds.). *Experimental Philosophy, Rationalism, and Naturalism*. London: Routledge. 85–109.

Collins, J. (2015b). Review of *the minimalist program: the nature and plausibility of Chomsky's biolinguistics* by Fahad Rashed Al-Mutairi. *Language* 91(3): 738–740.

Collins, J. (2020). Conjoining meanings without losing our heads. *Mind & Language* 35: 224–236.

Comrie, B. (1992). Before complexity. In Hawkins, J. A. & Gell-Mann, M. (eds.). *The Evolution of Human Language. Proceedings of the Workshop on the Evolution of Human Languages, August 1989, Santa Fe, New Mexico*. Santa Fe, NM: Addison-Wesley Publishing Company. 193–211.

Constantinescu, A. O., O'Reilly, J. X., & Behrens, T. E. J. (2016). Organizing conceptual knowledge in humans with a gridlike code. *Science* 352(6292): 1464–1468.

Copernicus, N. (1952). *On the Revolutions of the Heavenly Spheres*. Hutchins, R. M. (ed.), *Great Books of the Western World*. Chicago: Encyclopaedia Britannica.

Corcoran, A. W., Alday, P. M., Schlesewsky, M., & Bornkessel-Schlesewsky, I. (2018a). Toward a reliable, automated method of individual alpha frequency (IAF) quantification. *Psychophysiology* 55(7):e13064.

Corcoran, A. W., Pezzulo, G., & Hohwy, J. (2018b). Commentary: respiration-entrained brain rhythms are global but often overlooked. *Frontiers in Systems Neuroscience* 12: 25.

Cornélio, A. M., de Bittencourt-Navarrete, R. E., de Bittencourt Brum, R., Queiroz, C. M., & Costa, M. R. (2016). Human brain expansion during evolution is independent of fire control and cooking. *Frontiers in Neuroscience* 10: 167.

Covington, N. V. & Duff, M. C. (2016). Expanding the language network: direct contributions from the hippocampus. *Trends in Cognitive Sciences* 20(12): 869–870.

Cowan, N. (2001). The magical number 4 in short-term memory: a reconsideration of mental storage capacity. *Behavioral and Brain Sciences* 24(1): 87–114.

Cowan, N., Blume, C. L., & Saults, J. S. (2013). Attention to attributes and objects in working memory. *Journal of Experimental Psychology: Learning, Memory, and Cognition* 39(3): 731–747.

Crandall, S. R., Cruikshank, S. J., & Connors, B. W. (2015). A cortico-thalamic switch: Controlling the thalamus with dynamic synapses. *Neuron* 86: 768–782.

Crick, F. & Koch, C. (1995). Why neuroscience may be able to explain consciousness. *Scientific American* 273: 84–85.

Cross, Z. R., Kohler, M. J., Schlesewsky, M., Gaskell, M. G., & Bornkessel-Schlesewsky, I. (2018). Sleep-dependent memory consolidation and incremental sentence comprehension: computational dependencies during language learning as revealed by neuronal oscillations. *Frontiers in Human Neuroscience* 12: 18.

Cruikshank, S. J., Ahmed, O. J., Stevens, T. R., Patrick, S. L., Gonzalez, A. N., Elmaleh, M., & Connors, B. W. (2012). Thalamic control of layer 1 circuits in prefrontal cortex. *Journal of Neuroscience* 32(49): 17813–17823.

Crunelli, V., David, F., Lőrincz, M. L., & Hughes, S. W. (2015). The thalamocortical network as a single slow wave-generating unit. *Current Opinion in Neurobiology* 31: 72–80.

Cynx, J. (1990). Experimental determination of a unit of song production in the zebra finch (Taeniopygia guttata). *Journal of Comparative Psychology* 104: 3–10.

Daffertshofer, A., Ton, R., Kringelbach, M. L., Woolrich, M., & Deco, G. (2018). Distinct criticality of phase and amplitude dynamics in the resting brain. *NeuroImage* 180(B): 442–447.

Darwin, C. (1871). *The Descent of Man and Selection in Relation to Sex*. London: John Murray.

Davey, J., Thompson, H. E., Hallam, G., Karapanagiotidis, T., Murphy, C., De Caso, I., & Jefferies, E. (2016). Exploring the role of the posterior middle temporal gyrus in semantic cognition: integration of anterior temporal lobe with executive processes. *NeuroImage* 137: 165–177.

David, O., Maess, B., Eckstein, K., & Friederici, A. D. (2011). Dynamic causal modeling of subcortical connectivity of language. *Journal of Neuroscience* 31: 2712–2717.

Davidson, D. J. & Indefrey, P. (2007). An inverse relation between event-related and time frequency violation responses in sentence processing. *Brain Research* 1158: 81–92.

Davis, H. (2010). A unified analysis of relative clauses in St'at'imcets. *North-West Journal of Linguistics* 4: 1–43.

Dawkins, R. (1976). Hierarchical organization: a candidate principle for ethology. In Bateson, P. P. G. & Hinde, R. A. (eds.). *Growing Points in Ethology*. Cambridge: Cambridge University Press. 7–54.

Dawkins, R. (2006). *Climbing Mount Improbable*. Oxford: Oxford University Press.

Dawkins, R. (2015). *A Brief Candle in the Dark: My Life in Science*. New York: Harper Collins.

Dayan, P. & Abbott, L. F. (2001). *Theoretical Neuroscience: Computational and Mathematical Modeling of Neural Systems*. Cambridge, MA: MIT Press.

De Diego-Balaguer, R., Martinez-Alvarez, A., & Pons, F. (2016). Temporal attention as a scaffold for language development. *Frontiers in Psychology* 7: 44.

De Heer, W. A., Huth, A. G., Griffiths, T. L., Gallant, J. L., & Theunissen, F. E. (2017). The hierarchical cortical organization of human speech processing. *Journal of Neuroscience* 37(27): 6539–6557.

De Lange, S. C., van den Heuvel, M. P., & de Reus, M. A. (2016). The role of symmetry in neural networks and their Laplacian spectra. *NeuroImage* 141: 357–365.

De Pasquale, F., Della Penna, S., Snyder, A. Z., Marzetti, L., Pizzella, V., Luca Romani, G., & Corbetta, M. (2012). A cortical core for dynamic integration of functional networks in the resting human brain. *Neuron* 74: 753–764.

Dean, H. L., Hagan, M. A., & Pesaran, B. (2012). Only coherent spiking in posterior parietal cortex coordinates looking and reaching. *Neuron* 73(4): 829–841.

Deco, G., Cabral, J., Woolrich, M. W., Stevner, A. B. A., van Hartevelt, T. J., & Kringelbach, M. L. (2017). Single or multi-frequency generators in on-going brain activity: a mechanistic whole-brain model of empirical MEG data. *NeuroImage* 152: 538–550.

Deco, G., van Hartevelt, T. J., Fernandes, H. M., Stevner, A., & Kringelbach, M. L. (2017). The most relevant human brain regions for functional connectivity: evidence for a dynamical workspace of binding nodes from whole-brain computational modelling. *NeuroImage* 146: 197–210.

Dehaene, S. & Cohen, L. (2007). Cultural recycling of cortical maps. *Neuron* 56: 384–398.

Dehaene, S., Charles, L., King, J-R., & Marti, S. (2014). Toward a computational theory of conscious processing. *Current Opinion in Neurobiology* 25: 76–84.

Dehaene-Lambertz, G. (2017). The human infant brain: a neural architecture able to learn language. *Psychonomic Bulletin & Review* 24: 48.

Dehaene-Lambertz, G. & Spelke, E. S. (2015). The infancy of the human brain. *Neuron* 88: 93–109.

Deisz, R. A. & Prince, D. A. (1989). Frequency-dependent depression of inhibition in guinea-pig neocortex in vitro by GABAB receptor feed-back on GABA release. *Journal of Physiology* 412: 513–541.

Dejean, C., Arbuthnott, G., Wickens, J. R., Le Moine, C., Boraud, T. & Hyland, B. I. (2011). Power fluctuations in beta and gamma frequencies in rat globus pallidus: association with specific phases of slow oscillations and differential modulation by dopamine D1 and D2 receptors. *Journal of Neuroscience* 31: 6098–6107.

Dennett, D. (1987). *The Intentional Stance*. Cambridge, MA: MIT Press.

Dennett, D. (1995). *Darwin's Dangerous Idea: Evolution and the Meaning of Life*. New York: Simon & Schuster.

Dennett, D. (2018). *From Bacteria to Bach and Back: The Evolution of Minds*. London: Penguin Books.

Deutscher, G. (2005). *The Unfolding of Language: The Evolution of Mankind's Greatest Invention*. London: Arrow Books.

Di Liberto, G. M., Lalor, E. C., & Millman, R. E. (2018). Causal cortical dynamics of a predictive enhancement of speech intelligibility. *NeuroImage* 166: 247–258.

Di Sciullo, A. M., Nicolis, M., & Somesfalean, S. (2013). Evo-devo language universals. Paper presented at the International Linguists Conference 19, University of Geneva.

Diaz, M. T. & McCarthy, G. (2009). A comparison of brain activity evoked by single content and function words: an fMRI investigation of implicit word processing. *Brain Research* 1282: 38–49.

Ding, N. & Simon, J. Z. (2013). Adaptive temporal encoding leads to a background insensitive cortical representation of speech. *Journal of Neuroscience* 33(13): 5728–5735.

Ding, N. & Simon, J. Z. (2014). Cortical entrainment to continuous speech: functional roles and interpretations. *Frontiers in Human Neuroscience* 8: 311.

Ding, N., Melloni, L., Zhang, H., Tian, X., & Poeppel, D. (2016). Cortical tracking of hierarchical linguistic structures in connected speech. *Natural Neuroscience* 19: 158–164.

Ding, N., Melloni, L., Yang, A., Wang, Y., Zhang, W., & Poeppel, D. (2017). Characterizing neural entrainment to hierarchical linguistic units using electroencephalography (EEG). *Frontiers in Human Neuroscience* 11: 481.

Dipoppa, M. & Gutkin, B. S. (2013). Flexible frequency control of cortical oscillations enables computations required for working memory. *PNAS* 110(31): 12828–12833.

Dipoppa, M., Szwed, M., & Gutkin, B. S. (2016). Controlling working memory operations by selective gating: the roles of oscillations and synchrony. *Advances in Cognitive Psychology* 12(4): 209–232.

Dobson, C. W. & Lemon, R. E. (1979). Markov sequences in songs of American thrushes. *Behaviour* 68: 86–105.

Doelling, K. B. & Poeppel, D. (2015) Cortical entrainment to music and its modulation by expertise. *PNAS* 112(45),E6233–6242.

Doesburg, S. M., Vinette, S. A., Cheung, M. J., & Pang, E. W. (2012). Theta-modulated gamma-band synchronization among activated regions during a verb generation task. *Frontiers in Psychology* 3: 195.

Dor, D. (2017). The role of the lie in the evolution of human language. *Language Sciences* 63: 44–59.

Doumas, L. A. A., Hummel, J. E., & Sandhofer, C. M. (2008). A theory of the discovery and predication of relational concepts. *Psychological Review* 115: 1–43.

Dragoi, G. & Tonegawa, S. (2013). Selection of preconfigured cell assemblies for representation of novel spatial experiences. *Philosophical Transactions of the Royal Society B* 369(1635): 20120522.

Dubbledam, J. L. & den Boer-Visser, A. M. (2002). The central mesencephalic grey in birds: nucleus intercollicularis and substantia grisea centralis. *Brain Research Bulletin* 57: 349–352.

Dubois, J., de Berker, A. O., & Tsao, D. Y. (2015). Single-unit recordings in the macaque face patch system reveal limitations of fMRI MVPA. *Journal of Neuroscience* 35(6): 2791–2802.

Duff, M. C. & Brown-Schmidt, S. (2012). The hippocampus and the flexible use and processing of language. *Frontiers in Human Neuroscience* 6: 69.

Duffy, J. R. (2005). *Motor Speech Disorders: Substrates, Differential Diagnosis, and Management*. 2nd ed. St. Louis, MO: Elsevier Mosby.

Duncan, J. (2013). The structure of cognition: attentional episodes in mind and brain. *Neuron* 80: 35–50.

Edelman, G. M. (1989). *The Remembered Present: A Biological Theory of Consciousness*. New York: Basic Books.

Egidi, G. & Caramazza, A. (2014). Mood-dependent integration in discourse comprehension: happy and sad moods affect consistency processing via different brain networks. *NeuroImage* 103: 20–32.

Eklund, A., Nichols, T. E., & Knutsson, H. (2016). Cluster failure: why fMRI inferences for spatial extent have inflated false-positive rates. *PNAS* 113: 7900–7905.

Eliav, T., Geva-Sagiv, M., Yartsev, M. M., Finkelstein, A., Rubin, A., Las, L., & Ulanovsky, N. (2018). Nonoscillatory phase coding and synchronization in the bat hippocampal formation. *Cell* 175: 1–12.

Ellamil, M., Fox, K. C., Dixon, M. L., Pritchard, S., Todd, R. M., Thompson, E., & Christoff, K. (2016). Dynamics of neural recruitment surrounding the spontaneous arising of thoughts in experienced mindfulness practitioners. *NeuroImage* 136: 186–196.

Elmer, S. & Kühnis, J. (2016). Functional connectivity in the left dorsal stream facilitates simultaneous language translation: an EEG study. *Frontiers in Human Neuroscience* 10: 60.

Embick, D. & Poeppel, D. (2015). Towards a computational(ist) neurobiology of language: correlational, integrated and explanatory neurolinguistics. *Language, Cognition and Neuroscience* 30(4): 357–366.

Enel, P., Procyk, E., Quilodran, R., & Dominey, P. F. (2016). Reservoir computing properties of neural dynamics in prefrontal cortex. *PLoS Computational Biology* 12 (6): e1004967.

Engel, A. K. & Fries, P. (2010). Beta-band oscillations – signalling the status quo? *Current Opinion in Neurobiology* 20(2): 156–165.

Epstein, R. A., Patai, E. Z., Julian, J. B., & Spiers, H. J. (2017). The cognitive map in humans: spatial navigation and beyond. *Nature Neuroscience* 20(11): 1504–1513.

Epstein, S., Kitahara, H., & Seely, D. (2014). Labeling by minimal search: implications for successive-cyclic A-movement and the conception of the postulate 'phase'. *Linguistic Inquiry* 45(3): 463–481.

Epstein, S. D., Kitahara, H., & Seely, T. D. (2017a). Is the faculty of language a 'perfect solution' to the interface systems? In McGilvray, J. (ed.). *The Cambridge Companion to Chomsky*. 2nd ed. Cambridge: Cambridge University Press. 50–68.

Epstein, S. D., Kitahara, H., & Seely, T. D. (2017b). Merge, labeling and their interactions. In Bauke, L. & Blümel, A. (eds.). (2017). *Labels and Roots*. Berlin: Walter de Gruyter. 17–46.

Esghaei, M., Mohammad Reza, D., & Stefan, T. (2015). Attention decreases phase-amplitude coupling, enhancing stimulus discriminability in cortical area MT. *Frontiers in Neural Circuits* 9: 82.

Everaert, M. B. H., Huybregts, M. A. C., Chomsky, N., Berwick, R. C., & Bolhuis, J. J. (2015). Structures, not strings: Linguistics as part of the cognitive sciences. *Trends in Cognitive Sciences* 19(12): 729–743.

Ewerdwalbesloh, J. A., Palva, S., Rösler, F., & Khader, P. H. (2016). Neural correlates of maintaining generated images in visual working memory. *Human Brain Mapping* 37 (12): 4349–4362.

Farias-Virgens, M. & White, S. A. (2017). A sing-song way of vocalizing: generalization and specificity in language and birdsong. *Neuron* 96(5): 958–960.

Fecteau, S., Armony, J. L., Joanette, Y., & Belin, P. (2004). Is voice processing species-specific in human auditory cortex? An fMRI study. *Neuroimage* 23: 840–848.

Fedorenko, E. & Thompson-Schill, S. L. (2014). Reworking the language network. *Trends Cognitive Sciences* 18: 120–126.

Fedorenko, E. & Varley, R. (2016). Language and thought are not the same thing: evidence from neuroimaging and neurological patients. *Annals of the New York Academy of Sciences* 1369(1): 132–153.

Fedorenko, E., Scott, T. L., Brunner, P., Coon, W. G., Pritchett, B., Schalk, G., & Kanwisher, N. (2016). Neural correlate of the construction of sentence meaning. *PNAS* 113(41): E6256–E6262.

Fell, J. & Axmacher, N. (2011). The role of phase synchronization in memory processes. *Nature Neuroscience* 12: 105–118.

Fellner, M-C., Gollwitzer, S., Rampp, S., Kreiselmeyr, G., Bush, D., Diehl, B., Axmacher, N., Hamer, H., & Hanslmayr, S. (2019). Spectral fingerprints or spectral tilt? Evidence for distinct oscillatory signatures of memory formation. *PLoS Biology* 17(7): e3000403.

Fernández-Ruiz, A. & Oliva, A. (2016). Distributed representation of 'what' and 'where' information in the parahippocampal region. *Journal of Neuroscience* 36 (32): 8286–8288.

Fernández-Ruiz, A., Oliva, A., Fermino de Oliveira, E., Rocha-Almeida, F., Tingley, D., & Buzsáki, G. (2019). Long-duration hippocampal sharp wave ripples improve memory. *Science* 364(6445): 1082–1086.

Fiebach, C. J., Schlesewsky, M., Lohmann, G., Von Cramon, D. Y., & Friederici, A. D. (2005). Revisiting the role of Broca's area in sentence processing: syntactic integration versus syntactic working memory. *Human Brain Mapping* 24: 79–91.

Fiebach, C. J., Vos, S. H., & Friederici, A. D. (2004). Neural correlates of syntactic ambiguity in sentence comprehension for low and high span readers. *Journal of Cognitive Neuroscience* 16: 1562–1575.

Fiebelkorn, I. C., Pinsk, M. A., & Kastner, S. (2018). A dynamic interplay within the frontoparietal network underlies rhythmic spatial attention. *Neuron* 99: 842–853.

Finlay, B. L., Darlington, R. B., & Nicastro, N. (2001). Developmental structure in brain evolution. *Behavioral and Brain Sciences* 24: 263–278.

Fisher, S. E. (2016). A molecular genetic perspective on speech and language. In Hickok, G. & Small, S. (eds.). *Neurobiology of Language*. Amsterdam: Elsevier. 13–24.

Fisher, S. E. & Vernes, S. (2015). Genetics and the language sciences. *Annual Review of Linguistics* 1: 289–310.

Fitch, W. T. (2009). Prolegomena to a future science of biolinguistics. *Biolinguistics* 3: 283–320.

Fitch, W. T. (2010a). *The Evolution of Language*. Cambridge: Cambridge University Press.

Fitch, W. T. (2010b). Three meanings of 'recursion': key distinctions for biolinguistics. In Larson, R., Deprez, V., & Yamakido, H. (eds.). *The Evolution of the Human Language Faculty: Biolinguistic Perspectives*. Cambridge: Cambridge University Press. 73–90.

Fitch, W. T. (2014a). Toward a computational framework for cognitive biology: unifying approaches from cognitive neuroscience and comparative cognition. *Physics of Life Reviews* 11: 329–364.

Fitch, W. T. (2014b). Attending to the forest and the trees. Reply to comments on 'Toward a computational framework for cognitive biology: Unifying approaches from cognitive neuroscience and comparative cognition'. *Physics of Life Reviews* 11: 391–399.

Fitch, W. T. (2017). On externalization and cognitive continuity in language evolution. *Mind & Language* 32: 597–606.

Fitch, W. T. & Friederici, A. D. (2012). Artificial grammar learning meets formal language theory: an overview. *Philosophical Transactions of the Royal Society B* 367(1598): 1933–1955.

Fitch, W. T. & Hauser, M. (2004). Computational constraints on syntactic processing in a nonhuman primate. *Science* 303(337): 377–80.

Fitch, W. T. & Martins, M. D. (2014). Hierarchical processing in music, language, and action: Lashley revisited. *Annals of the New York Academy of Sciences* 1316: 87–104.

Fitch, W. T., de Boer, B., Mathur, N., & Ghazanfar, A. A. (2016). Monkey vocal tracts are speech-ready. *Science Advances* 2(12): e1600723.

Flanagan, S. & Goswami, U. (2018). The role of phase synchronisation between low frequency amplitude modulations in child phonology and morphology speech tasks. *The Journal of the Acoustical Society of America* 143: 1366–1375.

Florez, C. M., McGinn, R. J., Lukankin, V., Marwa, I., Sugumar, S., Dian, J. et al. (2013). *In vitro* recordings of human neocortical oscillations. *Cerebral Cortex* 25: 578–597.

Fogerson, P. M. & Huguenard, J. R. (2016). Tapping the breaks: cellular and synaptic mechanisms that regulate thalamic oscillations. *Neuron* 92: 687–704.

Foubet, O., Trejo, M., & Toro, R. (2019). Mechanical morphogenesis and the development of neocortical organisation. *Cortex* 118: 315–326.

Frank, S. L. & Christiansen, M. H. (2018). Hierarchical and sequential processing of language. *Language, Cognition and Neuroscience* 33(9): 1213–1218.

Frank, S. L. & Yang, J-B. (2017). Non-syntactic processing explains cortical entrainment during speech perception. Talk presented at the 30th CUNY Conference on Human Sentence Processing, Massachusetts Institute of Technology: http://tedlab.mit.edu/cuny_abstracts/12_Final_Manuscript.pdf

Frank, S. L. & Yang, J-B. (2018). Lexical representation explains cortical entrainment during speech comprehension. *PLoS ONE* 13(5): e0197304.

Frankland, S. M. & Greene, J. D. (2020). Two ways to build a thought: distinct forms of compositional semantic representation across brain regions. *Cerebral Cortex* doi.org/10.1093/cercor/bhaa001

Freedman, D. J., Riesenhuber, M., Poggio, T., & Miller, E. K. (2003). A comparison of primate prefrontal and inferior temporal cortices during visual categorization. *Journal of Neuroscience* 23(12): 5235–5246.

Freeman, W. J. (2015). Mechanism and significance of global coherence in scalp EEG. *Current Opinion in Neurobiology* 31: 199–205.

Freidin, R. (2012). A brief history of generative grammar. In Russell, G. & Fara, D. G. (eds.). *The Routledge Companion to Philosophy of Language.* New York: Routledge. 895–916.

Freiwald, W., Tsao, D. Y., & Livingston, M. S. (2009). A face feature space in the macaque temporal lobe. *Nature Neuroscience* 12: 1187–1196.

Frey, S., Mackey, S., & Petrides, M. (2014). Cortico-cortical connections of areas 44 and 45b in the macaque monkey. *Brain & Language* 131: 36–55.

Fridriksson, J., Yourganov, G., Bonilha, L., Basilakos, A., Den Ouden, D-B., & Rorden, C. (2016). Revealing the dual streams of speech processing. *PNAS* 113 (52): 15108–15113.

Friederici, A. D. (2011). The brain basis of language processing: from structure to function. *Physiological Reviews* 91: 1357–1392.

Friederici, A. D. (2012). The cortical language circuit: from auditory perception to sentence comprehension. *Trends in Cognitive Sciences* 5: 262–268.

Friederici, A. D. (2016). Evolution of the neural language network. *Psychonomic Bulletin & Review* 41(1): 41–47.

Friederici, A. D. (2017). *Language in Our Brain.* Cambridge, MA: MIT Press.

Friederici, A. D., Bahlmann, J., Heim, S., Schubotz, R. I., & Anwander, A. (2006). The brain differentiates human and non-human grammars: functional localization and structural connectivity. *PNAS* 103: 2458–63.

Friederici, A. D., Chomsky, N., Berwick, R. C., Moro, A., & Bolhuis, J. J. (2017). Language, mind and brain. *Nature Human Behaviour* 1: 713–722.

Fries, P. (2009). Neuronal gamma-band synchronization as a fundamental process in cortical computation. *Annual Review of Neuroscience* 32: 209–224.

Fries, P., Womelsdorf, T., Oostenveld, R., & Desimone, R. (2008). The effects of visual stimulation and selective visual attention on rhythmic neuronal synchronization in macaque area V4. *Journal of Neuroscience* 28: 4823–4835.

Friese, U., Köster, M., Hassler, U., Martens, U., Trujillo-Barreto, N., & Gruber, T. (2013). Successful memory encoding is associated with increased cross-frequency coupling between frontal theta and posterior gamma oscillations in human scalp-recorded EEG. *NeuroImage* 66: 642–647.

Frisch, S. A., Pierrehumbert, J. B., & Broe, M. B. (2004). Similarity avoidance and the OCP. *Natural Language & Linguistic Theory* 22: 179–228.

Friston, K. (2008). Hierarchical models in the brain. *PLoS Computational Biology* 4 (11): e1000211.

Friston, K. (2010). The free-energy principle: a unified brain theory? *Nature Reviews Neuroscience* 11: 127–138.

Friston, K. J., Rosch, R., Parr, T., Price, C., & Bowman, H. (2017). Deep temporal models and active inference. *Neuroscience and Biobehavioral Reviews* 77: 388–402.

Fromont, L. A., Steinhauer, K., & Royle, P. (2020). Verbing nouns and nouning verbs: using a balanced design provides ERP evidence against 'syntax-first' approaches to sentence processing. *PLoS ONE* 15(3): e0229169.

Fuentes, A. (2016). The extended evolutionary synthesis, ethnography, and the human Niche: toward an integrated anthropology. *Current Anthropology* 57(S13): S13-S26.

Fujioka, T., Trainor, L. J., Large, E. W., & Ross, B. (2012). Internalized timing of isochronous sounds is represented in neuromagnetic beta oscillations. *Journal of Neuroscience* 32(5): 1791–1802.

Fujita, K. (2009). A prospect for evolutionary adequacy: merge and the evolution and development of human language. *Biolinguistics* 3(2): 128–153.

Fujita, K. (2016). On certain fallacies in evolutionary linguistics and how one can eliminate them. In Fujita, K. & Boeckx, C. (eds.). *Advances in Biolinguistics: The Human Language Faculty and its Biological Basis.* London: Routledge. 220–237.

Fujita, K. (2018). Placing too much weight on animal communication can be harmful. In Cuskley, C., Flaherty, M., McCrohon, L., Little, H., Ravignani, A., & Verhoef, T. (eds.). *The Evolution of Language: Proceedings of the 12th International Conference (Evolang 12).* Torun: Nicolaus Copernicus University. 131–133.

Fukuda, T., Takahashi, J., & Tanaka, J. (1999). Tyrosine hydroxylase-immunoreactive neurons are decreased in number in the cerebral cortex of Parkinson's disease. *Neuropathology* 19(1): 10–13.

Fukui, N. (2015). A note on weak vs. strong generation in human language. *Studies in Chinese Linguistics* 36(2): 59–68.

Fukui, N. (2017). *Merge in the Mind-Brain: Essays on Theoretical Linguistics and the Neuroscience of Language.* London: Routledge.

Fyshe, A., Sudre, G., Wehbe, L., Rafidi, N., & Mitchell, T. M. (2016). The semantics of adjective noun phrases in the human brain. *bioRxiv.* http://dx.doi.org/10.1101/089615

Gabi, M., Neves, K., Masseron, C., Ribeiro, P. F. M., Ventura-Antunes, L., Torres, L., Mota, B., & Herculano-Houzel, S. (2016). No relative expansion of the number of prefrontal neurons in primate and human evolution. *PNAS* 113(34): 9617–9622.

Gągol, A., Magnuski, M., Kroczek, B., Kałamała, P., Ociepka, M., Santarnecchi E., & Chuderski, A. (2018). Delta-gamma coupling as a potential neurophysiological mechanism of fluid intelligence. *Intelligence* 66: 54–63.

Gallego, Á. J. & Orús, R. (2017). The physical structure of grammatical correlations: equivalences, formalizations and consequences. *arXiv* 1708.01525v2.

Gallistel, C. R. (2017a). What memory must look like. Talk presented at the Big Ideas in Cognitive Neuroscience, CNS 2017.

Gallistel, R. (2017b). The coding question. *Trends in Cognitive Sciences* 21(7): 498–508.

Gallistel, C. R. & King, A. P. (2009). *Memory and the computational brain: Why cognitive science will transform neuroscience.* Malden, MA: Wiley-Blackwell.

Gallistel, C. R. & Matzel, L. D. (2013). The neuroscience of learning: beyond the Hebbian synapse. *Annual Review of Psychology* 64: 169–200.

Garey, M. & Johnson, D. (1979). *Computers and Intractability: A Guide to the Theory of NP-Completeness.* New York: W.H. Freeman.

Gärtner, H.-M. & Sauerland, U. (eds.). (2007). *Interfaces + Recursion = Language? Chomsky's Minimalism and the View from Syntax-Semantics.* Berlin: De Gruyter Mouton.

Garvert, M. M., Dolan, R. J., & Behrens, T. E. (2017). A map of abstract relational knowledge in the human hippocampal-entorhinal cortex. *Elife* 6: e17086.

Gehrig, J., Michalareas, G., Forster, M-T., Lei, J., Hok, P., Laufs, H., Senft, C., Seifert, V., Schoffelen, J-M., Hanslmayr, S., & Kell, C. A. (2019). Low frequency oscillations code speech during verbal working memory. *Journal of Neuroscience* 39 (33): 6498–6512.

Genç, E., Fraenz, C., Schlüter, C., Friedrich, P., Hossiep, R., Voelkle, M. C., Ling, J. M., Güntürkün, O., & Jung, R. E. (2018). Diffusion markers of dendritic density and arborization in gray matter predict differences in intelligence. *Nature Communications* 9: 1905.

Genon, S., Reid, A., Langner, R., Amunts, K., & Eickhoff, S. B. (2019). How to characterize the function of a brain region. *Trends in Cognitive Sciences* 22(4): 350–364.

Gentner, T. Q. & Hulse, S. (1998). Perceptual mechanisms for individual vocal recognition in European starlings, Sturnus vulgaris. *Animal Behavior* 56: 579–594.

Gentner, T. Q., Fenn, K. M., Margoliash, D., & Nusbaum, H. C. (2006). Recursive syntactic pattern learning by songbirds. *Nature* 440: 1204–1207.

Geschwind, D. H. & Rakic, P. (2013). Cortical evolution: Judge the brain by its cover. *Neuron* 80: 633–47.

Ghazanfar, A. A. & Eliades, S. J. (2014). The neurobiology of primate communication. *Current Opinion in Neurobiology* 28: 128–135.

Ghirlanda, S., Lind, J., & Enquist, M. (2017). Memory for stimulus sequences: a divide between humans and other animals? *Royal Society Open Science* 4: 161011.

Giahi Saravani, A., Forseth, K. J., Tandon, N., & Pitkow, X. (2019). Dynamic brain interactions during picture naming. *eNeuro* 6(4): ENEURO.0472-18.2019.

Gibson, K. R. & Jessee, S. (1999). Language evolution and expansions of multiple neural processing areas. In B. King (ed.). *The Evolution of Language: Assessing the Evidence from the Non-Human Primates*. Santa Fe, NM: School for American Research. 189–228.

Giere, R. (2006). Perspectival pluralism. Kellert, S., Longino, H., & Waters, C. K. (eds.). *Scientific Pluralism*. Minneapolis: University of Minnesota Press. 167–190.

Gips, B., van der Eerden, J. P. J. M., & Jensen, O. (2016). A biologically plausible mechanism for neuronal coding organized by the phase of alpha oscillations. *European Journal of Neuroscience* 44(4): 2147–2161.

Giraud, A.-L. & Poeppel, D. (2012). Cortical oscillations and speech processing: emerging computational principles and operations. *Nature Neuroscience* 15(4): 511–517.

Goldin-Meadow, S. & Yang, C. (2016). Statistical evidence that a child can create a combinatorial linguistic system without external linguistic input: implications for language evolution. *Neuroscience and Biobehavioral Reviews* 81(B): 150–157.

Gollo, L. L., Roberts, J. A., & Cocchi, L. (2017). Mapping how local perturbations influence systems-level brain dynamics. *NeuroImage* 160: 97–112.

Golston, C. (2018). φ-features in animal cognition. *Biolinguistics* 12: 55–98.

Gomez, J., Barnett, M., & Grill-Spector, K. (2019). Extensive childhood experience with Pokémon suggests eccentricity drives organization of visual cortex. *Nature Neuroscience* 3: 611–624.

Gomez-Marin, A. & Mainen, Z. F. (2016). Expanding perspectives on cognition in humans, animals, and machines. *Current Opinion in Neurobiology* 37: 85–91.

Gorišek, V. R., Isoski, V. Z., Belič, A., Manouilidou, C., Koritnik, B., Bon, J., Meglič, N. P., Vrabec, M., Žibert, J., Repovš, G., & Zidar, J. (2016). Beyond aphasia:

altered EEG connectivity in Broca's patients during working memory task. *Brain & Language* 163: 10–21.

Goswami, U. (2019). Speech rhythm and language acquisition: an amplitude modulation phase hierarchy perspective. *Annals of the New York Academy of Sciences* 1453(1): 67–78.

Goswami, U. & Leong, V. (2013). Speech rhythm and temporal structure: converging perspectives? *Laboratory Phonology* 4(1): 67–92.

Goucha, T., Anwander, A., & Friederici, A. D. (2015). How language shapes the brain: cross-linguistic differences in structural connectivity. Poster presented at 45th Annual Meeting of the Society for Neuroscience (SfN 2015), Chicago, IL, USA.

Goucha, T. & Friederici, A. D. (2015). The language skeleton after dissecting meaning: a functional segregation within Broca's area. NeuroImage 114(6): 294–302.

Goucha, T., Zaccarella, E., & Friederici, A. D. (2017). A revival of Homo loquens as a builder of labeled structures: neurocognitive considerations. *Neuroscience and Biobehavioral Reviews* 81: 213–224.

Gould, S. J. &, Vrba, E. S. (1982). Exaptation: a missing term in the science of form. *Paleobiology* 8, 4–15.

Gould, S. J. (1997). Evolution: the pleasures of pluralism. New York Review of Books, June 26.

Gould, S. J. (2002). *The Structure of Evolutionary Theory.* Cambridge, MA: Harvard University Press.

Goyal, A., Miller, J., Qasim, S., Watrous, A. J., Stein, J. M., Inman, C. S., Gross, R. E., Willie, J. T., Lega, B., Lin, J.-J., et al. (2018). Functionally distinct high and low theta oscillations in the human hippocampus. *bioRxiv.* doi.org/10.1101/498055

Grabot, L., Kononowicz, T. W., Dupré la Tour, T., Gramfort, A., Doyère, V., van Wassenhove, V. (2019). The strength of alpha–beta oscillatory coupling predicts motor timing precision. *Journal of Neuroscience* 39(17): 3277–3291.

Gray, A. (1982). *The Neuropsychology of Anxiety: An Enquiry into the Septo-Hippocampal System.* Oxford: Oxford University Press.

Gray, C. M. & Singer, W. (1989). Stimulus-specific neuronal oscillations in orientation columns of cat visual cortex. *PNAS* 86: 1698–1702.

Greenhill, S. J., Wu, C.-H., Hua, X., Dunn, M., Levinson, S. C., & Gray, R. D. (2017). Evolutionary dynamics of language systems. *Proceedings of the National Academy of Sciences of the United States of America* 114: E8822–E8829.

Gregoriou, G. G., Gotts, S. J., Zhou, H., & Desimone, R. (2009). High-frequency, long-range coupling between prefrontal and visual cortex during attention. *Science* 324: 1207–1210.

Griffiths, B. J. & Fuentemilla, L. (2020). Event conjunction: how the hippocampus integrates episodic memories across event boundaries. *Hippocampus* 30(2): 162–171.

Grillner, S. (2006) Biological pattern generation: the cellular and computational logic of networks in motion. *Neuron* 52: 751–766.

Grimaldi, M. (2012). Toward a neural theory of language: old issues and new perspectives. *Journal of Neurolinguistics* 25: 304–327.

Grimaldi, M. (2019). From brain noise to syntactic structures: a formal proposal within the oscillatory rhythms perspective. Franco, L. & Lorusso, P. (eds.). *Linguistic Variation: Structure and Interpretation – A Festschrift in Honour of M. Rita Manzini in Occasion of Her 60th Birthday.* New York: Mouton de Gruyter.

Grodzinsky, Y. & Friederici, A. D. (2006). Neuroimaging of syntax and syntactic processing. *Current Opinion in Neurobiology* 16(2): 240–246.

Gross, J., Hoogenboom, N., Thut, G., Schyns, P., Panzeri, S., Belin, P., & Garrod, S. (2013). Speech rhythms and multiplexed oscillatory sensory coding in the human brain. *PLoS ONE* 11(12): e1001752.

Gu, B-M., van Rijn, H., & Meck, W. H. (2015). Oscillatory multiplexing of neural population codes for interval timing and working memory. *Neuroscience and Biobehavioral Reviews* 48: 160–165.

Guevara Erra, R., Perez Velazquez, J.L., & Rosenblum, M. (2017). Neural synchronization from the perspective of non-linear dynamics. *Frontiers in Computational Neuroscience* 11: 98.

Güntekin, B. & Başar, E. (2016). Review of evoked and event-related delta responses in the human brain. *International Journal of Psychophysiology* 103: 43–52.

Gunz, P., Neubauer, S., Golovanova, L., Doronichev, V., Maureille, B., & Hublin, J.-J. (2012). A uniquely modern human pattern of endocranial development: insights from a new cranial reconstruction of the Neandertal newborn from Mezmaiskaya. *Journal of Human Evolution* 62(2): 300–313.

Guo, W., Clause, A. R., Barth-Maron, A., & Polley, D. B. (2017). A corticothalamic circuit for dynamic switching between feature detection and discrimination. *Neuron* 95(1): 180–194.

Haber, S. N. & Calzavara, R. (2009). The cortico-basal ganglia integrative network: the role of the thalamus. *Brain Research Bulletin* 78: 69–74.

Hackett, T. A., Preuss, T. M., & Kaas, J. H. (2001). Architectonic identification of the core region in auditory cortex of macaques, chimpanzees, and humans. *Journal of Comparative Neurology* 441: 197–222.

Haegens, S., Osipova, D., Oostenveld, R., & Jensen, O. (2010). Somatosensory working memory performance in humans depends on both engagement and disengagement of regions in a distributed network. *Human Brain Mapping* 31 (1): 26–35.

Hage, S. R. & Nieder, A. (2016). Dual neural network model for the evolution of speech and language. *Trends in Neurosciences* 39(12): 813–829.

Hagoort, P. (2005). On Broca, brain, and binding: a new framework. *Trends in Cognitive Sciences* 9: 416–423.

Hagoort, P. (2019). The neurobiology of language beyond single-word processing. *Science* 366: 55–58.

Hahn, T. T., Sakmann, B., & Mehta, M. R. (2006). Phase-locking of hippocampal interneurons' membrane potential to neocortical up-down states. *Nature Neuroscience* 9: 1359–1361.

Halassa, M. M., Chen, Z., Wimmer, R. D., Brunetti, P. M., Zhao, S., Zikopoulos, B., Wang, F., Brown, E. N., & Wilson, M. A. (2014). State-dependent architecture of thalamic reticular subnetworks. *Cell* 158(4): 808–821.

Halgren, M., Fabo, D., Ulbert, I., Madsen, J. R., Erőss, L., Doyle, W. K., Devinsky, O., Schomer, D., Cash, S. S., & Halgren, E. (2017). Superficial slow rhythms integrate cortical processing in humans. *Scientific Reports* 8: 2055.

Hall, D. C. (2012). Book review: Bridget D. Samuels. *Phonological Architecture: A Biolinguistic Perspective. Journal of Linguistics* 48(3): 736–741.

Hamilton, J. D. (1994). *Time Series Analysis*. Princeton, NJ: Princeton University Press.

Handjaras, G., Ricciardi, E., Leo, A., Lenci, A., Cecchetti, L., Cosottini, M., Marotta, G., & Pietrini, P. (2016). How concepts are encoded in the human brain: a modality independent, category-based cortical organization of semantic knowledge. *NeuroImage* 135: 232–242.

Hanna, J., Mejias, S., Schelstraete, M.-A., Pulvermüller, F., Shtyrov, Y., & van der Lely, H. K. J. (2014). Early activation of Broca's area in grammar processing as revealed by the syntactic mismatch negativity and distributed source analysis. *Cognitive Neuroscience* 5(2): 66–76.

Hanslmayr, S., Axmacher, N., & Inman, C. S. (2019). Modulating human memory via entrainment of brain oscillations. *Trends in Neuroscienes* 42(7): 485–499.

Hanslmayr, S., Matuschek, J., & Fellner, M-C. (2014). Entrainment of prefrontal beta oscillations induces an endogenous echo and impairs memory formation. *Current Biology* 24: 904–909.

Hanslmayr, S., Staresina, B. P., & Bowman, H. (2016). Oscillations and episodic memory: addressing the synchronization/desynchronization conundrum. *Trends in Neurosciences* 39(1): 16–25.

Hanslmayr, S. & Staudigl, T. (2014). How brain oscillations form memories – a processing based perspective on oscillatory subsequent memory effects. *Neuroimage* 85(Part 2): 648–655.

Hardingham, G. E., Pruunsild, P., Greenberg, M. E., & Bading, H. (2018). Lineage divergence of activity-driven transcription and evolution of cognitive ability. *Nature Reviews Neuroscience* 19: 9–15.

Harmony, T. (2013). The functional significance of delta oscillations in cognitive processing. *Frontiers in Integrative Neuroscience* 7: 83.

Harris, K. D. (2015). Cortical computation in mammals and birds. *PNAS* 112(11): 3184–3185.

Hasson, U., Egidi, G., Marelli, M., & Willems, R. M. (2018). Grounding the neurobiology of language in first principles: the necessity of non-language-centric explanations for language comprehension. *Cognition* 180: 135–157.

Hauser, M. & Watumull, J. (2017). The Universal Generative Faculty: The source of our expressive power in language, mathematics, morality, and music. *Journal of Neurolinguistics* 43(B): 78–94.

Hauser, M., Chomsky, N., & Fitch, W. T. (2002). The faculty of language: what is it, who has it, and how did it evolve? *Science* 298(5598): 1569–1579.

Hauser, M., Yang, C., Berwick, R. C., Tattersall, I., Ryan, M. J., Watumull, J., Chomsky, N., & Lewontin, R. C. (2014). The mystery of language evolution. *Frontiers in Psychology* 5: 401.

Hauser, M. D., MacNeilage, P., & Ware, M. (1996). Numerical representations in primates. *PNAS* 93(4): 1514–1517.

Hauser, M. (2016). Challenges to the what, when, and why? *Biolinguistics* 10: 1–6.

Haynes, W. I. A. & Haber, S. N. (2013). The organization of prefrontal-subthalamic inputs in primates provides an anatomical substrate for both functional specificity and integration: implications for basal ganglia models and deep brain stimulation. *Journal of Neuroscience* 33(11): 4804–4814.

Headley, D. B. & Paré, D. (2017). Common oscillatory mechanisms across multiple memory systems. *npj Science of Learning* 2: 1.

Hebb, D. O. (1949). *The Organization of Behavior.* New York: John Wiley & Sons.

Hecht, E. E., Murphy, L. E., Gutman, D. A., Votaw, J. R., Schuster, D. M., Preuss, T. M., Orban, G. A., Stout, D., & Parr, L. A. (2013). Differences in neural activation for object-directed grasping in chimpanzees and humans. *Journal of Neuroscience* 33 (35): 14117–14134.

Heffner, H. E. & Heffner, R. S. (1986). Effect of unilateral and bilateral auditory cortex lesions on the discrimination of vocalizations by Japanese macaques. *Journal of Neurophysiology* 56: 683–701.

Heine, B. & Kuteva, T. (2002). On the evolution of grammatical forms. In Wray, A. (ed.). *The Transition to Language*. Oxford: Oxford University Press. 376–397.

Heinz, A. J. (2016) *A unitary framework defining the functional significance of neural oscillations in the alpha frequency*. PhD thesis, North Dakota State University.

Heinz, J., Kobele, G., & Riggle, J. (2009). Evaluating the complexity of optimality theory. *Linguistic Inquiry* 40: 277–288.

Helfrich, R. F., Fiebelkorn, I. C., Szczepanski, S. M., Lin, J. J., Parvizi, J., Knight, R. T., & Kastner, S. (2018). Neural mechanisms of sustained attention are rhythmic. *Neuron* 99: 854–865.

Helfrich, R. F. & Knight, R. T. (2016). Oscillatory dynamics of prefrontal cognitive control. *Trends in Cognitive Sciences* 20(12): 916–930.

Henderson, J. M., Choi, W., Lowder, M. W., & Ferreira, F. (2016). Language structure in the brain: a fixation-related fMRI study of syntactic surprisal in reading. *NeuroImage* 132: 293–300.

Herrmann, C. S., Strüber, D., Helfrich, R. F., & Engel, A. K. (2016). EEG oscillations: from correlation to causality. *International Journal of Psychophysiology* 103: 12–21.

Heusser, A. C., Poeppel, D., Ezzyat, Y., & Davachi, L. (2016). Episodic sequence memory is supported by a theta-gamma phase code. *Nature Neuroscience* 19: 1374–1380.

Hickok, G. (2014). *The Myth of Mirror Neurons: The Real Neuroscience of Communication and Cognition*. London: W.W. Norton & Company.

Hickok, G., Buchsbaum, B., Humphries, C., & Muftuler, T. (2003). Auditory-motor interaction revealed by fMRI: speech, music, and working memory in area Spt. *Journal of Cognitive Neuroscience* 15: 673–682.

Hickok, G., Rogalsky, C., Chen, R., Herskovits, E. H., Townsley, S., & Hillis, A. E. (2014). Partially overlapping sensorimotor networks underlie speech praxis and verbal short-term memory: evidence from apraxia of speech following acute stroke. *Frontiers in Human Neuroscience* 8: 649.

Hinaut, X. & Dominey, P. (2013). Real-time parallel processing of grammatical structure in the fronto-striatal system: a recurrent network simulation study using reservoir computing. *PLoS ONE* 8(2): e52946.

Hinzen, W. (2006). *Mind Design and Minimal Syntax*. Oxford: Oxford University Press.

Hinzen, W. (2009). The successor function + LEX = Human language? In Grohmann, K. (ed.). *InterPhases: Phase-Theoretic Investigations of Linguistic Interfaces*. Oxford: Oxford University Press. 25–47.

Hinzen, W. (2016). On the grammar of referential dependence. *Studies in Logic, Grammar and Rhetoric* 46(1): 11–33.

Hinzen, W. & Sheehan, M. (2013). *The Philosophy of Universal Grammar*. Oxford: Oxford University Press.

Hiraiwa, K. (2017). The faculty of language integrates the two core systems of number. *Frontiers in Psychology* 8: 351.

Hobhouse, L. T. (1901). *Mind in Evolution*. London: Macmillan.

Hochstein, E. (2016). Categorizing the mental. *The Philosophical Quarterly* 66(265): 745–759.

Hochstein, E. (2018). Why one model is never enough: a defense of explanatory holism. *Biology & Philosophy* 32(6): 1105–1125.

Hoepfner, A. R. & Goller, F. (2013). Atypical song reveals spontaneously developing coordination between multi-modal signals in brown-headed cowbirds (*Molothrus ater*). *PLoS ONE* 8(6): e65525.

Holmberg, A. & Roberts, I. (2014). Parameters and three factors of language design. In Picallo, C. (ed.). *Linguistic Variation in the Minimalist Framework*. Oxford: Oxford University Press. 61–81.

Honkanen, R., Rouhinen, S., Wang, S. H., Palva, J. M., & Palva, S. (2015). Gamma oscillations underlie the maintenance of feature-specific information and the contents of visual working memory. *Cerebral Cortex* 25(10): 3788–3801.

Horgan, J. (2017). The neural code. *Edge*. www.edge.org/response-detail/27011

Hornstein, N. (2009). *A Theory of Syntax: Minimal Operations and Universal Grammar*. Cambridge: Cambridge University Press.

Hornstein, N. & Pietroski, P. (2009). Basic operations: minimal syntax-semantics. *Catalan Journal of Linguistics* 8: 113–139.

Hosaka, R., Nakajima, T., Aihara, K., Yamaguchi, Y., & Mushiake, H. (2016). The suppression of beta oscillations in the primate supplementary motor complex reflects a volatile state during the updating of action sequences. *Cerebral Cortex* 26(8): 3442–3452.

Hoshi, K. (2019). More on the relations among categorization, merge and labeling, and their nature. *Biolinguistics* 13: 1–21.

Howard, S. R., Avargues-Weber, A., Garcia, J. E., Greentree, A. D., & Dyer, A. G. (2019). Numerical cognition in honeybees enables addition and subtraction. *Science Advances* 5: eaav0961.

Hülsemann, M. J., Naumann, E., & Rasch, B. (2019). Quantification of phase-amplitude coupling in neuronal oscillations: comparison of phase-locking value, mean vector length, modulation index, and generalized-linear-modeling-cross-frequency-coupling. *Frontiers in Neuroscience* 13: 573.

Hume, D. (1902). An enquiry concerning human understanding. In L. A. Selby-Bigge (ed.). *Enquiries Concerning the Human Understanding and Concerning the Principles of Morals*, 2nd ed. Oxford: Clarendon Press. 5–168.

Hunt, B. A. E., Tewarie, P. K., Mougin, O. E., Gaedes, N., Jones, D. K., Singh, K. D., Morris, P. G., Gowland, P. A., & Brookes, M. J. (2016). Reltionships between cortical myeloarchitecture and electrophysiological networks. *PNAS* 113(47): 13510–13515.

Hunter, T., Stanojević, M., & Stabler, E. P. (2019). The active-filler strategy in a move-eager left-corner minimalist grammar parser. Proceedings of the Workshop on

Cognitive Modeling and Computational Linguistics (CMCL). Association for Computational Linguistics, Minneapolis, Minnesota. 1–10.

Hurford, J. R. (2011). *The Origins of Grammar.* Oxford: Oxford University Press.

Hurford, J. R. (2014). *The Origins of Language: A Slim Guide.* Oxford: Oxford University Press.

Huth, A. G., de Heer, W. A., Griffiths, T. L., Theunissen, F. E., & Gallant, J. L. (2016). Natural speech reveals the semantic maps that tile human cerebral cortex. *Nature* 532: 453–458.

Huybregts, M. A. C. (2017). Phonemic clicks and the mapping asymmetry: how language emerged and speech developed. *Neuroscience and Biobehavioral Reviews* 81: 279–294.

Hyafil, A., Fontolan, L., Kabdebon, C., Gutkin, B., & Giraud, A.-L. (2015). Speech encoding by coupled cortical theta and gamma oscillations. *eLife* 10: 7554.

Iaria, G. & Burles, F. (2016). Developmental topological disorientation. *Trends in Cognitive Neurosciences* 20(10): 720–722.

Idsardi, W. (2018). Why is phonology different? No recursion. In Gallego, Á. J. & Martin, R. (eds.). *Language, Syntax, and the Natural Sciences.* Cambridge: Cambridge University Press. 212–223.

Itzkovitz, S. & Alon, U. (2007). The genetic code is nearly optimal for allowing additional information within protein-coding sequences. *Genome Research* 17: 405–412.

Iwabuchi, T., Nakajima, Y., & Makuuchi, M. (2019). Neural architecture of human language: hierarchical structure building is independent from working memory. *Neuropsychologia* 132: 107137.

Jackendoff, R. (2007). *Language, Consciousness, Culture: Essays on Mental Structure.* Massachusetts: MIT Press.

Jackendoff, R. (2017). In defense of theory. *Cognitive Science* 41(2): 185–212.

Jäger, G. & Rogers, J. (2012). Formal language theory: refining the Chomsky hierarchy. *Philosophical Transactions of the Royal Society B* 367: 1956–1970.

Jahanshahi, M., Obeso, I., Rothwell, J. C., & Obeso, J. A. (2015). A fronto-striato-subthalamicpallidal network for goal-directed and habitual inhibition. *Nature Reviews Neuroscience* 16: 719–732.

Jansen, B. H. & Rit, V. G. (1995). Electroencephalogram and visual-evoked potential generation in a mathematical-model of coupled cortical columns. *Biological Cybernetics* 73(4): 357–366.

Jardim-Messeder, D., Lambert, K., Noctor, S., Pestana, F. M., de Castro Leal, M. E., Bertelsen, M. F., Alagaili, A. N., Mohammad, O. B., Manger, P. R., & Herculano-Houzel, S. (2017). Dogs have the most neurons, though not the largest brain: trade-off between body mass and number of neurons in the cerebral cortex of large carnivoran species. *Frontiers in Neuroanatomy* 11: 118.

Jarvis, E., Gunturkun, O., Bruce, L., Csillag, A., Karten, H., Kuenzel, W. et al. (2005). Avian brains and a new understanding of vertebrate brain evolution. *Nature Reviews Neuroscience* 6: 151–159.

Jenkins, L. (2000). *Biolinguisitcs: Exploring the Biology of Language.* Cambridge: Cambridge University Press.

Jensen, O. & Mazaheri, A. (2010). Shaping functional architecture by oscillatory alpha activity: gating by inhibition. *Frontiers in Human Neuroscience* 4: 186.

Jensen, O., Bonnefond, M., & VanRullen R. (2012). An oscillatory mechanism for prioritizing salient unattended stimuli. *Trends in Cognitive Sciences* 16(4): 200–206.

Jensen, O., Gelfand, J., Kounios, J., Lisman, J. E. (2002). Oscillations in the alpha band (9–12 Hz) increase with memory load during retention in a short-term memory task. *Cerebral Cortex* 12: 877–882.

Jensen, O., Gips, B., Bergmann, T. O., & Bonnefond, M. (2014). Temporal coding organized by coupled alpha and gamma oscillations prioritize visual processing. *Trends in Neurosciences* 37(7): 357–369.

Jensen, O., Idiart, M., & Lisman, J. (1996). Physiologically realistic formation of autoassociative memory in networks with theta/gamma oscillations: role of fast NMDA channels. *Learning & Memory* 3: 243–256.

Jensen, O., Spaak, E., & Park, H. (2016). Discriminating valid from spurious indices of phase-amplitude coupling. *eNeuro* 3(6): ENEURO.0334-16.2016.

Jessen, N. A., Munk, A. S. F., Lundgaard, I., & Nedergaard, M. (2015). The glymphatic system: a beginner's guide. *Neurochemical Research* 40(12): 2583–2599.

Jiang, H., Bahramisharif, A., van Gerven, M. A. J., & Jensen, O. (2015). Measuring directionality between neuronal oscillations of different frequencies. *Neuroimage* 118: 359–367.

Jiang, X., Long, T., Cao, W., Li, J., Dehaene, S., & Wang, L. (2018). Production of supraregular spatial sequences by macaque monkeys. *Current Biology* 28: 1851–1859.

Jin, J. & Maren, S. (2015). Prefrontal-hippocampal interactions in memory and emotion. *Frontiers in Systems Neuroscience* 9: 170.

Jin, P., Zhou, T., & Ding, N. (2019). Low-frequency neural activity reflects rule-based chunking during speech. Poster presented at the 49th Meeting of the Society for Neuroscience, Chicago, 19–23 October.

Jin, X., Tecuapetla, F., & Costa, R. M. (2014). Basal ganglia subcircuits distinctively encode the parsing and concatenation of action sequences. *Nature Neuroscience* 17: 423–430.

Jirenhed, D.-A., Rasmussen, A., Johansson, F., & Hesslow, G. (2017). Learned response sequences in cerebellar Purkinje cells. *PNAS* 114(23): 6127–6132.

Johansson, S. (2013). Biolinguistics or psycholinguistics? Is the third factor helpful or harmful in explaining language? Biolinguistics 7: 249–275.

Johnson, C. D. (1972). *Formal Aspects of Phonological Description*. The Hague: Mouton.

Johnson, E. J. & Knight, R. T. (2015). Intracranial recordings and human memory. *Current Opinion in Neurobiology* 31: 18–25.

Jonas, E. & Kording, K. (2017). Could a neuroscientist understand a microprocessor? *PLoS Computational Biology*. doi.org/10.1371/journal.pcbi.1005268

Jones, E. G. (2007). *The Thalamus*. 2nd ed. Cambridge: Cambridge University Press.

Joshi, A. K. (1985). Tree adjoining grammars: how much context-sensitivity is required to provide reasonable structural descriptions? In Dowty, D. R., Karttunen, L., & Zwicky, A. M. (eds.). *Natural Language Parsing*. Cambridge: Cambridge University Press. 206–250.

Jost, K., Bryck, R. L., Vogel, E. K., & Mayr, U. (2011). Are old adults just like low working memory young adults? Filtering efficiency and age differences in visual working memory. *Cerebral Cortex* 21: 1147–1154.

Jouen, A-L., Verwey, W. B., van der Helden, J., Scheiber, C., Neveu, R., Dominey, P. F., & Ventre-Dominey, J. (2013). Discrete sequence production with and without a pause: the role of cortex, basal ganglia, and cerebellum. *Frontiers in Human Neuroscience* 7: 492.

Jung, R. E. & Haier, R. J. (2007). The parieto-frontal integration theory (P-FIT) of intelligence: converging neuroimaging evidence. *Behavioral and Brain Sciences* 30: 135–154.

Jutras, M. J., Fries, P., & Buffalo, E. A. (2013). Oscillatory activity in the monkey hippocampus during visual exploration and memory formation. *PNAS* 110(32): 13144–13149.

Kaas, J. H. & Stepniewska, I. (2015). Evolution of posterior parietal cortex and parietal-frontal networks for specific actions in primates. *Journal of Comparative Neurology* 524(3): 595–608.

Kaiser, J., Heidegger, T., Wibral, M., Altmann, C. F., & Lutzenberger, W. (2008). Distinct gamma-band components reflect the short-term memory maintenance of different sound lateralization angles. *Cerebral Cortex* 18: 2286–2295.

Kaiser, J., Rahm, B., & Lutzenberger, W. (2009). Temporal dynamics of stimulus-specific gamma-band activity components during auditory short-term memory. *NeuroImage* 44(1): 257–264.

Kamigaki, T. & Dan, Y. (2017). Delay activity of specific prefrontal interneuron subtypes modulates memory-guided behavior. *Nature Neuroscience* 20: 854–863.

Kamiński, J., Brzezicka, A., Mamelak, A. N., & Rutishauser, U. (2020). Combined phase-rate coding by persistently active neurons as a mechanism for maintaining multiple items in working memory in humans. *Neuron* 106(2): 256–264.

Kamiński, J., Brzezicka, A., & Wróbel, A. (2011). Short-term memory capacity (7 ± 2) predicted by theta to gamma cycle length ratio. *Neurobiology of Learning and Memory* 95(1): 19–23.

Kang, A. M., Constable, R. T., Gore, J. C., & Avrutin S. (1999). An event-related fMRI study of implicit phrase-level syntactic and semantic processing. *NeuroImage* 10: 555–561.

Kaplan, R., Adhikari, M. H., Hindriks, R., Mantini, D., Murayama, Y., Logothetis, N. K., & Deco, G. (2016). Hippocampal sharp-wave ripples influence selective activation of the default mode network. *Current Biology* 26: 1–6.

Kaplan, R., Bush, D., Bonnefond, M., Bandettini, P. A., Barnes, G. R., Doeller, C. F., & Burgess, N. (2014). Medial prefrontal theta phase coupling during spatial memory retrieval. *Hippocampus* 24(6): 656–665.

Karakaş, S. & Barry, R. J. (2017). A brief historical perspective on the advent of brain oscillations in the biological and psychological disciplines. *Neuroscience and Biobehavioral Reviews* 75: 335–347.

Kastellakis, G., Silva, A. J., & Piorazi, P. (2016). Linking memories across time via neuronal and dendritic overlaps in model neurons with active dendrites. *Cell Reports* 17: 1491–1504.

Kato, T., Kuno, M., Narita, H., Zushi, M., & Fukui, N. (2014). Generalized search and cyclic derivation by phase. *Sophia Linguistica* 61: 203–222.

Katz, P. S. & Harris-Warrick, R. M. (1999). The evolution of neuronal circuits underlying species-specific behavior. *Current Opinion in Neurobiology* 9: 628–633.

Kayser, C., Wilson, C., Safaai, H., Sakata, S., & Panzeri, S. (2014). Rhythmic auditory cortex activity at multiple timescales. *Journal of Neuroscience* 35(20): 7750–7762.

Kayser, S. J., Ince, R. A., Gross, J., & Kayser, C. (2015). Irregular speech rate dissociates auditory cortical entrainment, evoked responses, and frontal alpha. *Journal of Neuroscience* 35(44): 14691–14701.

Ke, A. H. (2017). Full phase transfer. Ms. University of Michigan. 10.13140/RG.2.2.14833.79209.

Keene, C. S., Bladon, J., McKenzie, S., Liu, C. D., O'Keefe, J., Eichenbaum, H. (2016). Complementary functional organization of neuronal activity patterns in the perirhinal, lateral entorhinal, and medial entorhinal cortices. *Journal of Neuroscience* 36: 3660–3675.

Keitel, A., Gross, J., & Kayser, C. (2018). Perceptually relevant speech tracking in auditory and motor cortex reflects distinct linguistic features. *PLOS Biology* 16(3): e2004473.

Keitel, A., Ince, R. A. A., Gross, J., & Kayser, C. (2017). Auditory cortical delta-entrainment interacts with oscillatory power in multiple fronto-parietal networks. *NeuroImage* 147: 32–42.

Keller, G. B. & Mrsic-Flogel, T. D. (2018). Predictive processing: a canonical cortical computation. *Neuron* 100(2): 424–435.

Kelso, J. A. S., Dumas, G., & Tognoli, E. (2013). Outline of a general theory of behavior and brain coordination. *Neural Networks* 37: 120–131.

Kenet, T., Bibitchkov, D., Tsodyks, M., Grinvald, A., & Ariell, A. (2003). Spontaneously emerging cortical representations of visual attributes. *Nature* 425: 954–956.

Kenneally, C. (2007). *The First Word: The Search for the Origins of Language.* New York: Penguin Books.

Kepecs, A., Uchida, N., & Mainen, Z. F. (2006). The sniff as a unit of olfactory processing. *Chemical Senses* 31: 167–179.

Kepinska, O., de Rover, M., Caspers, J., & Schiller, N. O. (2018). Connectivity of the hippocampus and Broca's area during acquisition of a novel grammar. *NeuroImage* 165: 1–10.

Kershenbaum, A., Bowles, A. E., Freeberg, T. M., Jin, D. Z., Lameira, A. R., & Bohn, K. (2014). Animal vocal sequences: not the Markov chains we thought they were. *Proceedings of the Royal Society B* 281: 20141370.

Kessler, K., Seymour, R. A., & Rippon, G. (2016). Brain oscillations and connectivity in autism spectrum disorders (ASD): new approaches to methodology, measurement and modelling. *Neuroscience and Biobehavioral Reviews* 71: 601–620.

Ketz, N. A., Jensen, O., & O'Reilly, R. C. (2015). Thalamic pathways underlying prefrontal cortex–medial temporal lobe oscillatory interactions. *Trends in Neurosciences* 38(1): 3–12.

Khodagholy, D., Gelinas, J. N., & Buzsáki, G. (2017). Learning-enhanced coupling between oscillations in association cortices and hippocampus. *Science* 358: 369–372.

Kielar, A., Meltzer, J., Moreno, S., Alain, C., & Bialystok, E. (2014). Oscillatory responses to semantic and syntactic violations. *Journal of Cognitive Neuroscience* 26: 2840–2862.

Kielar, A., Panamsky, L., Links, K. A., & Meltzer, J. A. (2015). Localization of electrophysiological responses to semantic and syntactic anomalies in language comprehension with MEG. *NeuroImage* 105: 507–524.

Kikuchi, Y., Attaheri, A., Wilson, B., Rhone, A. E., Nourski, K. V. et al. (2017). Sequence learning modulates neural responses and oscillatory coupling in human and monkey auditory cortex. *PLoS Biology* 15(4): e2000219.

Killingsworth, M. A. & Gilbert, D. T. (2010). A wandering mind is an unhappy mind. *Science* 330: 932.

Kingsolver, J. G. & Koehl, M. A. R. (1985). Aerodynamics, thermoregulation, and the evolution of insect wings: differential scaling and evolutionary change. *Evolution* 39: 488–504.

Kinzler, K. & Spelke, E. (2007). Core systems in human cognition. *Progress in Brain Research* 164: 257–64.

Kiran, S. & Thompson, C. K. (2019). Neuroplasticity of language networks in aphasia: advances, updates, and future challenges. *Frontiers in Neurology* 10: 295.

Kirmayer, L. J. (2017). Ontologies of life: From thermodynamics to teleonomics. Comment on 'Answering Schrödinger's question: A free-energy formulation' by Maxwell James Désormeau Ramstead et al. *Physics of Life Reviews*. https://doi.org/10.1016/j.plrev.2017.11.022

Klausberger, T., Marton, L. F., O'Neill, J., Huck, J. H., Dalezios, Y., Fuentealba, P., Suen, W. Y., Papp, E., Kaneko, T., Watanabe, M., Csicsvari, J., Somogyi, P. (2005). Complementary roles of cholecystokinin- and parvalbumin-expressing GABAergic neurons in hippocampal network oscillations. *Journal of Neuroscience* 25(42): 9782–9793.

Kleen, J. K., Testorf, M. E., Roberts, D. W., Scott, R. C., Jobst, B. J., Holmes, G. L., & Lenck-Santini, P-P. (2016). Oscillation phase locking and late ERP components of intracranial hippocampal recordings correlate to patient performance in a working memory task. *Frontiers in Human Neuroscience* 10: 287.

Klimesch, W., Doppelmayr, M., Wimmer, H., Gruber, W., Rohm, D., Schwaiger, J., & Hutzler, F. (2001). Alpha and beta band power changes in normal and dyslexic children. *Clinical Neurophysiology* 112: 1186–1195.

Klimesch, W., Sauseng, P., & Hanslmayr, S. (2007). EEG alpha oscillations: the inhibition-timing hypothesis. *Brain Research Reviews* 53: 63–88.

Klimesch, W., Schack, B., Schabus, M., Doppelmayr, M., Gruber, W., & Sauseng, P. (2004). Phase-locked alpha and theta oscillations generate the P1-N1 complex and are related to memory performance. *Cognitive Brain Research* 19: 302–316.

Klostermann, F., Krugel, L. K., & Ehlen, F. (2013). Functional roles of the thalamus for language capacities. *Frontiers in Systems Neuroscience* 7: 32.

Koehler, O. (1951). Der Vogelgesang als Vorstufe von Musik und Sprache. *Journal of Ornithology* 93(1): 3–20.

Koene, R. A. & Hasselmo, M. E. (2007). First-in-first-out item replacement in a model of short-term memory based on persistent spiking. *Cerebral Cortex* 17: 1766–1781.

Kolodny, O. & Edelman, S. (2018). The evolution of the capacity for language: the ecological context and adaptive value of a process of cognitive hijacking. *Philosophical Transactions of the Royal Society B* 373: 20170052.

König, P. (1994). A method for the quantification of synchrony and oscillatory properties of neuronal. *Journal of Neuroscience Methods* 54: 31–37.

König, P., Engel, A. K., & Singer, W. (1995). Relation between oscillatory activity and long-range synchronization in cat visual cortex. *PNAS* 92: 290–294.

Konopka, G. & Roberts, T. F. (2016). Insights into the neural and genetic basis of vocal communication. *Cell* 164: 1269–1276.

Kopell, N., Börgers, C., Pervouchine, D., Malerba, P., & Tort, A. (2010). Gamma and theta rhythms in biophysical models of hippocampal circuits. In Cutsuridis, V., Graham, B. P., Cobb, S., & Vida, I. (eds.). *Hippocampal Microcircuits: A Computational Modeler's Resource Book*. New York: Springer. 423–457.

Kopell, N. J., Gritton, H. J., Whittington, M. A., & Kramer, M. A. (2014). Beyond the connectome: the dynome. *Neuron* 83: 1319–1328.

Kopell, N. J., Kramer, M. A., Malerba, P., & Whittington, M. A. (2010). Are different rhythms good for different functions? *Frontiers in Human Neuroscience* 4: 187.

Korotkova, T., Fuchs, E. C., Ponomarenko, A., von Engelhardt, J., & Monyer, H. (2010). NMDA receptor ablation on parvalbumin-positive interneurons impairs hippocampal synchrony, spatial representations, and working memory. *Neuron* 68(3): 557–569.

Kösem, A. & van Wassenhove, V. (2016). Oscillatory neural activity controls the encoding of continuous speech. Talk presented at the 20th International Conference on Biomagnetism (BioMag 2016), Seoul.

Kösem, A. & van Wassenhove, V. (2017). Distinct contributions of low- and high-frequency neural oscillations to speech comprehension. *Language, Cognition and Neuroscience* 32(5): 536–544.

Kotz, S. A., Schwartze, M., & Schmidt-Kassow, M. (2009). Non-motor basal ganglia functions: a review and proposal for a model of sensory predictability in auditory language perception. *Cortex* 45: 982–990.

Koziol, L. F., Budding, D. E., & Suth, A. (2009). *Subcortical Structures and Cognition: Implications for Neuropsychological Assessment*. New York: Springer.

Krakauer, J. W., Ghazanfar, A. A., Gomez-Marin, A., MacIver, M. A., & Poeppel, D. (2017). Neuroscience needs behaviour: correcting a reductionist bias. *Neuron* 93: 480–490.

Kramer, M. A. & Eden, U. T. (2013). Assessment of cross-frequency coupling with confidence using generalized linear models. *Journal of Neuroscience Methods* 220 (1): 64–74.

Kriegeskorte, N. & Storrs, K. R. (2016). Grid cells for conceptual space? *Neuron* 92: 280–284.

Kristan Jr., W. B. (2016). Early evolution of neurons. *Current Biology* 26: R949–R954.

Kropotkin, P. (2010[1908]). *Modern Science and Anarchism*. Whitefish, MT: Kessinger Publishing.

Kucyi, A. (2018). Just a thought: how mind-wandering is represented in dynamic brain connectivity. *NeuroImage* 180(B): 505–514.

Kuhlwilm, M. & Boeckx, C. (2019). A catalog of single nucleotide changes distinguishing modern humans from archaic hominins. *Scientific Reports* 9: 8463.

Kuhnke, P., Meyer, L., Friederici, A., & Hartwigsen, G. (2017). Left posterior inferior frontal gyrus is causally involved in reordering during sentence processing. *NeuroImage* 148: 254–263.

Kujala, J., Pammer, K., Cornelissen, P., Roebroeck, A., Formisano, E., & Salmelin, R. (2007). Phase coupling in a cerebro-cerebellar network at 8–13 Hz during reading. *Cerebral Cortex* 17: 1476–1485.

Kurth, S., Riedner, B. A., Dean, D. C., O'Muircheartaigh, J., Huber, R., Jenni, O. G., Deoni, S. C. L., & LeBourgeois, M. K. (2017). Travelling slow oscillations during sleep: a marker of brain connectivity in childhood. *Sleep* 40: zsx121.

Lachaux, J. P., Rodriguez, E., Martinerie, J., & Varela, F. J. (1999). Measuring phase synchrony in brain signals. *Human Brain Mapping* 8: 194–208.

Lakatos, I. (1970). Falsification and the methodology of scientific research programmes. In Lakatos, I. & Musgrave, A. (eds.). *Criticism and the Growth of Knowledge.* Cambridge: Cambridge University Press. 8–11.

Lakatos, P., Karmos, G., Mehta, A. D., Ulbert, I., & Schroeder, C. E. (2008). Entrainment of neuronal oscillations as a mechanism of attentional selection. *Science* 320(5872): 110–113.

Lakatos, P., Shah, A. S., Knuth, K. H., Ulbert, I., Karmos, G., & Schroeder, C. E. (2005). An oscillatory hierarchy controlling neuronal excitability and stimulus processing in the auditory cortex. *Journal of Neurophysiology* 94: 1904–1911.

Lam, N. H. L., Hultén, A., Hagoort, P., & Schoffelen, J.-M. (2018). Robust neuronal oscillatory entertainment to speech displays individual variation in lateralisation. *Language, Cognition and Neuroscience* 33(8): 943–954.

Lam, N. H. L., Schoffelen, J-M., Udden, J., Hulten, A., & Hagoort, P. (2016). Neural activity during sentence processing as reflected in theta, alpha, beta, and gamma oscillations. *NeuroImage* 142: 43–54.

Lametti, D. R., Wijdenes, L. O., Bonaiuto, J., Bestmann, S., & Rothwell, J. C. (2016). Cerebellar tDCS dissociates the timing of perceptual decisions from perceptual change in speech. *Journal of Neurophysiology* 116: 2023–2032.

Lane, C., Kanjlia, S., Omaki, A., & Bedny, M. (2015). 'Visual' cortex of congenitally blind adults responds to syntactic movement. *Journal of Neuroscience* 35(37): 12859–12868.

Lapray, D., Lasztoczi, B., Lagler, M., Viney, T. J., Katona, L., Valenti, O., Hartwich, K., Borhegyi, Z., Somogyi, P., & Klausberger, T. (2012). Behavior-dependent specialization of identified hippocampal interneurons. *Nature Neuroscience* 15: 1265–1271.

Lara, A. H. & Wallis, J. D. (2015). The role of prefrontal cortex in working memory: a mini review. *Frontiers in Systems Neuroscience* 9: 173.

Larkum, M. (2013). A cellular mechanism for cortical associations: an organizing principle for the cerebral cortex. *Trends in Neurosciences* 36(3): 141–151.

Larson, B. (2015). Minimal search as a restriction on merge. *Lingua* 156: 57–69.

Larson-Prior, L. J., Oostenveld, R., Della Penna, S., Michalareas, G., Prior, F., Babajani-Feremi, A., Schoffelen, J. M., Marzetti, L., de Pasquale, F., Di Pompeo, F. et al. (2013). Adding dynamics to the human connectome project with MEG. *NeuroImage* 80: 190–201.

Lasnik, H. (2017). The locality of transformation movement: progress and prospects. In McGilvray, J. (ed.). *The Cambridge Companion to Chomsky.* 2nd ed. Cambridge: Cambridge University Press. 29–49.

Lau, E., Phillips, C., & Poeppel, D. (2008). A cortical network for semantics: (de) constructing the N400. *Nature Reviews Neuroscience* 9: 920–933.

Le May, M. & Geschwind, N. (1975). Hemispheric differences in the brains of great apes. *Brain, Behavior, and Evolution* 11: 48–52.

Le Van Quyen, M. & Bragin, A. (2007). Analysis of dynamic brain oscillations: methodological advances. *Trends in Neurosciences* 30: 365–373.

Lee, H., Simpson, G. V., Logothetis, N. K., & Rainer, G. (2005). Phase locking of single neuron activity to theta oscillations during working memory in monkey extrastriate visual cortex. *Neuron* 45: 147–156.

Lee, S. H., Kwan, A. C., Zhang, S., Phoumthipphavong, V., Flannery, J. G., Masmanidis, S. C., et al. (2012). Activation of specific interneurons improves V1 feature selectivity and visual perception. *Nature* 488: 379–383.

Lefebvre, J. L., Kostadinov, D., Chen, W. V., Maniatis, T., & Sanes, J. R. (2012). Protocadherins mediate dendritic self-avoidance in the mammalian nervous system. *Nature* 488: 517–521.

Leivada, E. (2017). What's in (a) label? Neural origins and behavioural manifestations of identity avoidance in language and cognition. *Biolinguistics* 11.SI.

Lemasson, A., Outtara, K., & Zuberbühler, K. (2013). Exploring the gaps between primate calls and human language. Botha, R. & Everaert, M. (eds.). *The Evolutionary Emergence of Language: Evidence and Inference*. Oxford: Oxford University Press. 181–203.

Lenneberg, E. H. (1964). A biological perspective of language. In Lenneberg, E. H. (ed.). *New Directions in the Study of Language*. Cambridge, MA: MIT Press. 65–88.

Lenneberg, E. H. (1967). *Biological Foundations of Language*. New York: John Wiley & Sons.

Leong, V., Byrne, E., Clackson, K., Harte, N., Lam, S., Barbaro, K. D., & Wass, S. (2017). Infants' neural oscillatory processing of theta-rate speech patterns exceeds adults'. *bioRxiv*. http://dx.doi.org/10.1101/108852

Leong, V. & Goswami, U. (2015). Acoustic-emergent phonology in the amplitude envelope of child-directed speech. *PLoS ONE* 10(12): 1–37.

Leszczynski, M., Barczak, A., Kajikawa, Y., Ulbert, I., Falchier, A., Tal, I., Haegens, S., Melloni, L., Knight, R., & Schroeder, C. (2019). Dissociation of broadband high-frequency activity and neuronal firing in the neocortex. *bioRxiv*. https://doi.org/10.1101/531368

Leszczyński, M., Fell, J., & Axmacher, N. (2015). Rhythmic working memory activation in the human hippocampus. *Cell Reports* 13: 1–11.

Leszczynski, M., Fell, J., Jensen, O., & Axmacher, N. (2017). Alpha activity in the ventral and dorsal visual stream controls information flow during working memory. *bioRxiv*. http://dx.doi.org/10.1101/180166

Letinic, K. & Rakic, P. (2001). Telencephalic origin of human thalamic gabaergic neurons. *Nature Neuroscience* 4: 931–936.

Leung, S., Mareschal, D., Rowsell, R., Simpson, D., Iaria, L., Grbic, A., & Kaufman, J. (2016). Oscillatory activity in the infant brain and the representation of small numbers. *Frontiers in Systems Neuroscience* 10: 4.

Leventhal, D. K., Gage, G. J., Schmidt, R., Pettibone, J. R., Case, A. C., & Berke, J. D. (2012). Basal ganglia beta oscillations accompany cue utilization. *Neuron* 73: 523–536.

Lever, C., Kaplan, R., & Burgess, N. (2014). The function of oscillations in the hippocampal formation. Derdikman, D. & Knierim, J. J. (eds.). *Space, Time and Memory in the Hippocampal Formation*. Wein: Springer. 303–350.

Levins, R. & Lewontin, R. (1985). *The Dialectical Biologist*. Cambridge, MA: Harvard University Press.

Levitis, D. A., Lidicker, W. Z., & Freund, G. (2009). Behavioural biologists don't agree on what constitutes behaviour. *Animal Behavior* 78: 103–110.

Lewis, A. G. & Bastiaansen, M. (2015). A predictive coding framework for rapid neural dynamics during sentence-level language comprehension. *Cortex* 68: 155–168.

Lewis, A. G., Lemhöfer, K., Schoffelen, J.-M., & Schriefers, H. (2016). Gender agreement violations modulate beta oscillatory dynamics during sentence comprehension: a comparison of second language learners and native speakers. *Neuropsychologia* 89: 254–272.

Lewis, A. G., Schoffelen, J-M., Schriefers, H., & Bastiaansen, M. (2016). A predictive coding perspective on beta oscillations during sentence-level language comprehension. *Frontiers in Human Neuroscience* 10: 85.

Lewis, A. G., Wang, L., & Bastiaansen, M. (2015). Fast oscillatory dynamics during language comprehension: unification versus maintenance and prediction? *Brain & Language* 148: 51–63.

Lewis, D. (1969). *Convention: A Philosophical Study.* Cambridge: Harvard University Press.

Lewis, L. D., Setsompop, K., Rosen, B. R., & Polimeni, J. R. (2016). Fast fMRI can detect oscillatory neural activity in humans. *PNAS* 113(43): E6679–E6685.

Lewis, S. & Phillips, C. (2015). Aligning grammatical theories and language processing models. *Journal of Psycholinguistic Research* 44: 27–46.

Lewontin, Richard C. (1983). Gene, organism, and environment. In Bendall, D. S. (ed.). *Evolution from Molecules to Men.* Cambridge: Cambridge University Press. 273–285.

Li, M. & Tsien, J. Z. (2017). Neural code – *neural self-information theory* on how cell-assembly code rises from spike time and neuronal variability. *Frontiers in Cellular Neuroscience* 11: 236.

Li, X., Crow, T. J., Hopkins, W. D., Gong, Q., & Roberts, N. (2018). Human torque is not present in chimpanzee brain. *NeuroImage* 165: 285–293.

Li, X., Shao, X., Xia, J., & Xu, X. (2019). The cognitive and neural oscillatory mechanisms underlying the facilitating effect of rhythm regularity on speech comprehension. *Journal of Neurolinguistics* 49: 155–167.

Lieberman, P. (2000). *Human Language and Our Reptilian Brain: The Subcortical Bases of Speech, Syntax, and Thought.* Cambridge, MA: Harvard University Press.

Lieberman, P. (2006). *Toward an Evolutionary Biology of Language.* Cambridge, MA: Harvard University Press.

Lieberman, P. (2015). Language did not spring forth 100,000 years ago. *PLoS Biology* 13(2): e1002064.

Lightfoot, D. (2011). Natural selection-itis. In Gibson, K. R. & Tallerman, M. (eds.). *The Oxford Handbook of Language Evolution.* Oxford: Oxford University Press. 313–317.

Lightfoot, D. (2020). *Born to Parse: Invention and Variation.*

Lim, S.-J., Wöstmann, M., & Obleser, J. (2015). Selective attention to auditory memory neurally enhances perceptual precision. *Journal of Neuro-science* 35(49): 16094–16104.

Lisman, J. E. & Buzsáki, G. (2008). A neural coding scheme formed by the combined function of gamma and theta oscillations. *Schizophrenia Bulletin* 34 (5): 974–980.

Lisman, J. E. & Idiart, M. A. (1995). Storage of 7 +/- 2 short-term memories in oscillatory subcycles. *Science* 267(5203): 1512–1515.

Lisman, J. E. & Jensen, O. (2013). The theta-gamma neural code. *Neuron* 77: 1002–1016.

Liu, Z., Fukunaga, M., de Zwart, J. A., & Duyn, J. H. (2010). Large-scale spontaneous fluctuations and correlations in brain electrical activity observed with magnetoencephalography. *NeuroImage* 51(1): 102–111.

Llinás, R. (2001). *I of the Vortex: From Neurons to Self.* Cambridge, MA: MIT Press.

Lobina, D. J. (2017). *Recursion: A Computational Investigation into the Representation and Processing of Language.* Oxford: Oxford University Press.

Longuet-Higgins, H. C. (1972). The algorithmic description of natural language. *Proceedings of the Royal Society of London B Biological Sciences* 182: 255–276.

Lopes-dos-Santos, V., Conde-Ocazionez, S., Nicolelis, M. A. L., Ribeiro, S. T., & Tort, A. B. L. (2011). Neuronal assembly detection and cell membership specification by principal component analysis. *PLoS ONE* 6(6): e20996.

Lourenço, J. & Bacci, A. (2017). Human-specific cortical synaptic connections and their plasticity: is that what makes us human? *PLoS Biology* 15(1): e2001378.

Lowet, E., Roberts, M. J., Bonizzi, P., Karel, J., & De Weerd, P. (2016). Quantifying neural oscillatory synchronization: a comparison between spectral coherence and phase-locking value approaches. *PLoS ONE* 11(1): e0146443.

Lu, M., Donamayor, N., Münte, T. F., & Bahlmann, J. (2017). Event-related potentials and neural oscillations dissociate level of cognitive control. *Behavioural Brain Research* 320: 154–164.

Lucas, B. & Hardin, J. (2017). Mind the (sr)GAP – roles of Slit-Robo GAPs in neurons, brains and beyond. *Journal of Cell Science* 130: 3965–3974.

Luck, S.J. (2014). An Introduction to the Event-Related Potential Technique. 2nd ed. Cambridge, MA: MIT Press.

Lundqvist, M., Herman, P., & Lansner, A. (2011). Theta and gamma power increases and alpha/beta power decreases with memory load in an attractor network model. *Journal of Cognitive Neuroscience* 23: 3008–3020.

Lundqvist, M., Rose, J., Herman, P., Brincat, S. L., Buschman, T. J., Miller, E. K. (2016). Gamma and beta bursts underlie working memory. *Neuron* 90: 1–13.

MacDonald, C. J., Lepage, K. Q., Eden, U. T., & Eichenbaum, H. (2011). Hippocampal 'time cells' bridge the gap in memory for discontiguous events. *Neuron* 71: 737–749.

Machens, C. K., Romo, R., & Brody, C. D. (2005). Flexible control of mutual inhibition: a neural model of two-interval discrimination. *Science* 307(5712): 1121–1124.

MacSweeney, M., Campbell, R., Woll, B., Brammer, M. J., Giampietro, V., David, A. S., Calvert, G. A., Machens, C. K., Romo, R., & Brody, C. D. (2005). Flexible control of mutual inhibition: a neural model of two-interval discrimination. *Science* 307(5712): 1121–1124.

Mai, G., Minett, J. W., Wang, W. S-Y. (2016). Delta, theta, beta, and gamma brain oscillations index levels of auditory sentence processing. *NeuroImage* 113: 516–528.

Maidenbaum, S., Miller, J., Stein, J. M., & Jacobs, J. (2018). Grid-like hexadirectional modulation of human entorhinal theta oscillations. *PNAS* 115(42): 10798–10803.

Maier, A., Adams, G. K., Aura, C., & Leopold, D. A. (2010). Distinct superficial and deep laminar domains of activity in the visual cortex during rest and stimulation. *Front. Syst. Neurosci.* 4: 31.

Mainen, Z. F. & Sejnowski, T. J. (1995). Reliability of spike timing in neocortical neurons. *Science* 268(5216): 1503–1506.

Makeig, S., Westerfield, M., Jung, T. P., Enghoff, S., Townsend, J., Courchesne, E., & Sejnowski, T. J. (2002). Dynamic brain sources of visual evoked responses. *Science* 295: 690–694.

Makuuchi, M., Bahlmann, J., Anwander, A., & Friederici, A. D. (2009). Segregating the core computational faculty of human language from working memory. *PNAS* 106: 8362–8367.

Malekmohammadi, M., Elias, W. J., & Pouratian, N. (2015). Human thalamus regulates cortical activity via spatially specific and structurally constrained phase-amplitude coupling. *Cerebral Cortex* 25: 1618–1628.

Mancini, S. (2018). When grammar and parsing agree. *Frontiers in Psychology* 9: 336.

Männel, C. & Friederici, A. D. (2011). Intonational phrase structure processing at different stages of syntax acquisition: ERP studies in 2-, 3-, and 6-year-old children. *Developmental Science* 14(4): 786–798.

Maris, E., Fries, P., & van Ede, F. (2016). Diverse phase relations among neuronal rhythms and their potential function. *Trends in Neurosciences* 39(2): 86–99.

Maris, E., van Vugt, M., & Kahana, M. (2011). Spatially distributed patterns of oscillatory coupling between high-frequency amplitudes and low-frequency phases in human iEEG. *NeuroImage* 54: 836–850.

Mariscal, M. G., Levin, A. R., Gabard-Durnam, L. J., Tager-Flusberg, H., & Nelson, C. A. (2019). Developmental changes in EEG phase amplitude coupling and phase preference over the first three years after birth. *bioRxiv.* https://doi.org/10.1101/818583

Marler, P. (1998). Animal communication and human language. In Jablonski, N. G. & Aiello, L. C. (eds.). *The Origin and Diversification of Language.* San Francisco, CA: California Academy of Sciences. 1–19.

Marr, D. (1982). *Vision: A Computational Investigation into the Human Representation and Processing of Visual Information.* New York: Freeman.

Marr, D. & Poggio, T. (1976). *From Understanding Computation to Understanding Neural Circuitry.* AI Memos (1959–2004).

Mars, R. B., Eichert, N., Jbabdi, S., Verhagen, L. & Rushworth, M. F. S. (2018). Connectivity and the search for specializations in the language-capable brain. *Current Opinion in Behavioral Sciences* 21: 19–26.

Martin, A. (2016). Language processing as cue integration: grounding the psychology of language in perception and neurophysiology. *Frontiers in Psychology* 7: 120.

Martin, A., & Doumas, L. A. A. (2017). A mechanism for the cortical computation of hierarchical linguistic structure. *PLoS Biology* 15: e2000663.

Martin, C. (2016). The cryptic cortex. *Current Biology* 26: R941–R945.

Martin, C. & Ravel, N. (2014). Beta and gamma oscillatory activities associated with olfactory memory tasks: different rhythms for different functional networks? *Frontiers in Behavioral Neuroscience* 8: 218.

Martins, M. D. & Villringer, A. (2018). The human arcuate fasciculus provides specific advantages to process complex sequential stimuli, not hierarchies in general. In Cuskley, C., Flaherty, M., McCrohon, L., Little, H., Ravignani, A., & Verhoef, T. (eds.). *The Evolution of Language: Proceedings of the 12th International Conference (Evolang 12)*. Torun: Nicolaus Copernicus University. 287–289.

Martins, P. T. (2017). There is no place for markedness in biologically-informed phonology. In Samuels, B. D. (ed.). *Beyond Markedness in Formal Phonology*. Amsterdam: John Benjamins.

Martins, P. T. & Boeckx, C. (2014). Attention mechanisms and the mosaic evolution of speech. *Frontiers in Psychology* 5: 1463.

Martorell, J. (2018). Merging generative linguistics and psycholinguistics. *Frontiers in Psychology* 9: 2283.

Martorell, J., Morucci, P., Mancini, S., & Molinaro, N. (2020). Sentence processing: how words generate syntactic structures in the brain. *PsyArXiv* doi.org/10.31234/osf .io/3utpv

Mas-Herrero, E. & Marco-Pallarés, J. (2016). Theta oscillations integrate functionally segregated sub-regions of the medial prefrontal cortex. *NeuroImage* 143: 166–174.

Matchin, W. (2016). Brain and syntax: part 2. *Faculty of Language*, 3 September: http:// facultyoflanguage.blogspot.co.uk/2016/09/brains-and-syntax-part-2.html

Matchin, W. (2018). A neuronal retuning hypothesis of sentence-specificity in Broca's area. *Psychonomic Bulletin & Review* 25: 1682–1694.

Matchin, W., Hammerly, C., & Lau, E. (2017). The role of the IFG and pSTS in syntactic prediction: Evidence from a parametric study of hierarchical structure in fMRI. *Cortex* 88: 106–123.

Matchin, W. & Hickok, G. (2016). 'Syntactic perturbation' during production activates the right IFG, but not Broca's area or the ATL. *Frontiers in Psychology* 7: 241.

Matchin, W. & Hickok, G. (2019). The cortical organization of syntax. *To appear in Cerebral Cortex*.

Matchin, W., Sprouse, J., & Hickok, G. (2014). A structural distance effect for backward anaphora in Broca's area: an fMRI study. *Brain and Language* 138: 1–11.

Matsunaga, E. & Okanoya, K. (2014). Cadherins: potential regulators in the faculty of language. *Current Opinion in Neurobiology* 28: 28–33.

Mayberry, R. I., Davenport, T., Roth, A., & Halgren, E. (2018). Neurolinguistic processing when the brain matures without language. *Cortex* 99: 390–403.

Mazaheri, A., Coffey-Corina, S., Mangun, G. R., Bekker, E. M., Berry, A. S., & Corbett, B. A. 2010. Functional disconnection of frontal cortex and visual cortex in attention-deficit/hyperactivity disorder. *Biological Psychiatry* 67: 617–623.

McCauley, S. M., Isbilen, E. S., & Christiansen, M. H. (2017). Chunking ability shapes sentence processing at multiple levels of abstraction. Gunzelmann, G., Howes, A., Tenbrink, T., & Davelaar, E. J. (eds.). *Proceedings of the 39th Annual Conference of the Cognitive Science Society*. Austin, TX: Cognitive Science Society. 2681–2686.

McCormick, D. A., McGinley, M. J., & Salkoff, D. B. (2015). Brain state dependent activity in the cortex and thalamus. *Current Opinion in Neurobiology* 31: 133–140.

McGhee, G. (1998). *Theoretical Morphology*. Columbia University Press.

McGilchrist, I. (2010). *The Master and His Emissary: The Divided Brain and the Making of the Western World*. Yale University Press.

McGilvray, J. (2013). The philosophical foundations of biolinguistics. In Boeckx, C. & Grohmann, K. (eds.). *The Cambridge Handbook of Biolinguistics* Cambridge: Cambridge University Press. 22–46.

Medeiros, D. P. (2008). Optimal growth in phrase structure. *Biolinguistics* 2(3): 152–195.

Meltzoff, A. N. & Moore, M. K. (1997). Explaining facial imitation: a theoretical model. *Early Development and Parenting* 6: 179–192.

Mendoza, G. & Merchant, H. (2014). Motor system evolution and the emergence of high cognitive functions. *Progress in Neurobiology* 122: 73–93.

Merchant, J. (2001). *The Syntax of Silence: Sluicing, Islands, and the Theory of Ellipsis*. Oxford: Oxford University Press.

Mesgarani, N., Cheung, C., Johnson, K., & Chang, E. F. (2014). Phonetic features encoding in human superior temporal gyrus. *Science* 343: 1006–1010.

Mesulam, M. M, Thompson, C. K., Weintraub, S., & Rogalski, E. J. (2015). The Wernicke conundrum and the anatomy of language comprehension in primary progressive aphasia. *Brain* 138(8): 2423–2437.

Meyer, L. (2018). The neural oscillations of speech processing and language comprehension: state of the art and emerging mechanisms. *European Journal of Neuroscience* 48(7): 2609–2621.

Meyer, L. (2019). The neural oscillations of language processing: Examples from German. Talk presented at Public Lecture. University of Georgia, Athens, GA. 2019-02-20-2019-02-20.

Meyer, L., Grigutsch, M., Schmuck, N., Gaston, P., & Friederici, A. D. (2015). Frontal-posterior theta oscillations reflect memory retrieval during sentence comprehension. *Cortex* 71: 205–218.

Meyer, L. & Gumbert, M. (2018). Synchronization of electrophysiological responses with speech benefits syntactic information processing. *Journal of Cognitive Neuroscience* 11: 1–9.

Meyer, L., Henry, M. J., Gaston, P., Schmuck, N., & Friederici, A. (2017). Linguistic bias modulates interpretation of speech via neural delta-band oscillations. *Cerebral Cortex* 7(9): 4293–4302.

Meyer, L., Obleser, J., & Friederici, A. (2013). Left parietal alpha enhancement during working memory-intensive sentence processing. *Cortex* 49(3): 711–721.

Meyer, L., Sun, Y., & Martin, A. E. (2019). Synchronous, but not entrained: exogenous and endogenous cortical rhythms of speech and language processing. *Language, Cognition, and Neuroscience*. DOI:10.1080/23273798.2019.1693050

Michelmann, S., Bowman, H., & Hanslmayr, S. (2016). The temporal signature of memories: identification of a general mechanism for dynamic memory replay in humans. *PLoS Biology* 14(8): e1002528.

Miłkowski, M. (2012). Limits of computational explanation of cognition. In Müller, V. C. (ed.). *Philosophy and Theory of Artificial Intelligence*. New York: Springer. 69–84.

Miller, I. F., Barton, R. A., & Nunn, C. L. (2019). Quantitative uniqueness of human brain evolution revealed through phylogenetic comparative analysis. *eLife* 8: e41250.

Miller, K. J., Hermes, D., Honey, C. J., Sharma, M., Rao, R. P., den Nijs, M., Fetz, E. E., Sejnowski, T. J., Hebb, A. O., Ojemann, J. G., Makeig, S., & Leuthardt, E. C. (2010). Dynamic modulation of local population activity by rhythm phase in human occipital cortex during a visual search task. *Frontiers in Human Neuroscience* 4: 197.

Milne, A. E., Wilson, B., & Christiansen, M. H. (2018). Structured sequence learning across sensory modalities in humans and nonhuman primates. *Current Opinion in Behavioral Sciences* 21: 39–48.

Mišić, B. & Sporns, O. (2016). From regions to connections and networks: new bridges between brain and behavior. *Current Opinion in Neurobiology* 40: 1–7.

Mišić, B., Goni, J., Betzel, R. F., Sporns, O., & McIntosh, A. R. (2014). A network convergence zone in the hippocampus. *PLoS Computational Biology* 10: e1003982.

Mithun, M. (2015). Gender and culture. In Corbett, G. G. (ed.). *The Expression of Gender*. Berlin: Walter de Gruyter. 131–160.

Miyagawa, S., Berwick, R. C., & Okanoya, K. (2013). The emergence of hierarchical structure in human language. *Frontiers in Psychology* 4: 71.

Mohammad-Rezazadeh, I., Frohlich, J., Loo, S. K., & Jeste, S. S. (2016). Brain connectivity in autism spectrum disorder. *Current Opinion in Neurobiology* 29: 137–147.

Mohr J. P., Pessin, M. S., Finkelstein, S., Funkenstein, H. H., Duncan, G. W., & Davis K. R. (1978). Broca aphasia: pathologic and clinical. *Neurology* 28: 311–324.

Molinaro, N. & Lizarazu, M. (2018). Delta(but not theta)-band cortical entrainment involves speech-specific processing. *European Journal of Neuroscience* 48(7): 2642–2650.

Molinaro, N., Paz-Alonso, P. M., Duñabeitia, J. A., & Carreiras, M. (2015). Combinatorial semantics strengthens angular-anterior temporal coupling. *Cortex* 65: 113–127.

Mollo, G., Cornelissen, P. L., Millman, R. E., Ellis, A. W., & Jefferies, E. (2017). Oscillatory dynamics supporting semantic cognition: MEG evidence for the contribution of the anterior temporal lobe hub and modality-specific spokes. *PLoS ONE* 12(1): e0169269.

Molnár, G., Oláh, S., Komlósi, G., Füle, M., Szabadics, J., Varga, C., Barzó, P., & Tamás, G. (2008). Complex events initiated by individual spikes in the human cerebral cortex. *PLoS Biology* 6(9): e222.

Moltmann, F. (Forthcoming). Levels of ontology and natural language: the case of the ontology of parts and wholes. In Miller, J. (ed). *The Language of Ontology*. Oxford: Oxford University Press.

Momenian, M., Nilipour, R., Samar, R. G., Oghabian, M. A., & Cappa, S. (2016). Neural correlates of verb and noun processing: an fMRI study of Persian. *Journal of Neurolinguistics* 37: 12–21.

Momma, S. (2016). Parsing, generation, and grammar. PhD dissertation. University of Maryland.

Montalbetti, M. (1984). *After Binding*. PhD thesis, MIT.

Montgomery, S. H., Mundy, N. I., & Barton, R. A. (2016). Brain evolution and development: adaptation, allometry and constraint. *Proceedings of the Royal Society B* 283: 20160433.

Moore, R. (2017). Gricean communication and cognitive development. *Philosophical Quarterly* 67(267): 303–326.

Moore, R. (2018). Gricean communication, joint action, and the evolution of cooperation. *Topoi* 37: 329–341.

Moreno, A., Limousin, F., Dehaene, S., & Pallier, C. (2018). Brain correlates of constituent structure in sign language comprehension. *NeuroImage* 167: 151–161.

Moro, A. (2006). Copular sentences. In Everaert, M. & van Riemsdijk, H. (eds.). *The Blackwell Companion to Syntax II*. Oxford: Blackwell. 1–23.

Moro, A. (2014). On the similarity between syntax and actions. *Trends in Cognitive Sciences* 18(3): 109–110.

Moro, A. (2015). *The Boundaries of Babel: The Brain and the Enigma of Impossible Languages*. 2nd ed. Cambridge, MA: MIT Press.

Morton, N. W., Sherrill, K. R., & Preston, A. R. (2017). Memory integration constructs maps of space, time, and concepts. *Current Opinion in Behavioral Sciences* 17: 161–168.

Müller, F. M. (1866). *Lectures on the Science of Language: Delivered at the Royal Institution of Great Britain in April, May, & June 1861*. London: Longmans, Green.

Müller, G. B. (2008). EvoDevo as a discipline. In Minelli, A. & Fusco, G. (eds.). *Evolving Pathways: Key Themes in Evolutionary Developmental Biology*. Cambridge: Cambridge University Press. 3–29.

Muller, L., Chavane, F., Reynolds, J., & Sejnowski, T. J. (2018). Cortical travelling waves: mechanisms and computational principles. *Nature Reviews Neuroscience* 19: 255–268.

Murakami, S. & Okada, Y. (2006). Contributions of principal neocortical neurons to magnetoencephalography and electroencephalography signals. *Journal of Physiology* 575: 925–936.

Murphy, E. (2015a). Labels, cognomes and cyclic computation: an ethological perspective. *Frontiers in Psychology* 6: 715.

Murphy, E. (2015b). The brain dynamics of linguistic computation. *Frontiers in Psychology* 6: 1515.

Murphy, E. (2016a). A theta-gamma neural code for feature set composition with phase-entrained delta nestings. *UCL Working Papers in Linguistics* 28: 1–23.

Murphy, E. (2016b). Evolutionary monkey oscillomics: generating linking hypotheses from preserved brain rhythms. *Theoretical Linguistics* 42(1–2): 117–137.

Murphy, E. (2016c). The human oscillome and its explanatory potential. *Biolinguistics* 10: 6–20.

Murphy, E. (2016d). A pragmatic oscillome: aligning visual attentional mechanisms with language comprehension. *Frontiers in Systems Neuroscience* 10: 72.

Murphy, E. (2017a). Acquiring the impossible: developmental stages of copredication. *Frontiers in Psychology* 8: 1072.

Murphy, E. (2017b). Implications of travelling weakly coupled oscillators for the cortical language circuit. *UCL Working Papers in Linguistics* 29: 24–29.

Murphy, E. (2018a). A domesticated code: on the emergence of the oscillatory basis of phrase structure. Cuskley, C., Flaherty, M., McCrohon, L., Little, H., Ravignani, A., & Verhoef, T. (eds.). *The Evolution of Language: Proceedings of the 12th International Conference (Evolang 12)*. Torun: Nicolaus Copernicus University. 335–338.

Murphy, E. (2018b). Interfaces (travelling oscillations) + recursion (delta-theta code) = language. In Luef, E. & Manuela, M. (eds.). *The Talking Species: Perspectives on the Evolutionary, Neuronal and Cultural Foundations of Language*. Graz: Unipress Graz Verlag. 251–269.

Murphy, E. (2019). No country for Oldowan men: emerging factors in language evolution. *Frontiers in Psychology* 10: 1448.

Murphy, E. & Benítez-Burraco, A. (2016). Bridging the gap between genes and language deficits in schizophrenia: an oscillopathic approach. *Frontiers in Human Neuroscience* 10: 422.

Murphy, E. & Benítez-Burraco, A. (2017). Language deficits in schizophrenia and autism as related oscillatory connectomopathies: an evolutionary account. *Neuroscience and Biobehavioral Reviews* 83: 742–764.

Murphy, E. & Benítez-Burraco, A. (2018). Paleo-oscillomics: inferring aspects of Neanderthal language abilities from gene regulation of neural oscillations. *Journal of Anthropological Sciences* 96: 111–124.

Murphy, E., & Shim, J.-Y. (2020). Copy invisibility and (non)categorial labeling. *Linguistic Research* 33(1): 177–198.

Muthukumaraswamy, S. D., Edden, R. A. E., Jones, D. K., Swettenham, J. B., & Singh, K. D. (2009). Resting GABA concentration predicts peak gamma frequency and fMRI amplitude in response to visual stimulation in humans. *PNAS* 106: 8356–8361.

Nadeau, S. E. & Crosson, B. (1997). Subcortical aphasia. *Brain and Language* 58: 355–402, discussion 418–423.

Najjar, R. & Brooker, R. J. (2017). Delta-beta coupling is associated with paternal caregiving behaviors during preschool. *International Journal of Psychophysiology* 112: 31–39.

Nandi, B., Swiatek, P., Kocsis, B., & Ding, M. (2019). Inferring the direction of rhythmic neural transmission via inter-regional phase-amplitude coupling (ir-PAC). *Scientific Reports* 9: 6933.

Narita, H. (2009). Full interpretation of optimal labeling. *Biolinguistics* 3(2–3): 213–254.

Narita, H. (2011). Phasing in full interpretation. PhD thesis, Harvard University.

Narita, H. (2012). Phase cycles in service of projection-free syntax. In Gallego, Á. J. (ed.). *Phases: Developing the Framework*. Boston: Walter de Gruyter. 125–172.

Narita, H. (2014a). *Endocentric Structuring of Projection-free Syntax*. Amsterdam: John Benjamins.

Narita, H. (2014b). *{t, t}. Poster presented at the 32nd West-Coast Conference on Formal Linguistics (WCCFL 32), University of Southern California.

Narita, H. & Fujita, K. (2010). A naturalist reconstruction of minimalist and evolutionary biolinguistics. *Biolinguistics* 4(4): 356–376.

Narita, H. & Fujita, K. (2016). Feature-equilibria in syntax. In Fujita, K. & Boeckx, C. (eds.). *Advances in Biolinguistics: The Human Language Faculty and its Biological Basis*. London: Routledge. 20–50.

Narita, H., Kasai, H., Kato, T., Zushi, M., & Fukui, N. (2017). 0-Search and 0-Merge. In Fukui, N. (ed.). *Merge in the Mind-Brain*. New York: Routledge. 127–154.

Neeleman, A. (2013). Comments on Pullum. *Mind & Language* 28(4): 522–531.

Nelson, M. J., Karoui, I. E., Giber, K., Yang, X., Cohen, L., Koopman, H., Cash, S. S., Naccache, L., Hale, J. T., Pallier, C., & Dehaene, S. (2017). Neurophysiological dynamics of phrase-structure building during sentence processing. *PNAS* 114(18): E3669–E3678.

Neubauer A. C. & Fink, A. (2009). Intelligence and neural efficiency. *Neuroscience and Biobehavioral Reviews* 33: 1004–1023.

Neubauer, S., Hublin, J-J., & Gunz, P. (2018). The evolution of modern human brain shape. *Science Advances* 4: eaao5961.

Neubert, F. X., Mars, R. B., Sallet, J., & Rushworth, M. F. (2015). Connectivity reveals relationship of brain areas for reward-guided learning and decision making in human and monkey frontal cortex. *PNAS* 112: E2695–E2704.

Neuper, C., Wortz, M., & Pfurtscheller, G. (2006). ERD/ERS patterns reflecting sensorimotor activation and deactivation. *Progress in Brain Research* 159: 211–222.

Nevins, A. (2010). Two case studies in phonological universals: a view from artificial grammars. *Biolinguistics* 4: 218–233.

Nevins, A. (2016). Lectures on postsyntactic morphology. Ms. University College London.

Newman, S. A., Forgacs, G., & Müller, G. D. (2006). Before programs: the physical origination of multicellular forms. *International Journal of Developmental Biology* 50: 289–299.

Newton, I. (1687). *Philosophiae Naturalis Principia Mathematica*. London.

Neymotin, S. A., Lazarewicz, M. T., Sherif, M., Contreras, D., Finkel, L. H., & Lytton, W. W. (2011). Ketamine disrupts theta modulation of gamma in a computer model of hippocampus. *Journal of Neuroscience* 31(32): 11733–11743.

Neymotin, S. A., Lee, H., Park, E., Fenton, A. A., & Lytton, W. W. (2011). Emergence of physiological oscillation frequencies in a computer model of neocortex. *Frontiers in Computational Neuroscience* 5: 19.

Nieuwland, M. S. & Martin, A. E. (2017). Neural oscillations and a nascent cortico-hippocampal theory of reference. *Journal of Cognitive Neuroscience* 29(5): 896–910.

Ninomiya, T., Dougherty, K., Godlove, D. C., Schall, J. D., & Maier, A. (2015). Microcircuitry of a granular frontal cortex: contrasting laminar connectivity between occipital and frontal areas. *Journal of Neurophysiology* 113: 3242–3255.

Noguchi, Y. & Kakigi, R. (2020). Temporal codes of visual working memory in the human cerebral cortex. *bioRxiv* doi.org/10.1101/2020.04.26.062752

Nosarti, C., Rushe, T. M., Woodruff, P. W. R., Stewart, A. L., Rifkin, L., & Murray, R. M. (2004). Corpus callosum size and very preterm birth: relationship to neuropsychological outcome. *Brain* 127: 2080–2089.

Noser, R. & Byrne, R. W. (2015). Wild chacma baboons (Papio ursinus) remember single foraging episodes. *Animal Cognition* 18(4): 921–929.

Novick, J. M., Trueswell, J. C., & Thompson-Schill, S. L. (2010). Broca's area and language processing: evidence for the cognitive control connection. *Language and Linguistics Compass* 4: 906–924.

Nusbaum, M. P. & Beenhakker, M. P. (2002). A small-systems approach to motor pattern generation. *Nature* 417(6886): 343–350.

O'Keefe, J. & Nadal, L. (1978). *The Hippocampus as a Cognitive Map*. Oxford: Oxford University Press.

O'Meara, D. J. (ed.). (1981). *Neoplatonism and Christian Thought*. Albany, NY: State University of New York Press.

O'Neill, J., Boccara, C. N., Stella, F., Schoenenberger, P., & Csicsvari, J. (2017). Superficial layers of the medial entorhinal cortex replay independently of the hippocampus. *Science* 355: 184–188.

Odden, D. (1986). On the role of the Obligatory Contour Principle in phonological theory. *Language* 62: 353–383.

Oettler, J., Schmid, V. S., Zankl, N., Rey, O., Dress, A., & Heinze, J. (2013). Fermat's principle of least time predicts refraction of ant trails at substrate borders. *PLoS ONE* 8(3): e59739.

Ohira, T. & Uzawa, T. (eds.) (2015). *Mathematical Approaches to Biological Systems: Networks, Oscillations, and Collective Motions*. New York: Springer.

Ohki, T., Gunji, A., Takei, Y., Takahashi, H., Kaneko, Y., Kita, Y., Hironaga, N., Tobimatsu, S., Kamio, Y., Hanakawa, T., Inagaki, M., & Hiraki, K. (2016). Neural oscillations in the temporal pole for a temporally congruent audio-visual speech detection task. *Scientific Reports* 6: 37973.

Ohki, T. & Takei, Y. (2018). Neural mechanisms of mental schema: a triplet of delta, low beta/spindle, and ripple. *European Journal of Neuroscience* 48(7): 2416–2430.

Ohta, S., Fukui, N., & Sakai, K. (2013). Syntactic computation in the human brain: the degree of merger as a key factor. *PLoS ONE* 8(2): e56230.

Ojemann, G. A. (1990). Organization of language cortex derived from investigations during neurosurgery. *Seminars in Neuroscience* 2: 297–306.

Ojima, S. & Okanoya, K. (2014). The non-hierarchical nature of the Chomsky hierarchy-driven artificial-grammar learning. *Biolinguistics* 8: 163–180.

Okanoya, K. (2012). Behavioural factors governing song complexity in Bengalese finches. *International Journal of Comparative Psychology* 25(1): 44–59.

Okanoya, K. (2013). Finite-state song syntax in Bengalese finches: sensorimotor evidence, developmental processes, and formal procedures for syntax extraction. In Bolhuis, J. J. & Everaert, M. (eds.). *Birdsong, Speech, and Language: Exploring the Evolution of Mind and Brain*. Cambridge, MA: MIT Press. 229–242.

Okanoya, K. & Merker, B. (2007). Neural substrates for string-context mutual segmentation: a path to human language. In Lyon, C., Nehaniv, C. L., & Cangelosi, A. (eds.). *Emergence of Communication and Language*. London: Springer. 421–434.

Onton, J., Delorme, A., & Makeig, S. (2005). Frontal midline EEG dynamics during working memory. *NeuroImage* 27: 341–356.

Oseki, Y. (2015). Eliminating pair-Merge. *Proceedings of WCCFL* 32: 303–312.

Oseki, Y. & Marantz, A. (2017). Hierarchical vs. linear syntactic models of morphological processing. Poster presented at the 30th CUNY Conference on Human Sentence Processing, Massachussets Institute of Technology.

Ossandón, T., Jerbi, K., Vidal, J. R., Bayle, D. J., Henaff, M. A., Jung, J., Minotti, L., Bertrand, O., Kahane, P., & Lachaux, J. P. (2011). Transient suppression of broadband gamma power in the default-mode network is correlated with task complexity and subject performance. *Journal of Neuroscience* 31: 14521–14530.

Ota, M. & Skarabela, B. (2016). Reduplicated words are easier to learn. *Language Learning and Development* 12: 380–397.

Ota, M. & Skarabela, B. (2018). Reduplication facilitates early word segmentation. *Journal of Child Language* 45(1): 204–218.

Ott, D. (2017). Strong generative capacity and the empirical base of linguistic theory. *Frontiers in Psychology* 8: 1617.

Ouattara, K., Lemasson, A., & Zuberbühler, K. (2009). Campbell's monkeys concatenate vocalizations into context-specific call sequences. *PNAS* 106: 22026–31.

Overath, T., McDermott, J. H., Zarate, J. M., & Poeppel, D. (2015). The cortical analysis of speech-specific temporal structure revealed by responses to sound quilts. *Nature Neuroscience* 18(6): 903–911.

Pääbo, S. (2014). The human condition – a molecular approach. *Cell* 157: 216–226.

Pajevic, S., Basser, P. J., & Fields, R. D. (2014). Role of myelin plasticity in oscillations and synchrony of neuronal activity. *Neuroscience* 276: 135–147.

Palmer, C., Zapparoli, L., & Kilner, J. M. (2016). A new framework to explain sensorimotor beta oscillations. *Trends in Cognitive Sciences* 20(5): 321–323.

Palomero-Gallagher, N. & Zilles, K. (2019). Differences in cytoarchitecture of Broca's region between human, ape and macaque brains. *Cortex* 118: 132–153.

Palva, J. M. & Palva, S. (2018). Functional integration across oscillation frequencies by cross-frequency phase synchronization. *European Journal of Neuroscience* 48(7): 2399–2406.

Panagiotidis, P. (2014). A minimalist approach to roots. In Kosta, P., Schürcks, L., Franks, S., & Radeva-Bork, T. (eds.). *Minimalism and Beyond: Radicalizing the Interfaces*. Amsterdam: John Benjamins. 287–303.

Panagiotidis, P. (2015). *Categorial Features: A Generative Theory of Word Class Categories*. Cambridge: Cambridge University Press.

Panoz-Brown, D., Corbin, H. E., Dalecki, S. J., Gentry, M., Brotheridge, S., Sluka, C. M., Wu, J-E., & Crystal, J. D. (2016). Rats remember items in context using episodic memory. *Current Biology* 26: 2821–2826.

Panzeri, S., Harvey, C. D., Piasini, E., Latham, P. E., & Fellin, T. (2017). Cracking the neural code for sensory perception by combining statistics, intervention, and behavior. *Neuron* 93: 491–507.

Papadimitriou, C. H., & Vempala, S. S. (2019). Random projection in the brain and computation with assemblies of neurons. Blum, A. (Ed). *Leibniz International Proceedings in Informatics* 57: 1–19.

Papathanasiou, I., & Coppens, P.(2017). *Aphasia and Related Neurogenic Communication Disorders*. 2nd ed. Burlington, MA: Jones & Bartlett Publishers.

Park, H., Ince, R. A. A., Schyns, P. G., Thut, G., & Gross, J. (2018). Representational interactions during audiovisual speech entrainment: redundancy in left posterior superior temporal gyrus and synergy in left motor cortex. *PLoS Biology* 16(8): e2006558.

Park, H., Lee, D. S., Kang, E., Kang, H., Hahm, J., Kim, J. S., Chung, C. K., Jiang, H., Gross, J., & Jensen, O. (2016). Formation of visual memories controlled by gamma power phrase-locked to alpha oscillations. *Scientific Reports* 6: 28092.

Parker, S. T. & McKinney, M. L. (1999). *Origins of Intelligence: The Evolution of Cognitive Development in Monkeys, Apes, and Humans*. Baltimore, MD: Johns Hopkins University Press.

Parnaudeau, S., O'Neill, P. K., Bolkan, S. S., Ward, R. D., Abbas, A. I., Roth, B. L., Balsam, P. D., Gordon, J. A. & Kellendonk, C. (2013). Inhibition of mediodorsal thalamus disrupts thalamofrontal connectivity and cognition. *Neuron* 77: 1151–1162.

Pascanu, R. & Jaeger, H. (2011). A neurodynamical model for working memory. *Neural Networks* 24(2): 199–207.

Pattamadilok, C., Dehaene, S., & Pallier, C. (2016). A role for left inferior frontal and posterior superior temporal cortex in extracting a syntactic tree from a sentence. *Cortex* 75: 44–55.

Patten, T. M., Rennie, C. J., Robinson, P. A., & Gong, P. (2012). Human cortical traveling waves: dynamical properties and correlations with responses. *PLoS ONE* 7: e38392.

Pearce, E., Stringer, C., & Dunbar, R. I. M. (2013). New insights into differences in brain organization between Neanderthals and anatomically modern humans. *Proceedings of the Royal Society B* 280: 20130168.

Pearson, J. (1790). *A Plain and Rational Account of the Nature and Effects of Animal Magnetism: in a Series of Letters*. With Notes and an Appendix. By the editor. Eighteenth Century Collections Online, London.

Peelle, J. E. & Davis, M. H. (2012). Neural oscillations carry speech rhythm through to comprehension. *Frontiers in Psychology* 3: 320.

Peelle, J. E., Gross, J., & Davis, M. H. (2013). Phase-locking responses to speech in human auditory cortex are enhanced during comprehension. *Cerebral Cortex* 23: 1378–1387.

Pefkou, M., Arnal, L. H., Fontolan, L., & Giraud, A.-L. (2017). Theta- and beta-band neural activity reflect independent syllable tracking and comprehension of time-compressed speech. *Journal of Neuroscience* 37(33): 7930–7938.

Penn, D. C., Holyoak, K. J., & Povinelli, D. J. (2008). Darwin's mistake: Explaining the discontinuity between human and nonhuman minds. *Behavioral and Brain Sciences* 31(2): 109–178.

Pepperberg, I. M. (2007). Emergence of linguistic communication: studies on grey parrots. In Lyon, C., Nehaniv, C. L., & Cangelosi, A. (eds.). *Emergence of Communication and Language*. London: Springer. 355–386.

Perani, D., Saccuman, M. C., Scifo, P., Anwander, A., Spada, D., Baldoli, C., Poloniato, A., Lohmann, G., & Friederici, A. D. (2011). Neural language networks at birth. *PNAS* 108: 16056–16061.

Perdomo-Sabotal, A., Kanton, S., Walter, M. B., & Nowick, K. (2014). The role of gene regulatory factors in the evolutionary history of humans. *Current Opinion in Genetics & Development* 29 C: 60–67.

Perrodin, C., Kayser, C., Logothetis, N. K., & Petkov, C. I. (2015). Natural asynchronies in audiovisual communication signals regulate neuronal multisensory interactions in voice-sensitive cortex. *PNAS* 112: 273–278.

Pesaran, B., Nelson, M. J., & Andersen, R. A. (2008). Free choice activates a decision circuit between frontal and parietal cortex. *Nature* 453: 406–409.

Pessoa, L. (2016). Beyond disjoint brain networks: overlapping networks for cognition and emotion. *Behavioral and Brain Sciences* 39: e120.

Petersen, S. E. & Sporns, O. (2015). Brain networks and cognitive architectures. *Neuron* 88: 207–219.

Petersson, K. M. & Hagoort, P. (2012). The neurobiology of syntax: beyond string sets. *Philosophical Transactions of the Royal Society B* 367: 1971–1983.

Petersson, K. M., Folia, V., & Hagoort, P. (2012). What artificial grammar learning reveals about the neurobiology of syntax. *Brain & Language* 120(2): 83–95.

Petkov, C. I., Kayser, C., Steudel, T., Whittingstall, K., Augath, M., & Logothetis, N. K. (2008). A voice region in the monkey brain. *Nature Neuroscience* 11: 367–374.

Petrides, M. & Pandya, D. N. (2009). Distinct parietal and temporal pathways to the homologues of Broca's area in the monkey. *PLoS Biology* 7: e1000170.

Pérez, A., Molinaro, N., Mancini, S., Barraza, P., & Carreiras, M. (2012). Oscillatory dynamics related to the Unagreement pattern in Spanish. *Neuropsychologia* 50(11): 2584–2597.

Pezzulo, G. & Levin, M. (2017). Embodying Markov blankets. Comment on 'Answering Schrödinger's question: Afree-energy formulation' by Maxwell James Désormeau Ramstead et al. *Physics of Life Reviews*.https://doi.org/10.1016/j.plrev.2017.09.001

Pfenning, A. R., Hara, E., Whitney, O., Rivas, M. V., Wang, R., Roulhac, P. L., Howard, J. T., Wirthlin, M., Lovell, P. V., Ganapathy, G. et al. (2014). Convergent transcriptional specializations in the brains of humans and song-learning birds. *Science* 346(6215): 1256846.

Phillips, C. (2003). Linear order and constituency. *Linguistic Inquiry* 34: 37–90.

Piai, V., Meyer, L., Dronkers, N. F., & Knights, R. T. (2016). Neuroplasticity of language in left-hemisphere stroke: evidence linking subsecond electrophysiology and structural connectivity. Poster presented at the Society for the Neurobiology of Language Annual Meeting 2016. 17–20 August.

Piattelli-Palmarini, M. (1974). *A Debate on Bio-linguistics, Endicott House, Dedham, MA (May 20–21, 1974)*. Paris: Centre Royaumont pour une Science de l'Homme.

Piattelli-Palmarini, M. (1989). Evolution, selection, and cognition: from 'learning' to parameter setting in biology and in the study of language. *Cognition* 31: 1–44.

Piattelli-Palmarini, M. (2017). From zero to fifty: considerations on Eric Lenneberg's *Biological Foundations of Language and updates. Biolinguistics* 11.SI.

Piattelli-Palmarini, M., & Uriagereka, J.(2008). Still a bridge too far? Biolinguistic questions for grounding language on brains. *Physics of Life Reviews* 5: 207–224.

Piattelli-Palmarini, M. & Vitiello, G.(2015). Linguistics and some aspects of its underlying dynamics. *Biolinguistics* 9: 96–115

Piattelli-Palmarini, M. & Vitiello, G. (2017). Quantum field theory and the linguistic minimalist program: a remarkable isomorphism. *Journal of Physics: Conference Series* 880(1): 012016.

Pietroski, P. (2002). Function and concatenation. In Preyer, G. & Peter, G. (eds.). *Logical Form and Language*. Oxford: Oxford University Press. 91–117.

Pietroski, P. (2005). *Events and Semantic Architecture*. Oxford: Oxford University Press.

Pietroski, P. (2008). Minimalist meaning, internalist interpretation. *Biolinguistics* 2(4): 317–341.

Pietroski, P. (2018). *Conjoining Meanings: Semantics without Truth Values*. Oxford: Oxford University Press.

Pigliucci, M. & Müller, G. B. (2010). Elements of an extended evolutionary synthesis. In Pigliucci, M. & Müller, G. B. (eds.). *Evolution – The Extended Synthesis*. Cambridge, MA: MIT Press. 3–17.

Pignatelli, M., Beyeler, A., & Leinekugel, X. (2012). Neural circuits underlying the generation of theta oscillations. *Journal of Physiology-Paris* 106: 81–92.

Pika, S. & Bugnyar, T. (2011). The use of referential gestures in ravens (*Corvus corax*) in the wild. *Nature Communications* 2: 560.

Pillay, S. B., Binder, J. R., Humphries, C., Gross, W. L., & Book, D. S. (2017). Lesion localization of speech comprehension deficits in chronic aphasia. *Neurology* 88: 970–975.

Pina, J. E., Bodner, M., & Ermentrout, B. (2018). Oscillations in working memory and neural binding: a mechanism for multiple memories and their interactions. *PLoS Computational Biology* 14(11): e1006517.

Pinker, S. (1999). *How the Mind Works*. New York: W. W. Norton & Company.

Pinker, S. (2015). *Language, Cognition, and Human Nature: Selected Articles*. Oxford: Oxford University Press.

Pinker, S. & Bloom, P. (1990). Natural language and natural selection. *Behavioral and Brain Sciences* 13: 707–784.

Pinotsis, D. A., Buschman, T. J., & Miller, E. K. (2019). Working memory load modulates neuronal coupling. *Cerebral Cortex* 29(4): 1670–1681.

Plato. (1945). *The Republic of Plato*. Trans. F. M. Cornford. Oxford: Oxford University Press.

Poeppel, D. (1996). Neurobiology and linguistics are not yet unifiable. *Behavioral and Brain Sciences* 19: 642–643.

Poeppel, D. (2008). The cartographic imperative: confusing localization and explanation in human brain mapping. *In Bildwelten des Wissens: Vol. 6.1. Bildwelten des wissens*. Akademie Verlag, Berlin, Germany. 13.

Poeppel, D. (2011). Genetics and language: a neurobiological perspective on the missing link(-ing hypothesis). *Journal of Neurodevelopmental Disorders* 3(4): 381–387.

Poeppel, D. (2012). The maps problem and the mapping problem: two challenges for a cognitive neuroscience of speech and language. *Cognitive Neuropsychology* 29: 34–55.

Poeppel, D. (2014). The neuroanatomic and neurophysiological infrastructure for speech and language. *Current Opinion in Neurobiology*. 28C, 142–149.

Poeppel, D. (2017). The influence of Chomsky on the neuroscience of language. In McGilvray, J. (ed.). *The Cambridge Companion to Chomsky*. 2nd ed. Cambridge: Cambridge University Press. 155–174.

Poeppel, D. & Assaneo, M. F. (2020). Speech rhythms and their neural foundations. *Nature Neuroscience*. https://doi.org/10.1038/s41583-020-0304-4

Poeppel, D. & Embick, D. (2005). Defining the relation between linguistics and neuroscience. In Cutler, A. (ed.). *Twenty-First Century Psycholinguistics: Four Cornerstones*. New Jersey: Lawrence Erlbaum. 103–118.

Postle, B. R. (2006). Working memory as an emergent property of the mind and brain. *Neuroscience* 139: 23–38.

Poulisse, C., Wheeldon, L., & Segaert, K. (2019). Evidence against preserved syntactic comprehension in healthy aging. *Journal of Experimental Psychology: Learning, Memory and Cognition* 45(12): 2290–2308.

Powys, J. C. ([1951]2007). *Porius: A Romance of the Dark Ages*. Bond, J. & Krisdóttir, M. (eds.). London: Overlook Duckworth.

Pratt, J., Dawson, N., Morris, B. J., Grent-'t-Jong, T., Roux, F., & Uhlhaas, P. J. (2017). Thalamo-cortical communication, glutamatergic neurotransmission and neural oscillations: a unique window into the origins of ScZ? *Schizophrenia Research* 180: 4–12.

Price, C. J. (2010). The anatomy of language: a review of 100 fMRI studies published in 2009. *Annals of the New Yorks Academy of Sciences* 119: 62–88.

Prindle, A., Liu, J., Asally, M., Ly, S., Garcia-Ojalvo, J., & Süel, G. M. (2015). Ion channels enable electrical communication in bacterial communities. *Nature* 527: 59–63.

Proskovec, A. L., Heinrichs-Graham, E., & Wilson, T. W. (2019). Load modulates the alpha and beta oscillatory dynamics serving verbal working memory. *NeuroImage* 184: 256–265.

Prystauka, Y. & Lewis, A. G. (2019). The power of neural oscillations to inform sentence comprehension: a linguistic perspective. *Language and Linguistics Compass* 13: e12347.

Pu, Y., Cheyne, D., Sun, Y., & Johnson, B. W. (2020). Theta oscillations support the interface between language and memory. *NeuroImage* 215: 116782.

Pulvermüller, F. (2014). The syntax of action. *Trends in Cognitive Sciences* 18(5): 219–220.

Pulvermüller, F., Preissl, H., Eulitz, C., Pantev, C., Lutzenberger, W., Elbert, T., & Birbaumer, N. (1994). Brain rhythms, cell assemblies and cognition: evidence from the processing of words and pseudowords. *Psycoloquy* 5(48): 1–30.

Pylkkänen, L. (2019). The neural basis of combinatory syntax and semantics. *Science* 366: 62–66.

Pylyshyn, Z. W. (1984). *Computation and Cognition*. Cambridge, MA: MIT Press.

Quax, S., Jensen, O., & Tiesinga, P. (2017). Top-down control of cortical gamma-band communication via pulvinar induced phase shifts in the alpha rhythm. *PLoS Computational Biology* 13(5): e1005519.

Quian Quiroga, R. (2012). Concept cells: the building blocks of declarative memory functions. *Nature Reviews Neuroscience* 13: 587–597.

Quian Quiroga, R., Kraskov, A., Koch, C. & Fried, I. (2009). Explicit encoding of multimodal percepts by single neurons in the human brain. *Current Biology* 19: 1308–1313.

Quian Quiroga, R., Reddy, L., Kreiman, G., Koch, C., & Fried, I. (2005). Invariant visual representation by single neurons in the human brain. *Nature* 435: 1102–1107.

Raghavachari, S., Kahana, M. J., Rizzuto, D. S., Caplan, J. B., Kirschen, M. P, Bourgeois, B., Madsen, J. R., & Lisman, J. E. (2001). Gating of human theta oscillations by a working memory task. *Journal of Neuroscience* 21(9): 3175–3183.

Raichle, M. E, MacLeod, A. M., Snyder, A. Z., Powers, W. J., Gusnard, D. A., & Shulman, G. L. (2001). A default mode of brain function. *PNAS* 98: 676–682.

Rakic, P. & Kornack, D. R. (2001). Neocortical expansion and elaboration during primate evolution. In Falk, D. & Gibson, K. R. (eds.). *Evolutionary Anatomy of the Primate Cerebral Cortex*. Cambridge: Cambridge University Press. 30–56.

Ramirez-Villegas, J. F., Logothetis, N. K., & Besserve, M. (2015). Sharp wave-ripple complexes in a reduced model of the hippocampal CA3-CA1 network of the macaque monkey. *BMC Neuroscience* 16(Suppl 1): P15.

Ramkumar, P., Acuna, D. E., Berniker, M., Grafton, S. T., Turner, R. S., & Kording, K. P. (2016). Chunking as the result of an efficiency computation trade-off. *Nature Communications* 7: 12176.

Räsänen, O., Doyle, G., & Frank, M. C. (2017). Pre-linguistic segmentation of speech into syllable-like units. *Cognition* 171: 130–150.

Rauschecker, J. P. (1998). Cortical processing of complex sounds. *Current Opinion in Neurobiology* 8: 516–521.

Rauschecker, J. P. (2018). Where did language come from? Precursor mechanisms in nonhuman primates. *Current Opinion in Behavioral Sciences* 21: 195–204.

Ravignani, A., Bowling, D. L., & Fitch, W. T. (2014). Chorusing, synchrony, and the evolutionary functions of rhythm. *Frontiers in Ecology and Evolution* 5: 1118.

Ravignani, A. & Norton, P. (2017). Measuring rhythmic complexity: a primer to quantify and compare temporal structure in speech, movement, and animal vocalizations. *Journal of Language Evolution* 2(1): 4–19.

Ravignani, A., Thompson, B., & Filippi, P. (2018). The evolution of musicality: what can be learned from language evolution research? *Frontiers in Neuroscience* 12: 20.

Ray, S. & Maunsell, J. H. R. (2015). Do gamma oscillations play a role in cerebral cortex? *Trends in Cognitive Sciences* 19(2): 78–85.

Rayner, K., Pollatsek, A., Ashby, J., & Clifton, C. Jr. (2012). *Psychology of Reading*. 2nd ed. New York: Psychology Press.

Reale, M. E., Webb, I. C., Wang, X., Baltazar, R. M., Coolen, L. M., & Lehman, M. N. (2013). The transcription factor Runx2 is under circadian control in the suprachiasmatic nucleus and functions in the control of rhythmic behavior. *PLoS ONE* 8: e54317.

Reboul, A. C. (2015). Why language really is not a communication system: a cognitive view of language evolution. *Frontiers in Psychology* 6: 1434.

Reboul, A. (2017). *Cognition and Communication in the Evolution of Language*. Oxford: Oxford University Press.

Regel, S., Meyer, L., & Gunter, T. C. (2014). Distinguishing neurocognitive processes reflected by P600 effects: evidence from ERPs and neural oscillations. *PLoS ONE* 9 (5): e96840.

Reimann, M. W., Muller, E. B., Ramaswamy, S., & Markram, H. (2015). An algorithm to predict the connectome of neural microcircuits. *Frontiers in Neural Circuits* 9: 28.

Reinhart, T. (2002). The theta system: an overview. *Theoretical Linguistics* 28: 229–290.

Reiss, C. (2003). Quantification in structural descriptions: attested and unattested patterns. *Linguistic Review* 20: 305–338.

Revonsuo, A. (2001). On the nature of explanation in the neurosciences. In Machamer, P. K., Grush, R., & McLaughlin, P. (eds.). *Theory and Method in the Neurosciences*. Pittsburgh, PA: University of Pittsburgh Press. 45–69.

Richards, M. (2011). Deriving the edge: what's in a phase? *Syntax* 14: 74–95.

Richards, N. (2010). *Uttering Trees*. Cambridge, MA: MIT Press.

Richter, C., Thompson, W. H., Bosman, C. A., & Fries, P. (2017). Top-down beta enhances bottom-up gamma. *The Journal of Neuroscience* 37(28): 6698–6711.

Riddle, J., McFerren, A., & Frohlich, F. (2019). Causal evidence for delta-beta and theta-gamma cross-frequency coupling in different dimensions of cognitive control. Poster presented at the 49th Meeting of the Society for Neuroscience, Chicago, 19–23 October.

Riddle, J., Scimeca, J. M., Cellier, D., Dhanani, S., & D'Esposito, M. (2020). Causal evidence for a role of theta and alpha oscillations in the control of working memory. *Current Biology* 30: 1–7.

Riebel, K. & Slater, P. J. B. (2003). Temporal variation in male chaffinch song depends on the singer and the song type. *Behaviour* 140: 269–288.

Riecke, L., Formisano, E., Sorger, B., Baskent, D., & Gaudrain, E.(2018). Neural entrainment to speech modulates speech intelligibility. *Current Biology*. 28: 161–169.

Rieke, F., Warland, D., van Steveninck, R. D. R., & Bialek, W. (1997). *Spikes: Exploring the Neural Code*. Cambridge, MA: MIT Press.

Rimmele, J. M., Sun, Y., Michalareas, G., Ghitza, O., & Poeppel D. (2019). Dynamics of functional networks for syllable and word-level processing. *bioRxiv 584375*. https://doi.org/10.1101/584375

Rizzi, L. (2012). Core linguistic computations: how are they expressed in the mind/brain? *Journal of Neurolinguistics* 25: 489–499.

Rizzi, L. (2016). Monkey morpho-syntax and merge-based systems. *Theoretical Linguistics* 42(1–2): 139–145.

Rizzuto, D. S., Madsen, J. R., Bromfield, E. B., Schulze-Bonhage, A., & Kahana, M. J. (2006). Human neocortical oscillations exhibit theta phase differences between encoding and retrieval. *NeuroImage* 31: 1352–1358.

Rodrigues, F. A., Peron, T. K. DM., Ji, P., & Kurths, J. (2016). The Kuramoto model in complex networks. *Physics Reports* 610: 1–98.

Rodríguez-Martínez, E. I., Barriga-Paulino, C. I., Rojas-Benjumea, M. A., & Gómez, C. M. (2015). Co-maturation of theta and low-beta rhythms during child development. *Brain Topography* 28: 250–260.

Roehm, D., Bornkessel-Schlesewsky, I., & Schlesewsky, M. (2007). The internal structure of the N400: frequency charactersitics of a language related ERP component. *Chaos and Complexity Letters* 2: 365–395.

Rogalsky, C., Rong, F., Saberi, K., & Hickok, G. (2011). Functional anatomy of language and music perception: Temporal and structural factors investigated using fMRI. *Journal of Neuroscience* 31(10): 3843–3852.

Rogers, J. & Hauser, M. (2010). The use of formal language theory in studies of artificial language learning: a proposal for distinguishing the differences between human and nonhuman animal learners. In Hulst, H. (ed.). *Recursion and Human Language*. New York: de Gruyter. 213–232.

Rogers, J., Heinz, J., Bailey, G., Edlefsen, M., Visscher, M., Wellcome, D., & Wibel, S. (2010). On languages piecewise testable in the strict sense. In Ebert, C., Jager, G., & Michaelis, J. (eds.). *Proceedings of the 11th Meeting of the Mathematics of Language Association*. New York: Springer-Verlag. 255–265.

Roll, M., Lindgren, M., Alter, K., & Horne, M. (2012). Time-driven effects on parsing during reading. *Brain & Language* 121: 267–272.

Rommers, J., Dickson, D. S., Norton, J. J. S., Wlotko, E. W., & Federmeier, K. D. (2017). Alpha and theta band dynamics related to sentential constraint and word expectancy. *Language, Cognition and Neuroscience* 32(5): 576–589.

Roux, F. & Uhlhaas, P. J. (2014). Working memory and neural oscillations: alpha-gamma versus theta-gamma codes for distinct WM information? *Trends in Cognitive Sciences* 18: 16–25.

Royer, S., Zemelman, B. V., Losonczy, A., Kim, J., Chance, F., Magee, J. C., & Buzsáki, G. (2012). Control of timing, rate and bursts of hippocampal place cells by dendritic and somatic inhibition. *Nature Neuroscience* 15: 769–775.

Rubio-Garrido, P., Pérez-De-Manzo, F., Porrero, C., Galazo, M. J. & Clascá, F. (2009). Thalamic input to distal apical dendrites in neocortical layer 1 is massive and highly convergent. *Cerebral Cortex* 19: 2380–2395.

Rugani, R., Vallortigara, G., Vallini, B., & Regolin, L. (2011). Asymmetrical number-space mapping in the avian brain. *Neurobiology of Learning and Memory* 95: 231–238.

Russell, B. (1919). *Introduction to Mathematical Philosophy*. London: George Allen & Unwin.

Russell, B. (1948). *Human Knowledge: Its Scope and Limits*. London: George Allen & Unwin.

Russell, E. S. (1916). *Form and Function*. London: John Murray.

Ryan, T. J., Roy, D. S., Pignatelli, M., Arons, A., & Tonegawa, S. (2015). Engram cells retain memory under retrograde amnesia. *Science* 348: 1007–1013.

Saalmann, Y. B., Pinsk, M. A., Wang, L., Li, X., & Kastner, S. (2012). The pulvinar regulates information transmission between cortical areas based on attention demands. *Science* 337: 753–756.

Saalmann, Y. B. (2014). Intralaminar and medial thalamic influence on cortical synchrony, information transmission and cognition. *Frontiers in Systems Neuroscience* 8: 83.

Sabeti, P. C., Schaffner, S. F., Fry, B., Lohmueller, J., Varilly, P., Shamovsky, O., Palma, A., Mikkelsen, T. S. et al. (2006). Positive natural selection in the human lineage. *Science* 312: 1614–1620.

Sadagopan, S., Temiz-Karayol, N. Z., & Voss, H. U. (2015). High-field functional magnetic resonance imaging of vocalization processing in marmosets. *Scientific Reports* 5: 10950.

Salami, M., Itami, C., Tsumoto, T., & Kimura, F. (2003). Change of conduction velocity by regional myelination yields constant latency irrespective of distance between thalamus and cortex. *PNAS* 100: 6174–6179.

Saleem, A. B., Lien, A. D., Krumin, M., Haider, B., Roman Roson, M., Ayaz, A., Reinhold, K., Busse, L., Carandini, M., & Harris, K. D. (2017). Subcortical source and modulation of the narrowband gamma oscillation in mouse visual cortex. *Neuron* 93: 315–322.

Salimpour, Y. & Anderson, W. S. (2019). Cross-frequency coupling based neuro-modulation for treating neurological disorders. *Frontiers in Neuroscience* 13: 125.

Samuels, B. (2015). Biolinguistics in phonology: a prospectus. *Phonological Studies* 18: 161–171.

Samuels, B. D. (2011). *Phonological Architecture: A Biolinguistic Perspective*. Oxford: Oxford University Press.

Sanchez-Vives, M. V., Massimini, M., & Mattia, M. (2017). Shaping the default activity pattern of the cortical network. *Neuron* 94: 993–1001.

Sanchez-Vives, M. V. & McCormick, D. A. (2000). Cellular and network mechanisms of rhythmic recurrent activity in neocortex. *Nature Neuroscience* 3: 1027–1034.

Sanides, F. (1962). *Die Architektonik des Menschlichen Stirnhirns: Zugleich eine Darstellung der Prinzipien Seiner Gestaltung als Spiegel der Stammesgeschichtlichen Differenzierung der Grosshirnrinde*. Berlin/Heidelberg: Springer-Verlag.

Santi, A. & Grodzinsky, Y. (2010). fMRI adaptation dissociates syntactic complexity dimensions. *NeuroImage* 51(4): 1285–1293.

Santi, A. & Grodzinsky, Y. (2012). Broca's area and sentence comprehension: a relationship parasitic on dependency displacement or predictability? *Neuropsychologia* 50: 821–832.

Santi, A., Friederici, A. D., Makuuchi, M., & Grodzinsky, Y. (2015). An fMRI study dissociating distance measures computed by Broca's area in movement processing: clause boundary vs. identity. *Frontiers in Psychology* 6: 654.

Sato, J. R., Biazoli, C. E., Salum, G. A., Gadelha, A., Crossley, N., Vieira, G., & Anés, M. (2016). Connectome hubs at resting state in children and adolescents: reproducibility and psychopathological correlation. *Developmental Cognitive Neuroscience* 20: 2–11.

Sauseng, P., Klimesch, W., Doppelmayr, M., Pecherstorfer, T., Freunberger, R., & Hanslmayr, S. (2005). EEG alpha synchronization and functional coupling during top-down processing in a working memory task. *Human Brain Mapping* 26(2): 148–155.

Sauseng, P., Klimesch, W., Gruber, W. R., Hanslmayr, S., Freunberger, R., & Doppelmayr, M. (2007). Are event-related potential components generated by phase resetting of brain oscillations? A critical discussion. *Neuroscience* 146: 1435–1444.

Sauseng, P., Peylo, C., Lena Biel, A., Friedrich, E. V. C., & Romberg-Taylor, C. (2019). Does cross-frequency phase coupling of oscillatory brain activity contribute to a better understanding of visual working memory? *British Journal of Psychology* 110(2): 245–255.

Saygin, Z. M., Osher, D. E., Norton, E. S., Youssoufian, D. A., Beach, S. A., Feather, S., Gaab, N., Gabrieli, J. D. E., & Kanwisher, N. (2016). Connectivity precedes function in the development of the visual word form area. *Nature Neuroscience* 19: 1250–1255.

Schapiro, A. C., Turk-Browne, N. B., Botvinick, M. M., & Norman, K. A. (2017). Complementary learning systems within the hippocampus: a neural network modeling approach to recomciling episodic memory with statistical learning. *Philosophical Transactions of the Royal Society B* 372(1711): 20160049.

Scharinger, C., Soutschek, A., Schubert, T., & Gerjets, P. (2017). Comparison of the working memory load in N-back and working memory span tasks by means of EEG frequency band power and P300 amplitude. *Frontiers in Human Neuroscience* 11: 6.

Scharinger, M., Bendixen, A., Herrmann, B., Henry, M. J., Mildner, T., & Obleser, J. (2015). Predictions interact with missing sensory evidence in semantic processing areas. *Human Brain Mapping* 37(2): 704–716.

Scheeringa, R. & Fries, P. (2019). Cortical layers, rhythms and BOLD signals. *NeuroImage* 197: 689–698.

Schenker, N. M., Buxhoeveden, D. P., Blackmon, W. L., Amunts, K., Zilles, K., & Semendeferi, K. (2008). A comparative quantitative analysis of cytoarchitecture and minicolumnar organization in Broca's area in humans and great apes. *Journal of Comparative Neurology* 510: 117–128.

Schlenker, P., Chemla, E., Arnold, K., Lemasson, A., Ouattara, K., Keenan, S., Stephan, C., Ryder, R., & Zuberbühler, K. (2014). Monkey semantics: two 'dialects' of Campbell's monkey alarm calls. *Linguistics and Philosophy* 37(6): 439–501.

Schlenker, P., Chemla, E., Schel, A. M., Fuller, J., Gautier, J.-P., Kuhn, J., Veselinović, D., Arnold, K., Cäsar, C., Keenan, S., Lemasson, A., Ouattara, K., Ryder, R., & Zuberbühler, K. (2016). Formal monkey linguistics. *Theoretical Linguistics* 42(1–2): 1–90.

Schmitt, L. I., Wimmer, R. D., Nakajima, M., Happ, M., Mofakham, S., & Halassa, M. M. (2017). Thalamic amplification of cortical connectivity sustains attentional control. *Nature* 545: 219–223.

Schneider, J. M., Abel, A. D., Ogiela, D. A., Middleton, A. E., & Maguire, M. J. (2016). Developmental differences in beta and theta power during sentence processing. *Developmental Cognitive Neuroscience* 19: 19–30.

Schneider, J. M. & Maguire, M. J. (2019). Developmental differences in the neural correlates supporting semantics and syntax during sentence processing. *Developmental Science* 22(4): e12782.

Schoch, S., Riedner, B., Dean, D., O'Muircheartaigh, J., Deoni, S., Huber, R., Jenni, O., LeBourgeois, M., & Kurth, S. (2017). EEG signatures of brain maturation in children: age-related and across-night dynamics in spatial propagation of slow oscillations. *Sleep Medicine* 40: e174.

Schoenemann, P. T. (2012). Evolution of brain and language. *Progress in Brain Research* 195: 443–459.

Schomburg, E. W., Fernandez-Ruiz, A., Mizuseki, K., Berenyi, A., Anastassiou, C. A., Koch, C., & Buzsáki, G. (2014). Theta phase segregation of input-specific gamma patterns in entorhinal-hippocampal networks. *Neuron* 84: 470–485.

Schroeder, C. E. & Lakatos, P. (2008). Low-frequency neuronal oscillations as instruments of sensory selection. *Trends in Neurosciences* 32(1): 9–18.

Schroeter, M. S., Charlesworth, P., Kitzbichler, M. G., Paulsen, O., & Bullmore, E. T. (2015). Emergence of rich-club topology and coordinated dynamics in development of hippocampal functional networks in vitro. *The Journal of Neuroscience* 35: 5459–5470.

Scott-Phillips, T. C. (2015). *Speaking Our Minds: Why Human Communication is Different, and How Language Evolved to Make It Special.* New York: Palgrave Macmillan.

Scott-Phillips, T. C. & Blythe, R. A. (2013). Why is combinatorial combination rare in the natural world, and why is language an exception to this trend? *Journal of the Royal Society Interface* 10: 2015020.

Sedivy, J. (2019). *Language in Mind: An Introduction to Psycholinguistics*. 2nd ed. Oxford: Oxford University Press.

Segaert, K., Mazaheri, A., & Hagoort, P. (2018). Binding language: structuring sentences through precisely timed oscillatory mechanisms. *European Journal of Neuroscience* 48(7): 2651–2662.

Sengupta, B., Stemmler, M. B., & Friston, K. J. (2013). Information and efficiency in the nervous system – a synthesis. *PLoS Computational Biology* 9(7): e1003157.

Sennert, D. (1650). *Tractatus de consensu et dissensu Galenicorum et Peripateticorum cum Chymicis, Opera omnia*. Vol. 3. Lyons.

Seung, S. (2012). *Connectome: How the brain's wiring makes us who we are*. Boston: Houghton, Mifflin, Harcourt.

Seyfarth, R. M. & Cheney, D. L. (2017). Precursors to language: social cognition and pragmatic inference in primates. *Psychonomic Bulletin & Review* 24: 79–84.

Shain, C., Blank, I. A., Schijndel, M. V., Schuler, W., & Fedorenko, E. (2020). fMRI reveals language-specific predictive coding during naturalistic sentence comprehension. *Neuropsychologia* 138: 107307.

Sheng, J., Zheng, L., Lyu, B., Cen, Z., Qin, L., Tan, L. H., Huang, M-X., Ding, N., & Gao, J-H. (2019). The cortical maps of hierarchical linguistic structures during speech perception. *Cerebral Cortex* 29(8): 3232–3240.

Shieber, S. (1985). Evidence against the context-freeness of natural language. *Linguistics and Philosophy* 8: 333–343.

Shim, J.-Y. (2013). External merge by phase: its implications for feature-inheritance, transfer and internal merge. In Lee, I.-J. & Uujinbai, D. (eds.). *Proceedings of the 15th Seoul International Conference on Generative Grammar (SICOGG): Universals and Parameters*. Seoul: Hankuk Publishing Co. 359–387.

Shim, J.-Y. (2018). <φ, φ>-less labeling. *Language Research* 54(1): 23–39.

Shine, J. M., Eisenberg, I., & Poldrack, R. A. (2016). Computational specificity in the human brain. *Behavioral and Brain Sciences* 39: e131.

Siebenhühner, F., Wang, S. H., Arnulfo, G., Nobili, L., Palva, J. M., & Palva, S. (2020). Genuine cross-frequency coupling networks in human resting-state electrophysiological recordings. *PLoS Biology* 18(5): e3000685.

Siegel, M., Buschman, T. J., & Miller, E. K. (2015). Cortical information flow during flexible sensorimotor decisions. *Science* 348(6241): 1352–1355.

Siegelman, M., Mineroff, Z., Blank, I., & Fedorenko, E. (2017). An attempt to replicate a dissociation between syntax and semantics during sentence comprehension reported by Dapretto & Bookheimer (1999, Neuron). *bioRxiv*. https://doi.org/10.1101/110791

Siegelmann, H. T. (1999). *Neural Networks and Analog Computation: Beyond the Turing Limit*. Basel, Switzerland: Springer.

Sikela, J. M. & Searles Quick, V. B. (2018). Genomic trade-offs: are autism and schizophrenia the steep price of the human brain? *Human Genetics* 137: 1–13.

Singer, W. (2013). Cortical dynamics revisited. *Trends in Cognitive Sciences* 17: 616–626.

Singer, W. (2018). Neural oscillations: unavoidable and useful? *European Journal of Neuroscience* 48(7): 2389–2398.

Skeide, M. A. & Friederici, A. D. (2016). The ontogeny of the cortical language network. *Nature Reviews Neuroscience* 17: 323–332.

Skeide, M. A., Brauer, J., & Friederici, A. D. (2016). Brain functional and structural predictors of language performance. *Cerebral Cortex* 26: 2127–2139.

Skelton, A. E., Catchpole, G., Abbott, J. T., Bosten, J. M., & Franklin, A. (2017). Biological origins of color categorization. *PNAS* 114(21): 5545–5550.

Sklar, R. (1968). Chomsky's revolution in linguistics. *The Nation*. 9 September.

Snyder, J. S. (2015). Sound perception: Rhythmic brain activity really is important for auditory segregation. *Current Biology* 25: R1166–R1185.

Solomon, E. A., Kragel, J. E., Sperling, M. R., Sharan, A., Worrell, G., Kucewicz, M. et al. (2017). Widespread theta synchrony and high-frequency desynchronization underlies enhanced cognition. *Nature Communications* 8: 1704.

Soma, M. & Mori, C. (2015). The songbird as a percussionist: syntactic rules for non-vocal sound and song production in java sparrows. *PLoS One* 10(5): e0124876.

Somel, M., Liu, X., & Khaitovich, P. (2013). Human brain evolution: transcripts, metabolites and their regulators. *Nature Reviews Neuroscience* 14: 112–127.

Somogyi, P. & Klausberger, T. (2005). Defined types of cortical interneurone structure space and spike timing in the hippocampus. *The Journal of Physiology* 562(1): 9–26.

Sotero, R. C. (2015). Modeling the generation of phase-amplitude coupling in cortical circuits: from detailed networks to neural mass models. *BioMed Research International* 2015: 915606.

Sotero, R. C., Sanchez-Rodriguez, L. M., Dousty, M., Iturria-Medina, Y., & Sanchez-Bornot, J. M. (2019). Cross-frequency interactions during information flow in complex brain networks are facilitated by scale-free properties. *Frontiers in Physics* 7: 107.

Sousa, A. M. M., Zhu, Y., Raghanti, M. A., Kitchen, R. R., Onorati, M., Tebbenkamp, A. T. N., Stutz, B., Meyer, K. A. et al. (2017). Molecular and cellular reorganization of neural circuits in the human lineage. *Science* 358: 1027–1032.

Spaak, E., Bonnefond, M., Maier, A., Leopold, D. A., & Jensen, O. (2012). Layer-specific entrainment of gamma-band neural activity by the alpha rhythm in monkey visual cortex. *Current Biology* 22: 2313–2318.

Spaak, E., Zeitler, M., & Gielen, S. (2012). Hippocampal theta modulation of neocortical spike times and gamma rhythm: a biophysical model study. *PLoS ONE* 7(10): e45688.

Spelke, E. (2010). Innateness, choice, and language. In Bricmont, J. & Franck, J. (eds.). *Chomsky Notebook*. New York: Columbia University Press. 203–210.

Sporns, E. (2013). The human connectome: origins and challenges. *NeuroImage* 80: 53–61.

Sporns, O., Tononi, G., & Kötter, R. (2005). The human connectome: A structural description of the human brain. *PLoS Computational Biology* 1: e42.

Sprouse, J. & Almeida, D. (2013). The empirical status of data in syntax: a reply to Gibson and Fedorenko. *Language and Cognitive Processes* 28(3): 222–228.

Stabler, E. P. (1997). Derivational minimalism. Retoré, C. (ed.). *Logical Aspects of Computational Linguistics*. LNCS 1328. New York: Springer-Verlag. 68–95.

Stankovski, T., Ticcinelli, V., McClintock, P. V. E., & Stefanovska, A. (2017). Neural cross-frequency coupling functions. *Frontiers in Systems Neuroscience* 11: 33.

Stanley, G. B. (2013). Reading and writing the neural code. *Nature Neuroscience* 16(3): 259–263.

Staudigl, T., Hartl, E., Noachtar, S., Doeller, C. F., & Jensen, O. (2017). Saccades are phase-locked to alpha oscillations in the occipital and medial temporal lobe during successful memory encoding. *PLoS ONE* 15(12): e2003404.

Steinhauer, K., Alter, K., & Friederici, A. D. (1999). Brain potentials indicate immediate use of prosodic cues in natural speech processing. *Nature Neuroscience* 2: 191–196.

Steinmetzger, K. & Rosen, S. (2017). Effects of acoustic periodicity and intelligibility on the neural oscillations in response to speech. *Neuropsychologia* 95: 173–181.

Steriade, M. (1993). Cellular substrates of brain rhythms. In Niedermeyer, E. & Lopez Da Silva, F. (eds.). *Electroencephalography: Basic Principles, Clinical Application, and Related Fields*. Baltimore: Williams & Wilkins. 27–62.

Steriade, M., Curro Dossi, R., & Contreras, D. (1993). Electrophysiological properties of intralaminar thalamocortical cells discharging rhythmic (~40 Hz) spike-bursts at ~1000 Hz during waking and rapid eye movement sleep. *Neuroscience* 56: 1–9.

Sterling, P. & Laughlin, S. (2015). *Principles of Neural Design*. Cambridge, MA: MIT Press.

Sternberg S. (1966). High-speed scanning in human memory. *Science* 153(736): 652–654.

Sternberg, S. (1969). Memory-scanning: mental processes revealed by reaction-time experiments. *American Scientist* 57: 421–457.

Sternberg, S. (2011). Modular processes in mind and brain. *Cognitive Neuropsychology* 28: 156–208.

Storchi, R., Bedford, R. A., Martial, F. P., Allen, A. E., Wynne, J., Montemurro, M. A., Petersen, R. S., & Lucas, R. J. (2017). Modulation of fast narrowband oscillations in the mouse retina and dLGN according to background light intensity. *Neuron* 93: 299–307.

Storm, J. F. (1990). Potassium currents in hippocampal pyramidal cells. *Progress in Brain Research* 83: 161–187.

Stowe, L. A., Kaan, E., Sabourin, L., & Taylor, R. C. (2018). The sentence wrap-up dogma. *Cognition* 176: 232–247.

Strauss, A., Henry, M. J., Scharinger, M., & Obleser, J. (2015). Alpha phase determines successful lexical decision in noise. *Journal of Neuroscience* 35(7): 3256–3262.

Strawson, G. (2008). *Real Materialism and Other Essays*. Oxford: Oxford University Press.

Strawson, G. (2010). *Mental Reality*. 2nd ed. Cambridge, MA: MIT Press.

Strawson, P. F. (1966). *The Bounds of Sense: An Essay on Kant's Critique of Pure Reason*. London: Methuen.

Strub, R. L. (1989). Frontal lobe syndrome in a patient with bilateral globus pallidus lesions. *Archives of Neurology* 46: 1024–1027.

Sugisaki, K. (2016). Structure dependence in child English. In Fujita, K. & Boeckx, C. (eds.). *Advances in Biolinguistics: The Human Language Faculty and its Biological Basis*. London: Routledge. 111–132.

Sukhinin, D. I., Engel, A. K., Manger, P., & Hilgetag, C. C. (2016). Building the ferretome. *Frontiers in Neuroinformatics* 10: 16.

Sun, C., Yang, W., Martin, J., & Tonegawa, S. (2020). Hippocampal neurons represent events as transferable units of experience. *Nature Neuroscience* 23(5): 651–663.

Suzuki, T. N., Wheatcroft, D., & Griesser, M. (2016). Experimental evidence for compositional syntax in bird calls. *Nature Communications* 7: 10986.

Svensson, E. I. (2018). On reciprocal causation in the evolutionary process. *Evolutionary Biology* 45: 1–14.

Swanson, L. W. & Lichtman, J. W. (2016). From Cajal to connectome and beyond. *Annual Review of Neuroscience* 39: 197–216.

Sweeney-Reed, C. M., Zaehle, T., Voges, J., Schmitt, F. C., Buentjen, L., Kopitzki, K., Hinrichs, H., Heinze, H-J., Rugg, M. D., Knight, R. T., & Richardson-Klavehn, A. (2015). Thalamic theta phase alignment predicts human memory formation and anterior thalamic cross-frequency coupling. *eLife* 4: e07578.

Symons, A. E., El-Deredy, W., Schwartze, M., & Kotz, S. A. (2016). The functional role of neural oscillations in non-verbal emotional communication. *Frontiers in Human Neuroscience* 10: 239.

Szalisznyó, K., Silverstein, D., Teichmann, M., Duffau, H., & Smits, A.(2017). Cortico-striatal language pathways dynamically adjust for syntactic complexity: a computational study. *Brain & Language*. 164: 53–62.

Szathmáry, E. (1996). From RNA to language. *Current Biology* 6(7): 764.

Szatloczki, G., Hoffmann, I., Vincze, V., Kalman, J., & Pakaski, M. (2015) Speaking in Alzheimer's disease, is that an early sign? Importance of changes in language abilities in Alzheimer's disease. *Frontiers in Aging Neuroscience* 7: 195.

Taglialatela, J. P., Russell, J. L., Schaeffer, J. A., & Hopkins, W. D. (2011). Chimpanzee vocal signaling points to a multimodal origin of human language. *PLoS ONE* 6(4): e18852.

Takahasi, M., Yamada, H., & Okanoya, K. (2010). Statistical and prosodic sues for song segmentation learning by Bengalese Finches (*Lonchura striata* var. *domestica*). *Ethology* 116: 481–489.

Takashima, A., Bakker, I., van Hell, J. T., Janzen, G., & McQueen, J. M. (2017). Interaction between episodic and semantic memory networks in the acquisition and consolidation of novel spoken words. *Brain & Language* 167: 44–60.

Tallerman, M. (2016). Against the emergent view of language evolution. In Roberts, S. G., Cuskley, C., McCrohon, L., Barceló-Coblijn, L., Feher, O., & Verhoef, T. (eds.). *The Evolution of Language: Proceedings of the 11th International Conference (EVOLANGXI)*. New Orleans, United States of America.

Tallon-Baudry, C. & Bertrand, O. (1999). Oscillatory gamma activity in humans and its role in object representation. *Trends in Cognitive Sciences* 3(4): 151–162.

Tamura, M., Spellman, T. J., Rosen, A. M., Gogos, J. A., & Gordon, J. A. (2017). Hippocampal-prefrontal theta-gamma coupling during performance of a spatial working memory task. *Nature Communications* 8: 2182.

Tass, P. A. (1999). *Phase Resetting in Medicine and Biology*. New York: Springer.

Tass, P. A. (2000). Stochastic phase resetting: a theory for deep brain stimulation. *Progress of Theoretical Physics Supplement* 139, 301–313.

Tattersall, I. (2017). How can we detect when language emerged? *Psychonomic Bulletin & Review* 24: 64–67.

Tavano, A., Blohm, S., Knoop, C., Muralikrishnan, R., Scharinger, M., Wagner, V., Thiele, D., Ghitza, O., Ding, N., Menninghaus, W., & Poeppel, D. (2020). Neural harmonics reflect grammaticality. *bioRxiv.* doi.org/10.1101/2020.04.08.031575

Ten Cate, C. & Okanoya, K. (2012). Revisiting the syntactic abilities of non-human animals: natural vocalizations and artificial grammar learning. *Philosophical Transactions of the Royal Society B* 367(1598): 1984–1994.

Teng, X., Ma, M., Yang, J., Blohm, S., Cai, Q., & Tian, X. (2020). Constrained structure of ancient Chinese poetry facilitates speech content grouping. *Current Biology* 30: 1299–1305.

Teng, X., Tian, X., Doelling, K., & Poeppel, D. (2018). Theta band oscillations reflect more than entrainment: behavioral and neural evidence demonstrates an active chunking process. *European Journal of Neuroscience* 48(8): 2770–2782.

Terporten, R., Schoffelen, J-M., Dai, B., Hagoort, P., & Kösem, A. (2019). The relation between alpha/beta oscillations and the encoding of sentence induced contextual information. *Scientific Reports* 9: 20255.

Terzi, A., Marinis, T., Zafeiri, A., & Francis, K. (2019). Subject and object pronouns in high-functioning children with ASD of a null-subject language. *Frontiers in Psychology* 10: 1301.

Tesche, C. D. & Karhu, J. (2000). Theta oscillations index human hippocampal activation during a working memory task. *PNAS* 97: 919–924.

Tettamanti, M. & Weniger, D. (2006). Broca's area: A supramodel hierarchical processor? *Cortex* 42(4): 491–494.

Teyler, T. J. & DiScenna, P. (1986). The hippocampal memory indexing theory. *Behavioural Neuroscience* 100(2): 147–154.

Theofanopoulou, C. (2015). Brain asymmetry in the white matter making and globularity. *Frontiers in Psychology* 6: 1355.

Theofanopoulou, C. & Boeckx, C. (2016). The central role of the thalamus in language and cognition. In Boeckx, C. & Fujita, K. (eds.). *Advances in Biolinguistics: The Human Language Faculty and its Biological Basis*. London: Routledge.

Theofanopoulou, C. & Boeckx, C. (2018). (Neural) syntax. In R. Martin, R. & Gallego, Á. (eds.). *Language, Syntax, and the Natural Sciences*. Cambridge: Cambridge University Press.

Theyel, B. B., Llano, D. A., & Sherman, S. M. (2010). The corticothalamocortical circuit drives higher-order cortex in the mouse. *Nature Neuroscience* 13(1): 84–88.

Theves, S., Fernandez, G., & Doeller, C. F. (2019). The hippocampus encodes distances in multidimensional feature space. *Current Biology* 29: 1226–1231.

Thompson, P., Kuttab-Boulos, H., Witonsky, D., Yang, L., Roe, B. A., & Di Rienzo, A. (2001). Genetic influences on brain structure. *Nature Neuroscience* 4: 1253–1258.

Tian, B., Reser, D., Durham, A., Kustov, A., & Rauschecker, J. P. (2001). Functional specialization in rhesus monkey auditory cortex. *Science* 292: 290–293.

Tian, L. Y. & Brainard, M. S. (2017). Discrete circuits support generalized versus context-specific vocal learning in the songbird. *Neuron* 96(5): 1168–1177.

Tinbergen, N. (1963). On the aims and methods of ethology. *Zeitschrift für Tierpsychologie* 20: 410–463.

Todt, D. & Hultsch, H. (1998). How songbirds deal with large amounts of serial information: retrieval rules suggest a hierarchical song memory. *Biological Cybernetics* 79: 487–500.

Tomalin, M. (2006). *Linguistics and the Formal Sciences: The Origins of Generative Grammar*. Cambridge: Cambridge University Press.

Tomalin, M. (2007). Reconsidering recursion in syntactic theory. *Lingua* 117: 1784–1800.

Tooby, J. & Cosmides, L. (1992). The psychological foundations of culture. In Barkow, J. H., Cosmides, L. & Tooby, J. (eds.). *The Adapted Mind: Evolutionary Psychology and the Generation of Culture*. Oxford: Oxford University Press. 19–136.

Torday, J. S. & Miller, W. B. Jr. (2016). On the evolution of the mammalian brain. *Frontiers in Systems Neuroscience* 10: 31.

Tort, A. B., Komorowski, R. W., Manns, J. R., Kopell, N. J., & Eichenbaum, H. (2009). Theta-gamma coupling increases during the learning of item-context associations. *PNAS* 106: 20942–20947.

Tort, A. B. L., Rotstein, H. G., Dugladze, T., Gloveli T., & Kopell, N. J. (2007). On the formation of gamma-coherent cell assemblies by oriens lacunosum-moleculare interneurons in the hippocampus. *Proceedings of the National Academy of Sciences of the United States of America* 104(33): 13490–13495.

Tremblay, P. & Dick, A. S. (2016). Broca and Wernicke are dead, or moving past the classic model of neurobiology. *Brain & Language* 162: 60–71.

Trettenbrein, P. C. (2016). The demise of the synapse as the locus of memory: a looming paradigm shift? *Frontiers Systems Neuroscience* 10: 88.

Trevisan, M. A., Mindlin, G. B., & Goller, F. (2006). Nonlinear model predicts diverse respiratory patterns of birdsongs. *Physical Review Letters* 96(5): 058103.

Trotzke, A. (2015). *Rethinking Syntacticentrism: Architectural Issues and Case Studies at the Syntax-Pragmatics Interface*. Amsterdam: John Benjamins.

Tsien, J. Z. (2016). Principles of intelligence: on evolutionary logic of the brain. *Frontiers in Systems Neuroscience* 9: 186.

Tsuda, I. (2013). Chaotic itinerancy. *Scholarpedia* 8: 4459.

Tsuda, I. (2015). Chaotic itinerancy and its roles in cognitive neurodynamics. *Current Opinion in Neurobiology* 31: 67–71.

Turken, A. U. & Dronkers, N. F. (2011). The neural architecture of the language comprehension network: converging evidence from lesion and connectivity analyses. *Frontiers in Systems Neuroscience* 5: 1.

Tutunjian, D. & Boland, J. E. (2008). Do we need a distinction between arguments and adjuncts? Evidence from psycholinguistic studies of comprehension. *Language and Linguistics Compass* 2: 631–646.

Tzourio-Mazoyer, N. & Mazoyer, B. (2017). Variations of planum temporale asymmetries with Heschl's Gyri duplications and association with cognitive abilities: MRI investigation of 428 healthy volunteers. *Brain Structure and Function* 222(6): 2711–2726.

Uddén, J., Hultén, A., Schoffelen, J.-M., Lam, N., Harbusch, K., van den Bosch, A., Kempen, G., Petersson, K. M., & Hagoort, P. (2019). Supramodal sentence processing in the human brain: fMRI evidence for the influence of syntactic complexity in more than 200 participants. *bioRxiv*. https://doi.org/10.1101/576769

Uddén, J., Ingvar, M., Hagoort, P., & Magnus Petersson, K. (2017). Broca's region: a causal role in implicit processing of grammars with crossed non-adjacent dependencies. *Cognition* 164: 188–198.

Ueda, M. (2016). On the current status of biolinguistics as a biological science. In Fujita, K. & Boeckx, C. (eds.). *Advances in Biolinguistics: The Human Language Faculty and its Biological Basis*. London: Routledge. 264–289.

Uhlhaas, P. J., Haenschel, C., Nikolić, D., & Singer, W. (2008). The role of oscillations and synchrony in cortical networks and their putative relevance for the pathophysiology of schizophrenia. *Schizophrenia Bulletin* 34(5): 927–943.

Underhill, J. W. (2009). *Humboldt, Worldview and Language*. Edinburgh: Edinburgh University Press.

Uriagereka, J. (2012). *Spell-Out and the Minimalist Program*. Oxford: Oxford University Press.

Ursini, F-A. (2011). Space and the vision-language interface: a model-theoretic approach. *Biolinguistics* 5(3): 170–225.

Vaas, R. (2001). It binds, therefore I am! Review of Rodolfo Llinás's *I of the Vortex*. *Journal of Consciousness Studies* 8(4): 85–88.

van de Cavey, J. & Hartsuiker, R. J. (2016). Is there a domain-general cognitive structuring system? Evidence from structural priming across music, math, action descriptions, and language. *Cognition* 146: 172–184.

van de Velde, F. (2011). Left-peripheral expansion of the English NP. *English Language and Linguistics* 15: 387–415.

van der Lely, H. K. & Pinker, S. (2014). The biological basis of language: insight from developmental grammatical impairments. *Trends in Cognitive Sciences* 18(11): 586–595.

van Driel, J., Gunseli, E., Meeter, M., & Olivers, C. N. L. (2017). Local and inter-regional alpha EEG dynamics dissociate between memory for search and memory for recognition. *NeuroImage* 149: 114–128.

van Gelderen, E. (2018). Problems of projection: the role of language change in labeling paradoxes. *Studia Linguistica* 72(1): 113–127.

van Le, Q., Isbell, L. A., Matsumoto, J., Nishimaru, H., Hori, E., Maior, R. S., Tomaz, C., Ono, T., & Nishijo, H. (2016). Snakes elicit earlier, and monkey faces, later, gamma oscillations in macaque pulvinar neurons. *Scientific Reports* 6: 20595.

van Petten, C. & Luka, B. J. (2006). Neural localization of semantic context effects in electromagnetic and hemodynamic studies. *Brain and Language* 97: 279–293.

van Riemsdijk, H. (2008). Identity avoidance: OCP effects in Swiss relatives. In Freidin, R., Otero, C. P., & Luisa Zubizarreta, M. (eds.). *Foundational Issues in Linguistic Theory: Essays in Honor of Jean-Roger Vergnaud*. Cambridge, MA: MIT Press. 227–250.

van Rooij, I. (2008). The tractable cognition thesis. *Cognitive Science* 32(6): 939–984.

Vanier, D., Sherwood, C., & Smaers, J. (2019). The evolution of hippocampal formation subregions in primates. Poster presented at the 49th Meeting of the Society for Neuroscience, Chicago, 19–23 October.

VanRullen, R. (2016). Perceptual cycles. *Trends in Cognitive Sciences* 20(10): 723–735.

VanRullen, R., Guyonneau, R., & Thorpe, S. J. (2005). Spike times make sense. *Trends in Neuroscience* 28(1): 1–4.

Varga, C., Golshani, P., & Soltesz, I. (2012). Frequency-invariant temporal ordering of interneuronal discharges during hippocampal oscillations in awake mice. *PNAS* 109: E2726–E2734.

Vaz, A. P., Yaffe, R. B., Wittig, J. H., Inati, S. K., & Zaghloul, K. A. (2017). Dual origins of measured phase-amplitude coupling reveal distinct neural mechanisms underlying human episodic memory in the human cortex. *NeuroImage* 148: 148–159.

Verguts, T. (2017). Binding by random bursts: a computational model of cognitive control. *Journal of Cognitive Neuroscience* 29(6): 1103–1118.

Vertes, R. P. & Kocsis, B. (1997). Brainstem-diencephalo-septohippocampal systems controlling the theta rhythm of the hippocampus. *Neuroscience* 81: 893–926.

Veselinovic, D., Candiotti, A., & Lemasson, A. (2014). Female Diana monkeys (Cercopithecus Diana) have complex calls. Ms. New York University.

Vetter, P., Edwards, G., & Muckli, L. (2013). Transfer of predictive signals across saccades. *Frontiers in Psychology* 3: 176.

Vicario, D. S. & Simpson, H. B. (1995). Electrical stimulation in forebrain nuclei elicits learned vocal patterns in songbirds. *Journal of Neurophysiology* 73: 2602–2607.

Vidaurre, D., Hunt, L. T., Quinn, A. J., Hunt, B. A. E., Brookes, M. J., Nobre, A. C., & Woolrich, M. W. (2018). Spontaneous cortical activity transiently organises into frequency specific phase-coupling networks. *Nature Communications* 9: 2987.

Vignali, L., Himmelstoss, N. A., Hawelka, S., Richlan, F., & Hutzler, F. (2016). Oscillatory brain dynamics during sentence reading: a fixation-related spectral perturbation analysis. *Frontiers in Human Neuroscience* 10: 191.

Vijayan, S. & Kopell, N. J. (2012). Thalamic model of awake alpha oscillations and implications for stimulus processing. *PNAS U.S.A.* 109(45): 18553–18558.

Vinogradov, S. & Herman, A. (2016). Psychiatric illnesses as oscillatory connectomopathies. *Neuropsychopharmacology* 41: 387–388.

Vitiello, G. (2015). The use of many-body physics and thermodynamics to describe the dynamics of rhythmic generators in sensory cortices engaged in memory and learning. *Current Opinion in Neurobiology* 31: 7–12.

Vollrath, M., Kazenwadel, J., & Krüger, H-P. (1992). A universal constant in temporal segmentation of human speech. *Naturwissenschaften* 79: 479–480.

Voloh, B. & Womelsdorf, T. (2016). A role of phase-resetting in coordinating large scale neural networks during attention and goal-directed behavior. *Frontiers in Systems Neuroscience* 10: 18.

von Lautz, A. H., Herding, J., Ludwig, S., Nierhaus, T., Maess, B., Villringer, A., & Blankenburg, F. (2017). Gamma and beta oscillations in human MEG encode the contents of vibrotactile working memory. *Frontiers in Human Neuroscience* 11: 576.

Vosskuhl, J., Huster, R. J., & Herrmann, C. S. (2015). Increase in short-term memory capacity induced by down-regulating individual theta frequency via transcranial alternating current stimulation. *Frontiers Human Neuroscience* 9: 257.

Vukovic, N. & Shtyrov, Y. (2017). Cortical networks for reference-frame processing are shared by language and spatial navigation systems. *NeuroImage* 161: 120–133.

Wahl, M., Marzinzik, F., Friederici, A. D., Hahne, A., Kupsch, A., Schneider, G. H., Saddy, D., Curio, G., & Klostermann, F. (2008). The human thalamus processes syntactic and semantic language violations. *Neuron* 59: 695–707.

Walsh, D. M. (2015). *Organisms, Agency, and Evolution*. Cambridge: Cambridge University Press.

Wang, L., Hagoort, P., & Jensen, O. (2018). Language prediction is reflected by coupling between frontal gamma and posterior alpha oscillations. *Journal of Cognitive Neuroscience* 30(3): 432–447.

Wang, L., Hua, L., Wu, E. X., & Chen, F. (2019). Cortical auditory responses index the contributions of different RMS-level-dependent segments to speech intelligibility. *Hearing Research* 383: 107808.

Wang, L., Jensen, O., van den Brink, D., Weder, N., Schoffelen, J., Magyari, L. et al. (2012). Beta oscillations relate to the N400m during language comprehension. *Human Brain Mapping* 33: 2898–2912.

Wang, L., Zhu, Z., & Bastiaansen, M. (2012). Integration or predictability? A further specification of the functional role of gamma oscillations in language comprehension. *Frontiers in Psychology* 3: 187.

Wang, Z., Wang, J., Zhang, H., Mchugh, R., Sun, X., Li, K., & Yang, Q. X. (2015). Interhemispheric functional and structural disconnection in Alzheimer's disease: a combined resting-state fMRI and DTI study. *PLoS ONE* 10: e0126310.

Ward, L. M. (2003). Synchronous neural oscillations and cognitive processes. *Trends in Cognitive Sciences* 7(12): 553–559.

Watanabe, H., Takahashi, K., & Isa, T. (2015). Phase locking of β oscillation in electrocorticography (ECoG) in the monkey motor cortex at the onset of EMGs and 3D reaching movements. Engineering in Medicine and Biology Society (EMBC), 37th Annual International Conference of the IEEE. 55–58.

Watrous, A. J., Deuker, L., Fell, J., & Axmacher, N. (2015). Phase-amplitude coupling supports phase coding in human ECoG. *eLife* 4: e07886.

Watumull, J., Hauser, M. D., & Berwick, R. B. (2014). Conceptual and methodological problems with comparative work on artificial language learning. *Biolinguistics* 8: 120–129.

Watumull, J., Hauser, M. D., Roberts, I. G., & Hornstein, N. (2014). On recursion. *Frontiers in Psychology* 4: 1017.

Webman-Shafran, R. & Fodor, J. D. (2015). Phrase length and prosody in on-line ambiguity resolution. *Journal of Psycholinguistic Research* 45: 447–474.

Weismann, A. (1893). The all-sufficiency of natural selection. *Contemporary Review* 64: 309–338, 596–610.

Welch, J. J. (2017). What's wrong with evolutionary biology? *Biology & Philosophy* 32 (2): 263–279.

Welle, C. G. & Contreras, D. (2017). New light on gamma oscillations. *Neuron* 93: 247–249.

West-Eberhard, M. J. (2003). *Developmental Plasticity and Evolution*. Oxford: Oxford University Press.

Westerlund, M. & Pylkkänen, L. (2014). The role of the left anterior temporal lobe in semantic composition vs. semantic memory. *Neuropsychologia* 57: 59–70.

Wexler, K. (1998). Very early parameter setting and the unique checking constraint: a new explanation of the optional infinitive stage. *Lingua* 106: 23–79.

White, J. A., Banks M. I., Pearce R. A., & Kopell, N. J. (2000). Networks of interneurons with fast and slow γ-aminobutyric acid type A (GABA$_A$) kinetics provide substrate for mixed gamma-theta rhythm. *Proceedings of the National Academy of Sciences of the United States of America* 97(14): 8128–8133.

Whitford, T. J., Jack, B. N., Pearson, D., Griffiths, O., Luque, D., Harris, A. W. F., Spencer, K. M., & Le Pelley, M. E. (2017). Neurophysiological evidence of efference copies to inner speech. *eLife* 6: e28197.

Whittington, M. A. & Traub, R. D. (2003). Interneuron diversity series: inhibitory interneurons and network oscillations in vitro. *Trends in Neuroscience* 26: 676–682.

Wianda, E. & Ross, B. (2019). The roles of alpha oscillation in working memory retention. *Brain and Behavior* DOI:10.1002/brb3.1263

Wiedmann, N. & Winkler, S. (2015). The influence of prosody on children's processing of ambiguous sentences. In Winkler, S. (ed.). *Ambiguity: Language and Communication*. Berlin: De Gruyter. 185–197.

Wilkinson, C. & Murphy, E. (2016). Joint interventions in autism spectrum disorder: relating oscillopathies and syntactic deficits. *UCL Working Papers in Linguistics* 28: 1–7.

Willer Gold, J., Arsenijević, B., Batinić, M., Becker, M., Čordalija, N., Kresić, M., Leko, N., Lanko Marušič, F. et al. (2017). When linearity prevails over hierarchy in syntax. *PNAS* 115(3): 495–500.

Wilsch, A., Henry, M. J., Herrmann, B., Maess, B., & Obleser, J. (2015). Alpha oscillatory dynamics index temporal expectation benefits in working memory. *Cerebral Cortex* 25(7): 1938–1946.

Wilson, B., Marslen-Wilson, W. D., & Petkov, C. I. (2017). Conserved sequence processing in primate frontal cortex. *Trends in Neurosciences* 40(2): 72–82.

Wilson, B., Slater, H., Kikuchi, Y., Milne, A. E., Marslen-Wilson, W. D., Smith, K., & Petkov, C. I. (2013). Auditory artificial grammar learning in macaque and marmoset monkeys. *Journal of Neuroscience* 33(48): 18825–18835.

Wilson, B., Kikuchi, Y., Sun, L., Hunter, D., Dick, F., Smith, K., Thiele, A., Griffiths, T. D., Marslen-Wilson, W. D., & Petkov, C. I. (2015). Auditory sequence processing reveals evolutionarily conserved regions of frontal cortex in macaques and humans. *Nature Communication* 6: 8901.

Wilson, B., Smith, K., & Petkov, C. (2015). Mixed-complexity artificial grammar learning in humans and macaque monkeys: evaluating learning strategies. *European Journal of Neuroscience* 41(5): 568–578.

Wilson, M. A., & Bower, J. M. (1991). A computer simulation of oscillatory behavior in primary visual cortex. *Neural Computation* 3: 498–509.

Wilson, S. M., DeMarco, A. T., Henry, M. L., Gesierich, B., Babiak, M., Mandelli, M. L., Miller, B. L., & Gorno-Tempini, M. L. (2014). What role does the anterior temporal lobe play in sentence-level processing? Neural correlates of syntactic processing in semantic variant primary progressive aphasia. *Journal of Cognitive Neuroscience* 26: 970–985.

Wilson, S. M., Molnar-Szakacs, I., & Iacoboni, M. (2008). Beyond superior temporal cortex: intersubject correlations in narrative speech comprehension. *Cerebral Cortex* 18(1): 230–242.

Winkler, M., Mueller, J. L., Friederici, A. D., & Männel, C. (2018). Infant cognition includes the potentially human-unique ability to encode embedding. *Science Advances* 4: eaar8334.

Wipf, D. P., Owen, J. P., Attias, H. T., Sekihara, K., & Nagarajan, S. S. (2010). Robust Bayesian estimation of the location, orientation, and time course of multiple correlated neural sources using MEG. *NeuroImage* 49: 641–655.

Witkowski, M., Garcia-Cossio, E., Chander, B. S., Braun, C., Birbaumer, N., Robinson, S. E., & Soekadar, S. R. (2016). Mapping entrained brain oscillations during transcranial alternating current stimulation (tACS). *NeuroImage* 140: 89–98.

Wojtecki, L., Elben, S., Vesper, J., & Schnitzler, A. (2017). The rhythm of the executive gate of speech: subthalamic low-frequency oscillations increase during verbal generation. *European Journal of Neuroscience* 45(9): 1200–1211.

Wolinski, N., Cooper, N., Sauseng, P., & Romei, V. (2018). The speed of parietal theta frequency drives visuospatial working memory capacity. *PLoS Biology* 16: e2005348.

Woolnough, O., Forseth, K. J., Rollo, P. S., & Tandon, N. (2020). Uncovering the functional anatomy of the human insula during speech. *eLife* 8: e53086.

Wöstmann, M., Herrmann, B., Wilsch, A., & Obleser, J. (2015). Neural alpha dynamics in younger and older listeners reflect acoustic challenges and predictive benefits. *Journal of Neuroscience* 35(4): 1458–1467.

Wu, C-Y., Zaccarella, E., & Friederici, A. D. (2019). Universal neural basis of structure building evidenced by network modulations emerging from Broca's area: the case of Chinese. *Human Brain Mapping* 40(6): 1705–1717.

Wutz, A., Loonis, R., Roy, J. E., Donoghue, J. A., & Miller, E. K. (2018). Different levels of category abstraction by different dynamics in different prefrontal areas. *Neuron* 97: 716–726.

Xie, K., Fox, G. E., Liu, J., Lyu, C., Lee, J. C., Kuang, H., Jacobs, S., Li, M., Liu, T., Song, S., & Tsien, J. Z. (2016). Brain computation is organized via power-of-two-based permutation logic. *Frontiers in Systems Neuroscience* 10: 95.

Yael, D., Vecht, J. J., & Bar-Gad, I. (2018). Filter-based phase shifts distort neuronal timing information. *eNeuro* 5(2): e0261–17.2018.

Yan, B. & Li, P. (2013). The emergence of abnormal hypersynchronization in the anatomical structural network of human brain. *NeuroImage* 65: 34–51.

Yang, C. (2018). The linguistic origin of the next number. Ms. University of Pennsylvania.

Yee, E. & Thompson-Schill, S. L. (2016). Putting concepts into context. *Psychonomic Bulletin & Review* 23(4): 1015–1027.

Yelnik, J., Percheron, G., & Francois, C. (1984). A Golgi analysis of the primate globus pallidus. II. Quantitative morphology and spatial orientation of dendritic arborizations. *Journal of Comparative Neurology* 227(2): 200–213.

Yener, G. G., Emek-Savaş, D. D., Lizio, R., Çavuşoğlu, B., Carducci, P., Ada, E., Güntekin, B., Babiloni, C., & Başar, E. (2016). Frontal delta event-related oscillations relate to frontal volume in mild cognitive impairment and healthy controls. *International Journal of Psychophysiology* 103: 110–117.

Yoshimi, J. (2012). Supervenience, dynamical systems theory, and non-reductive physicalism. *The British Journal for the Philosophy of Science* 63(20): 373–398.

Zaccarella, E. & Friederici, A. D. (2017). The neurobiological nature of syntactic hierarchies. *Neuroscience and Biobehavioral Reviews* 81(Pt B): 205–212.

Zaccarella, E. & Friederici, A. D. (2015). Merge in the human brain: a sub-region based functional investigation in the left pars opercularis. *Frontiers in Psychology* 6: 524.

Zaccarella, E., Meyer, L., Makuuchi, M., & Friederici, A. D. (2017). Building by syntax: the neural basis of minimal linguistic structures. *Cerebral Cortex* 27(1): 411–421.

Zador, A. M. (2019). A critique of pure learning and what artificial neural networks can learn from animal brains. *Nature Communications* 10: 3770.

Zalesky, A., Fornito, A., Cocchi, L., Gollo, L. L., & Breakspear, M. (2014). Time-resolved resting-state brain networks. *PNAS* 111: 10341–10346.

Zeder, M. A. (2017). Domestication as a model system for the extended evolutionary synthesis. *Interface Focus* 7: 20160133.

Zhang, H. & Jacobs, J. (2015). Traveling theta waves in the human hippocampus. *Journal of Neuroscience* 35: 12477–12487.

Zhang, H., Watrous, A. J., Patel, A., & Jacobs, J. (2018). Theta and alpha oscillations are travelling waves in the human neocortex. *Neuron* 98: 1269–1281.

Zhang, L. & Pylkkänen, L. (2018). Semantic composition of sentences word by word: MEG evidence for shared processing of conceptual and logical elements. *Neuropsychologia* 119: 392–404.

Zhang, Y. E. & Pylkkänen, L. (2015). The interplay of composition and concept specificity in the left anterior temporal lobe: an MEG study. *NeuroImage* 11: 228–240.

Zhang, Y. & Wang, Y. (2007). Neural plasticity in speech learning and acquisition. *Bilingualism: Language and Cognition* 10(2): 147–160.

Zielinski, M. C. Tang, W., & Jadhav, S. P. (2020). The role of replay and theta sequences in mediating hippocampal-prefrontal interactions for memory and cognition. *Hippocampus* 30(1): 60–72.

Zilles, K., Bacha-Trams, M., Palomero-Gallagher, N., Amunts, K., & Friederici, A. D. (2014). Common molecular basis of the sentence comprehension network revealed by neurotransmitter receptor fingerprints. *Cortex* 63: 79–89.

Zimmerer, V. C., Cowell, P. E., & Varley, R. A. (2014). Artificial grammar learning in individuals with severe aphasia. *Neuropsychologia* 53: 25–38.

Zipf, G. K. ([1949]1965). *Human Behavior and the Principle of Least Effort: An Introduction to Human Ecology.* New York: Hafner.

Zoefel, B., Costa-Faidella, J., Lakatos, P., Schroeder, C. E., & VanRullen, R. (2017). Characterization of neural entrainment to speech with and without slow spectral energy fluctuations in laminar recordings in monkey A1. *NeuroImage* 150: 344–357.

Zuberbühler, K. (2019). Evolutionary roads to syntax. *Animal Behaviour* 151: 259–265.

Zuidema, W. (2013). Context-freeness revisited. In Knauff, M., Pauen, M., Sebanz, N., & Wachsmuth, I. (eds.). *Proceedings of the 35th Annual Conference of the Cognitive Science Society*. Austin, TX: Cognitive Science Society. 1664–1669.

Index

For EU product safety concerns, contact us at Calle de José Abascal, 56–1°,
28003 Madrid, Spain or eugpsr@cambridge.org.

www.ingramcontent.com/pod-product-compliance
Ingram Content Group UK Ltd.
Pitfield, Milton Keynes, MK11 3LW, UK
UKHW020400140625
459647UK00020B/2569